Praise for the first edition of
Identifying and Managing Project Risk:

"Finally, we have a book on project risk that was written from the point of view of the manager rather than that of a mathematician. The author lays out a clear and concise program for identifying and minimizing project risk, and thus aiding in project success. This is done from the project manager's point of view and with a minimum of mathematical jargon. The author's clear exposition shows that he has spent many years explaining these concepts to many managers, and now many more project managers can benefit from this experience. Following the program explained in this book will help every project manager minimize their risk of project failure."

—Robert J. Graham, Ph.D., consultant and author of *Creating an Environment for Successful Projects, The Project Manager's MBA, Project Management As If People Mattered*, and others

"Anyone who—like me—has struggled to relate the abstract discussion of Risk Management in the PMBOK® to actual project management practice will welcome this down-to-earth presentation. This book shows how to incorporate risk management into the planning of your project along the way—the entire way—of the project development sequence."

—Al DeLucia, Director, Project Management Division, General Services Administration (GSA), Philadelphia, PA

"I found this excellent book on identifying and managing project risk to be well-grounded on strong fundamentals of project risk management. It is very comprehensive yet easy to read, filled with the spectrum of useful tools and approaches, and illustrated with numerous insightful practical examples. In particular, examples from the PERIL database and linkage to PMBOK® 2000 in every chapter were especially valuable.

"Overall, I expect that this book will become the benchmark reference guide on project risk management."

—Don White, Ph.D., MBA, Professor and Chair, Industrial and Manufacturing Engineering, Cal Poly, San Luis Obispo, CA

"I enjoyed the book very much—the combination of practical examples and user-friendly tools make application of the concepts possible. I like the High-Level Risk Assessment tool—we will pilot these tools on several teams. I really appreciate the real-life examples that help illustrate the key points."

—Paul T. Malinowski, Director of Corporate Engineering, Becton, Dickinson and Company

"This book addresses both the science and the art of project management. A great read for both new and experienced project managers, as well as aspiring project managers. The Panama Canal example provided discerning insights into why some projects fail and others succeed. I couldn't wait to read about how that project ultimately turned out!"

—Nancy McDonald, Associate Partner, Accenture

"Kendrick provides what is so often lacking in Project Management texts—real life experience as a project manager to bring the practical application of difficult theories to life. He explores the wide range of risk management techniques that are critical to successfully delivering complex projects. A delight to read and apply."

—Ted Lancaster, Director of Global
Engineering Services, Agilent Technologies

"This book is not only effective in minimizing risk in the design of projects, but helpful with prescriptive mitigation strategies to recover a project in need. The book has already found a place on my desk . . . like a good cookbook, it's starting to get marked up and dog-eared from frequent use."

—J. D. Watson, Manager, Global Telecommunications,
DuPont Textiles & Interiors

"It is a sad fact of life that most project managers do not have the liberty of choosing or selecting from among the projects to which they commit big chunks of their lives. Usually when it's dumped in their lap, they must manage or else. It's clear that Tom Kendrick understands this, and he gets immediately to the heart of the single biggest issue that all PMs must face—failure.

"Read [this book] slowly, scan it, or study it. Pick what works for you. There are gems everywhere. Coming from a broad business background, I was surprised and pleased with the comprehensive presentation of project management as a systemic whole."

—David O'Neal, PMP, business and IT consultant, Sunnyvale, CA

Identifying
and
Managing
Project Risk

Essential Tools for
Failure-Proofing Your Project

Second Edition

Tom Kendrick, PMP

▲AMACOM

American Management Association

New York • Atlanta • Brussels • Chicago • Mexico City • San Francisco
Shanghai • Tokyo • Toronto • Washington, D.C.

This publication is designed to provide accurate and authoritative information in regard to the subject matter covered. It is sold with the understanding that the publisher is not engaged in rendering legal, accounting, or other professional service. If legal advice or other expert assistance is required, the services of a competent professional person should be sought.

"PMI" and the PMI logo are service and trademarks of the Project Management Institute, Inc. which are registered in the United States of America and other nations; "PMP" and the PMP logo are certification marks of the Project Management Institute, Inc. which are registered in the United States of America and other nations; "PMBOK", "PM Network", and "PMI Today" are trademarks of the Project Management Institute, Inc. which are registered in the United States of America and other nations; ". . . building professionalism in project management . . ." is a trade and service mark of the Project Management Institute, Inc. which is registered in the United States of America and other nations; and the Project Management Journal logo is a trademark of the Project Management Institute, Inc.

PMI did not participate in the development of this publication and has not reviewed the content for accuracy. PMI does not endorse or otherwise sponsor this publication and makes no warranty, guarantee, or representation, expressed or implied, as to its accuracy or content. PMI does not have any financial interest in this publication, and has not contributed any financial resources.

Library of Congress Cataloging-in-Publication Data

Kendrick, Tom.
  Identifying and managing project risk : essential tools for failure-proofing your project / Tom Kendrick. — 2nd ed.
      p.   cm.
   Includes index.
   ISBN-13: 978-0-8144-1340-1 (hardcover)
   ISBN-10: 0-8144-1340-4 (hardcover)   1. Risk management.
  2. Project management.   I. Title.

  HD61.K46   2009
  658.4'04—dc22

                                    2008050808

Printing number

10   9   8   7   6   5   4   3   2   1

Contents

Acknowledgments

The second edition of this book is the result of even more decades of project work than the first edition, as well as thousands of hours of discussion about project management and project risk (including more than a little good-humored disagreement). It is also the consequence of many presentations and workshops on project risk management. Project work described in this book includes projects I have led at Hewlett-Packard, DuPont, and elsewhere as well as other projects done by colleagues, friends, and workshop participants from an enormous diversity of project environments. The large number of project situations that serves as the foundation of this book ensures that it is aligned with the real world and that it contains ideas that are practical and effective—not just based on interesting theories.

It is not possible to specifically acknowledge all of the people who have contributed useful content about projects and risk that are found in this book, but there are a few whom I need to single out. I spent twenty years at Hewlett-Packard, in a number of different roles, and there are many HP people who have helped to shape the ideas in this book, especially the members of the HP Project Management Initiative team. These folks served as a boundless source of wisdom and good examples, and they were always quick to point out anything that I said that was nonsense. Although most of us have now moved on, we remain close as friends, as critics, and as associates. From this group, I am particularly indebted to Richard Simonds, who diligently reads most of what I write and complains surprisingly little. I also owe big debts to Richard Bauhaus, Charlie Elman, Randy Englund, Patrick Neal, John Lamy, Ron Benton, Terry Ash, Ted Slater, Wolfgang Blickle, Denis Lambert, Patrick Schmid and Ashok Waran.

I am also grateful for support, guidance, and constructive criticism from the other officers and members of the PMI RiskSIG, especially Chuck Bosler, Karel de Bakker, Craig Peterson, David Hulett, David Hillson, Esteri Hinman, and Janice Preston.

I also need to acknowledge others who contributed to this book, particularly John Kennedy, who ensured that anything I said about statistics was within defendable confidence limits, and Peter de Jager, who bears many Y2K risk management scars.

Finally, my largest debt of gratitude in this endeavor goes to my wife, Barbara, who encouraged this project, supported it, warned me that a second edition would be at least as difficult as the first, and repeatedly read all the versions of the manuscript (including the boring parts). She provided the book with most of its clarity and a good deal of its logical structure. If the book proves useful to you, it is largely due to her efforts.

Although others have contributed significantly to the content of this book, any errors, omissions, or other problems are strictly my own. Should you run into any, let me know.

I also appreciate all the feedback and support from project risk management facilitators and participants, which has been enormously helpful in creating this second edition of *Identifying and Managing Project Risk*. If you are using this book to conduct training or university classes and are interested in supplemental materials, please feel free to contact me.

Tom Kendrick, San Carlos, CA
tkendrick@FailureProofProjects.com

1

Why Project Risk Management?

*"Those who cannot remember the past
are condemned to repeat it."*
—GEORGE SANTAYANA

Far too many technical projects retrace the shortcomings and errors of earlier work. Projects that successfully avoid such pitfalls are often viewed as "lucky," but there is usually more to it than that.

The Doomed Project

All projects involve risk. There is always at least some level of uncertainty in a project's outcome, regardless of what the Microsoft Project Gantt chart on the wall seems to imply. High-tech projects are particularly risky, for a number of reasons. First, technical projects are highly varied. These projects have unique aspects and objectives that significantly differ from previous work, and the environment for technical projects evolves quickly. There can be much more difference from one project to the next than in other types of projects. In addition, technical projects are frequently "lean," challenged to work with inadequate funding, staff, and equipment. To make matters worse, there is a pervasive expectation that however fast the last project may have been, the next one should be even quicker. The number and severity of risks on these technical projects continues to grow. To avoid a project doomed to failure, you must consistently use the best practices available.

Good project practices come from experience. Experience, unfortunately, generally comes from unsuccessful practices and poor project management. We tend to learn what *not* to do, all too often, by doing it and then suffering the consequences. Experience can be an invaluable resource, even when it is not your own. The foundation of this book is the experiences of others—a large collection of mostly plausible ideas that did not work out as hoped.

Projects that succeed generally do so because their leaders do two things well. First, leaders recognize that much of the work on any project, even a high-tech project, is not new. For this work, the notes, records, and lessons learned on earlier projects can be a road map for identifying, and in many cases avoiding, many potential problems. Second, they plan project work thoroughly, especially the portions that require innovation, to understand the challenges ahead and to anticipate many of the risks.

Effective project risk management relies on both of these ideas. By looking backward, past failures may be avoided, and by looking forward through project planning, many future problems can be minimized or eliminated.

Risk

In projects, a risk can be almost any uncertain event associated with the work. There are many ways to characterize risk. One of the simplest, from the insurance industry, is:

"Loss" multiplied by "Likelihood"

Risk is the product of these two factors: the expected *consequences* of the event and the *probability* that the event might occur. All risks have these two related, but distinctly different, components. Employing this concept, risk may be characterized in aggregate for a large population of events ("macro-risk"), or it may be considered on an event-by-event basis ("micro-risk").

Both characterizations are useful for risk management, but which of these is most applicable differs depending on the situation. In most fields, risk is primarily managed in the aggregate, in the "macro" sense. As examples, insurance companies sell a large number of policies, commercial banks make many loans, gambling casinos and lotteries attract crowds of players, and managers of mutual funds hold large portfolios of investments. The literature of risk management for these fields (which is extensive) tends to focus on large-scale risk management, with secondary treatment for managing single-event risks.

To take a simple example, consider throwing two fair, six-sided dice. In advance, the outcome of the event is unknown, but through analysis, experimenting, or guessing, you can develop some expectations. The only possible outcomes for the sum of the faces of the two dice are the integers between two and twelve. One way to establish expectations is to figure out the number of possible ways there are to reach each of these totals. (For example, the total 4 can occur three ways from two dice: 1 + 3, 2 + 2, and 3 + 1.) Arranging this analysis in a histogram results in Figure 1-1. Because each of the 36 possible combinations is equally likely, this histogram can be used to predict the relative probability for each possible total. Using this model, you can predict the average sum over many tosses to be seven.

If you throw many dice, the empirical data collected (which is another method for establishing the probabilities) will generally resemble the theoretical histogram, but because the events are random it is extraordinarily unlikely that your experiments rolling dice will ever precisely match the theory. What will emerge, though, is that the *average* sum generated in large populations (one hundred or more throws) will be close to the calculated average of seven, and the *shape* of the histogram will also resemble the predicted theoretical distribution. Risk analysis in the macro sense takes notice of the population mean of seven, and casino games of chance played with dice are designed by "the house" to exploit this fact. On the other hand, risk in the micro sense, noting the range of possible outcomes, dominates the analysis for the casino visitors, who may play such games only once; the risk associated with a single event—their next throw of the dice—is what matters to them.

Figure 1-1. Histogram of sums from two dice.

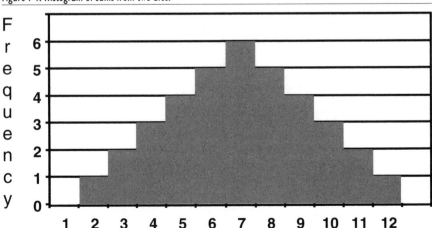

For projects, risk management in the large sense is useful to the organization, where many projects are undertaken. But from the perspective of the leader of a single project, there is only the one project. Risk management for the enterprise, or for a portfolio of projects, is mostly about risk in the aggregate (a topic explored in Chapter 13). Project risk management focuses primarily on risk in the small sense, and this is the dominant topic of this book.

Macro-Risk Management

In the literature of the insurance and finance industries, risk is described and managed using statistical tools: data collection, sampling, and data analysis. In these fields, a large population of individual examples is collected and aggregated, and statistics for the "loss and likelihood" can be calculated. Even though the individual cases in the population may vary widely, the average "loss times likelihood" tends to be fairly predictable and stable over time. When large numbers of data points from the population at various levels of loss have been collected, the population can be characterized using distributions and histograms, similar to the plot in Figure 1-2. In this case, each "loss" result that falls into a defined range is counted, and the number of observations in each range is plotted against the ranges to show a histogram of the overall results.

Various statistics and methods are used to study such populations, but the population mean is the main measure for risk in such a population. The mean represents the *typical* loss—the total of all the losses divided by the number of data points. The uncertainty, or the amount of

Figure 1-2. Histogram of population data.

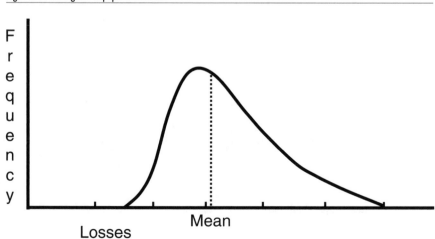

Losses   Mean

spread for the data on each side of the mean, also matters, but the mean sufficiently characterizes the population for most decisions.

In fields such as these, risk is mostly managed in the macro sense, using a large population to forecast the mean. This information may be used to set interest rates for loans, premiums for insurance policies, and expectations for stock portfolios. Because there are many loans, investments, and insurance policies, the overall expectations depend on the average result. It does not matter so much how large or small the extremes are; as long as the average results remain consistent with the business objectives, risk is managed by allowing the high and low values to balance each other, providing a stable and predictable overall result.

Project risk management in this macro sense is common at the project portfolio and enterprise levels. If all the projects undertaken are considered together, performance primarily depends on the results of the "average" project. Some projects will fail and others may achieve spectacular results, but the aggregate performance is what matters to the business bottom line.

Micro-Risk Management

Passive measurement, even in the fields that manage risk using large populations, is never the whole job. Studying averages is necessary, but it is never sufficient. Managing risk also involves taking action to influence the outcomes.

In the world of gambling, which is filled with students of risk on both sides of the table, knowing the odds in each game is a good starting point. Both parties also know that if they can shift the odds, they will be more successful. Casinos shift the game in roulette by adding zeros to the wheel, but not including them in the calculation of the payoffs. In casino games using cards such as blackjack, casino owners employ the dealers, knowing that the dealer has a statistical advantage. In blackjack the players may also shift the odds, by paying attention and counting the cards, but establishments minimize this advantage through frequent shuffling of the decks and barring known card counters from play. There are even more effective methods for shifting the odds in games of chance, but most are not legal; tactics like stacking decks of cards and loading dice are frowned upon. Fortunately, in project risk management, shifting the odds is not only completely fair, it is an excellent idea.

Managing risk in this small sense considers each case separately—every investment in a portfolio, each individual bank loan, each insurance policy, and in the case of projects, every exposure faced by the current project. In all of these cases, standards and criteria are used to minimize the possibility of large individual variances above the mean, and actions are taken to move the expected result. Screening criteria are applied at the bank to avoid making loans to borrowers who appear to be poor credit risks. (Disregarding these standards by offering "subprime" mortgages has recently led to the well-publicized consequences of deviating from this policy.) Insurers either raise the price of coverage or they refuse to sell insurance to people who seem statistically more likely to generate claims. Insurance firms also use tactics aimed at reducing the frequency or severity of the events, such as auto safety campaigns. Managers of mutual funds work to influence the boards of directors of companies whose stocks are held by the fund. All these tactics work to shift the odds—actively managing risk in the small sense.

For projects, risk management is almost entirely similar to these examples, considering each project individually. Thorough screening of projects at the overall business level attempts to select only the best opportunities. It would be excellent risk management to pick out and terminate (or avoid altogether) the projects that will ultimately fail—if only it were that easy. As David Packard noted, "Half the projects at Hewlett-Packard are a waste of time. If I knew which half, I would cancel them."

Project risk management—risk management in the small sense—works to improve the chances for each individual project. The leader of a project has no large population, only the single project; there will be only one outcome. In most other fields, risk management is primarily concerned with the mean values of large numbers of independent events. For project risk management, however, what generally matters most is predictability—managing the variation expected in the result *for this project.*

For a given project, you can never know the precise outcome in advance, but through review of data from earlier work and project planning, you can predict the range and frequency of potential outcomes that you can expect. Through analysis and planning, you can better understand the odds and take action to improve them. The goals of risk management for a single project are to establish a credible plan consistent with business objectives and then to minimize the range of possible outcomes.

One type of "loss" for a project may be measured in time. The distributions in Figure 1-3 compare timing expectations graphically for two similar projects. These plots are different from what was shown in Figure 1-2. In that case, the plot was based on empirical measurements of a large number of actual, historical cases. The plots in Figure 1-3 are *projections* of what might happen for these two projects, based on assumptions and data for each. These histograms are speculative and require you to pretend that you will execute the project many times, with varying results. Developing this sort of risk characterization for projects is explored in

Figure I-3. Possible outcomes for two projects.

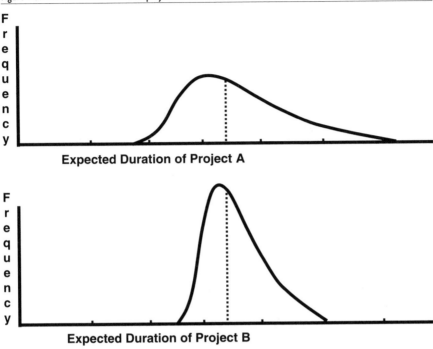

F
r
e
q
u
e
n
c
y

Expected Duration of Project A

F
r
e
q
u
e
n
c
y

Expected Duration of Project B

Chapter 9, where quantifying and analyzing project risk is discussed. For the present, assume that the two projects have expectations as displayed in the two distributions.

For these two projects, the average (or *mean*) duration is the same, but the range of expected durations for Project A is much larger. Project B has a much narrower spread (the statistical *variance*, or *standard deviation*), and so it will be more likely to complete close to the expected duration. The larger range of possible durations for Project A represents higher risk, even though it also includes a small possibility of an outcome even shorter than expected for Project B. Project risk increases with the level of uncertainty, both negative and positive.

Project risk management uses the two fundamental parameters of risk—likelihood and loss—just as any other area of risk management does. Likelihood is generally characterized as "probability" and may be estimated in several ways for project events (though often by guessing, so it can be quite imprecise). Loss is generally referred to for projects as "impact," and it is based on the consequences to the project if the risk does occur. Impact is usually measured in time (as in the examples in Figure 1-3) or cost, particularly for quantitative risk assessment. Other risk impacts include increased effort, issues with stated deliverable requirements, and a wide range of other more qualitative consequences that are not easily measured, such as team productivity and conflict and impact on other projects and other operations. Applying these concepts to project risk is covered in Chapter 7.

Managing project risk depends upon the project team understanding the sources of variation in projects, and then working to minimize threats and to maximize opportunities wherever it is feasible. Because no project is likely to be repeated enough times to develop distributions like those in Figure 1-3 using measured, empirical data, project risk analyses depend on projections and range estimates.

Benefits and Uses of Risk Data

Can you manage risk? This fundamental question is unfortunately not trivial, because uncertainty is always present, regardless of what we choose to do. For projects, we can at least answer "Yes, sometimes," depending on tactics such as those outlined earlier and throughout the second half of this book.

Because our ability to manage risk is imperfect, it's fair to ask a second question: Should you manage risk? As with any business decision, the answer has to do with cost and benefits. Developing a project plan with thorough risk analysis can involve significant effort, which may seem unnecessary overhead to many project stakeholders and even to some project leaders. There are many benefits from project risk management, though, and particularly for complex projects, they far outweigh the costs. Some of these benefits of project risk management follow, and each is amplified later in this book.

Project Justification

Project risk management is primarily undertaken to improve the chances of projects achieving their objectives. Although there are never any guarantees, broader awareness of common failure modes and ideas that make projects more robust can significantly improve the odds for success. The primary benefit of project risk management is either to develop a credible foundation for each project by showing that it is possible, or to demonstrate that the project is not feasible so it can be avoided, aborted, or transformed. Risk analysis can also reveal opportunities for improving projects that can result in increased project value.

Lower Costs and Less Chaos

Adequate risk analysis lowers both the overall cost and the frustration caused by avoidable problems. The amount of rework and unforeseen late project effort is reduced. Knowledge of the root causes of the potentially severe project problems enables project leaders and teams to work in ways that avoid these problems. Dealing with the causes of risk also minimizes "firefighting" and chaos during projects, much of which is focused short-term and deals primarily with symptoms rather than the intrinsic sources of the problems.

Project Priority and Management Support

Support from managers and other project stakeholders and commitment from the project team are more easily won when projects are based on thorough, understandable information. High-risk projects may begin with lower priority, but this can be raised using a thorough risk plan, displaying competence and good preparation for possible problems. Whenever you are successful in improving the priority of your project, you significantly reduce project risk—by opening doors, reducing obstacles, making resources available, and shortening queues for services.

Project Portfolio Management

Achieving and maintaining an appropriate mix of ongoing projects for an organization depends on risk data. The ideal project portfolio includes both lower- and higher-risk projects in proportions that are consistent with the business objectives. The process of project portfolio management and its relationship to project risk is covered in Chapter 13.

Fine-Tuning Plans to Reduce Risk

Risk analysis uncovers weaknesses in a project plan and triggers changes, new activities, and resource shifts that improve the project. Risk analysis at the project level may also reveal needed shifts in overall project structure or basic assumptions.

Establishing Management Reserve

Risk analysis demonstrates the uncertainty of project outcomes and is useful in justifying reserves for schedule and/or resources. It's more appropriate to define a window of time (or budget) instead of a single-point objective for risky projects. It is fine to set project targets on expected estimates (the "most likely" versions of the plans), but project commitments for high-risk projects are best established with less aggressive goals, reflecting the risks. The target and committed objectives set a range for acceptable project results and visibly communicate the uncertainty. For example, the target schedule for a risky project might be twelve months, but the committed schedule, reflecting potential problems, may be set at fourteen months. Completion within (or before) this range defines a successful project; only if the project takes more than fourteen months will it be considered a failure. Project risk assessment data provides both the rationale and the magnitude for the required reserve. More on this is found in Chapter 10.

Project Communication and Control

Project communication is most effective when there is a solid, credible plan. Risk assessments also build awareness of project exposures for the project team, showing when, where, and how painful the problems might be. This causes people to work in ways that avoid project difficulties. Risk data can also be useful in negotiations with project sponsors. Using information about the likelihood and consequences of potential problems gives project leaders more influence in defining objectives, determining budgets, obtaining staff, setting deadlines, and negotiating project changes.

The Project Risk Management Process

The overall structure of this book mirrors the information in the *Guide to the Project Management Body of Knowledge* (or *PMBOK® Guide*). This guide from the Project Management Institute (PMI) is widely used as a comprehensive summary of project management processes and principles, and it is the foundation for PMI certification. The *PMBOK® Guide* has nine Project Management Knowledge Areas:

1. Project Integration Management
2. Project Scope Management
3. Project Time Management
4. Project Cost Management
5. Project Quality Management
6. Project Human Resource Management

7. Project Communications Management
8. Project Risk Management
9. Project Procurement Management

Of these areas, Project Risk Management is the most central to this book, but all nine of these topics are strongly related.

The *PMBOK® Guide* is also built around five Process Groups: Initiating, Planning, Executing, Monitoring and Controlling, and Closing. In the *PMBOK® Guide*, the processes are related as shown in Figure 1-4. The six topics for Project Risk Management are included in two of these groups: the Planning Processes group and the Monitoring and Controlling Processes group.

In this book, the first of the six topics, "Plan Risk Management," is discussed in Chapter 2. "Identify Risks" is covered in Chapters 3 through 6, on scope risk, schedule risk, resource risk, and managing project constraints. The analysis and management of project risk is covered first at a detail level, and then for projects as a whole. (This is a distinction not explicit in the *PMBOK® Guide*, which addresses project-level risk only superficially.) The next two, "Perform Qualitative Risk Analysis" and "Perform Quantitative Risk Analysis," relate to risk assessment. Risk assessment is covered on two levels, for activity risks in Chapter 7, and for overall project risk in Chapter 9. "Plan Risk Responses" is also discussed twice, in Chapter 8 for activities and in Chapter 10 for the project as a

Figure 1-4. PMI PMBOK® links among process groups.

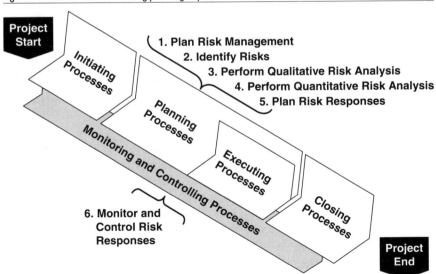

whole. "Monitor and Control Risk" is the topic of Chapter 11. The relation between risk management and Project Closing Processes is covered in Chapter 12.

As in the *PMBOK® Guide*, the majority of the book aligns with project planning, but the material here goes beyond the coverage in the *PMBOK® Guide* to focus on the "how to" of effective risk management, from the practitioner's standpoint. There is particular emphasis on ideas and tools that work well and can be easily adopted in technical projects. All risk management topics in the *PMBOK® Guide* are included here, for people who may be using this book to prepare for the PMP® Certification test, but not every topic will get equal coverage.

Anatomy of a Failed Project: The First Panama Canal Project

Risk management is never just about looking forward. Heeding the lessons learned on projects of all types—even some distant examples—can help you avoid problems on new projects. One such example, illustrating that people have been making similar mistakes for a long, long time, is the initial effort by the French to construct a canal across Panama.

The building of the Panama Canal was not an infeasible project; it was, after all, ultimately completed. However, the initial undertaking was certainly premature. The first canal project, begun in the late 1800s, was a massive challenge for the technology of the day. That said, lack of project management contributed significantly to the decision to go forward in the first place, the many project problems, and the ultimate failure.

Precise definition for the project was unclear, even years into the work. Planning was not thorough, and changes in the work were frequent and managed informally. Reporting on the project was sporadic and generally inaccurate (or even dishonest). Risks were not identified effectively or were ignored, and the primary risk management strategy seems to have been "hoping for the best."

Although there was speculation far earlier, the first serious investigation of a canal in Central America was in the mid-1800s. Estimates were that such a canal would provide US$48 million a year in shipping savings, and might be built for less than US$100 million. Further study on-site was less optimistic, but in 1850 construction of a railroad across the Isthmus of Panama started. The railroad was ultimately completed, but the US$1.5 million, two-year project swelled to US$8 million before it was finished, three years late in 1855. After a slow start, the railroad did prove to be a financial success, but its construction problems foreshadowed the canal efforts to come.

A few years later on the other side of the world, the Suez Canal was completed and opened in 1869. This project was sponsored and led successfully from Paris by Ferdinand de Lesseps. This triumph earned him the nickname "The Great Engineer," although he was actually a diplomat by training, not an engineer at all. He had no technical background and only modest skills as an administrator. However, he had completed a project many thought to be impossible and was now world famous. The Suez project was a huge financial success, and de Lesseps and his backers were eager to take on new challenges.

Examining the world map, de Lesseps decided a canal at Panama would be his next triumph, so in the late 1870s a French syndicate negotiated the necessary agreements in Bogota, Colombia, as Panama was then the northernmost part of Colombia. They were granted rights to build and operate a canal in exchange for a small percentage of the revenue to be generated over ninety-nine years.

Although it might seem curious today that these canal construction projects so far from France originated there, in the late 1800s Paris was the center of the engineering universe. The best schools in the world were there, and many engineering giants of the day lived in Paris, including Gustav Eiffel (then planning his tower). Such technical projects could hardly have arisen anywhere else.

The process of defining the Panama project started promisingly enough. In 1879 Ferdinand de Lesseps sponsored an International Congress to study the feasibility of a canal connecting the Atlantic and Pacific oceans through Central America. Over a hundred delegates gathered in Paris from a large number of nations, though most of the delegates were French. A number of routes were considered, and canals through Nicaragua and Panama both were recommended as possibilities. Construction ideas, including a realistic "lock-and-dam" concept (somewhat similar to the canal in service today), were also proposed. In the end, though, the Congress voted to support a sea-level canal project at Panama, even though nearly all the engineers present thought the idea infeasible and voted against it. Not listening to technical people is a perilous way to start a project. The Panama Canal was neither the first nor the last project to create its own problems through insufficient technical input.

Planning for the project was also a low priority. De Lesseps paid little attention to technical problems. He believed need would result in innovation as it had at Suez, and the future would take care of itself. He valued his own opinions and ignored the views of those who disagreed with him, even recognized authorities. An inveterate optimist, he was convinced, based only on self-confidence, that he could not fail. These attitudes are not conducive to good risk management; there are few things more dangerous to a project than an overly optimistic project leader.

The broad objective de Lesseps set for his Compagnie Universal du Canal Interoceanique was to build a sea-level canal in twelve years, to open in 1892. He raised US$60 million from investors through public offerings—a lot of money, but still less than one-third of the initial engineering cost estimate of more than US$200 million. In addition to this financial shortfall, there was little detailed planning done before work actually commenced, and most of that was done at the 1879 meeting in Paris. Even on the visits that de Lesseps made to Panama and New York to build support for the project, he failed to involve his technical people.

Eventually the engineers did travel to Panama, and digging started in 1882. Quickly, estimates of the volume of excavation required started to rise, to 120 million cubic meters—almost triple the estimates that were used for the decisions in 1879. As the magnitude of the effort rose, de Lesseps made no public changes to his cost estimates or to the completion date.

Management of risks on the project, inadequate at the start, improved little in the early stages of execution. There were many problems. Panama is in the tropics, and torrential rains for much of the year created floods that impeded the digging and made the work dangerous. The frequent rains turned Panama's clay into a flowing, sticky sludge that bogged down work, and the moist, tropical salt air combined with the viscous mud to destroy the machinery. There was also the issue of elevation. The continental divide in Panama is not too high by North or South American standards, but it does rise to more than 130 meters. For a canal to cross Central America, it would be necessary to dig a trench more than fifteen kilometers long to this depth, an unprecedented amount of excavation. Digging the remainder of the eighty-kilometer transit across the isthmus was nearly as daunting.

Adequate funding for the work was also a problem, as only a portion of the money that was raised was allocated to construction (most of the money went for publicity, including a impressive periodic *Canal Bulletin*, used to build interest and support). Worst of all, diseases, especially malaria and yellow fever, were lethal to many workers not native to the tropics, who died by the hundreds. As work progressed, the engineers, already dubious, increasingly believed the plan to dig a sea-level canal was doomed.

Intense interest in the project and a steady stream of new workers kept work going, and the *Canal Bulletin* reported good progress (regardless of what was actually happening). As the project progressed there were changes. Several years into the project, in 1885, the cost estimates were finally raised, and investors provided new funds that quadrupled the project budget to US$240 million. The expected opening of the canal was delayed "somewhat," but no specific date was offered. Claims were made at this time that the canal was half dug, but the truth was probably less than 15 percent. Information on the project was far from trustworthy.

In 1887, costs were again revised upward, exceeding US$330 million. The additional money was borrowed, as de Lesseps could find no new investors. Following years of struggle and frustration, the engineers finally won the debate over construction of a canal at sea level. Plans were shifted to construct dams on the rivers near each coast to create large lakes that would serve as much of the transit. Sets of locks would be needed to bring ships up to, and down from, these man-made lakes. Although this would slow the transit of ships somewhat, it significantly reduced the necessary excavation.

Even with these changes, problems continued to mount, and by 1889 more revisions and even more money were needed. After repeated failures to raise funding, de Lesseps liquidated the Compagnie Universal du Canal Interoceanique, and the project ended. This collapse caused complete financial losses for all the investors. By 1892 scandals were rampant, and the bad press and blame spread far and wide. Soon the lawyers and courts of France were busy dealing with the project's aftermath.

The French do not seem to have done a formal postproject analysis, but looking at the project in retrospect reveals over a decade of work, more than US$300 million spent, lots of digging, and no canal. Following the years of effort, the site was ugly and an ecological mess. The cost of this project also included at least 20,000 lives lost (many workers who came to Panama died so soon after their arrival that their deaths were never recorded; some estimates of the death toll run as high as 25,000). Directly as a result of this project failure, the French government fell in 1892, ending one of the messiest and most costly project failures in history.

The leader of this project did not fare well in the wake of this disaster. Ferdinand de Lesseps was not technical, and he was misguided in his beliefs that equipment and medicines would appear when needed. He also chronically reported more progress than was real (through either poor analysis or deception; the records are not clear enough to tell). He died a broken man, in poverty. Had he never undertaken the project at Panama, he would have been remembered as the heroic builder of the Suez Canal. Instead, his name is primarily linked to the failure at Panama.

Perhaps the one positive outcome from all this was clear evidence that building a sea-level canal at Panama was all but impossible because of rains, flooding, geology, and other challenges. These are problems that probably could not be surmounted even with current technology.

Although it is not possible ever to know whether a canal at Panama could have been constructed in the 1880s, better project and risk management practices, widely available at the time, would have helped substantially. Setting a more appropriate initial objective, or at least modifying it sooner, would have improved the likelihood of success. Honest, more frequent communication—the foundation of well-run projects—would almost certainly have either forced these changes or led to earlier abandonment of the work, saving thousands of lives and a great deal of money.

2

Planning for Risk Management

"You can observe a lot just by watching."
—Yogi Berra

Planning for risk involves paying attention. When we don't watch, projects fail.

How many? One frequently quoted statistic is 75 percent. The original source for this assertion is a study done in 1994 by the Standish Group and documented in "The CHAOS Report." There are reasons to be skeptical of this number, starting with the fact that if three of four projects actually did fail, there would be a lot fewer projects. What the Standish Group actually said in its study was that about a quarter of projects in the sample were cancelled before delivering a result. In addition to this, roughly half of the projects were "challenged," producing a deliverable but doing it late, over budget, or both. The remaining quarter of the projects they viewed as successful.

Although the Standish Group has done further research over the years with similar results, the actual picture for projects is probably not quite so bleak. The Standish Group studied only large IT projects, those with budgets more than US$2 million. In addition, the survey information did not come from the project leaders but was reported by the executives responsible for the organizations where the projects were undertaken. Larger projects are more prone to fail, and US$2 million is a big IT project (especially in 1994). The source of the data also raises a question about what was being compared to what. Were the projects in fact troubled, or were they doomed from the start by unrealistic expectations that were never validated? Whatever the true numbers for failed projects are, however, too many projects fail unnecessarily, and better risk management can help.

Although unanticipated "acts of God" doom some projects, most fail for one of three reasons:

- They are actually impossible.
- They are overconstrained ("challenged" in the Standish Group model).
- They are not competently managed.

A project is impossible when its objective lies outside of the technical capabilities currently available. "Design an antigravity device" is an example. Other projects are entirely possible, but not with the time and resources available. "Rewrite all the corporate accounting software so it can use a different database package in two weeks using two part-time university students" is an overconstrained project. Unfortunately, there are also projects that fail despite having a feasible deliverable and plausible time and budget expectations. These projects fail because of poor project management—simply because too little thought is put into the work to produce useful results.

Risk and project planning enable you to distinguish among and deal with all three of these situations. For projects that are demonstrably beyond the state of the art, planning and other analysis data generally provide sufficient information to terminate the project or at least to redirect the objective (buy a helicopter, for example, instead of developing the antigravity device). Chapter 3, on identifying project scope risks, discusses these situations. For projects with unrealistic timing, resource, or other constraints, risk and planning data provide you with a compelling basis for project negotiation, resulting in a more plausible objective (or, in some cases, the conclusion that a realistic project lacks business justification). Chapters 4, 5, and 6, on schedule, resource, and other risk identification, discuss issues common for these overconstrained projects. Dealing with "challenged" projects by negotiating a realistic project baseline is covered in Chapter 10.

The third situation, a credible project that fails because of faulty execution, is definitely avoidable. Through adequate attention to project and risk planning, these projects can succeed. Well-planned projects begin quickly, limiting unproductive chaos. Rework and defects are minimized, and people remain busy performing activities that efficiently move the project forward. A solid foundation of project analysis also reveals problems that might lead to failure and prepares the project team for their prompt resolution. In addition to making project execution more efficient, risk planning also provides insight for faster, better project decisions. Although changes are required to succeed with the first two types of projects mentioned earlier, this third type depends only on you, your project team, and application of the solid project management concepts in this book. The last half of this book, Chapters 7 through 13, specifically addresses these projects.

Project Selection

Project risk is a significant factor even before there is a project. Projects begin as a result of an organization's business decision to create something new or change something old. Projects are a large portion of the overall work done in organizations these days, and there are always many more attractive project ideas than can be funded or adequately staffed at any given time. The process for choosing projects both creates project risk and relies on project risk analysis, so the processes for project selection and project risk management are tightly linked. Selecting and maintaining an appropriate list of active projects requires project portfolio management.

Project selection affects project risk in a number of ways. Poor project portfolio management exacerbates a number of common project risks:

- Too many projects competing for scarce resources
- Project priorities that are misaligned with business and technical strategies
- Inadequately staffed or funded projects
- Unrealistically estimated organizational capabilities

Project risk management data is also a critical input to the project selection process. Project portfolio management uses project risk assessment as a key criterion for determining which projects to put into plan at any given time. Without high-quality risk data and realistic estimates for candidate projects, excessive numbers of projects will be undertaken and many of them will fail. The topic of project portfolio risk management is explored in Chapter 13.

Overall Project Planning Processes

The project selection process is a major source of risk for all projects, but the overall project management approach is even more significant. When projects are undertaken in organizations lacking adequate project management processes, risks will be unknown and probably unacceptably high. Without adequate analysis of projects, no one has much idea of what "going right" looks like, so it is not possible to identify and manage the risks—the things that may go wrong. The project management processes provide the magnifying glass you need to inspect your project to discover its possible failure modes.

Regular review of the overall methods and processes used to manage projects is an essential foundation for good risk management. If project information and control is sufficient across the organization and most of the projects undertaken are successful, then your processes are working well. For many high-tech projects, though, this is not the case. The methods used for managing project work are too informal and they lack adequate structure. Exactly what process you choose matters less than that you are using one. If elaborate, formal, PMBOK®-inspired heavyweight project management works for you, great. If agile, lightweight, adaptive methodologies provide what you need, that's fine too. The important requirement for risk management is that you adopt and *use* an effective project management process.

For too many technical projects, there is indifference or even hostility to planning. This occurs for a number of reasons, and it originates in organizations at several levels. At the project level, other types of work may carry higher priority, or planning may be viewed as a waste of time. Above the project level, project management processes may appear to be unnecessary overhead, or they may be discouraged to deprive project teams of data that could be used to win arguments with their managers. Whatever the rationalizations used, there can be little risk management without planning. Until you have a basic plan, most of the potential problems and failure modes for your project will remain undetected.

The next several pages provide support for the investment in project processes. If you or your management need convincing that project management is worthwhile, read on. If project planning and related management processes are adequate in your organization, skip ahead.

At the Project Level

A number of reasons are frequently cited by project leaders for avoiding project planning. Some projects are not thoroughly planned because the changes are so frequent that planning seems futile. Quite a few leaders know that project management methodology is beneficial, but with their limited time they feel they must do only "real work." An increasingly common reason offered is the belief that in "Internet time," thinking and planning are no longer affordable luxuries. There is a response for each of these assertions.

Inevitable project change is a poor reason not to plan. In fact, frequent change is one of the most damaging risk factors, and managing this risk requires good project information. Project teams that have solid planning data are better able to resist inappropriate change, rejecting or deferring proposed changes based on the consequences demonstrated using the project plan. When changes are necessary, it is easier to continue the work by modifying an existing plan than by starting over in a vacuum. In addition, many high-tech project changes directly result from faulty project assumptions that persist because of inadequate planning information. Better understanding leads to clearer definition of project deliverables and fewer reasons for change.

The time required to plan is also not a valid reason to avoid project management processes. Although it is universally true that no project has enough time, the belief that there is no time to plan is difficult to understand. All the work in any project must always be planned. There is a choice as to whether planning will be primarily done in a focused, early-project exercise, or by identifying the work one activity at a time, day by day, all through the project. All necessary analysis must be done by someone, eventually. The incremental approach requires comparable, if not more, overall effort, and it carries a number of disadvantages. First, tracking project progress will at best be guesswork. Second, most project risks, even those easily identified, come as unexpected surprises when they occur. Early, more thorough planning provides other advantages, and it is always preferable to have project information sooner than later. Why not invest in planning when the benefits are greatest?

Assertions about "Internet time" are also difficult to accept. Projects that must execute as quickly as possible need more, not less, project planning. Delivering a result with value requires sequencing the work for efficiency and ensuring that the activities undertaken are truly necessary and of high priority. There is no time for rework, excessive defect correction, or unnecessary activity on fast-track projects. Project planning, particularly on time-constrained projects, *is* real work.

Above the Project Level

Projects are undertaken based on the assumption that whatever the project produces will have value, but there is often little consideration of the type and amount of *process* that projects need. In many high-tech environments, little to no formal project management is mandated, and often it is even discouraged.

Whenever the current standards and project management practices are inadequate in an organization, strive to improve them. There are two possible ways to do this. Your best option is to convince the managers and other stakeholders that more formal project definition, planning, and tracking will deliver an overall benefit for the business. When this is successful, all projects benefit. For situations where this is unsuccessful, a second option is to adopt greater formalism just for your current project. It may even be necessary to do this in secret, to avoid criticism and comments like, "Why are you wasting time with all that planning stuff? Why aren't you working?"

In organizations where expenses and overhead are tightly controlled, it can be difficult to convince managers to adopt greater project formalism. Building a case for this takes time and requires metrics and examples, and you may find that some upper-level managers are highly resistant even to credible data. The benefits are substantial, though, so it is well worth trying; anything you can do to build support for project processes over time will help.

If you have credible, local data demonstrating the value of project management or the costs associated with inadequate process, assemble it. Most organizations that have such data also have good processes. If you have a problem that is related to inadequate project management, it is likely that you will also not have a great deal of information to draw from. For projects lacking a structured methodology, few metrics are established for the work, so mounting a compelling case for project management processes using your own data may be difficult.

Typical metrics that may be useful in supporting your case relate to achieving specifications, managing budgets, meeting schedules, and delivering business value. Project processes directly impact the first three, but only indirectly influence the last one. The ultimate value of a project deliverable is determined by a large number of factors in addition to the project management approach, many of which are totally out of the control of the project team. Business value data may be the best information you have available, though, so make effective use of what you can find.

Even if you can find or create only modest evidence that better project management processes will be beneficial, it is not hopeless. There are other approaches that may suffice, using anecdotal information, models, and case studies.

Determining which approaches to use depends on your situation. There is a wide continuum of beliefs about project management among upper-level managers. Some managers favor project management naturally. These folks will require little or no convincing, and any approach you use is likely to succeed. Other managers are highly skeptical about project management and will heavily focus on the visible costs (which are unquestionably real) while doubting the benefits. The best approach in this case is to gather local data, lots of it, that shows as clearly as possible how high the costs of *not* using better processes are. Trying to convince an extreme skeptic that project management is necessary may even be a waste of time, for both of you. Good risk management in such a skeptical environment is up to you, and it may be necessary to do it "below the radar."

Fortunately, most managers are somewhere in the middle, neither "true believers" in project management nor chronic process adversaries. The greatest potential for process improvement is with this ambivalent group. Using anecdotal information, models, case studies, and other information can be effective.

Anecdotal information Building a case for more project process with stories depends on outlining the benefits and costs, and showing there is a net benefit. Project management lore is filled with stated benefits, among them:

- Better communication
- Less rework
- Lowered costs, reduced time
- Earlier identification of gaps and inadequate specifications
- Fewer surprises
- Less chaos and firefighting

Finding situations that show where project management delivered on these or where lack of process created a related problem should not be hard.

Project management does have costs, some direct and some more subtle, and you will need to address these. One obvious cost is the "overhead" it represents: meetings, paperwork, time invested in project management activities. Another is the initial (and ongoing) cost of establishing good practices in an organization, such as training, job aids, and new process documentation. Do some assessment of the investment required and summarize the results.

There is a more subtle cost to managers in organizations that set high project management standards: the shift that occurs in the balance of power in an organization. Without project management processes, all the power in an organization is in the hands of management; all negotiations tend to be resolved using political and emotional tactics. Having little or no data, project teams are fairly easily backed into whatever corners their management chooses. With data, the discussion shifts and negotiations are based more on reality. Even if you choose not to directly address this "cost," be aware of it in your discussions.

Answering the question "Is project management worth it?" using anecdotal information depends on whether the benefits can be credibly shown to outweigh the costs. Your case will be most effective if you find the best examples you can, using projects from environments as similar to yours as possible.

Models Another possible approach for establishing the value of process relies on logical models. The need for process increases with scale and complexity, and managing projects is no exception to this. Scaling projects may be done in a variety of ways, but one common technique segregates them into three categories: small, medium, and large.

Small projects are universal; everyone does them. There is usually no particular process or formality applied, and more often than not these simple projects are successful. Nike-style ("Just Do It") project management is good enough, and although there may well be any number of slightly better ways to approach the work (apparent in hindsight, more often than not), the penalties associated with simply diving into the work are modest enough that it doesn't matter much. Project management processes are rarely applied with any rigor, even by project management zealots, as the overhead involved may double the work required for the project.

Medium-size projects last longer and are more complex. The benefits of thinking about the work, at least a little, are obvious to most people. At a minimum, there is a "to do" list. Rolling up your sleeves and beginning work with no advance thought often costs significant additional time and money. As the "to do" list spills over a single page, project management processes start to look useful. At what exact level of complexity this occurs has a lot to do with experience, background, and individual disposition. Many mid-size projects succeed, but the possibility of falling short of some key goal (or complete project failure) is increasing.

For large projects, the case for project management should never really be in doubt. Beyond a certain scale, all projects with no process for managing the work will fail to meet at least some part of the stated objective. For the largest of projects, success rates are low even *with* program management and systems engineering processes in addition to thorough project management practices.

For projects of different sizes, costs of execution with and without good project management will vary. Figure 2-1 shows the cost of a

Figure 2-1. Cost benefit for project management.

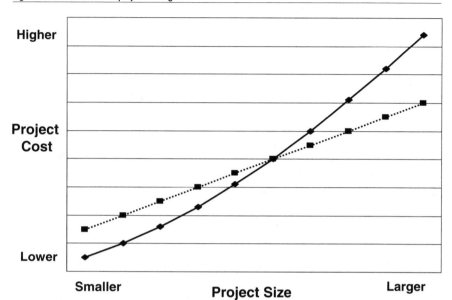

"best effort," or brute force, approach to a project contrasted with a project management approach. The assumption for this graph is that costs will vary linearly with project scale if project management is applied, and they will vary geometrically with scale if it is not. This figure, though not based on empirical data, is solidly rooted in a large amount of anecdotal information.

The figure has no units, because the point at which the crossover occurs (in total project size and cost) is highly situational. If project size is measured in effort-months, a common metric, a typical crossover might be between one and four total effort-months.

Wherever the crossover point is, the cost benefit is minor near this point, and negative below it. For these smaller projects, project management is a net cost or of small financial benefit. (Cost may not be the only, or even the most important, consideration, though. Project management methodologies may also be employed for other reasons, such as to meet legal requirements, to manage risk better, or to improve coordination between independent projects.)

A model similar to this, especially if it is accompanied by project success and failure data, can be a compelling argument for adopting better project management practices.

Case studies To offset the costs of project management, you need to establish measurable (or at least plausible) benefits. Many studies and cases have been developed over the years to assess this, including the one summarized in Figure 2-2. The data in this particular study was collected over a three-year period in the early 1990s from more than two hundred projects at Hewlett-Packard. For every project included, all schedule changes were noted and characterized. All changes attributed to the same root cause were aggregated, and the summations were sorted for the Pareto diagram in the figure, displaying the magnitude of the change on the vertical axis and the root causes along the horizontal axis.

Additional project effort—hundreds of engineer months—was associated with the most common root causes. The codes for the root causes, sorted by severity, were:

1. Unforeseen technical problems
2. Poor estimation of effort/top-down schedules
3. Poor product/system design or integration problems
4. Changing product definition
5. Other
6. Unforeseen activities/too many unrelated activities

Figure 2-2. Schedule change Pareto diagram.

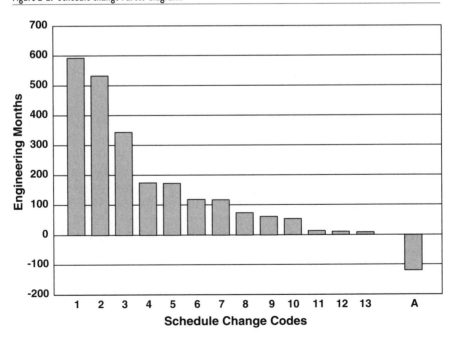

7. Understaffed, or resources not on time

8. Software development system/process problems

9. Related project slip (also internal vendor slip)

10. Insufficient support from service areas

11. Hardware development system/process problems

12. Financial constraints (tooling, capital, prototypes)

13. Project placed on hold

A. Acceleration

Not every one of these root causes directly correlates with project management principles, but most of them clearly do. The largest one is unforeseen technical problems, many of which were probably caused by insufficient planning. The second, faulty estimation, is also a project management factor. Although better project management would not have eliminated all these slippages, it surely would have reduced them. The top two reasons in the study by themselves represent an average of roughly five unanticipated engineer-months per project; reducing this by half would save thousands of dollars per project. Similar conclusions may be drawn from the analysis of the Project Experience Risk Information Library (PERIL) database later in this chapter and throughout this book.

Case study data such as these examples, particularly if it directly relates to the sort of project work you do, can be convincing. You likely have access to data similar to this, or could estimate it, for rework, fire-fighting, crisis management, missing work, and the cost of defects on recent projects.

Other reasons for project management One of the principal motivators in organizations that adopt project principles is reduction of uncertainty. Most technical people hate risk and will go to great lengths to avoid it. One manager who strongly supports project management practices uses the metaphor of going down the rapids of a white-water river. Without project management, you are down in the water—you have no visibility, it is cold, it is hard to breathe, and your head is hitting lots of rocks. With project management, you are up on a raft. It is still a wild ride, but you can see a few dozen feet ahead and steer around the worst obstacles. You can breathe more easily, you are not freezing and are less wet, and you have some confidence that you will survive the trip. In this manager's group, minimizing uncertainty is important and planning is never optional.

Another motivator is a desire (or requirement) to become more process oriented. Current standards and legal requirements for enterprise risk management in the United States and worldwide make adoption of formal processes for risk management obligatory. (The direct connection of this to project risk management is explored in Chapter 13.) In firms that provide solutions to customers, using a defined methodology is a competitive advantage that can help win business. In some organizations, evidence of process maturity is deemed important, and standards set by organizations such as the Software Engineering Institute for higher maturity are pursued. In other instances, specific process requirements may be tied to the work, as with many government contracts. In all of these cases, project management is mandatory, at least to some extent, whether the individuals and managers involved think it is a good idea or not.

The Project Management Methodology

Project risk management depends on thorough, sustained application of effective project management principles. The precise nature of the project management methodology can vary widely, but management of risk is most successful when consistent processes are adopted by the organization as a whole, because there will be more information to work with and more durable support for the ongoing effort required. If you need to manage risk better on your project and it proves impossible to gain support for more effective project management principles broadly, resolve to apply them project by project, with sufficient rigor to develop the information you need to manage risk.

Defining Risk Management for the Project

Beyond basic project planning, risk management also involves specific planning for risk. Risk planning begins by reviewing the initial project assumptions. Project charters, datasheets, or other documents used to initiate a project often include information concerning risk, as well as goals, staffing assumptions, and other information. Any risk information included in these early project descriptions is worth noting; sometimes projects believed to be risky are described as such, or there may be other evidence of project risk. Projects that are thought to be low risk may involve assumptions leading to unrealistically low staffing and funding. Take note of any differences in *your* perception of project risk and the stated (or implied) risks perceived by the project sponsors. Risk planning builds on a foundation that is consistent with the overall assumptions and project objectives. In particular, work to understand the expectations of the project stakeholders, and adopt an approach to risk management that reflects your environment.

Stakeholder Risk Tolerance

Organizations in different businesses deal with risk in their own ways. Start-ups and speculative endeavors such as oil exploration generally have a high tolerance for risk; many projects undertaken are expected to fail, but these are compensated for by a small number that are extremely successful. More conservative organizations, such as governments and enterprises that provide solutions to customers for a fee, are generally risk averse and expect consistent success but more modest returns on each project. Organizational risk tolerance is reflected in the organizational policies, such as pre-established prohibitions on pursuing fixed-price contract projects.

In addition, the stakeholders of the project may have strong individual opinions on project risk. Although some stakeholders may be risk tolerant, others may wish to staff and structure the work to minimize extreme outcomes. Technical contributors tend to prefer low risk. One often-repeated example of stakeholder risk preference is attributed to the NASA astronauts, who observed that they were sitting on the launch pad atop hundreds of systems, each constructed by the lowest bidder. Risk tolerance frequently depends on your perspective.

Planning Data

Project planning information supports risk planning. As you define the project scope and create planning documents such as the project work breakdown structure, you will uncover potential project risks. The planning processes also support your efforts in managing risk. The linkages between project planning and risk identification are explored in Chapters 3 through 6.

Templates and Metrics

Risk management is easier and more thorough when you have access to predefined templates for planning, project information gathering, and risk assessment. Templates that are preloaded with information common to most projects make planning faster and decrease the likelihood that necessary work will be overlooked. Consistent templates created for use with project scheduling applications organizationwide make sharing information easier and improve communication. If such templates exist, use them. If there are none, create and share proposed versions of common documents with others who do similar project work, and begin to establish standards.

Risk planning also relies on a solid base of historical data. Archived project data supports project estimating, quantitative project risk analysis, and project tracking and control. Examples of metrics useful for risk management are covered in Chapter 9.

Risk Management Plan

For small projects, risk planning may be informal, but for large, complex projects, you should develop and publish a written risk management plan. A risk management plan includes information on stakeholders, planning processes, project tools, and metrics, and it states the standards and objectives for risk management on your project. While much of the information in a risk plan can be developed generally for all projects in an organization, each specific project has at least some unique risk elements.

A risk plan usually starts by summarizing your risk management approach, listing the methodologies and processes that you will use, and defining the roles of the people involved. It may also include information such as definitions and standards for use with risk management tools; the frequency and agenda for periodic risk reviews; any formats to be used for required inputs and for risk management reports; and requirements for status collection and other tracking. In addition, each project may determine specific trigger events and thresholds for metrics associated with project risks, and the budgets for risk analysis, contingency planning, and risk monitoring.

Another aspect of risk planning is ensuring that risk management plans include adequate attention to project opportunities. The uncertainty inherent in projects means that some things may go better than expected. Considering project options that represent better opportunities can be at least as important to managing project risk as managing potential threats. Project opportunity management is discussed in more detail in Chapter 6.

The PERIL Database

Good project management is based on experience. Fortunately, the experience and pain need not all be personal; you can also learn from the experience of others, avoiding the aggravation of seeing everything firsthand. The Project Experience Risk Information Library (PERIL) database provides a step in that direction.

For more than a decade, in conducting workshops and classes on project risk management, I have been collecting data anonymously from hundreds of project leaders on their past project problems. Their descriptions included both what went wrong and the amount of impact it had on their projects. I have compiled this data in the PERIL database, which serves as the foundation for this book. The database describes a wide spectrum of things that have gone wrong with past projects, and it provides a sobering perspective on what future projects will face. Since the version of the PERIL database I used in the first edition of this book, the number of included cases has nearly tripled, to well over 600.

Some project risks are easy to identify because they are associated with familiar work. Other project risks are more difficult to uncover because they arise from new, unusual, or otherwise unique requirements. The PERIL database is valuable in helping to identify at least some of these otherwise invisible risks. In addition, the PERIL database summarizes the magnitude of the consequences associated with key types of project risk. Realistic impact information can effectively counteract the generally optimistic assessments typically used for project risks. Although some of the specific cases in the PERIL database relate only to certain types of projects or may be unlikely to recur, some close approximation of these situations will be applicable to most technical projects.

Sources for the PERIL Database

The information in the PERIL database comes primarily from participants in classes and workshops on project risk management, representing a wide range of project types. Slightly more than half the projects are product development projects, with tangible deliverables. The rest are information technology, customer solution, or process improvement projects. The projects in the PERIL database are worldwide, with a majority from the Americas (primarily United States, Canada, and Mexico). The rest of the cases are from Asia (mostly Singapore and India) and from Europe and the Middle East (from about a dozen countries, but largely from Germany and the United Kingdom). As with most modern projects, whatever their type or location the projects in the PERIL database share a strong dependence on new or relatively new technology. The majority of these projects also involved software development. There are both longer and shorter projects represented here, but the typical project in the database had a planned duration between six months and one year. Although there are some large programs in PERIL, typical staffing on these projects was rarely larger than about twenty people.

The raw project numbers in the PERIL database are presented in the following table.

	Americas	Asia	Europe/Middle East	Total
IT/Solution	256	57	18	331
Product Development	224	66	28	318
Total	**480**	**123**	**46**	**649**

Although the PERIL database represents many projects and their risks, with only 600 examples, it is far from comprehensive. The database contains only a small fraction of the thousands of projects undertaken by the project leaders from whom it was collected, and it does not even represent *all* the problems encountered on the projects that are included. Because of this, analysis of the data in the PERIL database is more suggestive of potential project risks than definitive. Despite this, the overall analysis of the current data corroborates the conclusions reached from the earlier, smaller database, so the broad trends appear to be holding up.

Also, as with any data based on nonrandom samples, there are inevitable sources of bias. The database contains a bias for major project risks, because the project leaders were asked to provide information on significant problems. Trivial problems are excluded from the data by design. There is also potential bias because each case was self-reported. Although all the information included is anonymous, some embarrassing details or impact assessment may well have been omitted or minimized. In addition, nearly all of the information was reported by people who were interested enough in project and risk management to invest their time participating in a class or workshop, so they are at the least somewhat skilled in project management. This could cause problems related to poor project management to be underrepresented.

Even considering these various limitations and biases, the PERIL database does illuminate a wide range of risks typical of today's projects. It is filled with constructive patterns, and the biggest source of bias—a focus on only major problems—accurately mirrors accepted strategies for risk management. Nonetheless, before blindly extending the following analysis to any particular situation, be aware that your mileage may vary.

Measuring Impact in the PERIL Database

The problem situations that make up the PERIL database resulted in a wide range of adverse consequences, including missed deadlines, significant overspending, scope reductions, and a long list of other undesirable outcomes that were not easily quantified. Although such an extensive assortment of misery may be fascinating, it is difficult to pummel into a useful structure. To this end, I chose to normalize all the quantitative data in the database using only time impact, measured in weeks of project slippage. This tactic makes sense in light of today's obsession with meeting deadlines, and it was an easy choice because by far the most prevalent serious impact reported in this data was deadline slip. Focusing on time is also appropriate because among the project triple constraints of scope, time, and cost, time is the only one that's completely out of our control—when it's gone, it's gone.

For cases where the impact reported was primarily something other than time, I either worked with the project leader to estimate an equivalent project slippage or excluded the case from the database. For example, when a project met its deadline by using significant overtime, we estimated the slippage equivalent to working all those nights, weekends, and holidays. If a project found it necessary to make significant cuts to the project scope, we estimated the additional duration that would have been required to retain the original scope. Where such transformations are included in the PERIL database, we used conservative methods in estimating the adjustments.

To better reflect the reality of typical projects, the time data in the PERIL database also excludes extremes. In keeping with the theme of focus on major risk, projects that reported a time slippage of less than a week were not included. On the assumption that there are probably better options for projects that overshoot their deadlines by six months or more, the cases included that reported longer slips are capped at twenty-six weeks. This prevents a single case or two from inordinately skewing the analysis, while retaining the root cause of the problem. Because of their enormous and disruptive potential impact, these and other significant cases will receive more detailed attention later in this book.

The average impact for all records was roughly seven weeks, representing almost a 20 percent slip for a typical nine-month project. The averages by project type were consistently close to the average for all of the data, with product development projects averaging a bit more than seven weeks and IT and solution projects slightly less than seven weeks. By region, projects in the Americas and in Europe and the Middle East averaged slightly more than seven weeks. Asian projects were slightly better, but still nearly six weeks. This data by region and project type includes average impact, in weeks.

	Americas	Asia	Europe/Middle East	Total
IT/Solution	7.0	6.0	7.5	6.8
Product Development	7.7	5.2	6.6	7.1
Total	**7.3**	**5.5**	**6.9**	**6.9**

Risk Causes in the PERIL Database

Although the consequences of the risks in the PERIL database are consistently reported based on time, the risk causes were varied and abundant. One approach to organizing this sort of data uses a risk breakdown structure (RBS) to categorize risks based on risk type. The categories and subcategories I have used to structure the database form an example of an RBS. Each reported problem in the database is characterized in the hierarchy based on its principal root cause. The top level of the hierarchy is organized similarly to the first half of this book, around the project triple constraints of scope, schedule (or time), and resource (or cost). The database subdivides these types of risks based on further breakdown of the root causes of the risks. For most of the risks, determining the principal root cause was fairly straightforward. For others, the problem reported was a result of several factors, but in each case, the risk was assigned to the project parameter that was most significant.

Across the board, risks related to scope issues were dominant. They were both most frequent and, on average, most damaging. Although schedule risks were next most numerous, on average resource risks were slightly more harmful. The typical slippage for risks within each major type represented from about a month and a half to two months.

	Count	Cumulative Impact (Weeks)	Average Impact (Weeks)
Scope	270	2114	7.8
Schedule	192	1141	5.9
Resource	187	1250	6.7
Total	**649**	**4,505**	**6.9**

The total impact of all the risks is a bit more than 4,500 weeks—almost ninety years—of slippage. A Pareto chart summarizing total impact by category is shown in Figure 2-3.

Within each of these three categories the data is further subdivided based on root-cause categories, using the following definitions.

Figure 2-3. Total project impact by root-cause category.

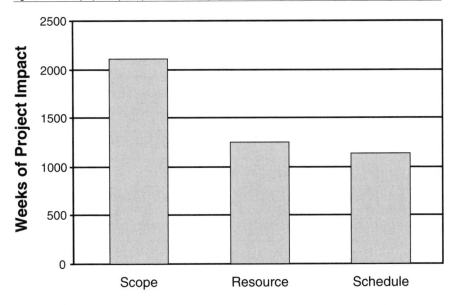

Root-Cause Subcategories	Definition	Cases	Cumulative Impact (Weeks)	Average Impact (Weeks)
Scope: Changes	Revisions made to scope during the project	177	1,460	8.2
Resource: People	Issues arising from internal staffing	123	706	5.7
Scope: Defects	Failure to meet deliverable requirements	93	654	7.0
Schedule: Delays	Project slippage due to factors under the control of the project	102	509	5.0
Schedule: Estimates	Inadequate durations allocated to project activities	49	370	7.6
Resource: Outsourcing	Issues arising from external staffing	47	316	6.7
Schedule: Dependencies	Project slippage due to factors outside the project	41	262	6.4
Resource: Money	Insufficient project funding	17	228	13.4

A Pareto of the cumulative impact data is shown in Figure 2-4. By far the largest source of slippage in this Pareto chart is scope change; it is more than twice as large as the next subcategory. One positive aspect

Figure 2-4. Total project impact by subcategory.

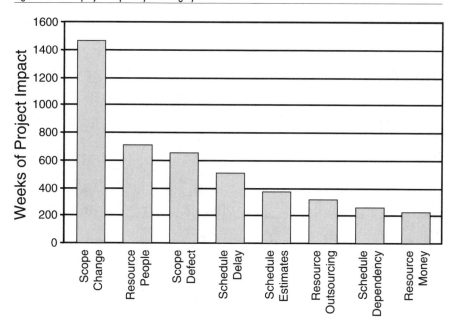

of this data is that the top five subcategories are all things that are at least partially within the purview of the project leader. This suggests that more focus on the things that you can control as a project leader can significantly reduce the number and magnitude of unpleasant surprises you'll encounter during your projects. This idea, along with further decomposition of these risk root-cause categories, is explored through the next three chapters, with scope risks discussed in Chapter 3, schedule risks in Chapter 4, and resource risks in Chapter 5.

Big Risks

Most books on project risk management spend a lot of time on theory and statistics. The first edition of this book departed from that tradition by focusing instead on what actually happens to real projects, using the PERIL database as its foundation. The point was to illuminate significant sources of actual project risk, with specific suggestions about what to do about the most serious problems—the "black swans."

Calling such risks "black swans" has been popularized of late by the writings of Nassim Nicholas Taleb. The notion of a black swan originated in Europe before there was much knowledge of the rest of the world.

In the study of logic, the statement "All swans are white" was used as the example of something that was incontrovertibly true. Because all the swans observed in Europe were white, a black swan was deemed impossible. It came as something of a shock when a species of black swans was later discovered in Australia. This realization gave rise to the metaphorical use of the term "black swan" to describe something erroneously believed to be impossible.

Taleb's primary subject matter (discussed in depth in his 2001 book, *Fooled by Randomness*) is financial risk, but his concept of a black swan as a "large-impact, hard-to-predict, rare event" is nonetheless applicable to project risk management. It is a mistake to consider a situation as impossible merely because it happens rarely or has not happened yet. In projects, it is common for project leaders to discount major project risks because they are estimated to have extremely low probabilities. But these risks do occur—the PERIL database is full of them—and the severity of problems they cause means that ignoring them can be unwise. When these risks do occur, the same project managers who initially dismissed them come to perceive them as much more predictable—sometimes even inevitable.

In the next three chapters, we will heighten visibility of these project-destroying "black swans" by singling out the most severe 20 percent of the risks in the PERIL database—the 127 cases representing the most schedule slippage. The definition of a "large-impact, hard-to-predict, rare event" is a useful starting point, but as the database shows, these most damaging risks are not as rare as might be thought, and they need not be so difficult for project managers to predict if they get appropriate attention in the risk management process.

Half of the "black swans," sixty-four, are scope risks. Schedule and resource risks are fewer, each constituting about a quarter of the total. These risks caused projects to slip at least three months, and they account for over half of the total damage in the PERIL database, almost 2,500 weeks of accumulated slip. The next three chapters will dig into the details of these risks, with the goal of improving your chances of identifying them in future projects. In the second half of the book, we will explore response tactics for dealing with these and other significant project risks.

Key Ideas for Project Risk Planning

- Project selection affects risk management and depends upon it.
- Project risk management builds on the foundation provided by your project definition and planning.
- A project risk plan summarizes your risk management approach.

A Second Panama Canal Project:
Sponsorship and Initiation (1902–1904)

"A man, a plan, a canal. Panama."

—FAMOUS PALINDROME

Successful projects are often not the first attempt to do something. Often, there is a recognized opportunity that triggers a project. If the first attempted project fails, it discourages people for a time. Soon, however, if the opportunity remains attractive another project will begin, building on the work and the experiences of the first project. A canal at Panama remained an attractive opportunity. When Theodore Roosevelt became president in 1901, he decided to make successful completion of a Central American canal part of his presidential legacy. (And so it is. He is the "man" in the famous palindrome.)

As much as the earlier French project failed because of lapses in project management, the U.S. project ultimately succeeded as a direct result of applying good project principles. The results of better project and risk management on this second project will unfold throughout the remainder of this book.

Unlike the initial attempt to build a canal, the U.S. effort was not a commercial venture. Maintaining separate U.S. navies on the East and West coasts had become increasingly costly. Consolidation into a single larger navy required easy transit between the Atlantic and Pacific, so Theodore Roosevelt saw the Panama Canal as a strategic military project, not a commercial one. The U.S. venture considered several routes, but as the French had done, they selected Panama.

Theodore Roosevelt was a more typical project sponsor than Ferdinand de Lesseps. He delegated the management of the project to others. His greatest direct contribution to the project was in "engineering" the independence of Panama from Colombia. (This "revolution" was accomplished by a pair of gunboats, one at Colon on the Gulf of Mexico and another at Panama City on the Pacific. Without the firing of a single shot, the independent nation of Panama was created in 1902. Repercussions of this U.S. foreign policy decision persist, more than a century later.) To get the project started quickly, Roosevelt also moved to acquire the assets of the Nouvelle Compagnie (which returned some relief to shareholders of the original company, but not much).

"I took the isthmus!" Roosevelt said. He then went to the U.S. Congress to get approval to go forward with the building of the canal. Following all this activity and the public support it generated, Congress had little choice but to support the project. Although the specifics for the project were still vague, the intention of the United States was clear: to build a canal at Panama capable of transporting even the largest U.S. warships, and to build it as quickly as was practical.

Insight into Roosevelt's thinking concerning the project is found in this quote from 1899, two years before his presidency:

> Far better it is to dare mighty things, to win glorious triumphs, even though checkered by failure, than to take rank with those poor spirits who neither enjoy much nor suffer much, because they live in the gray twilight that knows not victory nor defeat.

Project sponsors often aspire to "dare mighty things." They are much more risk tolerant than most project leaders and teams. Good risk management planning serves to balance the process of setting project objectives, so we undertake projects that are not only worthwhile and challenging but also *possible*.

3

Identifying Project Scope Risk

"Well begun is half done."
—ARISTOTLE

Although beginning well will never actually complete half of a project, beginning poorly will lead to disappointment, rework, stress, and potential failure. A great deal of project risk can be discovered at the earliest stages of project work, when defining the scope of the project.

For risks associated with the elements of the project management triple constraint (scope, schedule, and resources), scope risk generally will be considered first. Of the three types of projects that will fail—those that are beyond your capabilities, those that are overconstrained, and those that are ineffectively executed—the first type is the most significant, because this type of project is *literally* impossible. Identification of scope risks will reveal either that your project is feasible or that it lies beyond the state of your art. Early decisions to shift the scope or abandon the project are essential on projects with significant scope risks.

There is little consensus in project management circles on a precise definition of "scope." Broad definitions use scope to refer to everything in the project, and narrow definitions limit project scope to include only project deliverables. For the purposes of this chapter, project scope is defined to be consistent with the *Guide to the Project Management Body of Knowledge (PMBOK® Guide)*. The type of scope risk considered here relates primarily to the project deliverable(s). Other types of project risk are covered in later chapters.

Sources of Scope Risk

Scope risks are most numerous in the Project Experience Risk Information Library (PERIL) database, representing more than one-third of the data. Even more important, risks related to scope accounted for nearly half of the total schedule impact. The two broad categories of scope risk in PERIL relate to *changes* and *defects*. By far the most damage was due to poorly managed change (two-thirds of the overall scope impact and almost a third of all the impact in the entire database), but all the scope risks represented significant exposure for these projects. While some of the risk situations, particularly in the category of defects, were legitimately "unknown" risks, quite a few of the problems could have been identified in advance and managed as risks. The two major root-cause categories for scope risk are separated into more detailed subcategories.

Scope Root-Cause Subcategories	Definition	Count	Cumulative Impact (Weeks)	Average Impact (Weeks)
Changes: Creep	Any nonmandatory scope change	77	676	8.8
Changes: Gap	Legitimate scope requirements discovered late in project	87	731	8.4
Defects: Software	System or intangible deliverable problems that must be fixed	42	306	7.3
Defects: Hardware	Tangible deliverable problems that must be fixed	38	261	6.9
Defects: Integration	Program-level defects that require scope shifts in projects	13	87	6.7
Changes: Dependency	Scope changes necessary because of external dependencies	13	53	4.1

Scope changes due to gaps were the most frequent, but scope creep changes were the most damaging on average. A Pareto chart of overall impact by type of risk is summarized in Figure 3-1, and a more detailed analysis follows.

Change Risks

Change happens. Few if any projects end with the original scope intact. Managing scope risk related to change relies on minimizing the loose ends of requirements at project initiation and having (and using) a

Figure 3-1. Total project impact by scope root-cause subcategories.

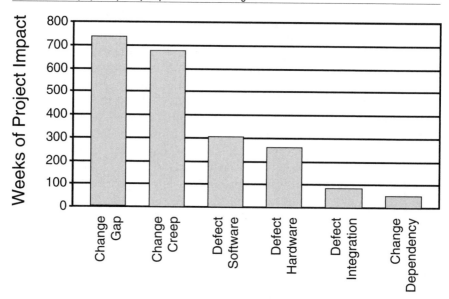

robust process for controlling changes throughout a project. In the PERIL database, there are three categories of scope change risks: *scope creep*, *scope gaps*, and *dependencies*.

Scope creep was the most damaging type of change risk, resulting in an average schedule slip of nearly nine weeks. Scope gaps were only slightly less damaging, at well over eight weeks of slippage, and were also both more common and had greater total impact. Each of these subcategories individually represented about one-sixth of all the problems in the PERIL database.

Scope gaps are the result of committing to a project before the project requirements are complete. When legitimate needs are uncovered later in the project, change is unavoidable. Some of the overlooked requirements were a consequence of the novelty of the project, and some were because of customers, managers, team members, or other project stakeholders who were not available at the project start. Although some of the scope gaps are probably unavoidable, in most of the cases these gaps were due to incomplete or rushed analysis. A more thorough scope definition and project work breakdown would have revealed the missing or poorly defined portions of the project scope.

Scope creep plagues all projects, especially technical projects. New opportunities, interesting ideas, undiscovered alternatives, and a wealth of other information emerges as the project progresses, providing a perpetual temptation to redefine the project and to make it "better."

Some project change of this sort may be justified through clear-eyed business analysis, but too many of these nonmandatory changes sneak into projects because the consequences either are never analyzed or are drastically underestimated. To make matters worse, the purported benefits of the change are usually unrealistically overestimated. In retrospect, much of scope creep delivers little or no benefit. In some particularly severe cases, the changes in scope delay the project so much that the ultimate deliverable has no value; the need is no longer pressing or has been met by other means. Scope creep represents unanticipated additional investment of time and money, because of both newly required effort and the need to redo work already completed. Scope creep is most damaging when entirely new requirements are piled on as the project runs. Such additions not only make projects more costly and more difficult to manage, they also can significantly delay delivery of the originally expected benefits. Managing scope creep requires an initial requirements definition process that thoroughly considers potential alternatives, as well as an effective process for managing specification changes throughout a project.

Scope creep can come from any direction, but one of the most insidious is from inside the project. Every day a project progresses you learn something new, so it's inevitable that you will see things that were not apparent earlier. This can lead to well-intentioned proposals by someone on the project team to "improve" the deliverable. Sometimes, scope creep of this sort happens with no warning or visibility until too late, within a portion of the project where the shift seems harmless. Only after the change is made do the real, and sometimes catastrophic, unintended consequences emerge. Particularly on larger, more complicated projects, all changes deserve a thorough analysis and public discussion, with a particularly skeptical analysis of all alleged benefits. Both scope creep and scope gaps are universal and pervasive issues for technical projects.

Scope dependencies are due to external factors that affect the project and are the third category of change risk. (Dependency risks that are primarily due to timing rather than requirements issues are characterized as schedule risks in the database.) Though less frequent in the PERIL database, compared with other scope change risks, scope dependencies did represent an average slippage of over a month. Admittedly, some of the cases in the database involved situations that no amount of realistic analysis would have uncovered in advance. Other examples, though, were a result of factors that should not have come as complete surprises. Although legal and regulatory changes do sometimes happen without notice, a little research will generally provide advance warning. Projects also depend on infrastructure stability, and periodic review of installation and maintenance schedules will reveal plans for new versions of application software, databases, telecommunications, hardware upgrades, or other changes that the project may need to anticipate and accommodate.

Defect Risks

Technical projects rely on many complicated things to work as expected. Unfortunately, new things do not always operate as promised or as required. Even normally reliable things may break down or fail to perform as desired in a novel application. Defects represent about a third of the scope risks and about one-seventh of all the risks in the PERIL database. The three categories of defect risks are *software*, *hardware*, and *integration*.

Software problems and *hardware* failures were the most common types of defect risk in the PERIL database, approximately equal in frequency. They were also roughly equal in impact, with software defects slightly exceeding seven weeks of delay on average and hardware problems a bit less than seven weeks. In several cases, the root cause was new, untried technology that lacked needed functionality or reliability. In other cases, a component created by the project (such as a custom integrated circuit, a board, or a software module) did not work initially and had to be fixed. In still other cases, critical purchased components delivered to the project failed and had to be replaced. Nearly all of these risks are visible, at least as possibilities, through adequate analysis and planning.

Some hardware and software functional failures related to quality or performance standards. Hardware may be too slow, require too much power, or emit excessive electromagnetic interference. Software may be too difficult to operate, have inadequate throughput, or fail to work in unusual circumstances. As with other defects, the definition, planning, and analysis of project work will help in anticipating many of these potential quality risks.

Integration defects were the third type of defect risk in the PERIL database. These defects related to system problems above the component level. Although they were not as common in the database, they were quite damaging. Integration defects caused an average of nearly seven weeks of project slip. For large programs, work is typically decomposed into smaller, related subprojects that can progress in parallel. Successful integration of the deliverables from each of the subprojects into a single system deliverable requires not only that each of the components delivered operates as specified but also that the combination of all these parts functions as a system. All computer users are familiar with this failure mode. Whenever all the software in use fails to play nicely together, our systems lock up, crash, or report some exotic "illegal operation." Integration risks, though relatively less common than other defect risks in the PERIL database, are particularly problematic, as they generally occur near the project deadline and are never easy to diagnose and correct. Again, thorough analysis relying on disciplines such as software architecture and systems engineering is essential to timely identification and management of possible integration risks.

Black Swans

Based on schedule impact, the worst 20 percent of the risks from each category in the PERIL database—defined as "black swans"—deserve more detailed attention. We'll explore these "large-impact, hard-to-predict, rare events" in this section. Each of the black swan risks represented at least three months of schedule slip, so each certainly qualifies as large impact. Black swan risks are rare; the PERIL database has an intentional bias in favor of the most serious risks, which are (or at least we hope are) not risks we expect to see frequently. The purpose of this section and the discussions in Chapters 4 and 5 is to make some of these black swans easier to predict.

Of the most damaging 127 risks in the PERIL database, 64—just over half—were scope risks. In the database as a whole, the black swans accounted for slightly more than half of the total risk impact. The top scope risks exceeded this with nearly 60 percent of the aggregate scope risk impact. The details are presented in the following table.

Scope Risks		Total Impact (Weeks)	Black Swan Impact (Weeks)	Black Swan Percentage
Changes	Creep	676	427	63%
	Dependency	53	26	49%
	Gap	731	480	66%
Defects	Hardware	261	137	52%
	Integration	87	26	30%
	Software	306	155	51%
Totals		**2,114**	**1,251**	**59%**

As the table shows, the black swan scope risks were dominated by change risk, with about three-quarters of these risks in terms of both quantity and impact. When major change risks occur, their effects are painful. Black swan defect risks were less common as well as somewhat less damaging overall, because recovery from these risks is generally more straightforward.

There were forty-seven black swan scope risks associated with change, dominated by scope gaps (with a total of twenty-five). Examples of the scope gap risks were:

- Project manager expected the solution to be one item, but it proved to be four.
- New technology required unanticipated changes to function.
- Development plans failed to include all of the 23 required applications.
- End users were too little involved in defining the new system.
- Requirements were understood differently by key stakeholders.
- Scope initially proposed for the project did not receive the upper management sign-off.
- Some countries involved provided incomplete initial requirements.
- Fit/gap analysis was poor.
- The architect determined late that the new design plan would be considerably more complex than expected.
- Lack of consensus on the specifications resulted in late project adjustments.
- When a survey required for the project was assigned to several people in different countries, each assumed someone else would do it but no one did.
- A midproject review turned up numerous additional regulations.
- Manufacturing problems were not seen in the original analysis.

Most of the rest of the change risk black swans were attributable to scope creep. Among these twenty-one risks were:

- Scoping for the project increased substantially after the award was won.
- New technology was introduced late in the project.
- The project team agreed to new requirements, some of which proved to be impossible.
- Late changes were poorly managed.
- The contract required state-of-the-art materials, which changed significantly over the project's two-year duration.

- Volume requirements increased late in the project, requiring extensive rework.
- Mid-project feature revisions had a major impact on effort and schedule, making the product late to market.
- A merger occurred during a companywide software refresh of all desktops and laptops, adding more systems and hugely complicating the project.
- A system for expense analysis expanded into redesign of most major internal systems.
- One partner on a Web design project expanded scope without communicating or getting approval from others.
- Late change required new hardware and a second phase.
- Application changed midproject to appeal to a prospective Chinese customer (who never bought).
- Project specifications changed, requiring material imported from overseas.

There was a single black swan change risk caused by an external dependency (in a pharmaceutical project, a significant study was unexpectedly mandated).

There were fewer black swans in the scope defect categories (seventeen total). Software and hardware defects each caused eight, and one was a consequence of poor integration. Examples of scope defect risks included:

- Redesign was required in a printer development project that failed to meet print quality goals.
- The system being developed had twenty major defects and eighty additional problems that had to be fixed.
- In user acceptance testing, a fatal flaw sent the deliverable back to development.
- During unit testing, performance issues arose with volume loads.
- Contamination of an entire batch of petri plates meant redoing them all.
- Server crashed with four months of information, none of it backed up, requiring everything to be reentered.
- Hardware failed near the end of a three-month final test, necessitating refabrication and retest.
- Purchased component failed, and continuing the project depended on a brute force and difficult-to-support workaround.

- System tool could not be scaled to a huge Web application.
- A software virus destroyed interfaces in two required languages, requiring rework.
- A purchased learning management system had unanticipated modular complexity.

Identifying scope risks similar to the examples given here can expose many potential problems. Reviewing these examples and the additional scope risks from the PERIL database listed in the Appendix can be a good starting point for uncovering possible scope-related problems on your next project.

Defining Deliverables

Scoping gaps were the top category of risk in the PERIL database. Defining deliverables thoroughly is a powerful tool for uncovering these potential project risks. The process for specifying deliverables for a project varies greatly depending on the type and the scale of the project.

For small projects, informal methods can work well, but for most projects, adopting a more rigorous approach is where good project risk management begins. For most projects, defining the deliverables is the initial opportunity for the project leader and team to begin uncovering risks. Whatever the process, the goal of deliverable definition is developing specific, written requirements that are clear, unambiguous, and agreed to by all project stakeholders and contributors.

A good, thorough process for defining project deliverables begins with identifying the people who should participate, including everyone who needs to agree. Project scope risk increases when key project contributors are not involved in the project early enough. Many scope gaps only become visible late in the project when these people do finally join the project team. Whenever it is not possible to work with the specific people who will later be part of the project team, locate and work with people who *are* available and who can represent all the needed perspectives and functional areas. If you need to, call in favors, beg, plead, or do whatever you need to do to get the right people involved.

Deliverable definition includes all of your core project team, but it rarely ends there. You will also need others from outside your team, from other functions such as marketing, finance, sales, and support. You are also likely to need input from outside your organization, from customers, users, other related project teams, and potential subcontractors. Consider the project over its entire development life cycle. Think about who will be involved with all stages of design, development, manufacturing or assembly, testing, documentation, marketing, sales, installation, distribution, support, and other aspects of the work.

Even when the right people are available and involved early in the initial project definition activities, it is difficult to be thorough. The answers for many questions may not yet be available, and some of your data may be ranges or even guesses. Specifics concerning new methods or technologies add more uncertainty. Three useful techniques for uncovering scope risk are using a documented definition process, developing a straw-man definition document, and adopting a rigorous evolutionary methodology.

Deliverable Definition Process

Processes for defining deliverables vary depending on the nature of the project. For product development projects, the following guidelines are a typical starting point. By reviewing such a list and documenting both what you know and don't know, you set the foundation for project scope and begin to identify activities for your project plan necessary to fill in the gaps.

Topics for a typical deliverable definition process are:

- Alignment with business strategy (How does this project contribute to stated high-level business objectives?)
- User and customer needs (Has the project team captured the ultimate end-user requirements that must be met by the deliverable?)
- Compliance (Has the team identified all relevant regulatory, environmental, and manufacturing requirements, as well as any relevant industry standards?)
- Competition (Has the team identified both current and projected alternatives to the proposed deliverable, including *not* undertaking the project?)
- Positioning (Is there a clear and compelling benefit-oriented project objective that supports the business case for the project?)
- Decision criteria (Does this project team have an agreed-upon hierarchy of measurable priorities for cost, time, and scope?)
- Delivery (Are logistical requirements understood and manageable? These include, but are not limited to, sales, distribution, installation, sign-off, and support.)
- Sponsorship (Does the management hierarchy collectively support the project and will they provide timely decisions and ongoing resources?)

- Resources (Does the project have, and will it continue to have, the staffing and funding needed to meet the project goals within the allotted time?)
- Technical risk (Has the team assessed the overall level of risk it is taking? Are technical and other exposures well documented?)

(This list is based on the 1972 SAPPHO Project at the University of Sussex, England.)

Although this list is hardly exhaustive, examining each criterion and documenting the information you already have provides the initial data for scoping and reveals what is missing. Determining the *degree* to which you understand each element (on a scale ranging from "Clueless" on one extreme to "Omniscient" on the other) reveals the biggest gaps. Although some level of uncertainty is inevitable, this analysis clarifies where the exposures are and helps you and the project sponsor decide whether the level of risk is inappropriately high. The last item on the list, technical risk, is most central to scope risk identification. High-level project risk assessment techniques are discussed in detail later in this chapter.

Straw-Man Definition Document

Most books on project management prattle on about identifying and documenting all the known project requirements. This is much easier said than done in the real world; it is hard to get users and stakeholders of technical projects to cooperate with this strategy. When too little about a project is clear, many people see only two options: accept the risks associated with incomplete definition (including inevitable scope creep), or abandon the project. Between these, however, lies a third option. By constructing a straw-man definition, instead of simply accepting the lack of data, the *project team* defines the specific requirements. These requirements can come from earlier projects, assumptions, or guesses, or they can come from your team's understanding of the problem that the project is supposed to solve. Any definition constructed this way is certain to be inaccurate and incomplete, but formalizing requirements leads to one of two beneficial results.

The first possibility is that these made-up requirements will be accepted and approved, giving you a solid basis for planning. Once sign-off has occurred, anything that is not quite right or deemed incomplete can still be changed, but only through a formal project change management process. Some contracting firms get rich using this technique. They win business by quoting fixed fees that are below the cost of delivering all the stated requirements, knowing full well that there will be changes. They then make their profits by charging for the inevitable changes that occur, generating large incremental project billings. Even for projects where the sponsors and project team are in the same organization, the sign-off process gives the project team a great deal of leverage when changes are proposed later in the project. (This whole process brings to mind the old riddle: How do you make a statue of an elephant? Answer: You get an enormous chunk of marble and chip off anything that does not look like an elephant.)

The second possible outcome is a flood of criticism, corrections, edits, and "improvements." Where most people are intimidated by a blank piece of paper or an open-ended question, *everyone* seems to be a critic. Once a straw-man requirements document is created, the project leader can circulate it far and wide as "pretty close, but not exactly right yet." Using such a document to gather comments (and providing big, red pens to get things rolling) is effective for the project, though it can be humbling to the original authors. In any case, it is always better to identify scoping issues early than to find you missed something during acceptance testing.

Evolutionary Methodologies

When the scope gaps are extremely large, a third approach to scope definition may be more productive. Evolutionary (or cyclic) methodologies are sometimes used for software development, where the end deliverable is truly novel and cannot be specified with much certainty. Rather than defining a system as a whole, these more organic approaches set out a general overall objective and then describe incremental stages, each producing a functional deliverable. Development projects have employed these step-by-step techniques since the 1980s, and they are still widely applied for innovative software development by small project teams that have ready access to their end users. The system built at the end of each development cycle adds more functionality, and each release brings the project closer to its destination. As the work continues, specific scope is defined for the next cycle or two using user feedback from testing of the previous cycle's deliverables. Cycles vary from about two to six weeks, depending on the specific methodology, and the deliverables for later cycles are defined only in general terms. The scoping will evolve as the project proceeds using user evaluations and other data collected along the way for course corrections.

Although this approach can be an effective technique for managing revolutionary projects where definition is not initially possible, it does carry the risk of institutionalizing scope creep. It can also result in "gold plating," or delivering additional functionality because it's possible, not because it's necessary.

Historically, evolutionary methodologies have carried higher costs than other project approaches. Compared with projects that are able to define project deliverables with good precision early using a more traditional "waterfall" life cycle, evolutionary development is both slower and more expensive. By avoiding a meandering definition process and eliminating the need to deliver to users every cycle and then evaluate their feedback, comparative costs for more traditionally run projects may be as little as a third, and timelines can be cut in half. From a risk standpoint, evolutionary methodologies focus primarily on scope risk, starting the project with no certain end date or budget. Without careful management, such projects might never end.

Risk management of these multicycle projects requires frequent reevaluation of the current risks as well as extremely disciplined scope management. To manage overall risk using evolutionary methodologies, set limits for both time and money, not only for the project as a whole but also for checkpoints no more than a few months apart.

Current thinking on evolutionary software development includes a number of methodologies described as agile, adaptive, or lightweight. These methods adopt more robust scope control and incorporate project management practices intended to avoid the "license to hack" nature of some of the earlier evolutionary development models. "Extreme programming" (XP) is a good example of this. XP is intended for use on relatively small software development projects by project teams collocated with their users. It adopts effective project management principles for estimating, managing scope, setting acceptance criteria, planning, and communicating. XP puts pressure on the users to determine the overall scope initially, and based on this the project team determines the effort required for the work. Development cycles of a few weeks are used to implement the scope incrementally, as prioritized by the users, but the amount of scope (which is carved up into "stories") delivered in each cycle is determined exclusively by the programmers. XP allows revision of scope as the project runs, but only as a zero-sum game—any additions cause something to be bumped out or deferred until later. XP also rigorously avoids scope creep in the current cycle.

Scope Documentation

However you go about defining scope, once it's defined you need to write it down. Managing scope risk requires a scope statement that clearly defines both what you will deliver and what you will not deliver. One problematic type of scope definition characterizes project requirements as "musts" and "wants." Although it may be fine to have some flexibility during the earliest project stages, carrying uncertainty into development work exacerbates scope risk. Retaining a list of "want to have" features remains common on many high-tech projects, and this makes planning chaotic and estimates inexact, and ultimately results in late (often expensive) scope changes. From a risk management standpoint, the "is/is not" technique is far superior to "musts and wants." The "is" list is equivalent to the "musts," but the "is not" list serves to limit scope. Determining what *is not* in the project specification is never easy, but if you fail to do it early many scope risks will remain hidden behind a moving target. An "is not" list does not cover every possible thing the project might include. It is generally a list of completely plausible, desirable features that could be included, and in fact might well be in scope for some future project—just not this one.

The "is/is not" technique is particularly important for projects that have a fixed deadline and limited resources, because it defines a boundary for scope consistent with the timing and budget limits. It is nearly always better to deliver the minimum requirements early than either to set aggressive scoping objectives that result in being late or to meet the deadline only by dropping promised features near the end of the project. As you document your project scope, establish limits that define what the project *will not* include, to minimize scope creep.

There are dozens of formats for a document that defines scope. In product development, it may be a reference specification or a product data sheet. In a custom solution project (and for many other types of projects), it may be a key portion of the project proposal. For information technology projects, it may be part of the project charter document. In other types of projects, it may be included in a statement of work or a plan of record. For agile software methodologies, it may be a brief summary on a Web page and a collection of index cards tacked to a wall or forms taped to a whiteboard. Whatever it may be called or be a part of, an effective definition for project deliverables must be *in writing*. Specific information typically includes:

- A description of the project (What are you doing?)
- Project purpose (Why are you doing it?)
- Measurable acceptance and completion criteria
- Planned project start
- Intended customer(s) or users
- What the project will and will not include ("is/is not")
- Dependencies (both internal and external)
- Staffing requirements (in terms of skills and experience)
- High-level risks
- Cost (at least a rough order-of-magnitude)

- Technology required
- Hardware, software, and other infrastructure required
- Detailed requirements, outlining functionality, usability, reliability, performance, supportability, and any other significant issues
- Other data customary and appropriate to your project

The third item on the list, acceptance criteria, is particularly important for identifying defect risks. When the requirements to be used at the end of the project are unclear or not defined, there is little chance that you will avoid problems, rework, and late project delay. The key for identifying scope risk is to capture what you know and, even more important, to recognize what you still need to find out.

High-Level Risk Assessment Tools

Technical project risk assessment is part of the earliest phase of project work, as mentioned in the discussion of the deliverable definition process earlier in this chapter. Even though there is usually little concrete information for initial project risk assessment, there are several techniques that provide useful insight into project risk even in the beginning stages. These tools are:

- Risk framework
- Risk complexity index
- Risk assessment grid

The first two are useful in any project that creates a tangible, physical deliverable through technical development processes. The third is appropriate for projects that have less tangible results, such as software modules, new processes, commercial applications, network architectures, or Internet service offerings. These tools all start with answering the same question: How much experience do you have with the work the project requires? How the tools use this information differs, and each builds on the assessment of technical risk in different directions. These tools are not mutually exclusive; depending on the type of project, more than one of them may be useful in characterizing risk.

Although any of these tools may be used at the start of a project to get an indication of project risk, none of the three is precise. The purpose of each is to provide information about the *relative* risk of a new project. Each of these three techniques is quick, though, and can provide insight into project risk early in a new project. None of the three is foolproof, but the results provide as good a basis as you are likely to have for deciding whether to go beyond initial investigation into further project work. (You may also use these three tools to reassess project risk later in the project. Chapter 9 discusses reusing these three tools, as well as several additional project risk assessment methods that rely on planning details to refine project risk assessment.)

Risk Framework

This is the simplest of the three high-level techniques. To assess risk, consider the following three project factors:

1. Technology (the work)
2. Marketing (the user)
3. Manufacturing (the production and delivery)

For each of these factors, assess the amount of change required by the project. For technology, does the project use only well-understood methods and skills, or will new skills be required (or developed)? For marketing, will the deliverable be used by someone (or by a class of users) you know well, or does this project address a need for someone unknown to you? For manufacturing, consider what is required to provide the intended end user with your project deliverable: are there any unresolved or changing manufacturing or delivery channel issues?

For each factor, the assessment is binary: change is either trivial (small) or significant (large). Assess conservatively; if the change required seems somewhere between these choices, treat it as significant.

Nearly all projects will require significant change to at least one of these three factors. Projects representing no (or little) change may not even be worth doing. Some projects, however, may require large changes in two or even all three factors. For technical projects, changes correlate with risk. The more change inherent in a project, and the more different types of change, the higher the risk.

In general, if your project has significant changes in only one factor, it probably has an acceptable, manageable level of risk. Evolutionary-type projects, where existing products or solutions are upgraded, leveraged, or improved, often fall into this category. If your project changes two factors simultaneously, it has higher relative risk, and the management decision to proceed, even into further investigation and planning, ought to reflect this. Projects that develop new platforms intended as the foundation of future project work frequently depend upon new methods for both technical development and manufacturing. For projects in this category, balance the higher risks against the potential benefits.

If your project requires large shifts in all three categories, the risks are greatest of all. Many, if not most, projects in this risk category are unsuccessful. Projects representing this much change are revolutionary and are justified by the substantial financial or other benefits that will result from successful completion. Often the risks seem so great—or so unknowable—that a truly revolutionary project requires the backing of a high-level sponsor with a vision.

A commonly heard story around Hewlett-Packard from the early 1970s involved a proposed project pitched to Bill Hewlett, the more technical of the two HP founders. The team brought a mock-up of a hand-held device capable of scientific calculations with ten significant digits of accuracy. The model was made out of wood, but it had all the buttons labeled and was weighted to feel like the completed device. Bill Hewlett examined the functions and display, lifted the device, slipped it in his shirt pocket, and smiled. The HP-35 calculator represented massive change in all three factors; the market was unknown, manufacturing for it was unlike anything HP had done before, and it was debatable whether the electronics could even be developed on the small number of chips that would fit in the tiny device. The HP-35 was developed primarily because Bill Hewlett wanted one. It was also a hugely successful product, selling more units in a month than had been forecasted for the entire year, and yielding a spectacular profit. The HP-35 also changed the direction of the calculator market completely, and it destroyed the market for slide rules and mechanical computing devices forever.

This story is known because the project was successful. Similar stories surround many other revolutionary products, like the Apple Macintosh, the Yahoo (and then Google) search engine, and home video cassette recorders. Stories around the risky projects that fail (or fall far short of their objectives) are harder to uncover; most people and companies would prefer to forget them. The percentage of revolutionary ideas that "crash and burn," based on the rate of Silicon Valley start-up company failures, is at least 90 percent. The higher risks of such projects should always be justified by substantial benefits and a strong, clear vision.

Risk Complexity Index

The risk complexity index is the second technique for assessing risk on technical projects. As in the risk framework tool, technology is the starting point. This tool looks more deeply at the technology being employed, separating it into three parts and assigning to each an assessment of difficulty. In addition to the technical complexity, the index looks at another source of project risk: the risk arising from larger project teams, or scale. The following formula combines these four factors:

Index = (Technology + Architecture + System) × Scale

For this index, *Technology* is defined as new, custom development unique to this project. *Architecture* refers to the high-level functional components and any external interfaces, and *System* is the internal software and hardware that will be used in the product. Assess each of these three against your experience and capabilities, assigning each a value from 0 to 5:

0—Only existing technology required

1—Minor extensions to existing technology needed in a few areas

2—Significant extensions to existing technology needed in a few areas

3—Almost certainly possible, but innovation needed in some areas

4—Probably feasible, but innovation required in many areas

5—Completely new, technological feasibility in doubt

The three technology factors will generally correlate, but some variation is common. Add these three factors, to a sum between 0 and 15.

For *Scale,* assign a value based on the number of people (including all full-time contributors, both internal and external) expected on the project:

0.8—Up to 12 people

2.4—13 to 40 people

4.3—41 to 100 people

6.6—More than 100 people

The calculation for the index yields a result between 0 and 99. Projects with an index below 20 are generally low-risk projects with durations of well under a year. Projects assessed between 20 and 40 are medium risk. These projects are more likely to get into trouble, and often take a year or longer. Most projects with an index above 40 are high risk, finishing long past their stated deadline, if they complete at all.

Risk Assessment Grid

The first two high-level risk tools are appropriate for hardware deliverables. Technical projects with intangible deliverables may not easily fit these models, so the risk assessment grid can be a better approach for early risk assessment.

This technique examines three project factors, similar to the risk framework. Assessment here is based on two choices for each factor, and technology is again the first. The other factors are different, and here the three factors carry different weights. The factors, in order of priority, are: Technology, Structure, and Size.

The highest weight factor, Technology, is based on required change, and it is rated either low or high, depending on whether the project team has experience using the required technology and whether it is well established in uses similar to the current project.

The second factor, Structure, is also rated either low or high, based on factors such as solid formal specifications, project sponsorship, and organizational practices appropriate to the project. Structure is rated low when there are significant unknowns in staffing, responsibilities, infrastructure issues, objectives, or decision processes. Good up-front definition indicates high structure.

The third factor, Size, is similar to the Scale factor in the risk complexity index. A project is rated either large or small. For this tool, size is not an absolute assessment. It is measured relative to the size of teams that the project leader has successfully led in the past. Teams that are only 20

Figure 3-2. Risk assessment grid.

Low	Medium	High
LOW Technology HIGH Structure SMALL Size **A**	LOW Technology LOW Structure LARGE Size **D**	HIGH Technology LOW Structure SMALL Size
LOW Technology HIGH Structure LARGE Size **B**	HIGH Technology HIGH Structure SMALL Size **E**	**G**
LOW Technology LOW Structure SMALL Size **C**	HIGH Technology HIGH Structure LARGE Size **F**	HIGH Technology LOW Structure LARGE Size **H**

A = Lowest Risk; H = Highest Risk

percent larger than the size a project leader has successfully led with should be considered large. Other considerations in assessing size are the expected length of the project, the overall budget for the project, and the number of separate locations where project work will be performed.

After you have assessed each of the three factors, the project will fall into one of the sections of the grid, A through H (see Figure 3-2). Projects in the right column are most risky; those to the left are more easily managed.

Beyond risk assessment, these tools may also guide early project risk management, indicating ways to lower project risk by using alternative technologies, making changes to reduce staffing, decomposing longer projects into a sequence of shorter projects with less aggressive goals, or improving the proposed structure. Use of these and other tools to manage project risk is the topic of Chapter 10.

Setting Limits

Although many scope risks come from specifics of the deliverable and the overall technology, scope risk also arises from failure to establish firm, early limits for the project.

In workshops on risk management, I demonstrate another aspect of scope risk using an exercise that begins with a single U.S. one-dollar bill. I show it to the group, setting two rules:

- The dollar bill will go to the highest bidder, who will pay the amount bid. All bids must be for a real amount—no fractional cents. The first bid must be at least a penny, and each succeeding bid must be higher than earlier bids. (This is the same as with any auction.)

- The second-highest bidder *also* pays the amount he or she bid (the bid just prior to the winning bid), but gets *nothing* in return. (This is unlike a normal auction.)

As the auctioneer, I start by asking if anyone wants to buy the dollar for one cent. Following the first bid, I solicit a second low bid, "Does anyone think the dollar is worth five cents?" After two low bids are made, the auction is off and running. The bidding is allowed to proceed to (and nearly always past) $1.00, until it ends. If $1.00 is bid and things slow down, a reminder to the person who has the next highest bid that he or she will spend almost one dollar to buy *nothing* usually gets things moving again. The auction ends when no new bids are made. The two final bids nearly always total well over $2.00.

By now everything is quite exciting. Someone has bought a dollar for more than a dollar. A second person has bought nothing but paid almost as much. To calm things down, I put the dollar away, explain that this is a lesson in risk management (not a scam), and apologize to people who seem upset.

So, what does the dollar auction have to do with risk management? This game's outcome is similar to what happens when a project that hits its deadline (or budget), creeps past, and just keeps going. "But we are *so* close. It's almost done; we *can't* stop now. . . ." The auction effectively models any case where people have, or think they have, too much invested in an undertaking to quit.

Dollar auction losses can be minimized by anticipating the possibility of an uncompensated investment, setting limits in advance, and then enforcing them. Rationally, the dollar auction has an expected return of half a dollar (the total return, one dollar, spread between the two active participants). If each participant set a bid limit of fifty cents, the auctioneer would always lose. For projects, clearly defining limits and then monitoring intermediate results will provide early indication that you may be in trouble. Project metrics such as earned value (described in Chapter 9), are useful in minimizing unproductive investments by detecting project overrun early enough to abort or modify unjustified projects. Defining project scope with sufficient detail and limits is essential for risk management.

Work Breakdown Structure (WBS)

Scope definition reveals some risks, but scope planning digs deeper into the project and uncovers even more. Product definition documents, scope statements, and other written materials provide the basis for decomposing of project work into increasingly finer detail, so it can be understood, delegated, estimated, and tracked. The process used to do this—to create the project work breakdown structure (WBS)—reveals potential defect risks.

One common approach to developing a WBS starts at the scope or objective statement and proceeds to carve the project into smaller parts, working "top down" from the whole project concept. Decomposition of work that is well understood is straightforward and quickly done. Whenever it is confusing or difficult to decompose project work into smaller, more manageable pieces, there is scope risk. If any part of the project resists breakdown using these ideas, that portion of the project is not well understood, and it is inherently risky.

Work Packages

The ultimate goal of the WBS process is to describe the entire project in much smaller pieces, often called "work packages." Each work package should be deliverable-oriented and have a clearly defined output. General guidelines for the size of the work represented by the work packages at the lowest level of a WBS are usually in terms of duration (between two and twenty workdays) or effort (roughly eighty person-hours or fewer). When breakdown to this level of detail is difficult, it is generally because of gaps in project understanding. These gaps either need to be resolved as part of project scoping or captured as scope risks. (These granularity guidelines foreshadow discussions on estimating risks discussed in Chapters 4 and 5.)

Work defined at the lowest level of a WBS may also be called "activities" or "tasks," but what really matters is that the effort be defined well enough that you understand how to complete it. If you cannot decompose the work into pieces within the guidelines, note it as a risk.

Aggregation

A WBS is a hierarchy and a useful method for detecting missing work. The principle of "aggregation" for a WBS ensures that the defined work at each level plausibly includes everything needed at the summary level above it. If the listed items under a higher-level work package do not represent its complete "to do" list, your WBS is incomplete. Either complete it by adding the missing work to the WBS, or note the WBS gaps as project scope risks. Any work in the WBS that you cannot adequately describe contributes to your growing accumulation of identified risks.

Parts of a project WBS that resist easy decomposition are rarely visible until you systematically seek them out. The WBS development process provides a tool for separating the parts of the project that you understand from those that you do not. Before proceeding into a project with significant unknowns, you also must identify these risks and determine whether the associated costs and other consequences are justified.

Ownership

There are many reasons why some project work is difficult to break into smaller parts, but the root cause is often a lack of experience with the work required. This is a common sort of risk discovered in developing a WBS, and it relates to delegation and ownership. A key objective in completing the project WBS is the delegation of each lowest-level work package (or whatever you may choose to call it) to someone who will own that part of the project. Delegation and ownership are well established in management theory as motivators, and they also contribute to team development and broader project understanding.

Delegation is most effective when it's voluntarily. It is fairly common on projects to allow people to assume ownership of project activities in the WBS by signing up for them, at least on the first pass. Although there is generally some conflict over activities that more than one person wants, sorting this out by balancing the workload, selecting the more experienced person, or using some other logical decision process usually works. But when the opposite occurs—when *no one* wants to be the owner—there are project risks to be identified. Activities without volunteers are risky, but you will need to investigate to find out why. There are a number of common root causes, including the one discussed before: no one understands the work well. Perhaps no one currently on the project has developed key skills that the work requires, or the work is technically so uncertain that no one believes it can be done at all. Or the work may be feasible, but no one believes that it can be completed in the "roughly two weeks" expected for activities defined at the lowest level of the WBS. In other cases, the description of deliverables may be so fuzzy that no one wants to be involved.

There are many other possible reasons, and these are also risks. Of these, availability is usually the most common. If everyone on the project is already working beyond full capacity on other work and other projects, no one will volunteer. Another possible cause might be that the activity requires working with people whom no one wants to work with. If the required working relationships are likely to be difficult or unpleasant, no one will volunteer, and successful completion of the work is uncertain. Some activities may depend on outside support or require external inputs that the project team is skeptical about. Few people willingly assume responsibility for work that is likely to fail because of issues beyond their control.

In addition, the work itself might be the problem. Even easy work can be risky, if people see it as thankless or unnecessary. All projects have at least some required work that no one likes to do. It may involve documentation or some other dull, routine part of the work. If done successfully, no one notices; this is simply expected. If something goes wrong, though, there is a lot of attention. The activity owner has managed to turn an easy part of the project into a disaster, and he or she will at least get yelled at. Most people avoid these activities.

Another situation is the "unnecessary" activity. Projects are full of these too, at least from the perspective of the team. Life-cycle, phase gate, and project methodologies place requirements on projects that seem to be (and in many cases, may actually be) unnecessary overhead. Other project work may be scheduled primarily because it is part of a planning template or because "That's the way we always do it." If the work is actually not needed, good project managers work to eliminate it.

To the project risk list, add clear descriptions of each risk identified while developing the WBS, including your best understanding of the root cause for each. These risks may emerge from difficulties in developing the WBS to an appropriate level of detail or in finding willing owners for the lowest-level activities. A typical risk listed might be: "The project requires conversion of an existing database from Sybase to Oracle, and no one on the current project staff has the needed experience."

WBS Size

Project risk correlates with size; when projects get too large, risk becomes overwhelming. Scope risk rises with complexity, and one measure of complexity is the size of the WBS. Once you have decomposed the project work, count the number of items at the lowest level. When the number exceeds about 200, project risk is high.

The more separate bits of work that a single project leader is responsible for, the more likely it becomes that something crucial to the project will be missed. As the volume of work and project complexity expand, the tools and practices of basic project management become more and more inadequate.

At high levels of complexity, the overall effort is best managed in one of two ways: as a series of shorter projects in sequence delivering what is required in stages, or as a program made up of a collection of smaller projects. In both cases, the process of decomposing the total project into sequential or parallel parts is done using a decomposition very like a WBS. In the case of sequential execution, the process is essentially similar to the evolutionary methodologies discussed previously in this chapter. For programs, the resulting decomposition creates a number of projects, each of which will be managed by a separate project leader using project management principles, and the overall effort will be the responsibility of a program manager. Project risk is managed by the project leaders, and overall program risk is the responsibility of the program leader. The relationship between managing project and program risk is discussed in Chapter 13.

When excessively lengthy or complex projects are left as the responsibility of a single project leader to plan, manage risk, and execute, the probability of successful completion is low.

Other Scope-Related Risks

Not all scope risks are strictly within the practice of project management. Examples are *market* risk and *confidentiality* risk. These risks are related, and although they may not show up in all projects, they are fairly common. Ignoring these risks is inappropriate and dangerous.

A business balance sheet has two sides: assets and liabilities. Project management primarily focuses on "liabilities," the expense and execution side, using measures related to the triple constraint of "scope/schedule/resources." Market and confidentiality risks tend to be on the asset, or *value*, side of the business ledger, where project techniques and teams are involved indirectly, if at all. Project management is primarily about delivering what you have been asked to deliver, and this does not always equate to "success" in the marketplace. Although it is obvious that "on time, on budget, within scope" will not necessarily make a project an unqualified success, managing these aspects alone is a big job and is really about all that a project leader should reasonably be held responsible for. The primary owners for market and confidentiality risks may not even be active project contributors, although many kinds of technical projects now engage cross-functional business teams—making these risks more central to the project. In any case, the risks are real, and they relate to scope. Unless identified and managed, they too contribute to project failure.

Market Risk

This first type of risk is about getting the definition wrong. Market risk can relate to features, timing, cost, or almost any facet of the deliverable. Various scenarios can trigger problems. When long development efforts are involved, the problem to be solved may change, go away, or be better addressed by an emerging new technology. A satisfactory deliverable may be brought to market a week after an essentially identical offering from a competitor. Even when a project produces exactly what was requested by a sponsor or economic buyer, it may be rejected by the intended end user. Sometimes the people responsible for promoting and selling a good product do not (or cannot) follow through. Many paths can lead to a result that meets the specifications and is delivered on time and on budget, yet is never deployed or fails to achieve expectations.

The longer and the more complicated the project is, the greater the market risk will tend to be. Project leaders contribute to the management of these risks through active, continuing participation in any market research and customer interaction, and by frequently communicating with (ideally, without annoying) all the people surrounding the project who will be involved with deployment of the deliverable.

Some of the techniques already discussed can help in managing this. A thorough process for deliverable definition probes for many of the sources of market risk, and the high-level risk tools outlined previously also provide opportunities to understand the environment surrounding the project.

In addition, ongoing contact with the intended users, through interviews, surveys, market research, and other techniques, will help to uncover problems and shifts in the assumptions the project is based upon. Agile methodologies employ ongoing user involvement in the definition of short, sequential project cycles, minimizing the "wrong" deliverable risk greatly for small project teams colocated with their users.

If the project is developing a product that will compete with similar offerings from competitors, ongoing competitive analysis to predict what others are planning can be useful (but, of course, competitors will not make this straightforward or easy—confidentiality risks are addressed next). Responsibility for doing this may be fully within the project, but if it is not, the project team should still review what is learned, and if necessary, encourage the marketing staff (or other stakeholders) to keep the information up to date.

The project team should always probe beyond the specific requirements (the *stated* need) to understand where the specifications come from (the *real* need). Understanding what is actually needed is generally much more important than simply understanding what was requested, and it is a key part of opportunity management. Early use of models, prototypes, mock-ups, and other simulations of the deliverable will help you find out whether the requested specifications are in fact likely to provide what is needed. Short cycles of development with periodic releases of meaningful functionality (and value) throughout the project also minimize this category of risk. Standards, testing requirements, and acceptance criteria need to be established in clear, specific terms, and periodically reviewed with those who will certify the deliverable.

Confidentiality Risk

A second type of risk that is generally not exclusively in the hands of the project team relates to secrecy. Although some projects are done in an open and relatively unconstrained environment, confidentiality is crucial to many high-tech projects, particularly long ones. If information about the project is made public, its value could decrease or even vanish. Better-funded competitors with more staff might learn of what you are working on and build it first, making your work irrelevant. Of course, managing this risk well will potentially *increase* the market risk, as you will be less free to gather information from end users. The use of prototypes, models, mock-ups, or even detailed descriptions can provide data to competitors that you want to keep in the dark. On some technical projects, the need for secrecy may also be a specific contractual obligation, as with government projects. Even if the deliverable is not a secret, you may be using techniques or methodologies that are proprietary competitive advantages, and loss of this sort of intellectual property also represents a confidentiality risk.

Within the project team, several techniques may help. Some projects work on a "need to know" basis and provide to team members only the information required to do their current work. Although this will usually hurt teamwork and motivation, and may even lead to substandard results (people will optimize only for what they know, not for the overall project), it is one way to protect confidential information.

Emphasizing the importance of confidentiality also helps. Periodically reinforce the need for confidentiality with all team members, and especially with contractors and other outsiders. Be specific about the requirements for confidentiality in contract terms when you bring in outside help, and make sure all nondisclosure terms are clearly understood. Any external market research or customer contact also requires effective nondisclosure agreements, again with enough discussion to make the need for secrecy clear.

In addition to all of this, project documents and other communication must be appropriately marked "confidential" (or according to the requirements set by your organization). Restrict distribution of project information, particularly electronic versions, to people who need it and who understand, and agree with, the reasons for secrecy. Protect information stored on computer networks or the Internet with passwords that are changed often enough to limit inappropriate access. Use legal protections such as copyrights and patents as appropriate to establish ownership of intellectual property. (Timing of patents can be tricky. On the one hand, they protect your work. On the other hand, they are public and may reveal to competitors what you are working on.)

Although the confidentiality risks are partially the responsibility of the project team, many lapses are well out of their control. Managers, sponsors, marketing staffs, and favorite customers are the sources for many leaks. Project management tools principally address execution of the work, not secrecy. Effective project management relies heavily on good, frequent communication, so projects with heavy confidentiality requirements can be difficult and even frustrating to lead. Managing confidentiality risk requires discipline, frequent reminders of the need for secrecy to all involved (especially those involved indirectly), limiting the number of people involved, and more than a little luck.

Documenting the Risks

As the requirements, scope definition documents, WBS, and other project data start to take shape, you can begin to develop a list of specific issues, concerns, and risks related to the scope and deliverables of the project. When the definitions are completed, review the risk list and inspect it for missing or incomplete information. If some portion of the project scope seems likely to change, note this as well. Typical scope risks involve performance, reliability, untested methods or technology, or combinations of deliverable requirements that are beyond your experience base. Make clear why each item listed is an exposure for the project; cite any relevant specifications and measures that go beyond those successfully achieved in the past in the risk description, using explicitly quantified criteria. An example might be, "The system delivered must execute at double the fastest speed achieved in the prior generation."

Sources of specific scope risks include:

- Requirements that seem likely to change
- Mandatory use of new technology
- Requirements to invent or discover new capabilities
- Unfamiliar or untried development tools or methods
- Extreme reliability or quality requirements
- External sourcing for a key subcomponent or tool
- Incomplete or poorly defined acceptance tests or criteria
- Technical complexity
- Conflicting or inconsistent specifications
- Incomplete product definition
- Large WBS

Using the processes for scope planning and definition will reveal many specific technical and other potential risks. List these risks for your project, with information about causes and consequences. The list of risks will expand throughout the project planning process and will serve as your foundation for project risk analysis and management.

> ## Key Ideas for
> ## Identifying Scope Risks
>
> - Clearly define all project deliverables, and note challenges.
> - Set limits on the project based on the value of the deliverables.
> - Decompose all project work into small pieces and identify work not well understood.
> - Assign ownership for all project work and probe for reasons behind any reluctance.
> - Note risk arising from expected project duration or complexity.

Panama Canal: Setting the Objective (1905–1906)

One of the principal differences between the earlier unsuccessful attempt to build the Panama Canal and the later project was the application of good project management practices. However, the second project had a shaky beginning. It was conceived as a military project and funded by the U.S. government, so the scope and objectives for the revived Panama Canal project should have been clear, even at the start. They were not.

The initial manager for the project when work commenced in 1904 was John Findlay Wallace, formerly the general manager of the Illinois Central Railroad. Wallace was visionary; he did a lot of investigating and experimenting but he accomplished little in Panama. His background included no similar project experience. In addition to his other difficulties, he could do almost nothing without the consent of a seven-man commission set up back in the United States, a commission that rarely agreed on anything. Also, nearly every decision, regardless of size, required massive amounts of paperwork. A year later, in 1905, US$128 million had been spent but still there was no final plan, and most of the workers were still waiting for something to do. The project had in most ways picked up just where the earlier French project had left off, problems and all. Even after a year, it was still not clear whether the canal would be at sea level or constructed with locks and dams. In 1905, mired in red tape, Wallace announced the canal was a mistake, and he resigned.

John Wallace was promptly replaced by John Stevens. Stevens was also from the railroad business, but his experience was on the building side, not the operating side. He built a reputation as one of the best engineers in the United States by constructing railroads throughout the Pacific frontier. Before appointing Stevens, Theodore Roosevelt eliminated the problematic seven-man commission, and he significantly reduced the red tape, complication, and delay. As chief engineer, Stevens, unlike Wallace, effectively had full control of the work. Arriving in Panama, Stevens took stock and immediately stopped all work on the canal, stating, "I was determined to prepare well before construction, regardless of clamor of criticism. I am confident that if this policy is adhered to, the future will show its wisdom." And so it did.

With the arrival of John Stevens, managing project scope became the highest priority. He directed all his initial efforts at preparation for the work. He built dormitories for workers to live in, dining halls to feed them, warehouses for equipment and materials, and other infrastructure for the project. The doctor responsible for health of the workers on the project, William Crawford Gorgas, had been trying for over a year to gain support from John Wallace for measures needed to deal with the mosquitoes, by then known to spread both yellow fever and malaria. Stevens quickly gave this work his full support, and Dr. Gorgas proceeded to eradicate these diseases. Yellow fever was conquered in Panama just six months after Dr. Gorgas received Stevens's support, and he made good progress combating malaria as well.

Under the guidance of Stevens, all the work was defined and planned employing well-established, modern project management principles. He said, "Intelligent management must be based on exact knowledge of facts. Guess work will not do." He did not talk much, but he asked lots of questions. People commented, "He turned me inside out and shook out the last drop of information." His meticulous documentation served as the basis for work throughout the project.

Stevens also determined exactly how the canal should be built, to the smallest detail. The objective for the project was ultimately set in 1907 according to his recommendations: The United States would build an eighty-kilometer (fifty-mile) lock-and-dam canal at Panama connecting the Atlantic and Pacific oceans, with a budget of US$375 million, to open in 1915. With the scope defined, the path forward became clear.

4

Identifying Project Schedule Risk

"Work expands so as to fill the time available for its completion."
—C. Northcote Parkinson, *Parkinson's Law*

Although Parkinson's observation was not backed up with any empirical data, its truth is rarely questioned. It seems particularly appropriate for technical projects, because in addition to all the obvious reasons that people have for using up the time available to complete their work, on technical projects there is an additional reason. Most people who are drawn to technical projects are analytical, and they like to be precise, accurate, and thorough. If there is time available to attempt to make something perfect, most engineers will try.

Projects, however, are rarely about perfection. They are about pragmatism, delivering a result that is "good enough." Practicality is not particularly motivating, and it is rarely much fun, so technical projects often diverge from the direct path and out into the weeds. Thoroughly identifying schedule risks requires awareness of this and disciplined use of project management planning tools to create appropriate schedules that avoid overengineering.

In the previous chapter, we considered factors that can make projects literally impossible. In this chapter, and in Chapter 5 concerning resource risks, our focus is on constraints—factors that transform otherwise reasonable projects into ones that will fail. Project processes for scheduling and resource planning provide a fertile source for discovery of project risks that arise from these constraints.

70

Sources of Schedule Risk

Schedule risks are second-most numerous in the PERIL database after scope risks, representing almost a third of the records. They fall into three categories: *delays*, *estimates*, and *dependencies*. Delay risks were most numerous; these are defined as schedule slips due to factors that are at least nominally under the control of the project. Estimate risks were on average the most damaging of the schedule risks; these are cases of inadequate durations assigned to project activities. Schedule dependency risks, also significant, relate to project slippage due to factors outside the project. (These dependencies all relate to timing—dependency problems primarily caused by deliverable requirements are grouped with the scope change risks.) Each root-cause category is further divided into subcategories, as demonstrated by the following table.

Schedule Root-Cause Subcategories	Definition	Count	Cumulative Impact (Weeks)	Average Impact (Weeks)
Estimates: Learning Curve	New work assumed to be easier than it turned out to be	21	207	9.9
Dependency: Legal	A shift in legal, regulatory, or standards	7	53	7.6
Estimates: Deadline	Top-down imposed deadlines that are unrealistic	9	64	7.1
Dependency: Project	Project interdependency delay in programs	17	119	7.0
Delay: Information	Slip due to unavailability of specification or other needed data	26	176	6.8
Dependency: Infrastructure	Infrastructure not ready or support not available (printing, IT, shipping, etc.)	17	90	5.3
Estimates: Judgment	Poor estimating process or inadequate analysis	19	99	5.2
Delay: Parts	Delay waiting for needed deliverable component	38	189	5.0
Delay: Hardware	Needed equipment arrives late or fails	23	98	4.3
Delay: Decision	Slip due to untimely decision for escalation, approval, phase exit	15	46	3.1

The overall impact of these schedule risk subcategories is summarized in Figure 4-1. The subcategory with the largest total impact was

Figure 4-1. Total project impact by schedule root-cause subcategories.

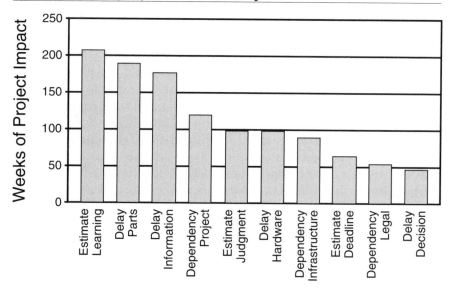

estimating new work, but several other subcategories were not far behind.

Delay Risks

Delay risks represent over half of the schedule risks and nearly a sixth of all the risks in the PERIL database. Impact from delays had the lowest average of any other subcategory in the database, but it was still more than one month. Types of delay risk in the PERIL database include *parts, information, hardware,* and *decisions.*

Parts that were required to complete the project deliverable were the most frequently reported source of delay, with an average schedule impact of five weeks. Delivery and availability problems were common sources for this delay, but there were also quite a few issues involving international shipping, including customs, paperwork, and related concerns. Delays also resulted from parts that arrived on time but were found to be defective. The time required to replace or repair components that did not work properly was a significant source of project slip.

Information needed by the project represented over a quarter of the cases of in the delay category. These were also the most damaging on average, representing an average of nearly seven weeks of project slip. Some of the information delay was due to time differences between parts of distributed global teams. Losing one or more days on a regular basis due to communication time lags and misunderstandings was common. In other cases, access to information was poor, or delivery of needed reports was interrupted.

About one-quarter of the delay risks was caused by *hardware* needed to perform project work, including systems and other equipment, that was late. Risks in this subcategory averaged more than one month for delay.

Slow *decisions* also caused project slippage. Roughly one-sixth of the delay examples were due to managers or other stakeholders who did not act as quickly as necessary to keep the project on schedule. Sometimes the cause was poor access to the decision makers, or their lack of interest in the project. For other projects, delays were the result of extended debates, discussions, or indecision. Projects facing these issues lost nearly three weeks on average waiting for a response to a project request.

Potential delay risks may be difficult to anticipate, and many of them seem to be legitimately "unknown" risks. Thorough analysis of the input requirements at each stage of the project plan, however, will highlight many of them.

Estimating Risks

Of all the types of schedule risk found in technical projects, estimating is the most visible. When you ask project managers what their biggest difficulties are, estimating is high on, if not on top of, the list. Despite this, the number of incidents in the PERIL database is not too large, about 8 percent of the records, and only about a quarter of the total schedule risks. The average impact of the estimating risks is only slightly above that of the PERIL database as a whole. One frequently cited issue with estimating in technical projects is the relatively rapid change in the work. The standard advice is that good estimates rely on history, but when the environment is in constant flux, history may not seem all that useful (more on this later in the chapter). The estimating risk subcategories relate to *learning curves, judgment,* and *imposed deadlines.*

Learning curve issues were the most common type of estimating risk. Their impact was well above the average for the database, nearly ten weeks. The quality of the estimates when new technology or new people (or even worse, both) are involved is not good. The portions of project work that require staff to do things they have never done before are always risky, and although thorough analysis of the work can show which parts of the project plan are most exposed, good estimating is difficult.

Judgment in estimating was the next most common estimating problem in the PERIL database. For most of these cases, the estimates were overoptimistic. Some of these estimates were too short by factors of three or four. Dealing with this source of estimating risk requires thorough planning, with appropriate understanding and decomposition of the work, so that the effort and steps required are known. It also requires good record keeping. Metrics and project data archives are invaluable in creating future estimates that are more consistent with reality than past estimates have been, even for projects where things change rapidly. Having *some* data always beats having to guess. Another powerful tool in revealing and combating optimistic estimates is worst-case analysis. The answer to the question "What might go wrong?" will not only reveal something about the likely duration, it will also uncover new potential sources of risk.

Imposed deadlines were the third subcategory of estimating risks. Although these estimates were poor, the root cause was outside the project. Technical projects frequently have aggressive deadlines set in advance with little or no input from the project team. Even when the project plan shows the deadline to be unrealistic, the objective is retained. These projects are often doomed from the start.

Dependency Risks

Dependency risks were about a fifth of the schedule risks. The impact from schedule dependency risks is a bit below the average for the PERIL database as a whole, averaging more than six weeks of slip per incident. There are three dependency risk subcategories: *other projects*, *infrastructure factors*, and *legal issues*.

Other projects with shared dependencies not only were the most numerous of the dependency risks, they also are quite damaging, with an average of seven weeks. In larger projects (often classified as programs), a number of smaller projects interact and link to each other. In addition to providing each other with information and deliverables that meet well-defined specifications (which is a scope risk exposure), each project within a larger program must also synchronize the timing of schedule dependencies to avoid being slowed down by (or slowing down) other projects. Managing all these connections is difficult in complex programs, and the amount of damage increases with time; many of these risks in the PERIL database were noticed only late in the project. Even for the interfaces that were defined in advance, delay was fairly common due to the uncertainty in each project and the high likelihood that at least one of the interconnected projects would encounter some sort of difficulty. With so many possible failure modes, it is all but certain that something will go wrong. Analysis of the connections and interfaces between projects is a key aspect of program management, and many of the risks faced by the projects become visible through interface management techniques.

Infrastructure dependencies also interfered with project schedules in the PERIL database. The frequency of these problems was equal to the project dependencies, but the impact was less on average, at slightly more than five weeks. These situations included interruption of technical services, such as computer systems or networks required by the project, and inadequate access to resources such as help desks, system support, and people who understood older but necessary applications. Several projects were delayed by maintenance outages that were not known to the project team, even though they had been scheduled in advance.

Legal and regulatory dependencies were also problematic. Though the number of cases was less than 20 percent of the dependency risks, the average impact was highest for this subcategory, at almost eight weeks. Legal and paperwork requirements for international shipments can cause problems when they change abruptly. Monitoring for planned or possible changes can forewarn of many potential regulatory problems.

Black Swans

The worst 20 percent of the risks in the PERIL database are deemed "black swans." These "large-impact, hard-to-predict, rare events" caused at least three months of schedule slip, and 30 of these most damaging 127 risks were schedule risks. As with the black swans as a whole, the most severe of the schedule risks account for slightly more than one-half of the total measured impact. The details are presented in the following table.

Schedule Risks		Total Impact (Weeks)	Black Swan Impact (Weeks)	Black Swan Percentage
Delay	Decision	46	0	0%
	Hardware	98	26	27%
	Information	176	91	52%
	Parts	189	88	47%
Dependency	Infrastructure	90	42	47%
	Legal	53	24	45%
	Project	119	82	69%
Estimates	Deadline	64	30	47%
	Judgment	99	44	44%
	Learning	207	150	72%
Totals		**1,141**	**577**	**51%**

As can be seen in the table, the black swan schedule risks were distributed relatively evenly, with a slight edge to *estimating* risks. There were thirteen estimating risks, with eight related to learning curve issues. The learning curve category of estimating risks also was dominated by these sizable impact risks. Well over two-thirds of the learning curve risks were caused by cases such as the following:

- Complexity of new software was significantly underestimated.
- Development team was staffed with no regard for business knowledge.
- Neophyte project staff was inexperienced and had inadequate training.
- Key developer proved to be incompetent.
- Remote team did not have the expertise for key intermediate testing.

There were three cases of major project slippage due to estimating judgment, all related to inordinately optimistic assessment of project work. Two black swan risks were caused by imposed deadlines:

- Adding project staff failed to cut the schedule in half.
- Commitments for a construction project were based on promises to customers, not planning.

Schedule *delays* in the PERIL database accounted for another ten black swans. Half of them were caused by late information, including these:

- Merging of multiple standards was required for reorganization, and lack of common definitions delayed the data conversion project.
- Software was developed in a country where a war broke out, limiting travel and inhibiting teleconferencing, so that needed information was always late.
- Poorly defined procedures for acceptance, quality, and communications inhibited distributed development.
- Legacy application that was to be modified had no documentation; reconstructing the original code was time consuming.

Four more significant risks were due to delayed parts:

- A component ordered was too long for international shipment, so it was cut and shipped in pieces. What arrived was useful only as raw material and replacing it was expensive.

- The required quantity of a new integrated circuit chip was unavailable, resulting in a major delay in delivery.
- A critical software component was delivered late.
- Insufficient material was sent to the contract lab to complete testing.

One black swan was hardware related, caused by a shipment of required servers that got stuck in customs. None of the black swan risks was due to tardy decision making, showing that even the slowest managers can eventually make up their minds.

Black swan *dependency* risks were even less numerous, with a total of seven. There were four black swan risks associated with programs in the PERIL database:

- The manager of a related project allowed stakeholders to make frequent scope changes, causing ripple effects and delay.
- Interdependencies in complex programs were detected late.
- The scope of work between related projects was poorly coordinated.
- Firmware needed for key project component was dropped by another project.

The two most significant *infrastructure* examples were:

- Development platforms had six-month validations; when a project slipped, required recertification delayed it further.
- The operating environment was upgraded to a new version, requiring rework and significant overhead.

There was also one project that encountered regulatory delay because of a process change that required an unexpected lengthy recertification.

Additional examples of schedule risks from the PERIL database may be found in the Appendix.

Activity Definition

Building a project schedule starts with defining project work at an appropriate level of decomposition. Both estimating and sequencing of work in a project are easier and less risky using small parts of the project. Although the entire project may be big, complicated, and confusing, the principle of "divide and conquer" allows for independent consideration of each little piece of work, and lets the project team bring order out of chaos. The starting point for schedule development (as well as for resource planning) is the project work breakdown structure (WBS), discussed in Chapter 3. If the work described at the lowest level of your WBS is consistent with the guidelines of "2 to 20 days duration" or "80 hours of effort," the lowest-level items may be used as the foundation for scheduling. If your WBS decomposition is not yet to that level of granularity, hidden risks and questionable estimates will remain until you do further analysis and decomposition. Managing risk depends upon knowing what "going right" looks like, so it's best to work with small, self-contained, deliverable-oriented bits of your project that you can competently estimate, schedule, and monitor.

The lowest level of the WBS hierarchy is the basis for developing a schedule, but the terminology used varies. Some call the items *work packages*, scheduling tools often use the term *tasks*, and agile software methodologies such as XP refer to *stories*. In "Project Time Management," the *PMBOK® Guide* refers to these pieces of work as *activities*, the term adopted in this book.

Creating a project schedule requires both duration estimating and activity sequencing. Which of these planning tasks you undertake first is largely a matter of personal preference. The *PMBOK® Guide* shows these two processes in parallel, which is realistic. Both estimating and activity sequencing are iterative processes, and there is a good deal of interaction between the two when building a project plan. If starting to sequence project activities prior to estimating them seems more natural for your projects, use the material in this chapter in that order. What is essential for risk management is that you do both thoroughly, as each reveals unique schedule risks.

Estimating Activity Duration

Estimating risk provides a substantial number of the entries in the PERIL database and represented the highest average impact, at nearly two months. A good estimating process is a powerful tool for identifying this type of schedule risk. When the estimates that are precise can be separated from those that are uncertain, the risky parts of the project are more visible. When estimates are "top down" or based on guesses, the exposures in the project plan remain hidden. Quite a few failed projects are a consequence of inaccurate estimates.

In the dictionary, an estimate is "a rough or approximate calculation." Projects require approximations of both time and cost. The focus of this section is on the risks associated with time estimates. All project estimates are related, though, and a number of concepts introduced here will be expanded in Chapter 5 and used there to identify resource risks through the process of estimating effort and cost. Estimates of varying accuracy are derived throughout a project, from the "rough-order-of-magnitude" estimates used to initiate projects to fairly precise estimates that are refined as the project runs to control and execute project work. Single-point estimates imply accuracy that is rarely justified in technical projects. Estimates that make risk visible are therefore stated as ranges, or with a percentage (plus or minus) to indicate the precision, or by using a probability distribution for expected possibilities.

Estimation Pitfalls

Estimating project work is challenging, and most people admit that they don't do it well. Understanding the factors that make accurate estimating hard to do for technical projects provides insight into sources of project risk and helps us to improve future estimates. Four key impediments to estimating well are:

1. Avoidance
2. Optimism
3. Lack of information
4. Granularity

Probably the most significant problem with estimating is that people who work on technical projects do not like to estimate, so they avoid it. The appeal of technical projects is the work—designing, programming, engineering, building, and other activities that the analytical people on these projects like to do. People avoid estimating (and planning in general) because it is seen as overhead, or boring "administrivia." Estimates are done quickly and only grudgingly. Most technical people have little estimating experience or training for estimating, so their skill level is low. Few people like doing things they do poorly. To make matters worse, because the estimates provided are so often inaccurate, most of the feedback they get is negative. It is human nature to avoid activities that are likely to result in criticism and punishment.

Too much optimism is another enemy of good estimates. In the PERIL database, the most common causes for poor estimating are learning curves and judgment, both of which may be symptoms of excessive optimism. Estimates that are too short create many additional project problems including severe increases in late-project work and deadline slippage.

Optimistic estimates are often based on best-case scenario analysis (each activity is scheduled assuming that nothing goes wrong), assumptions about the amount of time that people will have available to do project work, and overconfidence in the talent and speed of the project team. The third kind of estimating risk in the PERIL database is top-down deadline pressure. When sponsors and stakeholders are inappropriately optimistic, they impose unrealistic time constraints on the project, forcing the project team to create estimates in their plans based on the time available ("schedule to fit"), not based on the reality of the work.

A third issue is a lack of information. Initial project estimates are the product of early analysis, when the amount and quality of available project information is still low. Often, scope definition is still changing and incomplete, and significant portions of the work are poorly understood when these estimates are made. Compounding this, on most technical projects there is little (or no) historical information to use in estimating, and there are no defined estimating processes used. The estimating method used far too often is guessing.

A fourth factor contributing to poor estimates is the granularity of the work. Early estimates are often done for projects based on descriptions of the work and the deliverables while lacking much detail. Estimates are chronically inaccurate when they are based on high-level project deliverables without details or acceptance criteria. The quality of estimates for long-duration project activities is also poor. Guidelines for project activities at the lowest level of the WBS—roughly two weeks' duration, or eighty hours of effort—enable better estimating. When the activity duration extends beyond a month, duration assessments are generally inaccurate.

To recap, metrics, well-defined estimating procedures, clear scoping, disciplined planning, and periodic review of the project are all instrumental in improving estimates and decreasing estimation risk.

Estimating Techniques

Most of the estimating risks in the PERIL database are categorized as judgment and learning curve problems. The projects affected by these risks all had significant delays due to unrealistically short estimates. Many projects failed to account properly for the increasing complexity or new technologies in their work. Other projects chronically underestimated time for shipping and other commonplace project dependencies. Better processes and more attention to performance data will at least identify many of these risks, if not eliminate them.

Effective estimating techniques all rely on history. The best predictor of effort or duration for work on a project is the measurement made of the same (or similar) work done earlier. Project estimating either uses historical data directly or applies processes that have history as a foundation. Sources of appropriate data are essential to estimating well and reducing estimating risk. Good estimating relies on:

- Finding and using historical data
- Experts and expert judgment
- Experience-based rules and parametric formulas
- Delphi group estimating
- Further decomposition

For cases where none of these methods prove useful, there will be estimating risk.

Historical data The simplest estimating technique is to "look up the answer." The most useful historical information, for projects of all types, is solid empirical data, collected with discipline and care during earlier work. Unfortunately for most project leaders, project metric databases are still fairly rare for technical projects, so such information is sparse. Potential sources of activity effort and duration information for projects can be found by reviewing data from:

- Postproject analysis and "lessons learned" reports
- Personal notes and status reports from recent projects
- Notes from team members
- Published technical data (either inside your organization or public)
- Reference materials and engineering or other standards
- The Web (offering data of wildly varying reliability)

Anecdotal historical information is often plentiful. Discuss the project with others and probe their memories. Written historical data tends to be more reliable, but anecdotal information is easier to get. Memories may not be as trustworthy, but any historical information can serve as a good foundation for preliminary estimating, especially if the data is recent, relevant, and credible.

A lack of documented history is a problem that is easy to fix. Measurement and productivity analysis are essential to ongoing management of estimation risk, so resolve to begin, or to continue, collecting actual activity data at least for your own projects. Metrics useful for risk management are covered in detail in Chapter 9.

Experts Historical information need not be personal to be useful. Even when no one on the project has relevant experience or data, there may be others who do, outside of your project. Look to peers, managers, and technical talent elsewhere in your organization. Seek out the opinions of colleagues in professional societies who do similar work for other companies. Outside consultants in technical or management fields may have useful information that they will share for a fee. Even quotations and proposals from service suppliers may contain useful data that you can use for estimating project work.

Rules and formulas When a type of work is repeated often, the data collected over time may evolve into useful formulas for effort or for duration. These formulas may be informal "rules of thumb" providing approximate estimates that relate to measurable aspects of activity output, or they may be elaborate, precise (or at least precise-looking) analytical equations derived by regression analysis using data from past projects. One often-referenced parametric formula in the software development world is the Constructive Cost Model (COCOMO), developed several decades ago by Barry Boehm at TRW. If your organization supports such size-based estimation methods, use them, and contribute data from your projects to improve their accuracy and keep them current.

Delphi estimates What individuals can't tell you, groups sometimes can. The Delphi process uses inputs from several people (a minimum of four or five) to establish numerical estimate ranges and stimulate discussion. This method relies on the fact that although no one person may be able to confidently provide reliable estimates, a population of stakeholders can frequently provide a realistic prediction. Delphi is a "group intelligence" process to tap into information that would otherwise be unavailable, and because it is collaborative, it contributes to group buy-in, ownership, and motivation.

Further decomposition Another approach you can use when you lack historical data is to create some. Begin by breaking the activity to be estimated into even smaller pieces of work, and choose a representative portion. Perform this part of the work and measure the duration (or effort) required to complete it. Extrapolate from the actual measurements of the portion of the work to estimate the whole activity. Some activities can also be better estimated if thought of as small projects, with phases such as investigation, analysis, development, documentation, and testing
For activity estimates where none of these methods prove useful, you will face estimating risk.

The Overall Estimating Process

Good project estimating requires many inputs, starting with a comprehensive list of project activities. Another is a resource plan, information about the people and other resources available to the project. The resource plan is part of the "Project Resource Management" segment of the *PMBOK® Guide* and is a major topic in Chapter 5. One key reason for the resource information was mentioned in Chapter 3: You need to know the owners for activities at the lowest level of the project WBS. The activity owner is generally responsible for initial activity duration estimates. Whether the owner is the only contributor, or leads a team, or serves as a liaison to another group where the work will be done, the estimate is ultimately the owner's responsibility.

Accurate estimates require clear, specific information about each activity. Document the constraints on activity durations or project assumptions that might affect the estimates. Activities with more than one deliverable may be easier to manage and have less risk if they are broken down further, creating new, smaller activities for each deliverable. Acceptance criteria and unambiguous, measurable requirements also contribute to accurate estimates. If specifications are unclear, clarify them or note the project risks.

There are three types of project estimates:

- Duration estimates, measured in active work time (usually workdays)
- Effort estimates, measured using a combination of people and time (person-days or something similar)
- Calendar estimates, measured in elapsed time (calendar days)

Each type of estimate has its place in the planning process. Duration estimates are used as input to computer scheduling tools and for schedule analysis. Effort estimates are resource based and part of project costs. Calendar durations relate to project deadlines and support accurate tracking. Project planning requires all three types of estimate, generally starting either with duration estimates or effort estimates. The other estimates follow, ultimately generating calendar estimates that are used to define the project timeline. Whatever estimating sequence you prefer, good planning and risk management depends on estimates derived from bottom-up project analysis. Avoid "pegged-date" or arbitrary, politically specified estimates. Building a plan with unrealistic estimates creates risk and undermines your ability to negotiate necessary project changes.

Some project leaders prefer to derive duration estimates first,

Figure 4-2. Estimation process.

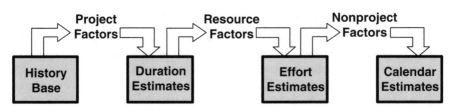

and then develop the effort estimates when other planning data, such as activity sequencing information, is available. Effort estimates are then used to validate and adjust the duration estimates, based upon the accumulating project information. This process is summarized in Figure 4-2. Other methods begin with effort estimating, but whatever sequence you use the same issues, factors, and risks are involved.

Project-specific factors and duration estimates As mentioned above, project estimating methods (including guessing) start with information derived in some way from history and experience. Beginning with the best available historical data for each activity, develop duration estimates. Use project-specific information to adjust these initial assessments, based on differences between the current project and earlier work. Project-specific factors include:

- Clarity of the project specifications
- Likelihood of significant specification change
- New resource requirements
- Longer overall project duration
- Unusual technical complexity
- New required technology
- Extreme requirements for reliability
- Geographic separation and cultural diversity on the project team
- Infrastructure and environment differences
- Training requirements

Every lowest-level activity in your WBS requires a duration estimate, measured in workdays (or some suitable units). In addition to providing input for adjusting historical data, these project-specific factors may also reveal significant project risks. If so, list them.

The estimates themselves may also reveal risks. Any activities with uncertain estimates are risky. However, lack of confidence in an estimate is a symptom of risk, not the risk itself. Whenever any of your project estimates seem untrustworthy, probe for why, and note the root cause as the risk. Two common sources of low-confidence estimates are lack of experience with the work and activities that may have several different outcomes, such as an investigation.

Resource factors and effort estimates Duration estimates, combined with project information on people and teams, provide the basis for effort estimates. Initial resource plans provide information on resource factors, such as:

- The amount of time each day each team member has for project work
- The number of people contributing to each activity
- The skills, experience, and productivity of each team member
- Training and mentoring requirements
- Nonproject responsibilities for each person
- Communication lags and other consequences of distributed teams
- Expected turnover or attrition of staff during the project
- The number and duration of project (and other) meetings
- The amount of project communication and reporting
- Travel requirements
- The number of required people not yet assigned to the project

The first factor in the list, the number of project hours in a day, is a common cause of underestimation. Not every hour that people work is available for project activities. Meetings, communication (both formal and informal), breaks, meals, and other interruptions take time. Even the common assumption of "five to six" hours per day for project activities is significantly higher than the reality available to many projects. Productivity is also a source of variation, and for individual team members it can vary wildly. Any estimates of effort or duration made in advance of assigning the specific people who will do the work are risky. These and other resource-related risks will be discussed in greater detail in Chapter 5.

By considering the effort required by each activity in light of the resource factors, you can determine activity effort in person-hours (or contributor-days or some other combination of staffing and time).

Nonproject factors and calendar estimates The final stage of estimation is to translate duration estimates into calendar estimates. To translate workday duration estimates into elapsed-time estimates, you need to account for all the days that are not available for project work. Computer scheduling tools simplify this process; many of the following factors can be entered into the calendar database, allowing the software to do the calculations. Some nonproject factors include:

- Holidays
- Weekends
- Vacations and other paid time off
- Other projects
- Other nonproject work
- Lengthy nonproject meetings
- Equipment downtime
- Interruptions and shutdowns
- Scheduled medical leave

Calendar estimates account for all the days between the start and end of each activity. Specific dates for each activity are derived by combining duration estimates, nonproject factors, and the activity sequencing information that we discuss later in this chapter. One particular risk common for global projects is a result of differences in scheduled time off for geographically separate parts of the project team. Frequent loss of some of the project team to various national and religious holidays is disruptive enough, but all too often these interruptions come as a surprise to the project leader, who may not be aware of all the relevant holidays.

Applying Estimating Techniques

Figure 4-3 summarizes estimation techniques that are applicable in various situations. For each project activity, the team either has experience or does not. For the type of work involved, relevant metrics will either be available or not.

Highest estimating risk is found in the worst case, lower right quadrant: no experience *and* no data. This case is far from unusual; on technical projects, it may be true for a number of activities you need to estimate. The most frequently used estimating methods involve guessing, sometimes with arcane rules, and in this situation a guess may be your best option. You can also consider alternatives such as getting someone who does have experience to consult on your project or even replanning the work to use an approach where your team does have experience.

Figure 4-3. Estimating techniques.

	Relevant Metrics Exist	No Data Available
Prior Activity Experience	• Retrospectives • Databases • Parametric formulas, experiential rules ("Size"methods) • Notes and status reports	• Task owner input • Peer inputs • Inspections • Delphi analysis • Short tasks (20-day maximum) in WBS • Further decomposition
No Activity Experience	• Published information • Vendor quotes • Expert consultation	• Guesses • Outside help • Older technology

Only slightly better than this is the case where you have no experience, but you have found some external information. Estimates based on someone else's measurements are better than nothing, but unless your project is similar to the project where the measurements were made, the data may not be relevant. In either of these cases, when a project activity requires work for which you lack experience, estimation risk is high, and your activity duration estimates belong on the project risk list.

The upper right quadrant is for activities that have been done before but for which no data exists. Although this should not happen, it is fairly common on technical projects. Thorough analysis and estimating methods such as Delphi may provide adequate estimates, but the results of these processes still contain estimation risk. Over time, more disciplined data collection will help you better manage these risks.

The best case is the upper left quadrant. The existence of both experience and measurements should provide credible, reliable estimates for project activities. Eventually, proactive risk management and disciplined application of other project processes will move many, if not most, activities here, even on high-tech projects.

One other significant source of estimation risk arises from the people who are assigned to do the work. "Good" estimates need to be believable, which means that they are derived from data and methods that make sense. This is a good foundation, but even the best estimating techniques yield unreliable estimates unless the project team buys in. To be accurate, estimates also must be *believed*. No matter how much data goes into creating estimates, if the people who will do the work do not agree with them, they are risky. Good estimates are both *believable* and *believed.*

Estimates Adjusted for Uncertainty

All the techniques just discussed generate deterministic, single-point estimates for project activities. This type of estimate implies a precision that is far from reality. To better deal with uncertainty and risk, the Program Evaluation and Review Technique (PERT) methodology was developed during the late 1950s by the U.S. military. The earliest forms of PERT used three-point range estimates for each activity: an optimistic estimate, a most likely estimate, and a pessimistic estimate. (PERT may be used for both time and cost analysis. This discussion concerns only time analysis.) Traditionally, PERT assumed a bell-type distribution that could skew toward either the optimistic or pessimistic estimate, similar to the Beta distribution in Figure 4-4. The three estimates were used to define a distribution of outcomes as in the figure, and calculations predicted an *expected* activity duration using the formula:

$$t_e = (t_o + 4t_m + t_p)/6, \text{ where}$$

t_e is the calculated "expected" duration—the mean

t_o is the "optimistic" duration (the "best case")

t_m is the "most likely" duration (the peak of the distribution)

t_p is the "pessimistic" duration (the "worst case")

Figure 4-4. Duration estimates for PERT analysis.

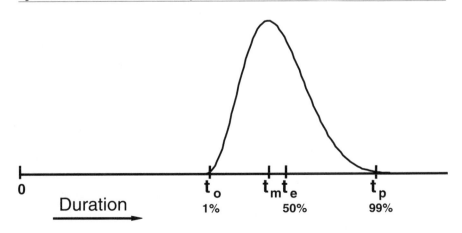

In addition to the "expected" estimate, PERT is also used to quantitatively assess estimation risk. For PERT, the range of possible outcomes allows you to approximate the standard deviation for each activity duration estimate, where:

$$\text{One standard deviation} = (t_p - t_o)/6$$

The theory behind PERT was a step in the right direction, but in practice PERT analysis does not always prove to be useful. The three most common problems people have with PERT are the time and effort required for the analysis, data quality, and misuse of the information.

PERT requires more data—three estimates. This requires more time to collect, enter, and analyze. The collection process is annoying to the project team, and the three estimates are not easily integrated using common project management tools. Because of this, the cost of PERT analysis may exceed the apparent value of the results.

Also, as discussed earlier, the quality of even one estimate can be problematic. The accuracy of the two additional estimates is usually worse. Definitions of optimistic and pessimistic can be inconsistent, arbitrary, and confusing. PERT initially defined the range limits as "1 percent tails." It was suggested that people imagine doing an activity 100 times and select estimates so that only once would the duration fall below the optimistic estimate and only once would it lie above the pessimistic estimate. For most activities, these estimates were generally wild guesses, or fixed plus/minus percentages. Because of this, PERT is often the victim of "garbage in, garbage out."

Probably the biggest reason that PERT is not more widely used for technical projects is the potential for misuse of the information involved. Many organizations experiment with PERT for a time before this issue surfaces, but it eventually does. Everything starts out well. Project teams do their best to figure out what the three estimates might be for each activity, using difficult-to-understand definitions involving Beta distributions and 1 percent tails (or 5 or 10 percent tails—there are many variants). Project PERT analysis proceeds for a time, and some insight into project uncertainty begins to emerge. This continues until some bright midlevel manager notices the optimistic estimates. Because the project teams have admitted that these estimates are not actually impossible, managers begin to insist that schedules be based only on these most aggressive estimates, which are used to define the project deadlines. The statistical underpinnings of PERT predict that such schedules have essentially no chance of success, and experience invariably proves it. If any interest in PERT remains after this, the battered project teams in self-defense start to use different definitions for optimistic estimates.

Although PERT methodology can be troublesome, especially in its traditional form, three-point estimates can be useful. "Optimistic" estimate analysis is an important tool for exploring project opportunities, and in Chapter 6 we will explore using this "best-case" analysis for project opportunity management.

Even more important, pessimistic (or worst-case) estimates are a particularly fertile source of project risk information. After collecting activity estimates, investigate worst cases using questions such as:

- What might go wrong?
- What are the likely consequences should any issues arise?
- Is the staff involved experienced in this area?
- Have we had problems with this kind of work before?
- Does this activity depend on inputs, resources, or other factors we don't control?
- Are there aspects of this work that we don't understand well?
- If you were betting money on the estimates, would they change?

The responses to these and related probing questions will provide two pieces of important project risk data. The potential consequences you uncover, including slippage, additional costs, and other information, will be useful for later project risk assessment. Even more revealing, the *sources* of the potential slip (or other significant impact) are project risks that belong on your risk list.

Schedule impact information can also be used for a simplified variation on PERT that provides insight into schedule risk. This analysis uses the initial activity estimates for both the optimistic and most likely PERT estimates, which Parkinson's Law, the quotation that opened this chapter, predicts anyway. The worst-case information that you collect on any activity durations provides data for your pessimistic estimates. The distribution this implies will be essentially triangular and similar to Figure 4-5. The formula approximating the expected duration is $t_e = (5t_m + t_p)/6$.

Although PERT techniques such as three-point estimating relate to activity estimating, PERT analysis and more sophisticated simulation techniques are really tools for *project* risk assessment. This use of PERT and related tools is explored in Chapter 9.

Activity Sequencing

Additional scheduling risks become visible as you develop your project schedule by combining sequencing information with the activity

Figure 4-5. "PERT-like" estimating.

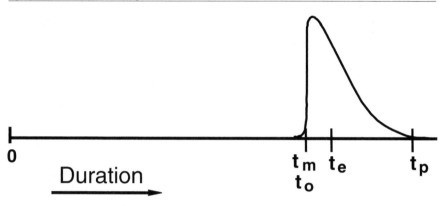

estimates. Activity sequencing requires you to determine the dependencies for each project activity, and these linkages reveal many potential sources of project delay. Delay and other dependency risks were responsible for most of the scheduling risks in the PERIL database.

One effective method for minimizing schedule risk related to sequencing is to break long, complex projects into a series of much shorter ones. This principle is fundamental to evolutionary, or cyclic, software development methodologies. If the cycles are sufficiently short—two to four weeks are a common cycle in methodologies such as XP—the dependencies either become irrelevant or are sufficiently simple that managing them is trivial. For the most part, XP ignores dependencies except as special cases within each iteration. The same principle applies generally; the shorter the overall arc of a project is, the fewer complications and risks there will be because of activity dependencies.

In more complex projects, there are many possible types of dependencies that may connect project activities, but most are linked by finish-to-start relationships—once one activity or a collection of activities is complete, other project activities can begin. Occasionally, some activities might need to be synchronized by either starting or finishing at the same time, and the logic of project work may also depend on interruptions and lags of various kinds. Although project plans may include some of these more exotic dependencies, the majority of the dependencies in a typical project network are finish-to-start linkages, and it is these sequential-activity dependencies that are most likely to cause work flow problems and delay risk.

Discovering risks arising from schedule dependencies requires all project activities to be linked both to predecessor and to successor activities. Schedule development requires a logical network of project activities (and milestones) that has *no gaps*. Establish a logical flow of work for your project so that each project activity, without exception, has a continuous path backward to your initial project milestone and a continuous path forward to the final project deadline. Project analysis and risk identification will be incomplete (and possibly worthless) if there are gaps or dangling connections. For project planning using a computer tool, avoid the use of features such as "must start on" and "must end on" pegged-date logic. The software will generate a Gantt chart that looks a lot like a project plan, but you will not be able to perform schedule analysis, do proper project tracking, or effectively identify schedule risk.

Critical Path Methodology

Critical path methodology (CPM) analysis combines duration estimates with dependency information and calculates the minimum project duration based on this data. For larger projects, the analysis is best done using a computer scheduling tool. Once all your activities, duration estimates, and dependencies are entered into the database of a scheduling tool, the software automatically analyzes the project network. The set (or sets) of activities that make up the longest sequence is the project *critical path*, which is generally highlighted using an appropriately scary red color. Each of the red activities carries schedule risk, because if it exceeds its duration estimate, everything that follows in the project can also be expected to slip, including the project deadline.

CPM also calculates "float" or "slack" for "noncritical" activities, revealing any flexibility available. If the float is small, even though the activity might be colored a soothing blue, it's also risky. Even project activities that have a large amount of float can be risky when their worst-case estimates exceed the calculated float. The other noncritical activities, those with significant float and reliable-looking estimates, are also relevant to risk management. They could represent opportunities for keeping the project on track.

Computer scheduling tools make it is easy to do "what if" analysis and reveal risky activities in addition to those on the project critical path. The first step is to make a copy of the database for the project (so you can manipulate the copy to identify additional schedule risks and leave your initial schedule intact). By deleting all the critical activities in your copy (relinking any resulting broken dependencies as you go), you can see what the resulting project looks like and generate a list of the next tier of risky activities to watch out for.

It's even more illuminating to replace all your initial estimates with worst-case estimates to see what happens. When you do this one activity at a time, you discover how sensitive the overall project is to each potential problem. If you enter all of your worst-case estimates, you get a version of the plan that shows a far longer schedule than is probable, but the end point displays just how bad things might get if *everything* goes wrong. (And remember, your analysis is based on only *known* risks; if there are significant unknown project risks, even your worst-case schedule could be optimistic.)

In reality, every activity in the project represents at least a small level of schedule risk. Any piece of work in the plan could be the one that causes a project to fail. CPM analysis is a useful technique for determining which schedule risks belong on your risk list.

Multiple Critical Paths

Projects can and often do have more than one critical path. Multiple critical paths further increase schedule risk. To see why, consider the simple network in Figure 4-6. Both paths "A-D-J" and "C-H-L" are marked as critical, and for this analysis we will assume "expected" durations where the probability of an activity finishing early (or on time) is the same as the chance of the activity finishing late. For a project with a single critical path, the project as a whole has identical probabilities—50/50. (This assumes all events and activities are independent—more on this later.) What can we say about the project in Figure 4-6, with two critical paths?

The expectation for each path being on time or early is the same as for the activities, 50 percent, but there are two of them. If the risks associated with the two paths are independent, the matrix in Figure 4-7 shows the probabilities for each possible outcome. The *project* has only one chance in four of finishing early or on time because this requires both paths to be early or on time, which is expected 25 percent of the time.

Figure 4-6. Project with two critical paths.

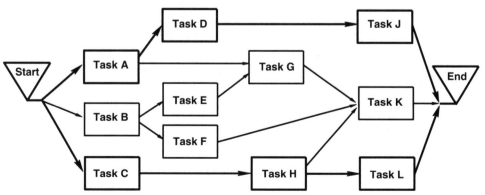

Figure 4-7. Result matrix for a project with two critical paths.

		A-D-J	
		Early/ on Time	Late
C H L	Early/ on Time	25%	25%
	Late	25%	25%

If there are more than two critical paths, the situation gets worse. With three critical paths, the chances fall to one in eight, and the fraction shrinks by a factor of two with each additional critical path. The more potential failure modes there are, the more likely it is that the project will be late. Although this picture is bleak, most technical projects face even higher risk. Few projects are planned using estimates that are equally likely to be slightly early or slightly late. Aggressive estimates are common on technical projects for all the reasons discussed earlier in the chapter, including overconfidence, lack of experience, and political pressure. If the estimates are actually 10 percent likely to be early or on time and 90 percent likely to be late, a matrix similar to Figure 4-7 for two critical paths will calculate only one chance of success in a hundred.

In addition, this analysis assumes statistical independence for all events. Although the assumption of independence may be valid for some project work, on most projects the work is all done by the same small team of people, and much of the work is interrelated. Assuming that the outcome of a given activity will have no effect on succeeding activities is unrealistic. Project problems tend to cascade, and there is often significant positive correlation between project activities. The upshot of all this is that schedule risk increases significantly when there are multiple parallel failure modes.

Scheduling Risky Work

The timing of activities may also increase project risk. Whenever an activity has high uncertainty, it is human nature to schedule it to start late in the project. If an activity requires the invention of something new, or the specifics of the work are far from obvious, you may be tempted to defer the work until later in the project, reasoning that the delay might give you a chance to figure it out. Also, scheduling risky work toward the end of your project will allow you to write at least a few weekly status reports that are not filled with bad news about troubled activities.

Tempting though this is, don't do it. Deferring riskier activities until late in the project can lead to both increased project risk and cost. By scheduling risky activities earlier, you can learn faster, and frequently with less effort, whether there are any show-stoppers—activities that make your whole project impossible. When you discover the problems earlier, project decision makers have more options, including shifting the objective, using the time still available to seek alternate ways to proceed with the project, or even abandoning the work altogether. If a risky activity is deferred until late in the project, changes may be impossible or much more costly, and there will be little or no time left to find another approach. Perhaps the worst case of all is discovering that the project is not feasible and canceling it after months (or even years) have elapsed. When risky work is scheduled earlier, a decision to cancel can be made after spending only a small portion of the project budget instead of nearly all of it. In addition to being a waste of time and money, late cancellation is demotivating for the project team and will make it difficult to find enthusiastic staff for future projects.

Schedule Path Convergence

Another project risk is due to "fan-in." Most places in a project network that have a large number of predecessor dependencies are milestones, but any point of convergence in a project network represents schedule risk. Because project work stops at a milestone or activity whenever any of the preceding activities are incomplete, each additional path in represents an additional failure mode, and increases the probability of delay. Milestones, phase exits, stage gates, and other life-cycle checkpoints are often delayed in large programs because of a single missing requirement; even when all the other work is satisfactorily completed, work may halt to wait for the final dependency.

The largest fan-in exposure for many projects is the final milestone, which usually has a large number of predecessor activities. Even in the simple project network in Figure 4-6, there are three predecessor dependencies for the finish milestone.

Interfaces

Dependency risks outside the project are also substantially represented in the PERIL database. Dependencies of all kinds may represent schedule risks, but interfaces—dependencies that connect one or more projects—are particularly problematic; the impact of these risks was among the highest for all schedule risks in the PERIL database, averaging seven weeks per project. Connections between projects are most common for projects that are part of a larger program. As each project team plans its work, dependencies on other projects are discovered and must be planned and managed. Dependencies that are wholly within a project carry schedule risk, but interfaces are even riskier. For a schedule interconnection, each project contains only half of the linkage, either the predecessor or the successor activity. The deliverables can be components, services, information, software, or almost anything that one project creates that is required by another project team. The project that expects to receive the deliverable potentially faces both schedule and scope risk. If the handoff is late, the dependent project may slip. Even when it is on time, if the deliverable is not acceptable, the project (and the whole program) may be in trouble. Interfaces are particularly important to identify and manage because of the limited visibility of progress in the project responsible for the deliverable.

The process for managing these interfaces and the risks related to them is best managed at the program level, and it is described in Chapter 13 in the section on program risk management.

Interface management requires agreement and commitments *in writing* between each involved project, and even then it's risky. Add each interface dependency for your project to your list of project risks.

Planning Horizon

Yet another source of schedule risk relates to project duration. When you drive an automobile at night on a dark road with no illumination other than your headlights, you can see only a limited distance ahead. The reach of the headlights is several hundred meters, so you must stay alert and frequently re-examine the road ahead to see things as they come into view.

Projects also have visibility constraints. Projects vary a good deal in how much accurate planning is possible, but all project planning has a limit. For some projects, planning even three months in advance is difficult. For others, the planning horizon might be longer, but technical project planning is rarely accurate more than six to nine months into the future. Uncertainty inherent in work planned more than a few months out is a source of significant schedule risk on any long duration project. Make specific note of any unusual, novel, or unstaffed activities more than three months away. On a regular basis, include explicit activities in the project plan to review estimates, risks, assumptions, and other project data. Risk management relies on periodic recommendations for project plan adjustments based on the results of these reviews.

Project reviews are most useful at natural project transitions: the end of each life-cycle phase, a major milestone or checkpoint, a significant change to the project objective, whenever key contributors leave or are added to the project team, or following business reorganizations. At a minimum, schedule reviews for longer projects at least every three to six months. A process for project review is detailed in Chapter 11.

Documenting the Risks

Schedule risks become visible throughout the planning and scheduling processes. The specific instances discussed in this chapter are all project risks:

- Long-duration activities
- Significant worst-case (or pessimistic PERT) estimates
- High uncertainty estimates
- Overly optimistic estimates
- All critical path (and near-critical path) activities
- Multiple critical paths
- Convergence points in the logical network
- External dependencies and interfaces
- Deadlines beyond the planning horizon
- Cross-functional and subcontracted work

Augment the list of project scope risks, adding each schedule risk identified with a clear description of the risk situation. The list of risks continues to expand throughout the project planning process and serves as the foundation for project risk analysis and management.

Key Ideas for Identifying Schedule Risks

- Determine the root causes of all uncertain estimates.
- Identify all estimates not based on historical data.
- Note dependencies that pose delay risks, including all interfaces.
- Identify risky activities and schedule them early in the project.
- Ascertain risks associated with multiple critical (or near-critical) paths.
- Recognize the riskiest dependencies at fan-in points in the project schedule.
- Note risks associated with lengthy projects.

Panama Canal: Planning (1905–1907)

Early in his work in Panama, John Stevens spent virtually all of his time among the workers, asking questions. His single-minded pursuit was thorough project planning. Stevens put all he learned into his plans, establishing the foundation he required to get the project moving forward.

The primary tool for construction was one Stevens was familiar with: the railroad. He recognized that digging enormous trenches was only part of the job. Excavated soil had to be moved out of the cut in central Panama where someday ships would pass, and it had to be deposited near the coasts to construct the required massive earthen dams. In the rain forests of Panama at the turn of the twentieth century, the railroad was not only the best way to do this, it was the only practical way. Much of the planning that Sevens did centered on using the railroad as a tool, and by early in 1906, he had documented exactly how this was to be done. When excavation resumed, his elaborate, "ingeniously elastic" use of the railroad enabled progress at a vigorous pace, and it continued virtually nonstop until the work was complete.

Once Stevens had broken the work down into smaller, easily understood activities, the canal project began to look possible. Each part of the job was now understood to be something that had been done, somewhere, before. It became a matter of getting it all done, one activity at a time.

For all his talents and capabilities, John Stevens never considered himself fully qualified to manage the entire project. His experience was with surveying and building railroads. The canal project involved building massive concrete locks (like enormous bath tubs with doors on each end) that would raise ships nearly 30 meters from sea level and lower them back again—twelve structures in all. The project also required a great deal of knowledge of hydraulics; moving enormous amounts of water quickly was essential to efficient canal operation. Stevens had no experience with either of these types of engineering. These gaps in his background, coupled with his dislike of the hot, humid climate and the omnipresent (and still dangerous) insects, led him to resign as chief engineer after two years, in 1907.

This did not sit well with Theodore Roosevelt. Losing such a competent project leader was a huge risk to the schedule. Both of his project leaders had now resigned before completing his most important project, and Roosevelt was determined that this would not happen again. To replace John Stevens, Roosevelt chose George Washington Goethals, an immensely qualified engineer. Goethals had been seriously considered for the job twice previously and was ideally qualified to complete the Panama Canal. He had built a number of similar, smaller projects, and he had a great deal of experience with nearly all the work required at Panama.

Theodore Roosevelt wanted more than competence, however. For this project, he wanted "men who will stay on the job until I get tired of having them there, or until I say they may abandon it." He was safe in his choice of a new chief engineer and project leader: George Goethals was a major (soon to be lieutenant colonel) in the U.S. Army Corps of Engineers, and if he tried to resign, he could be court-martialed and sent to jail.

5

Identifying Project Resource Risk

"If you want a track team to win the high jump,
you find one person who can jump seven feet,
not several people who can jump six feet."
—FREDERICK TERMAN, STANFORD UNIVERSITY
DEAN AND PROFESSOR OF ENGINEERING

Fred Terman is probably best known as the "father of Silicon Valley." He encouraged Bill Hewlett and Dave Packard, the Varian brothers, and hundreds of others to start businesses near Stanford University. Starting in the 1930s, alarmed at the paucity of job opportunities in the area, he helped his students start companies, set up the Stanford Industrial Park, and generally was responsible for the establishment of the world's largest high-tech center. He was good at identifying and nurturing technical talent, and he understood how critical it is in any undertaking.

A lack of technical skills or access to appropriate staff is a large source of project risk for complex, technical projects. Risk management on these projects requires careful assessment of needed skills and commitment of capable staff.

Sources of Resource Risk

Like schedule risks, resource risks represent less than one-third of the records in the PERIL database. Resource risks have an average impact of nearly seven weeks, intermediate between scope and schedule risks. There are three categories of resource risk: *people, outsourcing,* and *money. People* risks arise within the project team. *Outsourcing* risks are caused by using people and services outside the project team for critical project work. The third category, *money,* is the rarest risk subcategory for the PERIL database, as few of the problems reported were *primarily* about funding. Money, however, has the highest average impact and the effect of insufficient project funding has substantial impact on projects in many other ways. The root causes of people and outsourcing risk are further characterized by type, shown in the following summary.

Resource Root-Cause Subcategories	Definition	Count	Cumulative Impact (Weeks)	Average Impact (Weeks)
Money: Limitation	Slip due to funding limits	17	228	13.4
People: Motivation	Loss of team cohesion and interest; often on long projects	8	69	8.6
People: Late Start	Staff available late; often due to delayed finish of earlier projects	15	115	7.7
Outsourcing: Late or Poor Output	Deliverable late from vendor; includes queuing, turnover	34	260	7.6
People: Loss	Permanent staff member loss due to resignation, promotion, reassignment, health, etc.	40	277	6.9
People: Queuing	Slip due to bottleneck (includes specialized equipment)	27	117	4.3
Outsourcing: Delayed Start	Contracting-related delays	13	56	4.3
People: Temporary Loss	Temporary staff loss due to illness, hot site, support, etc.	33	128	3.9

A Pareto chart of overall impact by type of risk is in Figure 5-1. Although risks related to internal staffing dominate the listed resource risk subcategories, both outsourcing and money risks are included in the top three.

People Risks

Risks related to people represent the most numerous resource risks, constituting almost 20 percent of the entire database and nearly two-

Figure 5-1. Total project impact by resource root-cause subcategories.

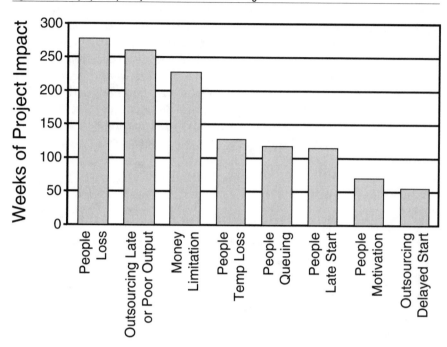

thirds of the resource category. People risks are subdivided into five subcategories:

1. *Loss*: Permanent staff member loss to the project due to resignation, promotion, reassignment, health, or other reasons
2. *Temporary loss*: Short-term staff loss due to illness, hot site, support priorities, or other reasons
3. *Queuing*: Slip due to other commitments for needed resources or expertise
4. *Late start*: Staff not available at project start; often because of late finish of previous projects
5. *Motivation*: Loss of team cohesion and interest; typical of long projects

Loss of staff permanently had by far the highest overall impact, resulting in an average slip of almost seven weeks. Permanent staff loss represented about one-third of the people risks. The reasons for permanent staff loss included resignations, promotions, reassignments to other work or different projects, and staffing cutbacks. Discovering these risks in advance is difficult, but good record-keeping and trend analysis are useful in setting realistic project expectations.

Temporary loss of project staff was the next most common people-related risk, with roughly another third of the total. Its overall impact was lower than for permanent staff loss, causing an average slip of nearly four weeks. The most frequently reported reason for short-term staff loss was a customer problem (a "hot site") related to the deliverable from an earlier project. Other reasons for short-term staff loss included illness, travel problems, and organizational reorganizations.

Queuing problems were about 20 percent of the people-related risks in the PERIL database. The average schedule impact due to queuing was just in excess of four weeks. Most organizations optimize operations by investing the bare minimum in specialized (and expensive) expertise, and in costly facilities and equipment. This leads to a potential scarcity of these individuals or facilities, and contention between projects for access. Most technical projects rely on at least some special expertise that they share with other projects, such as system architects needed at the start, testing personnel needed at the end, and other specialists needed throughout the project. If an expert happens to be free when a project is ready for the work to start, there is no problem, but if he or she has five other projects queued up already when your project needs attention, you will come to a screeching halt while you wait in queue. Queuing analysis is well understood, and it is relevant to a wide variety of manufacturing, engineering, system design, computer networks, and many other business systems. Any system subject to queues requires some excess capacity if it needs to increase throughput. Optimizing organizational resources needed for projects based only on cost drives out necessary capacity and results in project delay.

Late starts for key staff unavailable at the beginning of a project also caused a good deal of project delay. Although the frequency was only a little more than 10 percent of the people-related resource risks, the average impact was nearly eight weeks. Staff joining the project late had a number of root causes, but the most common was a situation aptly described by one project leader as the "rolling sledgehammer." Whenever a prior project is late, some, perhaps even all, of the staff for the new project is still busy working to get it done. As a consequence, the next project gets a slow and ragged start, with key people beginning their contributions to the new project only when they can break free of an earlier one. Even when these people become available, there may be additional delay, because the staff members coming from a late project are often exhausted from the stress and long hours typical of an overdue project. The "rolling sledgehammer" creates a cycle that self-perpetuates and is hard to break. Each late project causes the projects that follow also to be late.

Motivation issues were the smallest subcategory, at only a bit more than 5 percent of the people-related resource risks. However, these risks had an average impact of nearly nine weeks, among the highest for any of the subcategories in the PERIL database. Motivation issues are generally a consequence of lowering interest on long-duration projects, or due to interpersonal conflicts.

Thorough planning and credible scheduling of the work well in advance will reveal some of the most serious potential exposures regarding people. Histogram analysis of resource requirements may also provide insight into staffing exposures a project will face, but unless analysis of project resources is credibly integrated with comprehensive resource data for other projects and all the nonproject demands within the business, the results may not be useful. Aligning staffing capacity with project requirements requires ongoing attention. One significant root cause for understaffed projects is little or no use of project planning information to make or revise project selection decisions at the organization level, triggering the "too many projects" problem. Retrospective analysis of projects over time is also an effective way to detect and measure the consequences of inadequate staffing, especially when the problems are chronic.

Outsourcing Risks

Outsourcing risks account for more than a quarter of the resource risks. Though the frequency in the PERIL database is lower than for people risks, the impact of outsourcing risk was nearly seven weeks, about equal to the database average. Risks related to outsourcing are separated into two subcategories: *late or poor outputs* and *delayed start.*

Late or poor output from outsource partners is a problem that is well represented in the PERIL database. The growth of outsourcing in the recent past has been driven primarily by a desire to save money, and often it does. There is a trade-off, though, between this and predictability. Work done at a distance is out of sight, and problems that might easily be detected within a local team inside the organization may not surface as an issue until it is too late. Nearly three-quarters of the outsourcing risks involved receiving a late or unsatisfactory deliverable from an external supplier, and the average impact for these incidents was nearly eight weeks. These delays result from many of the same root causes as other people risks—turnover, queuing problems, staff availability, and other issues—but often a precise cause is not known. Receiving anything the project needs late is a risk, but these cases are compounded by the added element of surprise; the problem may be invisible until the day of the default (after weeks of reports saying, "Things are going just fine . . ."), when it is too late to do much about it. Lateness was often exacerbated in cases in the PERIL database because work that did not meet specifications caused further delay while it was being redone correctly.

Delayed starts are also fairly common with outsourced work, causing about one-quarter of the outsourcing problems. Before any external work can begin, contracts must be negotiated, approved, and signed. All these steps are time consuming. Beginning a new, complex relationship with people outside your organization can require more time than expected. For projects with particularly unusual needs, just finding an appropriate supplier may cause significant delays. The average impact from these delayed starts in the database was just over one month.

Outsourcing risks are detected through planning processes, and through careful analysis and thorough understanding of all the terms of the contract. Both the project team and the outsourcing partner must understand the terms and conditions of the contract, especially the scope of work and the business relationship.

Money Risks

The third category of resource risks was rare in the PERIL database, representing less than 10 percent of the resource risks and about 2 percent of the whole. It is significant, however, because when funding is a problem, it is often a big problem. The average impact was the highest for any subcategory, at over thirteen weeks. Insufficient funding can significantly stretch out the duration of a project, and it is a contributing root cause in many other subcategories (people turnover due to layoffs and outsourcing of work primarily for cost reasons, as examples).

"Black Swans"

The worst 20 percent of the risks in the PERIL database are deemed black swans. These "large-impact, hard-to-predict, rare events" caused at least three months of schedule slip, and 33 of these most damaging 127 risks were resource risks. As with the black swans as a whole, the most severe of the resource risks account for about one-half of the total measured impact. The details are given in the following table.

Resource Risks		Total Impact (Weeks)	Black Swan Impact (Weeks)	Black Swan Percentage
Money	Limitation	228	174	76%
Outsourcing	Delayed start	56	12	21%
	Late or poor output	260	152	58%
People	Late start	115	58	50%
	Loss	277	101	36%
	Motivation	69	53	77%
	Queuing	117	50	43%
	Temp loss	128	12	9%
Totals		**1,250**	**612**	**49%**

As can be seen in the table, the black swan resource risks were distributed unevenly. The money category represents a much higher portion of the total, with outsourcing about as expected and people-related risks much lower.

Not surprisingly, money issues were a substantial portion of the black swan resource risks. Eight cases, more than half of the risks reported in this category, were in this group, including such problems as:

- Project budget was limited to the bare minimum estimated.
- Important parts of scope were missed because of insufficient resources.
- Not enough staff was funded to cover the workload.
- Major cutbacks delayed fixes that lost time and ultimately also cost a lot of money.
- Only half the resources required were assigned to the project.

There were also ten outsourcing black swan risks. Nine were due to late or poor output, with these among them:

- The vendor was unable to control the subproject and the work had to be redone.
- The supplier was purchased and reorganized; the project had to find a new supplier.
- Outsourced research work was not managed well, and all work was ultimately redone.
- Changes were agreed to, but the supplier shipped late and it failed.

- The subcontractor failed to understand technology and requirements.
- The partner on the project defaulted.
- The supplier was not able to meet deadlines.

There was also a black swan outsourcing risk due to a delayed start when settling the terms of the agreement and negotiating the contracts took months and caused the project to begin late.

There were fifteen additional black swan *people* risks. This category had a smaller proportion of severe risks but did have the largest total number of these severe risks.

The three black swan risks associated with motivation were over one-third of all the motivation risks, and they account for nearly 80 percent of the impact from this category of risk. These risks were:

- Management mandated the project but never got team buy-in.
- Staff got along poorly and frequently quarreled.
- The product manager disliked the project manager.

Permanent staff loss also caused a lot of pain and led the list of black swan people risks with five examples:

- A key staff member resigned.
- The committed medical expert was no longer available.
- Staffing suffered cutbacks.
- Specialists were lost, including designers, business analysts, and QA/testers.
- There was a companywide layoff.

There were also three black swan project risks due to queuing, where projects were slowed by lack of access to specific resources:

- Insufficient QA resources were available to cover the auditing tasks and training tasks.
- Key decisions were stalled when no system architect was available.
- Several projects shared only one subject matter expert.

There were three more major people risks caused by late staffing availability. All were due to people who were trapped on a delayed prior project. Temporary loss of people caused only one back swan risk, because of an unexpectedly early start of conflicting peak-season responsibilities that resulted in a protracted loss of project staff.

Additional examples of resource risks are listed in the Appendix.

Resource Planning

Resource planning is a useful tool for anticipating many of the people, outsourcing, and money risks. Inputs to the resource planning process include the project work breakdown structure (WBS), scope definition, activity descriptions, duration estimates, and the project schedule. Resource requirements planning can be done in a number of ways, using manual methods, histogram analysis, or computer tools.

Resource Requirements

Based on the preliminary schedule and assumptions about each project activity, you will need to determine the skills and staffing required for each activity. It is increasingly common, even for relatively small projects, to use a computer scheduling tool for this. For all project work, identify staff *by name*. Although preliminary resource planning can start using functions or roles, effort estimates done without staffing information are imprecise, and there is significant resource risk until the project staff is named and committed. Identify as a risk any work depending on staff members who are not named during project planning.

For the project as a whole, also identify all holidays, scheduled time off, significant nonproject meetings, and other time that will not be available to the project. Do this for each person as well, and identify any scheduling differences for different regions, countries, and companies involved in the project. A computer scheduling tool is a good place to store calendar information, such as holidays, vacations, and any other important dates. If you do use a computer tool, enter all the calendar data into the database *before* you begin resource analysis.

You also need to determine the amount of effort available from each contributor. Even for "full-time" contributors, it is difficult to get more than five to six hours of project activity work per day, and "part-time" staff will contribute much less.

Particularly for project activities that are already identified as potential risks, such as those on the critical path, determine the total effort required and verify who will do the necessary work. Knowing the resources your project will need and how this compares with what is available is central to identifying and managing project risk.

Whether you do this analysis manually by inspection of the project plans, through a tabular or spreadsheet approach, or by using resource analysis functionality in a computer spreadsheet, your goal will be to detect resource shortfalls that could hurt your project. Work to uncover any resource overcommitments and undercommitments. Even if you do use a computer tool, and there are many, remember that a scheduling tool is primarily a database with specialized output reports. The quality of the information the tool provides can never be any better than the quality of the data that you put in. *You* and the project team must still do the thinking; a computer cannot plan your project or identify its risks.

Histogram Analysis Using Computer Tools

For more complicated projects, graphical resource analysis is useful. Resource histograms can be used to show graphically where project staffing is inadequate on an individual-by-individual or an overall project basis. The graphical format provides a visible way to identify places in the preliminary schedule where project staffing fails to support the planned workflow, as shown in Figure 5-2. In this case, the effort profile for a project team member expected to contribute to all these activities shows that this person must work a double shift where the activities overlap.

The benefits of entering resource data into a computer scheduling tool include:

- Identifying resource risks
- Improving the precision of the schedule
- Building compelling evidence for negotiating budgets and schedules
- Focusing more attention on project estimates

Figure 5-2. Histogram analysis for an individual.

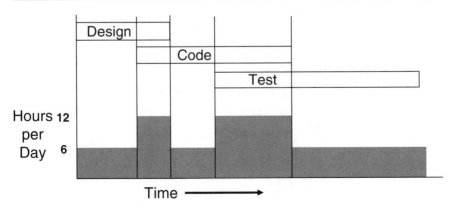

These benefits require some investment on your part. Histogram analysis adds complexity to the planning process, and it increases the effort for both planning and tracking. In your resource analysis, allocate sufficient effort for this into your overall project workload.

Be particularly wary of assumptions that contribute to project risk, such as the dependability of committed start dates for project contributors. Both late starts and queuing delays were significant sources of risk in the PERIL database.

Resource shortfalls are not limited to staffing. Early in your project, assess your project infrastructure: the equipment, software, and any other project assets. If required computers, software applications, test gear, instruments, communications and networking equipment, or other available hardware elements are not adequate or up to date, plan to replace, upgrade, or augment them. The effort and money to do this tends to be easiest to obtain during the planning and start-up phases of a new project. Getting familiar with new hardware and software is less disruptive early than it will be in the middle of the project, when it could disrupt high-priority project activities.

Staff Acquisition

Histograms and other project analysis are necessary, but rarely sufficient to determine whether the project has the staffing and skills required to do the work. Particularly for the riskiest project activities, revalidate both the skills needed and your effort estimates.

Skill Requirements

Through project scope definition and preliminary planning, identify specific skills and other needs required by your project. Your initial project staffing will often include adequate coverage for some or even most of these, but on many projects there are substantial gaps. These gaps will remain project resource risks until they are resolved.

Specific skills that are not available on the project team might be acquired by negotiating for additional staff, or through training or mentoring. In some cases, needed skills can be added through outsourcing. These options are most possible when the need is made known early and supported with credible planning data. You may also be able to replan the parts of the project that require unavailable skills to use other methods that require only skills already available on the project team. If there are knowledge gaps that can be filled through training, plan to do it early in the project. Postponing training until just before you need it increases two risks: that the time or money required for it will no longer be available, and that the "ramp-up time" to competence may exceed what you planned. (Learning curve issues were a major source of schedule risk in the PERIL database.) Building new skills can also be a powerful motivator and team builder—both of which can reduce risk for any project.

The ultimate goal of staff acquisition is to ensure that all project activities are aligned with specific individuals who are competent and can be counted on to get the work done. Two significant resource risks related to staff acquisition are unnamed staff members and contributors with unique skills. Every identified staffing need on your project roster that remains blank, identified only with a function or marked "to be hired," is a risk. Even if these people are later named, their productivity may not be consistent with your estimates and assumptions. It is also possible that the names will *still* be missing even after work is scheduled to begin—and some staffing requirements may never be filled. Plans completed with unassigned staffing are unreliable, and every project staffing requirement that lacks a credible commitment by an actual person is a project risk.

Unique skills also pose a problem. When project work can be assigned to one of several competent contributors, there is a good chance that it will be done adequately and on schedule. When only a single person knows how to do the work, the project faces risk. There are many reasons why a necessary person may not be available to the project when needed, including illness, resignation, injury, or reassignment to other higher priority work. There are no alternatives for the project when this happens; work on a key part of the project will halt. Whenever a key part of your project depends on access to a single specific individual, note it as a risk.

Revisiting Estimates

As noted in Chapter 4, resource planning and activity estimating are interrelated. As the staffing plan for the project comes together, additional resource risks become apparent through review of the assumptions you used for estimating. Project resource risks are usually most severe for activities that are most likely to impact the project schedule— activities that are on the critical path, or have little float, or have worst-case estimates that could put them on the critical path. Reviewing the effort estimates for these and other project activities reveals resource risks related to staff ability, staff availability, and the work environment.

Staff ability Individual productivity varies a great deal, so it matters who will be involved with each project activity. Even for very simple tasks, there can be very great differences in performance. Cooks often encounter the requirement for "one onion, chopped." The amount of time this task will take depends greatly on the person undertaking it. For a home cook, it might take two or three minutes (assuming that the majority of the chopping is restricted to the onion). A trained professional chef, as watchers of television cooking know, dispatches this task in seconds. On the other extreme one finds the perfectionist, who could make an evening out of ensuring that each fragment of onion is identical in size and shape.

Productivity measurements for "knowledge" work of most kinds show a similar wide spectrum. Research on productivity shows that people who are among the best at what they do typically work two to three times as fast as the average, and they are more than *ten times* as productive as the slowest. In addition to being faster, the best performers also make fewer errors and do much less rework.

Differences due to variations in productivity are a frequent source of inaccurate project estimates. Project leaders often plan the project using data from their own experience, and then delegate the work to others who may not be as skilled or as fast as they are (or think they are). When there are historical metrics that draw on a large population, you can accurately predict how fast an *average* person will be able to accomplish similar work. If your project contributors are significantly more (or less) productive than the average, your effort and duration estimates will be accurate only if they are adjusted accordingly. When you do not know who will be involved in the work, risks can be significant.

Staff availability No one can ever actually work on project activities "full time." Every project contributor has commitments even within the project that are above and beyond the scheduled project work, such as communications. Further, some team members will inevitably be responsible for significant work outside the project. Studying computer and medical electronics firms, Wheelwright and Clark (in *Revolutionizing Product Development*) reported the effect of assigning work on parallel projects to engineers. For engineers assigned to a single project or two projects, about 70 percent of the time spent went into project activities, roughly equivalent to the often-quoted "five or six" hours of project work per day. With three and more projects, useful time plummets precipitously. An engineer with five projects deals with so much overhead that only 30 percent of the time remains for project activities. Not all projects are equal, so when you are faced with this situation, find out how your overcommitted contributors prioritize their activities. Ask each part-time contributor about both the *importance* and the *urgency* of the work on your project. Both matter, but it's a lack of urgency that will hurt your project the most. When contributors see your project's work as low priority, it is a risk. If you are unable to adjust it, you may even need to consider alternative resources or other methods to do the project work.

The "too many projects" problem takes a heavy toll on project progress, and estimates of duration or effort that fail to account for the impact of competing priorities can be absurdly optimistic.

Project environment The project environment is yet another factor that has an impact on the quality of project estimates. Noise, interruptions, the workspace, and other factors may erode productivity significantly. When people can work undistracted, a lot gets done.

This is not typical, though. Frequent disturbances are commonplace, particularly with work done in an "open office" environment. The background noise level, nearby conversations, colleagues who drop by to chat, and other interruptions are actually much more disruptive than assumed in project estimates. People can't shift from one activity to a different one instantaneously. Studies of knowledge workers indicate that it takes twenty minutes, typically, for the human brain to come back to full concentration following an interruption as short as a few seconds. A programmer who gets three telephone calls, a few IMs, or "quick questions" from a peer each hour cannot accomplish much.

Once the staffing for your project is set, consider all these factors, particularly the talent, proportion of time dedicated to your project, and the effect of the environment on the estimates in your project plan. Make adjustments as necessary, identify the resource risks, and add them to your project risk list.

Outsourcing

Outsourcing was a significant source of resource risk in the PERIL database, causing an average project slip of nearly seven weeks. Better management of outsourcing and procurement can uncover many of these problems in advance.

Not all project staffing needs can be met with internal people. More and more work on technical projects is done using outside services. It is increasingly difficult (and expensive) to maintain competence in all the fields of expertise that might be required, especially for skills needed only infrequently. A growing need for specialization underlies the trend toward increased dependence on project contributors outside the organization. Other reasons for this trend are attempts to lower costs and a desire in many organizations to reduce the amount of permanent staff. In the *PMBOK® Guide,* Project Procurement Management has four components:

1. Plan procurements
2. Conduct procurements
3. Administer procurements
4. Close procurements

The first two of these provide significant opportunities for risk identification.

Planning Procurements

Outsourcing project work is most successful when the appropriate details and specifics are thoroughly incorporated into all the legal and other documentation used. Outsourced work must be specified in detail both in the initial request and in the contract, so that both parties have a clear definition for the work required and how it will be evaluated. Planning required to do this effectively is difficult, and it takes more effort and specificity than might ordinarily be applied to project planning.

Specific risks permeate all aspects of the procurement process, starting before any work directly related to outsourcing formally starts. The process generally begins with identification of any requirements that the project expects to have difficulty meeting with the existing staff. Procurement planning involves investigation of possible options, and requires a "make-or-buy" analysis to determine whether there are any reasons why using outside services may be undesirable or inappropriate. From the perspective of project risk, delegating work to dedicated staff whenever possible is almost always preferable. Communication, visibility, continuity, motivation, and project control are all easier and better for nonoutsourced work. Other reasons to avoid outsourcing may include higher costs, potential loss of confidential information, an ongoing significant need to maintain core skills (on future projects or for required support), and lack of confidence in the available service providers. Some outsourcing decisions are made because all the current staff is busy and there is no one available to do necessary project work. These decisions seem to be based on the erroneous assumption that project outsourcing can be done successfully with no effort. Ignoring the substantial effort required to find, evaluate, negotiate and contract with, routinely communicate with, monitor, and pay a supplier is a serious risk.

Although it may be desirable to avoid outsourcing, project realities may require it. Whenever the make-versus-buy decision comes out "buy," there will be risks to manage.

Conducting Procurements

The next step in the outsourcing process is to develop a request for proposal (RFP), also known as request for bid, invitation to bid, and request for quotation. In organizations that outsource project work on a regular basis, there are usually standard forms and procedures to be used for this, so the steps in assembling, distributing, and later analyzing the RFP responses are generally not up to the project team. This is fortunate, because using well-established processes, preprinted forms, and professionals in your organization who do this work regularly are all essential to minimizing risk. If you lack templates and processes for this, consult colleagues who are experienced with outsourcing and borrow theirs, customizing as necessary. Outsourcing is one aspect of project management where figuring things out as you proceed will waste a lot of time and money and result in significant project risk.

Risk management also requires that at least one member of the project team be involved with planning and contracting for outside services, so that the interests of the project are represented throughout the procurement process.

Ensure that each RFP includes a clear, unambiguous definition of the scope of work involved, including the terms and conditions for evaluation and payment. Although it is always risky for any project work to remain poorly defined, outsourced work deserves particular attention. Inadequate definition of outsourced work leads to all the usual project problems, but it may result in even more schedule and resource risk. Problems with outsourced deliverables often surface late in the project with no advance warning (generally, following a long series of "we are doing just fine" status reports) and frequently will delay the project deadline, as is evident in the PERIL database, where delivery of a late or inadequate deliverable led to almost two months of average project slippage. There can also be significant increased cost due to required changes and late-project expedited work. Minimize outsourcing risks through scrupulous definition of all deliverables involved, including all measurements and performance criteria you will use for their evaluation.

As part of solicitation planning, establish the criteria that you will use to evaluate each response. Determine what is most important to your project and ensure that these aspects are clearly spelled out in the RFP, with guidance for the responders on how to supply the information that you require. Because the specific work on technical projects tends to evolve and change quickly, there is a good chance that well-established criteria for selecting suppliers will, sooner or later, be out of date. In light of your emerging planning data for the project, review the proposed criteria to validate that they are still appropriate. If the list of criteria used in the past seems in need of updating, do it *before* sending out the RFP. Establish priorities and relative weights for each evaluation criterion, as well as how you will assess the responses you receive. Communicating your priorities and expectations clearly in the RFP will help responders to self-qualify (or disqualify) themselves and will better provide the data you need to make a sound outsourcing decision.

Relevant experience is also important to avoiding outsourcing risk. In the RFP, request specifics from responders on similar prior efforts that were successful, and ask for contact information so you can follow up and verify. Even for work that is novel, ask for reference information from potential suppliers that will at least allow you to investigate past working relationships. Although it may be difficult to get useful reference information, it never hurts to request it.

Once you have established the specifics of the work to be out-sourced, as well as the processes and documents you plan to use, the next step is to find potential suppliers and encourage them to respond. One of the biggest risks in this step is failure to contact enough suppliers. For some project work, networking and informal communications may be sufficient, but sending the RFP to lists of known suppliers, putting information on public Web sites, and even advertising may be useful in letting potential responders know of your needs. If too few responses are generated, the quality and cost of the choices available may not serve the project well.

Bringing the RFP process to closure is also a substantial source of risk. There are potential risks in decision making, negotiation, and the contracting process.

Decision-making risks include not doing adequate analysis to assess each potential supplier and making a selection based on something other than the needs of the project.

Inadequate analysis can be a significant source of risk. It is fairly common for the decisions on outsourcing to coincide with many other project activities, and writing and getting responses to an RFP often takes more time than expected. As a result, you may be left with little time to evaluate the proposals on their technical merit. Judging proposals by weight, appearance, or some other superficial criteria may save time, but is not likely to result in the best selection. Evaluating and comparing multiple complex proposals thoroughly takes time and effort. Before you make a decision, spend the time necessary to ensure a thorough evaluation. It's like the old saying, "Act in haste; repent at leisure," except in your case you will be repenting when you are *very* busy.

Another potential risk in the selection process is pressure from outside your project to make a choice for reasons unrelated to your project. Influences from other parts of the organization may come to bear during the decision process—to favor friends, to avoid some suppliers, to align with "strategic" partners of some other internal group, or to use a global (or a local) supplier. Because the decision will normally be signed and approved by someone higher in the organization, sometimes the project team may not even be aware of these factors until late in the process. Documenting the process and validating your criteria for supplier selection with your management can reduce this problem, but use of outside suppliers not selected by the project team represents significant, and sometimes disastrous, project risk.

Overall, you must diligently stay on top of the process to ensure that the selections made for each RFP are as consistent with your project requirements as possible.

Negotiation is the next step after selecting a supplier, to finalize the details of the work and finances. After a selection is made, the balance of power begins to shift from the purchaser to the supplier, raising additional risks. Once the work begins, the project will be dependent on the supplier for crucial, time-sensitive project deliverables. The supplier is primarily dependent on the project for money, which in the short run is neither crucial nor urgent. To a lesser extent, suppliers are also dependent on future recommendations from you (which can provide leverage for ongoing risk management), but from the supplier's perspective, the relationship is mainly based on cash.

Effective and thorough negotiation is the last opportunity for the project to identify (and manage) risks without high potential costs. All relevant details of the work and deliverables need to be discussed and clearly understood, so the ultimate contract will unambiguously contain a scope of work that both parties see the same way. Details concerning tests, inspections, prototypes, and other interim deliverables must also be clarified. Specifics concerning partial and final payments, as well as the process and cost for any required changes or modifications, are also essential aspects of the negotiation process. Failure to conduct thorough, principled negotiation with a future supplier is a potential source of massive risk. Shortening a negotiation process to save time is never a good idea.

Because the primary consideration on the supplier side is financial, the best tactic for risk management in negotiation is to strongly align payments with achievement of specific results. Payment for time, effort, or other less tangible criteria may allow suppliers to bill the project even while failing to produce what your project requires. When negotiating the work and payment terms, the least risky option for you as the purchaser is to establish a "payment for result" contract.

Outsourcing risk can also be lowered by negotiating contract terms that align with specific project goals. Although a contract must include consequences for supplier nonperformance, such as nonpay-ment, legal action, or other remedies, these terms do little to ensure proj-ect success. If the supplier fails to perform, your project will still be in trouble. Lack of a key deliverable will lead to project failure, so it is also use-ful to negotiate terms that more directly support your project objectives. If there is value in getting work done early, incentive payments are worth considering. If there are specific additional costs associated with late de-livery, establish penalties that reduce payments proportionate to the delay. For some projects, more complex financial arrangements than the simple "fee for result" may be appropriate, where percentages of favorable vari-ances in time or cost are shared with the supplier and portions of unfa-vorable ones may be deducted from the fees. Negotiating terms that more directly support the project objectives and involve suppliers more deeply in the project can significantly reduce outsourcing risks.

If the negotiation process, despite your best efforts, results in terms that represent potential project problems, note these as risks. In extreme cases, you may want to reconsider your selection decision, or even the decision to outsource the project work at all.

Contracting follows agreement on the terms and conditions for the work. These terms must be documented in a contract, signed, and put into force. One effective way to minimize risk is to use a well-established, preprinted contract format to document the relationship. This should in-clude all of the information that a complete, prudent contract must con-tain, so the chances of leaving out something critical, such as protection of confidential information or proprietary intellectual property, will be re-duced. For this reason, you can reduce project risk by using a standard contract form with no significant modifications or deletions. In addition, using standard formats will reduce the time and effort needed for con-tract approval. In large companies, contracts varying from the standard may take an additional month (or even more) for review, approval, and processing. Adding data to a contract is also generally a poor idea, with one big exception. Every contract needs to include a clear, unambiguous definition of the scope of work that specifies measurable deliverables and payment terms. A good contract also provides an explicit description of the process to be used if any changes are necessary.

One other source of risk in contracting is also fairly common for technical projects. The statement of work must be clear not only in defin-ing the results expected but also in specifying who will be responsible. It turns out that this is quite a challenge for engineers and other analytical people. Most engineering and other technical writing is filled with passive-voice sentences, such as, "It is important that the device be tested us-ing an input voltage varying between 105 and 250 volts AC, down to a temperature of minus 40 degrees Celsius." In a contract, there is no place for the passive voice. If the responsible party is not clearly specified, the sentence has no legal meaning. It fails to make clear who will do the testing and what, if any, consequences there may be should the testing fail. To minimize risks in contracts, write requirements in the active voice, spelling out all responsibilities in clear terms and *by name*.

Finally, when setting up a contract, minimize the resource risk by establishing a "not to exceed" limitation to avoid runaway costs. Set this limit somewhat higher than the expected cost, to provide some reserve for changes and unforeseen problems, but not a great deal higher. Many technical projects provide a reserve of about 10 percent to handle small adjustments. If problems or changes arise that require more than this, they will trigger review of the project, which is prudent risk management.

Outsourcing Risks

There are a variety of other risks that arise from outsourcing. One of the largest is cost, even if the work seems to be thoroughly defined. Unforeseen aspects of the work, which are never possible to eliminate completely, may trigger expensive change fees.

Continuity and turnover of contract staff is a risk. Although people who work for another company may be loyal to your project and stay with it through the end, the probabilities are lower than for the permanent staff on your project. Particularly with longer projects, turnover and retraining can represent major risks.

Outsourcing may increase the likelihood of turnover and demotivation of your permanent staff. If it becomes standard procedure to outsource all the new, "bleeding edge" project work, your permanent staff gets stuck doing the same old things, project after project, never learning anything new. It becomes harder to motivate and hold on to people who have no opportunity for development.

There may also be hidden effort for the project due to outsourcing, not visible in the plan. Someone must maintain the relationship, communicate regularly, deal with payments and other paperwork, and carry the other overhead of outsourcing. Although this may all run smoothly, if there are any problems it can become a major time sink. The time and effort this overhead requires is routinely overlooked or underestimated.

Finally, the nature of work at a distance requires significant additional effort. Getting useful status information is a lot of work. You will not get responses to initial requests every time, and verifying what is reported may be difficult. You can expect to provide much more information than you receive, and interpreting what you do get can be difficult. Even if the information is timely, it may not be completely accurate, and you may get little or no advance warning for project problems. Working to establish and maintain a solid working relationship with outsourcing partners can be a major undertaking, but it is prudent risk management.

Project-Level Estimates

Once you have validated the effort estimates for each activity in the project WBS, you can calculate the effort required in each project phase and total project effort. The "shape" of projects generally remains consistent over time, so the percentages of effort for each project phase derived from your planning process ought to be consistent with the measured results from earlier projects. Whatever the names and contents of the actual project phases, any significant deviation in the current plan compared with historical norms is good reason for skepticism. It's also evidence of risk; any plan that shows a lower percentage of effort in a given project phase than is normal has probably failed to identify some of the necessary activities or underestimated them.

Published industry norms may be useful, but the best information to use for comparison is local. How projects run in different environments varies a great deal, even for projects using a common life cycle or methodology. Historical data from peers can be helpful, but data directly from projects that you have run is better. Disciplined collection of project metrics is essential for accurate estimation, better planning, and effective risk management. If you have personal data, use it. If you lack data from past projects, this is yet another good reason to start collecting it.

Not all project phases are as accurately planned as others, because some project work is more familiar and receives more attention. The *middle* phases of most project life cycles contain most of the work that defines "what we do." Programmers program; hardware engineers build things; tech writers write; and in general, people do what it says on their business card. Whatever the "middle" phases are called (development, implementation, execution, and so forth), it is during this portion of the work where project contributors use the skills in which they have the most background and experience. These phases of project work are generally planned in detail, and activity estimates are often quite accurate. The phases that are earlier (such as investigation, planning, analysis, and proposal generation) and later (test, rollout, integration, and ramp-up) are generally less accurate. Using the life-cycle norm data, and assuming the "development" portion of the plan is fairly accurate, it is possible to detect whether project work may be missing or underestimated in the other phases. If this analysis shows inadequate effort allocated to the early (or late) phases based on historical profiles for effort, it is a good idea to find out why.

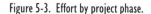

Figure 5-3. Effort by project phase.

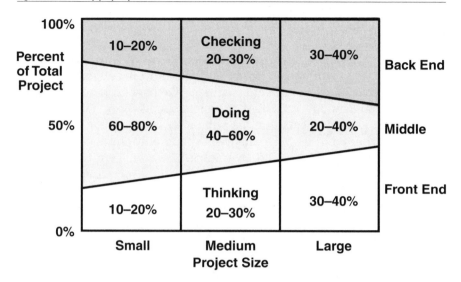

Effort profiles for projects also vary with project size. By mapping the data from a large number of projects with various life cycles into a simple, generic life cycle, a significant trend emerges. The simplified project life cycle in Figure 5-3 is far less detailed than any you are likely to use, but all life cycles and methodologies define phases or stages that map into these three broad categories:

1. *Thinking*: All the initial work on a project, such as planning, analysis, investigation, initial design, proposal generation, specification, and preparation for the business decision to commit to the project.

2. *Doing*: The work that generally defines the project, including development. This is where the team rolls up their sleeves and digs into the creation of the project deliverable.

3. *Checking*: Testing the results created by the project, searching for defects in the deliverable(s), correcting problems and omissions, and project closure.

As projects increase in size and complexity, the amount of work grows rapidly. Project effort tends to expand geometrically as projects increase in time, staffing, specifications, or other parameters. In addition to this overall rise in effort, the effort spent in each phase of the project, as a percentage, shifts. As projects become larger, longer, and more complex, the percentage of total project effort increases for both early front-end project work and for back-end activities at the end of the project. A graphical summary of this, based on data from a wide rage of projects, is in Figure 5-3.

Small projects (fewer than six months, most work done with a small collocated team) spend nearly all their effort in "doing"—creating the deliverable. Medium projects (six to twelve months long, with more than one team of people contributing) might spend about half of their effort in other work. Projects that are still larger (one year or longer, with several distributed or global teams) will spend only about a third of the total effort developing project deliverables. This rise in effort both in the early and late stages of project work stems from the increased amount of information and coordination required, and the significantly larger number of possible failure modes (and, therefore, statistically expected) in these more difficult projects. Fixing defects in complex systems requires a lot of time and effort. Software consultant Fred Brooks (author of *The Mythical Man-Month*) states that a typical software project is one-third analysis, one-sixth coding, and *one-half* testing.

All this bears on project risk for at least two reasons. The first is chronic underestimation of late project effort. If a complex project is planned with the expectation that 10 percent of the effort will be in up-front work, followed by 80 percent in development, the final phase will rarely be the expected 10 percent. It will balloon to another 80 percent (or more). This is a primary cause of the all-too-common "late project work bulge." Many entirely possible projects fail to meet their deadline (or fail altogether) due to underinvestment in early analysis and planning.

The second reason that life-cycle norms are valuable is found in the symmetry of Figure 5-3. The total effort required for a project tends to be lower when the initial and final phases of the work are roughly in balance. If the life-cycle norms for typical projects reveal that little effort is invested up front and a massive (generally unexpected) amount of effort is necessary at the end, then all projects are taking longer and costing more than necessary. Most projects that fail or are late because of end-of-project problems would benefit greatly from additional up-front work and planning.

Cost Estimating and Cost Budgeting

Inadequate funding was a major problem for nearly all the projects in the PERIL database with money risks, causing well over three months of average slippage. Project cost estimates are generally dominated by staffing and outsourcing costs, but also include expenses for equipment, services, travel, communications, and other project needs.

Staffing and Outsourcing Costs

Staffing costs can be calculated using the activity effort estimates, based on your histograms, spreadsheets, or other resource planning information. Using standard hourly rates for the project staff and your effort estimates, you can convert effort into project costs. For longer projects, you may also need to consider factors such as salary changes and the effect of inflation.

Estimate any outsourcing costs using the contracts negotiated for the services, working with figures about halfway between the minimum you can expect and the "not to exceed" amounts.

Equipment and Software Costs

The best time to request new equipment or upgrade older hardware, systems, and applications for a project is at the outset. You should assess the project's needs, and research the options that are available. Inspect all equipment and software applications already in place to determine any opportunities for replacement or upgrade. Document the project's needs and assemble a proposal including all potential purchases. As discussed earlier in the chapter, proposing the purchase and installation of new equipment at the start of the project has two benefits: getting approval from management when it is most likely, and allowing for installation when there is little other project work to conflict with it. Propose purchase of the best equipment available, so if purchase is approved you will be able to work as fast and efficiently as possible. If you propose the best options and only some of the budget is approved, you still may be able to find alternative hardware or systems that will enable you to complete your project. Estimate the overall project equipment expense by summing the cost of any approved proposals with other expected hardware and software costs.

Travel

The best time to get travel money for your project is at the beginning; midproject travel requests are often refused. As you plan the project work, determine when travel will be necessary and decide who will be involved. Travel planned and approved in advance is easier to arrange, less costly, and less disruptive for the project and the team members than last-minute, emergency trips. Request and justify face-to-face meetings with distant team members, getting team members from each site together at the project start, and for longer projects, at least every six months thereafter. Also budget for appropriate travel to interact with users, customers, and other stakeholders.

There are no guarantees that travel requested at the beginning of the project will be approved, or that it might not be cut back later, but if you do not estimate and request travel funds early, the chances get a lot worse.

Other Costs

Communication is essential on technical projects, and for distributed teams, it may be quite costly. Video- (and even audio-) conferencing technology may require up-front investments as well as usage fees. Schedule and budget for frequent status meetings, using the most appropriate technology you can find.

Projects that include team members outside of a single company may need to budget for setup and maintenance of a public-domain–secure Web site outside of corporate firewalls for project information that will be available to everyone. Other services such as shipping, couriers, and photocopying may also represent significant expenses for your project.

Cost Budgeting

Cost budgeting is the accumulation of all the cost estimates for the project. For most technical projects, the majority of the cost is for people, either permanent staff or workers under some kind of contract. The project cost baseline also includes estimated expenses for equipment, software and services, travel, communications, and other requirements. Whenever your preliminary project budget analysis exceeds the project cost objectives, the difference represents a significant project risk. Unless you are able to devise a credible lower-cost plan or negotiate a larger project budget, your project may prove to be impossible because of inadequate resources.

Documenting the Risks

Resource risks become visible throughout the planning and scheduling processes. Resource risks discussed in this chapter include:

- Activities with unknown staffing
- Understaffed activities
- Work that is outsourced
- Contract risks
- Activities requiring a unique resource

- Part-time team members
- Remote team members
- The impact of the work environment
- Budget requirements that exceed the project objectives

Add each specific risk discovered to the list of scope and schedule risks, with a clear description of the risk situation. This growing risk list provides the foundation for project risk analysis and management.

Key Ideas for Identifying Resource Risks

- Identify all required skills you need for which you lack named, committed staffing.
- Determine all situations in the project plan where people or other resources are overcommitted.
- Find all activities with insufficient resources.
- Identify uncertain activity effort estimates.
- Note outsourcing risks.
- Gain funding approval early for needed training, equipment purchases, and travel.
- Ascertain all expected project costs.

Panama Canal: Resources (1905–1907)

Project resource risk arises primarily from people factors, as demonstrated in the PERIL database, and this was certainly true on the Panama Canal project. Based on the experiences of the French during the first attempt, John Stevens realized project success required a healthy, productive, motivated workforce. For his project money was never an issue, but retaining people to do difficult and dangerous work in the hot, humid tropics certainly was. Stevens invested heavily, through Dr. Gorgas, in insect control and other public health measures. He also built an infrastructure at Panama that supported the productive, efficient progress he required. At the time of his departure from the project, Stevens had established a well-fed, well-equipped, well-housed, well-organized workforce with an excellent plan of attack.

This boosted productivity, but George Goethals realized that success also relied on continuity and motivation. He wanted loyalty, not to him, but to the project. The work was important, and Goethals used any opportunity he had to point this out. He worked hard to keep the workers engaged, and much of what he did remains good resource management practice today.

Goethals took a number of important steps to build morale. He started a weekly newspaper, the *Canal Record*. The paper gave an accurate, up-to-date picture of progress, unlike the *Canal Bulletin* periodically issued during the French project. In many ways, it served as the project's status report, making note of significant accomplishments and naming those involved to build morale. The paper also provided feedback on productivity. Publishing these statistics led to healthy rivalries, as workers strived to better last week's record for various types of work, so they could see their names in print.

It was crucial, Goethals believed, to recognize and reward service. Medals were struck at the Philadelphia Mint, using metal salvaged from the abandoned French equipment. Everyone who worked on the project for at least two years was publicly recognized and presented with a medal in a formal ceremony. People wore these proudly. In a documentary made many years after the project, Robert Dill, a former canal worker interviewed at age 104, was still wearing his medal, number 6726.

Goethals also sponsored weekly open-door sessions on Sundays when anyone could come with their questions. Some weeks over one hundred people would come to see him. If he could quickly answer a question or solve a problem, he did it then. If a request or suggestion was not something that would work, he explained why. If there were any open questions or issues, he committed to getting an answer, and he followed up. Goethals treated workers like humans, not brutes, and this engendered fierce loyalty.

Although all this contributed to ensuring a loyal, motivated, productive workforce, the most significant morale builder came early on, from the project sponsor. In 1906, Theodore Roosevelt sailed to Panama to visit his project. His trip was without precedent; never before had a sitting U.S. president left the country. The results of the trip were so noteworthy that one newspaper at the time conjectured that someday, a president "might undertake European journeys."

Roosevelt chose to travel in the rainy season, and the conditions in Panama were dreadful. This hardly slowed him down at all; he was in the swamps, walking the railroad ties, charging up the slopes, even operating one of the huge, 97-ton Bucyrus steam shovels. He went everywhere the workers were. The reporters who came along were exhausted, but the workers were hugely excited and motivated.

On Roosevelt's return to Washington, so much was written about the magnitude and importance of the project that interest and support for the canal spread quickly throughout the United States. People believed: "With Teddy Roosevelt, anything is possible."

Managing Project Constraints and Documenting Risks

> *"A good plan, violently executed right now, is better*
> *than the perfect plan executed next week."*
> —GENERAL GEORGE S. PATTON

Reviewing a plan to detect problems and make improvements generally ought to be a brief exercise done toward the end of initial project planning. This chapter is not about obsessive application of every single project management practice in an endless quest for the flawless plan (sometimes called "analysis-paralysis"). The topic here is realistic, common-sense project analysis. The principal objective of reviewing the plan is to find defects and omissions, deal with unmet constraints, and seek an improved plan, *quickly*. You are not after a perfect plan, just the best one possible using what you currently know about your project.

This part of the planning process relates to risk management in several ways, but two aspects are particularly important. First, the process of replanning to deal with constraints will nearly always *create* project risk—self-inflicted risk—as minimizing one parameter of a project often leads to more pressure on other aspects of the work, creating additional exposures, failure modes, and potential problems. These new risks result from trade-offs made by the project team, and they need to be recognized, documented, and added to the project risk list. A second type of project risk is that of not taking on the "right" project. All projects have alternatives, and examining at least some of these options is key to *opportunity* management, also discussed in this chapter.

Analyzing Constraints

As you proceed through preliminary project definition and planning, a coherent picture of your project starts to emerge. Although your project plan is still incomplete at this point, it does begin to provide insight into whether the project objective is possible or not. Often, it reveals the unpleasant fact that the project (at least as defined so far) *is* impossible, or at least overconstrained; the result of your bottom-up plan leaves at least part of the project objective unmet. Your preliminary analysis might reveal a schedule that extends beyond the deadline, resource requirements that exceed initial budgets, or other significant issues. Your planning process reveals just how much trouble you are in.

Failure of the preliminary plan to meet the overall project objective is not the only issue that emerges at this stage of planning. Above and beyond the high-level constraints, most projects also have other constraints that you must manage. Timing requirements for intermediate documents, prototypes, and other midproject deliverables may mandate fixed-date milestones within the project plan. The profile of available resources may be interrupted at specific times by the business cycle, by holidays and vacations, or by higher-priority projects. In addition, projects undertaken in lean organizations (where keeping everyone busy all the time in the name of efficiency is a top priority) will frequently run into a queue when access to a critical, unique resource is required. Delays for contract approvals, management sign-off, and other decisions are common. Identifying and managing risks from these other constraints is also part of risk management on high-tech projects.

Your primary goal in managing project constraints is to remove, or at least minimize, the differences between the project objective and your project plan, in terms of scope, schedule, and resources. The standard triangle diagram for examining project trade-offs is one way to show these differences, as in Figure 6-1. The plan, represented by the triangle with the dashed-line edges, is quite a bit larger than the objective, shown as the solid-edged triangle.

For this project, the initial plan suggests that the deliverable is probably feasible, so this project is not *literally* impossible—its scope is within your capabilities. However, as shown, the project will require both more time and more resources (people, money, etc.) than requested in the project objective, so based on the current plan, it is not feasible because of its *constraints*. For projects where the scope is plausible, the situation in Figure 6-1 is fairly common. Bottom-up project planning begins with a work breakdown structure (WBS) that is consistent with the desired

Figure 6-1. Objective versus plan.

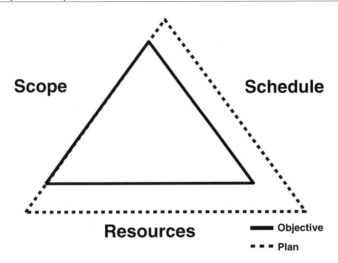

scope, but the initial schedule and resource plans fall wherever the WBS leads them—often at significant variance with the project objective.

For some projects, the objective is firm, based on hard limits that cannot be modified. For other projects, the objective may be based on softer constraints, goals that are desirable but not absolutely necessary. Each project is unique, so determining how to approach trade-off analysis for your project requires you to understand what the constraints and priorities are, and how they were determined. In the simplest form, project priorities boil down to the old saying, "Good, fast, cheap: Pick two." Every project requires at least one degree of freedom. Because of this, it is unrealistic to nail down all aspects of a project prior to completing a thorough analysis of the required work.

Any of the three parameters *could* be most flexible, but one of them *must* be. Although you can get a deliverable out of a project quickly and cheaply, it may fail to meet the need. This lesson was re-learned quite often in the late 1990s by projects executed in Internet time, as well as by NASA on several failed Mars missions. Similarly, excellent results are often possible in short time frames, but the cost of this compression is high and may not be justified by the result ("crashing" project activities in the project schedule is covered later in this chapter). You may even be able to deliver good results at low cost in projects where time is not limited (though this scenario could result in the "analysis-paralysis" mentioned earlier).

A slightly more sophisticated analysis rests on prioritizing the

Figure 6-2. Project priority matrix.

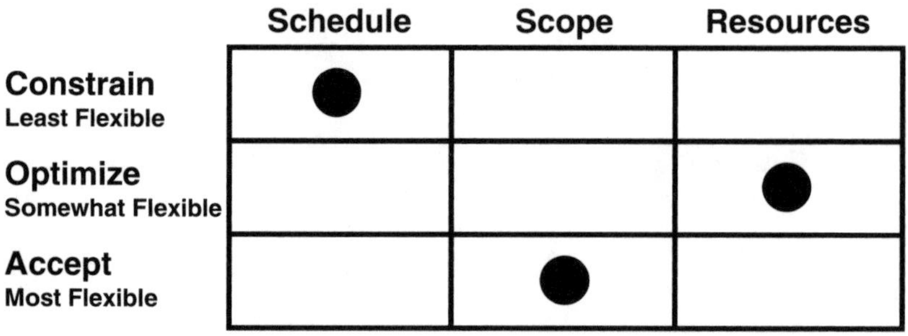

	Schedule	Scope	Resources
Constrain Least Flexible	●		
Optimize Somewhat Flexible			●
Accept Most Flexible		●	

triple constraint. Rank-ordering scope, schedule, and resources shows which of the three is most important for your project. A simple three-by-three grid is often used for this, as in Figure 6-2.

The project priorities shown here are common for high-tech projects, as timing dominates more and more of the work. In contract work, deadlines with financial penalties are often looming. In product development, pressure from competitors, trade show schedules, and other real constraints on timing are often at issue. Even in application development, delivery often must synchronize with fiscal accounting periods. Schedule in all these cases is the dominant priority, and failure to meet the project deadline will have significant, possibly dire consequences. Schedule is the parameter such projects *constrain*.

In Figure 6-2, the second priority is resources. This is also common, as the desire to minimize resources and execute as efficiently as possible is a key goal for many projects. In fact, many projects face significant limits on competent, available staff. In the time frame of many technical projects, the number of available people who are familiar with new or evolving technologies is fixed and can only increase gradually over time through training, mentoring, and other methods for hauling people up the learning curve. Projects such as this strive to *optimize* their resources.

The largest degree of freedom for the project in Figure 6-2 is for scope, indicating that there may be aspects or specifications set in the objective that, although desirable, may not be absolutely required. The project will *accept* small changes to the deliverable, particularly if not making the changes would require more time, more resources, or both. This prioritization is one of six possibilities, and good examples for each of the other five are easily imagined. Though all prioritizations are possible, today's technical projects frequently converge on "schedule/resources/scope," as in Figure 6-2.

Figure 6-3. Plan trade-offs.

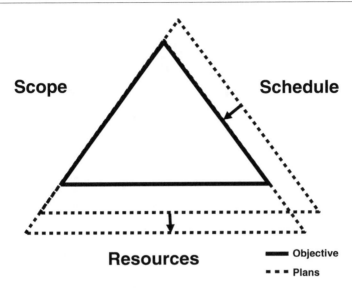

Scope   **Schedule**

Resources   ━━ Objective
                       ▪ ▪ ▪ Plans

For the example in Figure 6-1, the initial plan failed to meet the deadline and also was over budget. Doing some "what if" analysis, you may discover a way to use a top-notch group of consultants (with a credible track record) to perform more work in parallel, shortening the overall project. This approach will not be inexpensive; it makes the budget problem even bigger, and results in the shift shown in Figure 6-3. In this figure, the schedule has been compressed, bringing it in line with the objective, but the resources required for the project, which already exceeded the objective, are *even farther* out of line with the project expectations.

For projects where resources are the lowest priority, this tactic may be a good alternative. For projects with the priorities in Figure 6-2, however, this is not likely to be the best plan. It may be better to reevaluate the specifications and propose a plan that achieves its deadline within budget but falls slightly short on scope. Some projects may find some of the requested requirements are not actually needed. Other projects may propose delivering the most valuable functionality on time, and delivering the rest in a follow-on project somewhat later. The analysis for such a scope reduction might result in a shift similar to Figure 6-4.

In this case, changes proposed to the initial plan affect all three of the project parameters, with the most significant difference between the objective and the plan being a small reduction in the feature set for the deliverable.

Figure 6-4. Seeking the "best" plan.

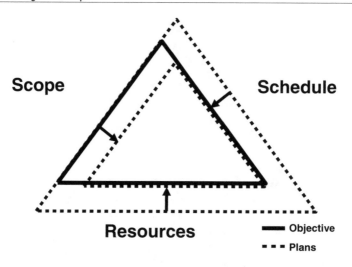

The overall objective of the plan review and "what if" analysis is to discover the options available as alternatives to the initial plan, and to see whether it might be desirable, or even necessary, to revisit the project objective and change the project definition. This triangle model can be thought of as a representation of projects in a two-dimensional state space, and the exploration of plan alternatives will reveal where in this space you can find realistic, feasible projects. For particularly ill-conceived projects, the analysis may fail to turn up any options close to the original objective. For such projects, you need to negotiate a major change to the objective, abandon the project, or at least think about updating your résumé.

In most cases, though, reasonable alternatives for your project are not difficult to find. Start your analysis of the project plan with the parameter that has the lowest priority, and explore possible changes related to that aspect of the project. These modifications are generally the easiest to negotiate, so it makes sense to focus first on that side of the triangle. For most projects, you will also want to examine alternatives for the other two parameters. The next sections describe using this "what if" technique for exploring project opportunities, and then for options related to scope, resources, and schedule (following the prioritization in Figure 6-2).

Managing Opportunities

When your preliminary plan falls short of the project objective, it might seem inappropriate to analyze opportunities, because this might make things worse. There are a number of good reasons for exploring these project options, though, and they relate directly to risk management. Where risk management seeks to understand what might go badly in a project, opportunity management looks for what might go better. In particular, opportunity management asks what similar, but superior, projects might be possible. Realizing halfway through the work that you could have achieved a more valuable result is not useful. It's too late at that point on most projects to do anything about it. Opportunity management also may result in a more interesting, more motivating project that can increase teamwork and provide development opportunities valued by contributors. Mostly, however, it helps to ensure that you are not working on the wrong project. As with risks, a good starting point for opportunity management is the triple constraint of scope, schedule, and resources.

Scope

Deliverables for high-tech projects are set using two kinds of input, user/market demand and technological possibilities. Most project work relies primarily on the first. The sponsors, economic buyers, managers, and others who get projects started are generally doing so to meet a need, solve a problem, or respond to some specific request. Although this may be sufficient, the requested deliverables in high-tech projects can fall well short of what is possible. Technology moves fairly quickly, so user requests may represent continued use of an older technology even after emerging new ideas and approaches are available. If you were collecting specifications for a project deliverable from people sitting on a river bank washing their clothes with two large stones, their requirements would probably involve developing lighter rocks. The concept of a washing machine might not occur to them if the technology is not part of their experience. Similarly, the project team may be able to see possibilities based on technology unknown to the users that would solve the problem or meet the need much more effectively than the original request. Opportunity management is about merging a deep understanding of user needs with the technical capabilities available to create the best deliverable—not necessarily the one initially envisioned.

Scope opportunity management often requires a counterproposal to the original objective, and may involve negotiation. Some project leaders for high-tech projects go to great effort to avoid this sort of confrontation, viewing it as unpleasant and usually unproductive. This is unfortunate, because this process represents one of the real sources of power and influence that the project leader has. There is an old saying, "If you are going to lose an argument, change the subject." Proposing an alternative that is demonstrably superior to the requested deliverable can effectively "change the subject," avoiding an otherwise doomed project by substituting a better, more realistic one.

The main motivation for opportunity management, though, is to increase the business value of the project. There are a number of ways to approach this. Surveying the current state of relevant and closely related technologies is a typical starting point. It may be that a new generation of hardware is available that could effectively be used. New technologies or methods may provide greater speed or reliability. New or existing standards may have application to your work, which could extend the possible uses of the deliverable, both in the current project and for future applications. It might be possible to develop a deliverable with capabilities that solve a whole class of problems instead of the single one that triggered the project. Conversely, it may be possible to break up an ambitious project into shorter stages, developing something that provides tangible value (perhaps most of what is actually needed) for a fraction of the time and cost that the entire project would require.

Resources

Explore options for efficiency or schedule reduction through the use of additional, more highly skilled, or outside contributors. If improvements to your tools, systems, or other aspects of your infrastructure will help performance, propose changes. Gain access to and use the best available facilities and methods for communications. Bringing distributed teams together and arranging other face-to-face collaborations may significantly boost progress and teamwork. If so, obtain funding for necessary travel. If additional training for contributors will help the project, schedule it.

If there are team members who have underallocated time during parts of the project, consider replanning to more effectively use the effort available (though this will add less resource reserve and increase potential failure modes).

Schedule

Schedule opportunities include revising the schedule to exploit float, revising logical dependencies, and "crashing" activities. Seek valid shortcuts and better, newer methods for the work. Although each of these can reduce the schedule, each also tends to increase risk. These concepts are discussed in the section on schedule modifications.

Some project leaders list opportunities with risks and assess them together using the processes outlined in Chapter 7. Although opportunities and risks are related, they are not exactly "opposites." Most people think of risks as threats, and the choice of whether to manage them or not is primarily the responsibility of the project team. Unmanaged risks that do occur are unquestionably going to be seen as the responsibility of the team.

Opportunities are not symmetric with risks. Adopting them, particularly when they involve significant scope changes, is not generally up to the project team, so proposals and approvals are part of the process. The consequences are not really symmetric either. It's often said, "Success has many fathers, while failure is an orphan." When things go better than expected, everyone takes credit—especially the managers. When things go badly, the project team will be left standing alone.

Opportunities that significantly change the project require sponsor support, and acceptance of them is nearly always more complex than the risk assessment process described in Chapter 7. Opportunities that do not represent substantial shifts to the overall project objective (including much of what follows in this chapter) mostly fall into the category of "good project planning." Some of the opportunities you uncover may reduce project risk, while others may increase it. Include all opportunities that you plan to consider, and note their effects on your risk list.

Scope Modification

Proposed changes to the project deliverable may be easily accepted, absolutely nonnegotiable, or anything in between. This depends on the project, the sponsors and users, and the type and magnitude of the change. Whatever the circumstances, a conscientious project team will spend at least a little time examining the effect on the project of adjusting the project deliverable. This "what if" exercise helps your team understand the work better and provides you with valuable information for decision making.

To meet project constraints, many projects will end up trimming scope. Before deciding what features or aspects of the project deliverable to drop or change, determine which requirements are absolute "must have" features, and which (if any) are more expendable. There are several techniques for prioritizing requirements. The simplest is to list the requirements and sort them into a sequence where the most essential ones are at the top of the list and the least important ones fall to the bottom. "Is/is not" analysis, described in Chapter 3, is another possible starting point. You will need to revisit the list of items on the "is" list to validate that each requirement is in fact essential. Determining what portions of scope can be demoted to the "is not" list effectively limits scope. This is particularly useful for projects that have hard limits on timing and budget; the "is/is not" technique establishes a firm boundary for scope that is consistent with the other limits.

The purpose of the exercise, however you approach it, is to capture and document the specifications that you *must* deliver, separating them from the portions of the requested deliverable that are desirable but not absolutely necessary. Accepting small decreases in reliability or performance may cause a significant reduction in project time and cost, and such trade-offs may result in a project that better meets its overall goals.

Project scope requirements are easiest to change early. Late changes are often painful and expensive, resulting in work that would have been unnecessary had the change been made earlier. Freezing scope early does not mean that project scope will never shift; it just means that any modifications will be subject to analysis and change control before being accepted. Determining the lowest-value features and requirements allows you to intelligently determine what to exclude (either permanently, or to be part of a follow-on project).

Resource Modification

Revisiting the resource plan also can lead to an overall plan that better fits the objective. Alternative approaches to staffing, cross-training, outsourcing, and other elements of the resource plan are all potentially useful options.

Resource Analysis

For some projects, there may be ways to get work done faster without increasing the overall required resources. One possibility is to rearrange the work assignments to use available staffing more fully and effectively. Schedules may be too long because of nonproject commitments. If the external work can be postponed or eliminated, it could have a significant impact on your schedule. You may also be able to find ways to improve the effectiveness of the project team by simply asking individuals what they need to work faster. Many people get more work done through telecommuting, working at times when they are more efficient, or being in a different work environment. Unless you ask, these possibilities will remain hidden.

You may even be able to minimize distractions and noise during some or most of the project through moving work off-site, collocating the team in a closed-off area, or relocating to space that is out of normal foot-traffic areas. One project team I worked with attributed much of their on-schedule performance to their location in a trailer (while new buildings were being completed). It was quiet there, and no one dropped by to visit.

Training Additional Staff

Another tactic that can potentially help the schedule as well as mitigate a source of project risk is mentoring and cross-training. Project timelines are often longer than theoretically necessary on high-tech projects because only one person knows how to do some part of the work. These activities must be scheduled in sequence, queued up for the expert. Work can be speeded up if others on the staff have an interest in this area of expertise and can be trained to take on activities in parallel. Of course, people new to a discipline will rarely work as fast as experienced staff. Duration estimates for activities assigned to them will generally be longer, due to training requirements and lower work efficiency. Activities assigned to the current expert will also take somewhat longer, because of the required mentoring. Despite this, the benefits to the schedule in getting the work done concurrently can be substantial. In addition, the project risk profile will improve, as the project will no longer be dependent on a single person. If the expert becomes unavailable to your project (because of illness, higher priority work, resignation, or any other reason), your project will not grind to a halt but can continue (although more slowly) using the newly trained staff.

Staffing Alternatives

For projects where schedule is much more important than budget, subcontracting work to outside service providers might speed things up, providing that a larger staff can work in parallel on activities that are currently planned in sequence. If the project priority is high, more staff from within the organization may also be an option. Some projects cannot run as quickly as theoretically possible because the experience and talent available on the original project team is low, so it is useful to explore the possibility of finding staff who are more efficient or who do not require any training before taking on project activities. Additional resources of other types, such as faster computers, newer equipment for test and other work, or systems to automate manual activities, can also potentially help to compress the project. New work methods require training and practice, but may still represent options for saving time. All of this will raise the resource cost of the project, but for some projects this trade-off may be justified.

Schedule Modification

Reexamining the schedule also provides alternative projects. Some ideas to consider include using float, revising activity dependencies, and "crashing" the schedule.

Using Float

One simple approach for shortening your project involves reducing the amount of float on noncritical activities. Float is derived from the critical path analysis of the schedule (discussed in Chapter 4), and it measures how much an activity can slip without impact to the project deadline.

To shorten your project using float, you shift some of the work on critical path activities to staff assigned to noncritical activities. These staffing shifts will cause changes to noncritical activities (such as delaying the start, interrupting the activity, or reducing productivity), but as long as the activities retain some float, the additional effort on the critical activities can shorten the project. Bear in mind that this sort of schedule compression comes with a price. Using all (or nearly all) of the float for an activity makes it more critical. This increases project risk by creating new failure modes.

Revising Activity Dependencies

A second, more elaborate idea involves revising activity dependencies. Here, the schedule is shortened through rearranging or redefining the work. The simplest possibility is to inspect the dependencies linking critical path activities, looking for opportunities to shorten the schedule using a more compact logical work flow.

If revising activity sequences is ineffective, you can reexamine the activities and brainstorm alternate ways to approach longer activities on the critical path by using a different breakdown or a completely new approach. This second method often involves breaking critical path activities down further to create smaller activities that can be executed in parallel, as in Figure 6-5.

This concept has a variety of names, including concurrent engineering, "fast tracking," and simultaneous development. For parallel execution to be effective, there are at least two requirements. First, you need to allow integration time in the estimates for the parallel activities, or define a new activity (as in Figure 6-5) during which all the separately developed components are assembled. The second requirement is often

Figure 6-5. Converting activities to parallel execution.

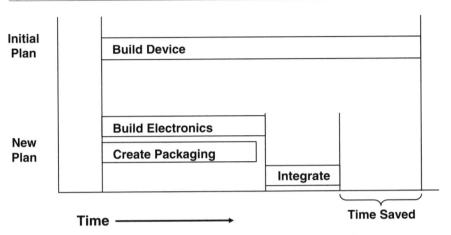

less visible, but it is even more important. Detailed up-front analysis is essential to ensure that the integration works. All the connections, interfaces, and relationships between the independently developed activity deliverables must be defined and thoroughly documented. Whatever this work is called—architecting, systems engineering, or something else—doing it well will be the difference between components that mesh properly and integration efforts that fail. When the system decomposition is done poorly, integration activities can consume all the time you expected to save, and more. Even worse, it may fail utterly, resulting in components that are completely unusable. Before committing to a plan that uses independent parallel development, explicitly identify when and by whom this analysis will be done, and note the integration risks on your project risk list.

Another approach for schedule compression through revising activity dependencies involves overlap of the work. In the plan, there may be finish-to-start dependencies on the critical path that can be converted to start-to-start dependencies with lags.

In Figure 6-6, the preliminary project plan includes a design activity scheduled for three weeks followed by a coding activity scheduled for four weeks. After thinking about it, the project team may decide that it would be possible to begin coding after only two weeks of design, because there will be enough information to start programming for some of the modules at that point, and staffing will be available to get going. Although it may seem that converting a finish-to-start dependency to start-to-start dependency with a lag of two weeks would save one week on the schedule, this is overly optimistic. There is an increased likelihood of

Figure 6-6. Modifying activity dependencies.

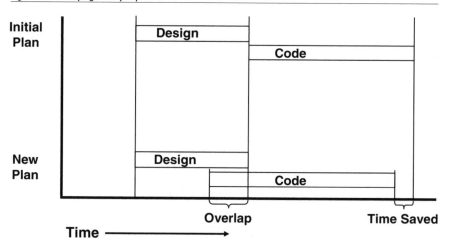

rework or discovery of something unexpected in the final week of design, so when you elect to make this sort of change, increase your duration estimates for any activities that you choose to begin early (in this case, about two days have been added to the coding activity), and also explicitly note the new risk.

"Crashing" the Schedule

An additional scheduling technique, common on projects with extreme schedule pressure, is "crashing." In this sense, crashing means applying additional resources to gain speed—as in a crash program. Not all activities can be crashed. It is not possible to crash activities where one person must do all the work, activities that cannot be partitioned, or activities with time constraints you do not control. A good example of an uncrashable activity is sailing a ship from New York to London. With one ship, it takes five days. With five ships, it *still* takes five days.

Even when crashing helps, it adds both additional cost and new risks to projects. If an activity is efficiently executed by a team of three people, a team of six will rarely be able to do it in half the time. Involving more people requires extra communication, overhead, and complexity, so resources and time do not vary linearly. This has been observed and documented for all types of projects for a long time, but the best discussion of this for high-tech projects remains *The Mythical Man-Month*, by Fred Brooks. Brooks covers in detail how people get in each other's way and how inefficiencies grow as the number of people working on a project increases. As efficiency drops, project risk increases because of the larger staff, potential confusion, work methods, and general complexity.

For all this, when time is critical to your project, these trade-offs may be justified. Crashing a project schedule requires you to locate the activities that can be shortened, and to estimate for each what the impact of compression will be, particularly on the project budget. Experienced project leaders usually have a good sense of how to do project work efficiently, so initial plans are generally built using assumptions for staffing and work methods that minimize effort and cost. For any given activity, though, other combinations of staffing and duration may be possible. One person working alone on an activity might take a long time; two working together could take quite a bit less. Adding more people will, for some activities, continue to reduce the activity duration even more. Eventually, though, you reach a point of diminishing returns, where adding more staff makes a negligible difference in the activity duration. A curve describing the relationship between staffing and time has a bend in it at that point, giving it an "L" shape, similar to the curve in Figure 6-7.

For any given activity, there is also a minimum possible duration; no amount of additional staffing, money, or other tactics will allow you to do the work in less time.

Because the initial estimates tend to be near the bend in the curve (where the cost is minimized), shortening projects by crashing can be quite expensive. Strategies for compressing projects by crashing begin by seeking a number of ideas, more than may be needed to meet the project deadline. Examine the schedule for activities that could be crashed, expedited, or otherwise changed in ways that could shorten the project,

Figure 6-7. Trade-off between effort and time.

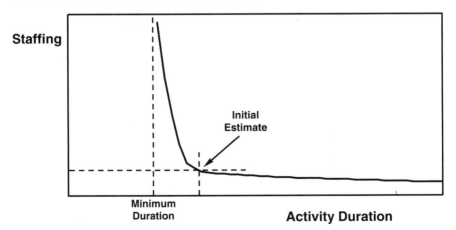

initially focusing on the critical path(s). Ideas for each activity can then be considered in turn and assessed for both effectiveness and cost.

If the next priority after schedule is resource, you will first adopt the strategies that have the least impact to the project budget. This will require you to estimate the "cost penalty" for each idea. The usual way to do this is to calculate the cost per time (usually per day) associated with the schedule reduction. For example, one idea might be to shorten a development activity, initially estimated to take fifteen work days and consume $4,000 of effort. You believe that this could be reduced to eleven days, saving four, if you bring in an outside contractor to help for a week at a rate of $6,000. Both the initial and compressed approaches to this activity are indicated in Figure 6-8, and the slope of the dotted line connecting them, $1,500 per day, defines the cost penalty for schedule compression.

Ideas for schedule compression can come from a variety of sources. The project team can brainstorm, you can consult peers or experts, or you can research what similar past projects did when they ran into trouble and were forced to work faster. In addition to providing a potentially rich source of ideas, project recovery information may offer data on costs and describe the work that will be required.

Typical methods that may prove effective in shortening project activity durations (for a price) include:

- Adding staff
- Paying for overtime

Figure 6-8. Estimates for crashed activity.

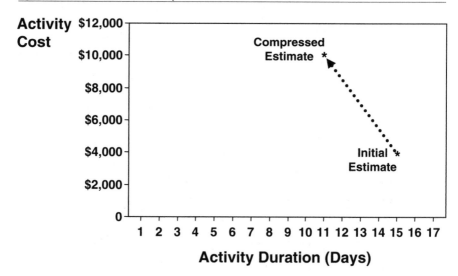

- Hiring outside staff to help or outsourcing whole project activities
- Paying to expedite shipping or other services
- Upgrading or replacing slower equipment
- Spreading work over more shifts

For each crashable activity idea you develop, estimate the total cost involved and assess the cost penalty—the expense for each day of schedule improvement—so you can arrange the ideas from least costly to most expensive, *per day*. Starting with the least costly strategies, make schedule changes affecting critical activities and note the cost of the additional resources. For each modification considered, check that the change does in fact provide a schedule improvement, and monitor for noncritical path activities that become critical. You can continue the process, crashing activities until it is no longer necessary, or is not possible.

Any schedule compression ideas that you do not use can be held in reserve as possible contingency plans for your project. (Contingency planning is discussed in detail in Chapter 8.) An alternative to adopting tactics for shortening the project based on cost takes this concept an additional step. Ideas for crashing can be useful as contingency plans only if they relate to future portions of the project. To maximize the potential utility of any crashing tactics you have developed, you might choose to apply them based on timing. If you start with the ideas that shorten the project by acting on the earliest activities, *any* leftover tactics will remain available as contingency plans. Although this will generally cost more, it will result in a more resilient plan.

Before leaving the topic of schedule changes, it's worth noting that a compressed schedule has a lot more failure modes and will generate a good deal more stress for the project. The trade-offs between time and cost and time and scope are visible throughout the process of managing project constraints. The trade-off between time and risk is more subtle, but nonetheless real. At the conclusion of this process, document any changes you made and list all the new risks introduced to your project plan, including the new critical and near-critical paths. Also be aware of the increased overall project risk contributed by the added complexity and stress.

Assessing Options and Updating Plans

After investigating possible scope, resource, and schedule changes, you have the information you need to assess your options and seek the plan that best meets the project objective. Your analysis may result in a credible project plan (including a detailed project schedule, resource plan, and description of major project deliverables) that supports the project objective and any other significant constraints. If so, your next step is risk analysis.

If the "best" plan you can develop is still far from the objective, it is evidence that you have an overconstrained project. In such a case, use your "what if" analysis of scope, schedule, and resource combinations and develop *at least* two additional plans that achieve slightly different project objectives, such as:

- Fewer resources needed, but longer schedule or reduced scope
- Increased scope (with higher demonstrable value), but more time or resources required
- Shorter schedule, but more resources needed (or scope reduced)

For each option, document relative advantages and risks. These alternative plans can be used in discussions and negotiations. (Negotiating project objective changes is a key topic of Chapter 10.)

Incorporate any plan changes that you are empowered to make into your preliminary schedule and other project documents. If you developed alternative plans, document them as well, with any proposed changes or opportunities that would require higher-level approval.

Seeking Missing Risks

Your list of project risks grows throughout the defining and planning processes, as noted in the preceding chapters. Although you have collected risk data throughout the planning of project work, it is useful to review your scope definition, preliminary schedule, and resource plan, using the ideas in Chapters 3 through 5. You may also want to review the selected risks from the PERIL database listed in the Appendix to further stimulate discovery of project risks. There are also a number of additional methods for detecting potential problems and risks.

Brainstorming

One powerful risk discovery process is brainstorming. With the project team, review the risk list that you have already constructed. Work together to brainstorm additional potential project problems. Examine the methods and processes you intend to use and consider any aspects that are new or that will be particularly difficult. Think about risk that would arise as a consequence of any organizational changes that are rumored or seem likely. Finally, focus on outside factors that might have an impact on your project, such as natural disasters, weather, government or legal changes, and actions of competitors.

Capture every idea without comment, questions, or criticism. Stimulate people to think of new risks triggered by the thoughts of others. List every risk that is mentioned, even those you think you can do nothing about. Keep the brainstorming going, striving to hear from every member of the project team, until the flow of ideas seems at an end. Conclude the process by restating any risks that are unclear, combining or eliminating risks where there is redundancy. Add all the new risks to the project risk list.

Retrospective Analysis

A second idea for finding risks in a new project is retrospective analysis of earlier projects. The old adage "Lightning never strikes twice in the same place" is demonstrably false; lightning strikes the same spot hundreds of times, always the highest place with the best electrical connection to the ground. (If this were not the case, lightning rods would not work.) On projects, the analogous statement *"That* can never happen again" is equally untrue. Risks tend to recur in project after project, unless you understand the root cause and do something differently to avoid the problem. Data from earlier work (in the form of project retrospectives, lessons learned, postmortems, postproject analyses, or close-out reports) is a rich source of risk information.

These reports generally contain two types of data useful for risk management: effective practices worth repeating and areas where improvement is possible. In the area of good practices, seek specific ideas from what was done well, practices to repeat or extend, and specific significant accomplishments. Examine your plan to see whether you are incorporating opportunities to take full advantage of known good practices. In the realm of things that did not go well, review previous project data for problems, assumptions, poor estimates, actual beginnings and ends of major activities compared to plans, complexity of activities undertaken, number of changes proposed and accepted, sources of delay, and other issues. Identify any aspects that impacted progress.

Scenario Analysis

Additional risks may come to light through scenario analysis. Discuss situations expected along the project timeline, step-by-step, asking questions such as, "What might go wrong here?" and "What will be keeping me up at night during this portion of the work?" You can close your eyes and "play a movie in your head" to gain insight into the project's work and the problems it may be exposed to. Techniques familiar to software development organizations such as inspections and structured walk-throughs may also be applied to the project plan to reveal weaknesses, omissions, and risks. As you think through project scenarios, test the project assumptions to uncover any that might change.

SWOT Analysis

A similar approach to scenario analysis is "Strengths, Weaknesses, Opportunities, and Threats" (SWOT) analysis. For many projects, particularly those involving delivering solutions, these aspects are examined early in the project. As the project planning process approaches closure, you should revisit both the identified weaknesses and threats for the project to ensure that any that have not been addressed in your planning are noted as risks.

Assumptions Analysis

Also related to scenario analysis is review of your assumptions. As you proceed with your project planning, assumptions analysis will show where initial expectations are no longer valid or could result in possible project failure modes.

Expert Interviews

Risk discovery sources outside your project can also be useful. Expert interviews both inside and outside of your organization can be a potentially rich source of information on risks that your project may encounter. Utilizing the experiences and perspectives of others is a potent technique for identifying and managing risks.

Root-Cause Analysis

Finally, root-cause analysis or "cause-and-effect" exercises may be used for risk discovery. Risk management requires knowledge of the root causes that lead to project problems. There are a number of effective techniques for discovering the sources of problems, and although they are most often applied retrospectively, they can also be used to examine future problems. These techniques include failure mode and effect analysis, fishbone diagrams, root-cause analysis, K-J analysis, or other varieties of cause-and-effect analysis. Using these processes to look for potential risks begins by stating an outcome the project intends to avoid—such as losing a key resource, delay in getting an important input, or significant increases in the cost of some portion of the project. The next step is to challenge the project team to work backward to uncover plausible sources that could cause the problem. In addition to uncovering specific risks that might not otherwise be detected, this exercise will often raise the perception of how probable certain problems are likely to be. Before the sources of trouble are articulated, most projects look fairly straightforward. After documenting the things that can contribute to project difficulty, you have a much more realistic view of the work, balancing the sometimes excessive optimism that is common early in a new project. Further discussion of root-cause analysis as a tool for managing risks is in Chapter 8.

Documenting the Risks

Every time you uncover a risk, write it down. Once all the risks identified have been added to the risk list, review the whole list in preparation for the next steps of analysis and assessment. For each listed risk, check that the description is clear, including a summary of the consequences. Specify the trigger event that signals the occurrence of the risk. For risks that are time-specific, also identify when in the project the risk is most likely to occur. The risk list with this added detail is also called a risk register.

Key Ideas for Constraint Management and Risk Discovery

- Minimize differences between project plans and objectives.
- Understand and clearly document project priorities.
- Explore project opportunities.
- Use priorities to identify project alternatives.
- Identify and explicitly remove unnecessary project scope.
- Determine risks and costs of proposed project changes.
- Minimize unknown risk through brainstorming, analysis, and research.

Panama Canal: Improving the Plan (1906)

Many projects, viewed in retrospect, failed because they could not manage the work within mandated constraints. In reviving the

Panama Canal project, a great deal of effort went into rethinking the approach to the work, to avoid the most significant issues that plagued the earlier project.

For projects of all types, it is beneficial to invest effort early, investigating whether there are better, faster, more efficient ways to do what is required. New technologies, methodologies, and approaches are born this way. Several key innovations were introduced in the U.S. canal project. Avoiding schedule and cost problems required changes to the equipment used and the methods employed to accomplish the work.

On the equipment side, twentieth-century technology made possible the huge, powerful steam shovels that gave the U.S. effort a big advantage over the earlier project. New technology also provided equipment suitable for use in the warm, damp, machine-destroying environment of Panama.

As important as the hardware was, however, the *way* the equipment was used made an even bigger difference. John Stevens, as a railroad engineer, saw the canal project as a railroad problem. To him, the canal was "the greatest of all triumphs in American railroad engineering." To keep the huge shovels digging continuously, Stevens developed a system so that shovel loads could be dropped onto railroad flatcars that ran along track adjacent to the shovels. The flatcars circulated in large loops out to the dams and other places where these loads could be deposited. Once there, huge fixed scoops (similar to the fronts of enormous snowplows) cleaned off the flatcars for their return to the shovels, with no need to stop or pause at any point for this enormous conveyor belt. Using this arrangement and the much larger steam shovels, the U.S. project was soon excavating more in one day than the earlier French project had accomplished in a month.

This system would have been sufficient for the project if the shovels had been simply digging deep holes in one place, but they were not. As the digging proceeded, the shovels had to move, and so did the railroad tracks that carried the flatcars. For this, John Stevens developed an elaborate, elastic method for moving the track, providing a constant, steady stream of empty flatcars flowing by the steam shovels. With his system, twelve men could move almost two kilometers of track in a single day. Using conventional track-laying methods, 600 men would have had difficulty equaling this performance. As the construction continued, excavation in the Culebra Cut widened and deepened, so these methods were used at multiple levels. Each level had its own railroad loop, shovels, and crews. The total track moved in one year approached 2,000 kilometers. Without these innovations, the canal project would have taken years longer to complete and cost far more, and it might well have been abandoned before completion, like the earlier project.

7

Quantifying and Analyzing Activity Risks

"When you know a thing, to hold that you know it,
and when you do not know a thing, to allow that
you do not know it—this is knowledge."
—CONFUCIUS

Project planning processes serve several purposes, but probably the most important for risk management is to separate the parts of the work that are well understood, and therefore less risky, from the parts that are less well understood. Often, what separates an impossible project from a possible one is isolating the most difficult work early, so it receives the attention and effort it requires. Risk assessment techniques are central to gaining an understanding of what is most uncertain about a project, and they are the foundation for managing risk. The focus of this chapter is analysis and prioritization of the identified project risks. Analysis of *overall* project risk will be addressed in Chapter 9.

Quantitative and Qualitative Risk Analysis

Risk analysis strives for deeper understanding of potential project problems. Techniques for doing this effectively may provide either qualitative information for prioritizing risks or quantitative risk measures.

Qualitative techniques are easier to apply and generally require less effort. Qualitative risk assessment is often sufficient for rank-ordering risks, allowing you to select the most significant ones to manage using the techniques discussed in Chapter 8.

Quantitative methods strive for greater precision, and they reveal more about each risk. These methods require more work, but quantitative analysis also provides data on the absolute magnitude of the risks and allows you to estimate schedule and/or budget reserves needed for risky projects.

Although the dichotomy between these approaches is explicit in the *PMBOK® Guide,* analysis methods fall into a continuum of possibilities. They range from qualitative assessment using a small number of categories, through methods that use progressively more and finer distinctions, to the extreme of determining specific quantitative data for each risk. If the primary goal of risk analysis is to prioritize risks to determine which ones are important enough to warrant further analysis and response, the easiest qualitative assessment methods generally suffice. If you need to assess project-level risk with maximum precision, then you will need quantitative assessment methods (though the nature of the available data usually puts a rather modest limit on your accuracy).

Whatever assessment method you apply, the foundation goes back to the simple formula discussed in Chapter 1: "loss" multiplied by "likelihood." The realm of likelihood is statistics and probability, topics that many project contributors find daunting and even counterintuitive. Loss in projects is measured in impact: time, money, and other project factors, including some that may be difficult to quantify. These two parameters characterize risk, and evaluating each poses challenges.

Risk Probability

At the beginning of a project, risks are uncertain. The likelihood, or probability, for any specific risk will always be somewhere between zero (no chance of occurrence) and one (inevitable occurrence). Looking backward from the end of a project, every risk has one of these two values; either it happened or it did not. Qualitative risk assessment methods divide the choices into probability ranges and require project team members to assign each risk to one of the defined ranges. Quantitative risk assessment assigns each risk a specific fraction between zero and one (or between zero and 100 percent).

Risk probabilities must all fall within this range, but picking a value between zero and one for a given risk poses difficulties. There are only three ways to estimate probabilities. For some situations, such as flipping coins and throwing dice, you can construct a *mathematical model* and calculate an expected probability. In other situations, a simple model does not exist, but there may be many historical events that are similar. In these cases statistical analysis of *empirical data* may be used to estimate probabilities. Analysis such as this is the foundation of the insurance industry. In all other cases, probability estimates are based on *guesses*. For complex events that seldom or perhaps never occur, you can neither calculate nor measure to determine a probability. Ideas such as referencing analogous situations, scenario analysis, and "gut feel" come into play. For most project risks, probabilities are not based on much objective data, so they are inexact.

We face yet an additional challenge because the human brain does not deal well with probabilities. In most cases there is a strong bias in favor of what we wish to happen. People tend to estimate desirable outcomes as more likely than is justified. ("This lottery ticket is sure to win.") Conversely, we estimate undesirable outcomes as less likely. ("That risk could never happen.") Effective risk management requires us to manage this bias, or at least to be wary of it.

Qualitative methods require less precision and do not use specific numerical values. They divide the complete range of possibilities into two or more nonoverlapping probability ranges. The simplest qualitative assessment uses two ranges: "more likely than not (.5 to 1)" and "less likely than not (0 to .4999)." Most project teams are able to select one of these choices for each risk with little difficulty, but the coarse granularity of the analysis makes selecting significant risks for further attention fairly arbitrary.

A more common method for qualitative assessment uses three ranges, assigning a value of high, medium, or low to each risk. The definitions for these categories vary, but these are typical:

- *High*: 50 percent or higher (likely)
- *Medium*: Between 10 and 50 percent (unlikely)
- *Low*: 10 percent or lower (very unlikely)

These three levels of probability are generally easy to determine for project risks without much debate, and the resulting characterization of risk allows you to discriminate adequately between likely and unlikely risks.

Other qualitative methods use four, five, or more categories. These methods tend to use linear ranges for the probabilities: quartiles for four, quintiles for five, and so forth. (The names assigned to five categories could be: Very high, High, Moderate, Low, and Very low.) The more ranges there are, the better the characterization of risk, at least in theory. More ranges do make it harder for the project team to achieve consensus, though.

The logical extension of this continues through increasingly quantitative assessments using integer percentages (100 categories) to continuous estimates allowing fractional percentages. Although the *apparent* precision improves, the process for determining numerical probabilities can require a lot of overhead, and you must remember that the probability estimates are often based on guesses. The illusion of precision can be a source of risk in itself; making subjective information look objective and precise can result in unwarranted confidence and poor decisions.

Depending on the project, the quality of data available, and the planned uses of the risk data, there are a number of ways to estimate probability. For qualitative assessment methods using five or fewer categories, experience, polling, interviewing, and rough analysis of the risk situation may be sufficient. For quantitative methods, a solid base of historical performance data is the best source, as it provides an empirical foundation for probability assessment and is less prone to bias. Estimating probabilities using methods such as the Delphi technique (mentioned in Chapter 4) or computer modeling (discussed later in this chapter) and employing knowledgeable experts (who may have access to more data than you do) can also potentially improve the quality of quantitative probabilities.

Measurement-based probabilities, when available, serve an additional purpose in project risk management: trend analysis. In hardware projects, statistics for component failure support decisions to retain or replace suppliers for future projects. If custom circuit boards, specialized integrated circuits, or other hardware components are routinely required on projects, quarter-by-quarter or year-by-year data across a number of projects will provide the fraction of components that are not accepted, and provide data on whether process changes are warranted to improve the yields and success rates. Managing risk over the long term relies heavily on metrics, which are discussed in Chapter 9.

Risk Impact

The loss, or project impact, for an individual risk is not as easily defined as the probability. Although the minimum is again zero, both the units and the maximum value are specific to the risk. The impact of a given risk may be relatively easy to ascertain and have a single, predictable value, or it may be best expressed as a distribution or histogram of possibilities. Qualitative risk assessment methods for impact again divide the choices into ranges. The project team assigns each risk to one of the ranges, based on the magnitude of the risk consequences. For quantitative risk assessment, impact may be estimated using units such as days of project slip, money, or some other suitable measure.

Qualitative impact assessment assigns each risk to one of two or more nonoverlapping options that include all the possible risk consequences. A two-option version uses categories such as "low severity" and "high severity," with suitable definitions of these terms related to attaining the project objective. As with probability analysis, the usefulness of only two categories is limited.

There will be better discrimination using three ranges, where each risk is assigned a value of high, medium, or low. The definitions for these categories vary, but commonly they relate to the project objective and plan as follows:

- High: Project objective is at risk (mandatory change to one or more of scope, schedule, or resources).
- Medium: Project objectives can be met, but significant replanning is required.
- Low: No major plan changes; the risk is an inconvenience or it will be handled through overtime or other minor adjustments.

These three levels of project impact are not difficult to assess for most risks and provide useful data for sequencing risks according to severity.

Other methods use additional categories, and some partition impact further into specific project factors, related to schedule, cost, and scope and other factors. Impact measurement is open-ended; there is no theoretical maximum for any of these parameters (in a literally impossible project, both time and cost may be considered infinite). Because the scale is not bounded, the categories used for impact are often geometric, with small ranges at the low end and progressively larger ranges for the upper categories. For an impact assessment using five categories, definitions might be:

1. *Very low*: Less than 1 percent impact on scope, schedule, cost, or quality
2. *Low*: Less than 5 percent impact on scope, schedule, cost, or quality
3. *Moderate*: Less than 10 percent impact on scope, schedule, cost, or quality
4. *High*: Less than 20 percent impact on scope, schedule, cost, or quality
5. *Very high*: 20 percent or more impact on scope, schedule, cost, or quality

Risks are assigned to one of these categories based on the most significant predicted variance, so a risk that represents a 10 percent schedule slip and negligible change to other project parameters would be categorized as "moderate." As with probability assessment, the more ranges there are, the better the characterization of risk, but the harder it is to achieve agreement among the project team.

Similar assessment may also be devised to look at specific kinds of risk separately, such as cost risk or schedule risk, to determine which are most likely to affect the highest project priorities.

The most precise assessment of impact requires quantitative estimates for each risk. Few risks relate only to a single aspect of the project, so there may be a collection of measurement estimates, generally including at least cost and schedule impact. Cost is conceptually the simplest, because it is unambiguously measured in dollars, yen, euros, or some other easily described unit, and any adverse variance will directly affect the project budget. Schedule impact is not as simple, because not every activity duration slippage will necessarily represent an impact to the schedule. Activities off the critical path will generate schedule impact only for adverse variances that exceed the available float. As with other project estimating, determining cost and schedule variances attributable to risks is neither easy nor necessarily accurate. Quantitative assessments of risk impact may look precise, but the accuracy of such estimates is often questionable.

The discussion of risk impact here so far has focused on measurable project information—even the qualitative categories tend to be based on numerical ranges. Limiting impact assessment to such factors overlooks risk impact that may be difficult to quantify. For some risks such an approach may ignore factors that may well be the most significant. Because the impact resulting from these other factors can be hard to determine with precision, it is generally ignored or assumed to be insignificant in project risk assessment. Categories for these more "qualitative" types of impact, listed in sequence from the most narrow perspective to the broadest, include:

- Personal consequences
- Career penalties
- Loss of team productivity
- Team discord
- Organizational impact
- Business and financial consequences

Measurable consequences for some of these factors may be roughly quantified, at least in the short term. Such analysis, however, may vastly underestimate true long-term overall effects. For other factors, it may seem impossible to incorporate these consequences in a way that permits straightforward assessment. Despite the challenges, it is worthwhile to list and carefully consider the potential consequences of these factors, because the true overall impact for many project risks may well be dominated by them. More detail follows, along with some suggestions about how to integrate these factors into your risk assessment. Although not exhaustive, the lists that follow should provide food for thought.

Many risks faced by projects include potential *personal consequences* that can be quite severe, ranging from inconveniences and aggravations to major impositions. These include:

- Marital problems, divorce, and personal relationship troubles
- Cancelled vacations
- Missed family activities
- Excessive unpaid overtime
- Fatigue and exhaustion
- Deterioration of health
- Exposure to unsafe conditions, poisonous or volatile chemicals, dangerous environments, or undesirable modes of travel
- Loss of face, embarrassment, lowered prestige, bruised egos, and reduced self-esteem
- Required apologies and "groveling"

Major project difficulties can lead to a variety of *career penalties*, and personal reputations may suffer, leading to:

- Job loss
- Lowered job security
- A bad performance appraisal
- Demotion
- No prospect for promotion

Both during and following a major risk, team members may work less efficiently. *Loss of team productivity* may result from:

- More meetings
- Burnout
- Increased communication overhead, especially if across multiple time zones

- Added stress, tension, pressure
- More errors, inaccuracies
- Chaos, confusion
- Rework
- Additional reporting, reviews, interruptions
- Individuals assuming responsibility for work assigned to others
- Exhaustion of project reserves, contingency

Even if productivity is unaffected, *team discord* may rise. The success of a project relies on maintaining good teamwork among your project contributors. When things start to unravel, the consequences can include:

- Conflict, hostility, resentment, and short tempers
- Lack of cooperation and strained relationships
- Low morale
- Frustration, disappointment, and discouragement
- Demoralization and disgruntlement

Project risk consequences may lead to *organizational impact* that extends well beyond your current project's prospects for success. Some of these include:

- Delayed concurrent projects
- Late starts for following projects
- Resignations and staff turnover
- Loss of sponsor (and stakeholder) confidence, trust, and goodwill
- Questioning of methods and processes
- Ruined team reputations
- Micromanagement and mistrust by supervisors
- Required escalations and expediting of work
- The need to get lawyers involved

Finally, some risks will have significant *business and financial consequences*. Although these effects may well be estimated and quantified, the true impact is generally measurable only after—and often well after—the project is closed. Some examples are:

- Loss of business to competitors and competitive disadvantage
- Bad press, poor public relations, and loss of organizational reputation
- Customer dissatisfaction and unhappy clients
- Loss of future business and lowered revenues
- Reduced margins and profits
- Loss of client trust, confidence
- Complications resulting from failure to meet legal, regulatory, industry standards, or other compliance requirements
- Damaged partner relationships
- Reduced performance of the project deliverable
- Compromised quality or reliability
- Rushed, inadequate testing
- Missed windows of opportunity
- Continued cost of obsolete systems or facilities
- Inefficient, unpleasant manual workarounds
- Service outages and missed service level agreements
- Bankruptcy and business failure (if the project is big enough)

Although for some risks the short-term quantifiable impact on your project's schedule or budget may be modest, the overall consequences, particularly some of the items on the last two lists, will have major impact on the organization. Even though these potential impacts may be primarily qualitative, it is desirable to integrate them into your risk assessment and prioritization. One way to do this is to apply impact criteria such as in the five-level assessment demonstrated in the following table.

Risk Impact	Criteria
Very Low	Any impact that can be handled within a single status cycle and would likely not be visible outside the project team
Low	Any impact that can be dealt with within the project team and would have no anticipated long-term effects
Moderate	Any impact that would result in significant project replanning or that could lead to a noticeable and inconvenient effect for the organization
High	Any impact that would threaten the project's objective (failure to meet one or more of the project's triple constraint parameters) or that might lead to significant, measurable longer-term business impact for the organization
Very High	A project "showstopper" that would result in cancellation, or a risk that has potential for overall long-term business impact in excess of the project's budget

Analysis based on these criteria remains subjective, but it provides a practical way to assess the relative importance of project risks—even risks where measurable impact is difficult to pin down.

Qualitative impact assessment using three to five categories is usually relatively easy, and it is sufficient for prioritizing risks based on severity. Techniques such as polling, interviewing, team discussion, and reviews of planning data are effective for assigning risks to impact categories. As with probability assessment for each risk, the best foundation for quantitative estimates of impact is history, along with techniques such as Delphi, computer modeling, and consulting peers and experts.

For quantitative assessments of impact in situations that frequently repeat, statistics may be available. A good way to provide credible quantitative impact data is to select the mean of the distribution for initial estimates of duration or cost and use the difference between that estimate and the measured "90 percent" point. This principle is the basis for Program Evaluation and Review Technique (PERT) analysis. The PERT estimating technique was discussed in Chapter 4, and other aspects of PERT and related techniques are covered later in this chapter and in Chapter 9.

Qualitative Risk Assessment

The minimum requirement for risk assessment is a sequenced list of risks, rank-ordered by perceived severity. You can sort the listed risks from most to least significant using your assessment of loss times likelihood. If your list of risks is short enough, you can quickly arrange the list based on few passes of pair-wise comparisons, switching any adjacent risks where the more severe of the two is lower on the list. The most serious risks will bubble to the top and the more trivial ones will sink to the bottom. This technique is generally done by a single individual.

A similar technique, related to Delphi, combines data from lists sorted individually by each member of a team. The risks on each list are assigned a score equal to their position on the list, and all the scores for each risk are summed. The risk with the lowest total score heads the composite list, and the rest of the list is sorted based on the aggregate scores. If there are significant variances in some of the lists, further discussion and an additional iteration may lead to better consensus. The resulting list will be more objective than a sequence created by an individual, and it represents the whole team.

Although these sorting techniques result in an ordered risk list, such a list shows only *relative* risk severity, without indication of the project exposure that each risk represents.

Risk Assessment Tables

Qualitative risk assessment based on categorization of both probability and impact provides greater insight into the *absolute* risk severity. A risk assessment table or spreadsheet where risks are listed with category assignments for both probability and impact, as in Figure 7-1, is one approach for this.

After listing each risk, assign a qualitative rating (such as High/Moderate/Low) for both probability and impact. Consider all potential impact, not just that which is easily measured, and be skeptical about probabilities. Fill in the last column, "Overall Risk," based on "loss times likelihood." Although any number of rating categories may be used, the quickest method that results in a meaningful sort uses three categories (defined as in the earlier discussions of probability and impact) and assigns either combinations of the categories or weights such as 1, 3, and 9 for low, moderate, and high, respectively. An example of a sorted qualitative assessment for five risks might look like Figure 7-2.

For the data in the last column, categories may be combined (as shown), factors multiplied (the numbers would be 27, 9, 9, 3, and 1), or "stoplight" icons displayed to indicate risk (red for high, yellow for moderate, and green for low). From a table such as Figure 7-2, you can select risks above a certain level, such as moderate, for further attention.

Figure 7-1. Risk assessment table.

Risks	Probability	Impact	Overall Risk

Figure 7-2. Qualitative risk assessment example.

Risks	Probability (H/M/L)	Impact (H/M/L)	Overall Risk
Software Guru Is Not Available	M	H	HM
Consultant Is Incompetent	M	M	M
Purchased Component Comes Late	L	H	M
Software Development Is Too Slow	L	M	ML
Needed Test Gear Is Not Available	L	L	L

Risk Assessment Matrices

An alternative method for qualitative risk assessment involves placing risks on a two-dimensional matrix, where the rows and columns represent the categories of probability and impact. The matrices may be two-by-two, three-by-three, or larger. Risk matrices are generally square, but they may have different numbers of categories for probability and impact. Figure 7-3 is an example of a five-by-five matrix.

The farther up and to the right a risk is assessed to be, the higher its overall assessment. Risks are selected for management based on whether the cell in the matrix represents a risk above some predetermined level of severity. An organization's risk tolerance (or appetite) is generally bounded by one of the sets of lighter gray cells in the matrix.

A matrix such as Figure 7-3 is usually applied to the analysis of risks having negative consequences (threats). It may also be used to assess *uncertain* project opportunities. Some of the opportunities discussed in Chapter 6 relate to scoping choices and planning decisions, where the only uncertainty is whether an opportunity is adopted as part of the project or not. Other opportunities, like most risks, hinge on circumstances that might or might not happen. For these opportunities assessment is based on likelihood and (instead of loss) gain. An example of this type of opportunity might be buying something needed by the project that occasionally goes on sale. Once the opportunity to purchase the item at a reduced price is recognized, managing this "risk" might involve delaying the purchase to potentially take advantage of a better price. For most projects, there are far fewer opportunities of this sort than there are risks.

Figure 7-3. Risk assessment matrix.

Probability

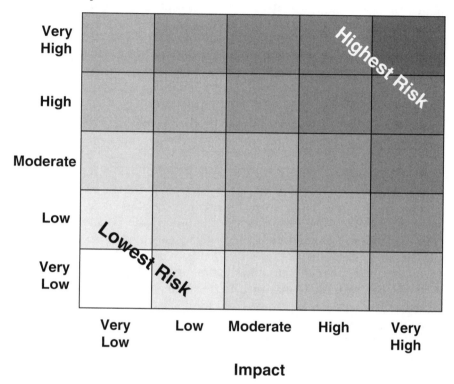

Impact

For analysis of uncertain opportunities, the definition of probability is unchanged. The impact is also similar, but for opportunities the categories relate to beneficial variances, not harmful ones. Using the same matrix, you can assess potentially positive events to determine those that deserve further attention—again by focusing near the corner representing the combination of highest impact and probability. Another variant on this matrix technique joins together the threat matrix and a mirror-image opportunity matrix into a single matrix (for this case, five cells high and ten cells wide). You find the highest impact in the middle using the combined matrix, so the uncertain events most deserving your attention will be those in the cells near the top and center of the matrix.

Assessing Options

Standard project network charts do not generally permit the use of conditional branching. Because it is not uncommon to have places in a project schedule where one of several possible alternatives, outcomes, or decisions will be chosen, you need some method for analyzing the situation. One qualitative way around this limitation is to construct a baseline plan using the assumption that seems most likely and deal with the other possible outcomes as risks. If it is not possible to determine which outcome may be most likely, a prudent risk manager will usually select the one with the longest duration (or highest cost) to include in the project baseline, but any one option may be selected. Assessing the risk associated with choosing incorrectly involves determining the estimated impact on the project if a different option is picked, weighted by the probability of this happening (loss times likelihood once again). List the significant ones on your risk register and sort them with your other project risks.

Data Quality Assessment

Not all risks are equally well understood. Some risks happen regularly, and data concerning them is plentiful. Other project risks arise from work that is unique compared with past projects. Assessment of probability and impact for these risks tends to be based on inadequate information, so it's common to underestimate overall risk.

Even with qualitative risk assessment, these poorly understood risks can be identified and singled out for special treatment. For each assessment, consider the quality, reliability, and integrity of the data used to categorize probability and impact. Where the information seems weak, seek out experts or other sources of better information. You can also err on the side of caution and bump up your probability and impact estimates to elevate the visibility of the risk.

Other Factors

Although a risk that has high probability and impact will require your attention, those that relate to work well into the future may not need it immediately. Other aspects of risk that may enter into qualitative assessment are urgency and surprise. The impact of even a modest risk can cause harm to your project overall if it happens early and affects the perception of your competence or the teamwork of your contributors. Risks tend to cascade, so early problems may lead to more trouble later in the project. If a risk relates to work that is imminent, factor this into your impact assessment, increasing it where justified.

Similarly, some risks are relatively easy to see coming. Other risks, such as the damaging example from the PERIL database of receiving a late deliverable from an outsourcing partner, are hard to detect in advance. Consider the trigger events for each risk when estimating impact, and increase it for risks where the harm may be amplified by the surprise factor.

Risks Requiring Further Attention

The main objective of qualitative risk assessment is to identify the major risks by prioritizing the known project risks and rank-ordering them from most significant to least. The sequenced list may be assembled using any of the methods described, but the use of three categories (low, moderate, and high) for both probability and impact generally provides a good balance of adequate analysis and minimal effort and debate. However you analyze and sort the list, you need to partition the risks that deserve further consideration from risks that seem too minor to warrant a planned response.

The first several risks on your prioritized list nearly always require attention, but the question of how far down the list to go is not necessarily simple. One idea is to read down the list, focusing on the consequences and the likelihood of each risk until you reach the first one that won't keep you awake at night. The "gut feel" test is not a bad way to select the boundary for a sorted risk list. A similar idea using consensus has team members individually select the cut-off point, and then discuss as a team where the line should be, based on individual and group experiences. You can also set an absolute limit, such as moderate overall risk, or you can use a diagonal stair-step boundary from the upper left to the lower right in a matrix. Whatever method you choose, review each of the risks that are *not* selected to ensure that there are none below the line that warrant a response.

Following this examination, you are ready to prepare an abridged list of risks for potential further quantitative analysis and management.

Quantitative Risk Assessment

As stated earlier in the chapter, quantitative risk assessment involves more effort than qualitative techniques, so qualitative methods are generally used for initial risk sorting and selection. This is not absolutely necessary, though, because each of the qualitative methods discussed has a quantitative analogue that could be used to sequence the risk list. Qualitative tables have their categories for probability and impact replaced by absolute numerical estimates. The cells in risk matrices are transformed into continuous two-dimensional graphs for plotting the estimates. Quantitative techniques such as sensitivity analysis, more rigorous statistical methods, decision trees, and simulations can provide further insight into project risk, and may also be used for overall project risk assessment.

Sensitivity Analysis

Not all risks are equally damaging. Schedule impact not affecting resources is significant only when the estimated slippage exceeds any available float. For simple projects, a quick inspection of the plan using the risk list will distinguish the risks that are likely to cause the most damage. For more complex networks of activities, using a copy of the project database that has been entered into a scheduling tool is a fast way to detect risks (and combinations of risks) that are most likely to result in project delay. Schedule "what if" analysis uses worst-case estimates to investigate the overall project impact for each risk. By sequentially entering your scheduling data and then backing it out, you can determine the quantitative schedule sensitivity for each schedule risk.

Unlike activity slippage, all adverse cost variances contribute to budget overruns. However, for some projects not all cost impact is accounted for in the same way. If a risk results in an out-of-pocket expense for the project, then it impacts the budget directly. If the cost impact involves a capital purchase, then the project impact may be only a portion of the actual cost, and in some cases the entire expense may be accounted for elsewhere. An increase in overhead cost, such as a conference room commandeered as a "war room" for a troubled project, is seldom charged back to the project directly. Increased costs for communications, duplication, shipping, and other services considered routine are frequently not borne directly by technical projects. Travel costs in some cases may also not be allocated directly. Although it is generally true that all cost and other resource impact is proportionate to the magnitude of the variance, it may be worthwhile to segregate potential direct cost variances from any that are indirect.

Quantitative Risk Assessment Tables

For quantitative assessment, the same sort of table or spreadsheet discussed previously can be filled in with numerical probabilities instead of the categories used for qualitative assessment. For each risk, estimate the impact in cost, effort, time (but only time in excess of any available scheduling flexibility), or other factors, and then assess overall risk as the product of the impact estimates and the selected probability. One drawback of using this method for sequencing risks is that for some risks it may be difficult to develop precise consensus for both the impact and probability. A second, more serious issue is that impact may be measured in more than one way (as examples, time and money), making it difficult to ascertain a single uniform quantitative assessment of overall risk.

Although you could certainly list impacts of various kinds, weighted using the estimated probabilities, you may find that sorting based on this data is not straightforward. This can be overcome by selecting one type of impact, such as time, and converting impact of other kinds into an equivalent project duration slip (as was done in the PERIL database). You could also develop several tables, one for cost, another for schedule, and others for scope, quality, safety, or any other type of impact for which you can develop meaningful numerical estimates. You can then sort each table on a consistent basis, and select risks from each for further attention. This multiple-table process also requires you to do a final check to detect any risks that are significant only when all factors are considered together.

Two-Dimensional Quantitative Analysis

The qualitative matrix converts to a quantitative tool by replacing the rows and columns with perpendicular axes. Probability may be plotted on the horizontal axis from zero to 100 percent, and impact may be plotted on the vertical axis. Each risk identified represents a point in the two-dimensional space, and risks requiring further attention will be found again in the upper right, beyond a boundary defined as "risky." As with tables, this method is most useful when all risks can be normalized to some meaningful single measure of impact such as cost or time.

A variation on this concept plots risks on a pair of axes that represent estimated project cost and project schedule variances, representing each risk using a "bubble" that is sized proportionately with estimated probability instead of a single point. Because impact is higher for bubbles farther from the origin, several boundaries are defined for the graph. A diagonal close to the origin defines significant risk for the large (very likely) bubbles, and other diagonals farther out define significant exposure for the smaller bubbles. In Figure 7-4, there are several risks that are clearly significant. Risk F has the highest impact, and Risk E is, well, risky. Others would be selected based on their positions relative to the boundaries of the graph.

PERT

PERT methodology, discussed earlier, has assumed a number of meanings. The most common, which actually has little to do with PERT methodology, is associated with the graphical network of activities used

Figure 7-4. Risk assessment graph.

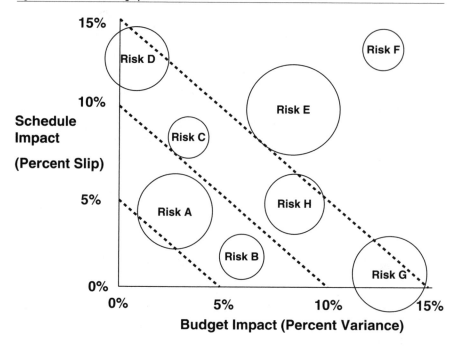

for project planning, often referred to as a PERT chart. Logical project networks are used for PERT analysis, but PERT methodology went beyond the deterministic, single-point estimates of duration to which "PERT charts" are generally limited. A second, slightly less common meaning for PERT relates to three-point estimating, which was discussed with identifying schedule risk in Chapter 4. The original purpose of PERT was actually much broader.

The principal reason PERT was originally developed in the late 1950s was to help the U.S. military quantitatively manage risk for large defense projects. PERT was used on the development of the Polaris missile systems, on the NASA manned space projects, including the Apollo moon missions, and on countless other government projects. The motivation behind all of this was the observation that as programs became larger, they were more likely to be late and to have significant cost overruns. PERT was created to provide a better basis for setting expectations on these massive, expensive endeavors.

PERT is a specific example of quantitative risk analysis, and it is applied to both schedule (PERT Time) and budget (PERT Cost) exposures. PERT is based on some statistical assumptions about the project plan, requiring both estimates of likely outcomes and estimates of the *uncertainty* for these outcomes. PERT techniques may be used to analyze all project activities or only those activities that represent high perceived risk. In either case, the purpose of PERT was to provide data on *overall* project risk. This application of PERT methodology is covered in Chapter 9.

PERT Time was mentioned in Chapter 4, using three estimates for each activity—an optimistic estimate, a most likely estimate, and a pessimistic estimate—to calculate an "expected estimate." PERT Cost also uses three estimates to derive an expected activity cost, using essentially the same formula:

$$c_e = (c_o + 4c_m + c_p)/6, \text{ where}$$
$$c_e \text{ is the "expected" cost}$$
$$c_o \text{ is the "optimistic" (lowest realistic) cost}$$
$$c_m \text{ is the "most likely" cost}$$
$$c_p \text{ is the "pessimistic" (highest realistic) cost}$$

As with PERT Time, the standard deviation is estimated to be $(c_p - c_o)/6$. A distribution showing this graphically is in Figure 7-5.

PERT Cost estimates are generally done in monetary units (pesos, rupees, euros), but they may also be evaluated in effort (person-hours, engineer-days) instead of, or in addition to, the financial estimates.

Whether for time or cost, PERT ideas are useful in gathering risk information about project activities, particularly concerning the pessimistic (or worst-case) estimates as discussed in Chapter 4. PERT also provided the basis for simulation-based project analysis techniques that

Figure 7-5. Cost estimates for PERT analysis.

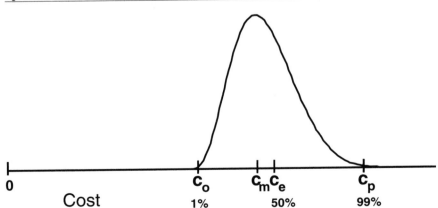

are better able to account for schedule fan-in risks and correlation factors. Project simulations are referenced later in this chapter and explored in more detail in Chapter 9.

Statistical Concepts and Probability Distributions

Risk impact discussed so far has been based primarily on single-point, deterministic estimates. PERT, as originally defined, assumed a continuum of possibilities. PERT used three-point estimates to define a Beta distribution, a bell-shaped probability density function that can skew to the right or left. Figure 7-5 is an example of a Beta distribution fitted to three estimates for activity cost. This example uses the traditional "1 percent tails" to bound the range of possibilities, but other variants are based on 5 or 10 percent tails.

Probability distribution functions, or even discrete data values defined by a histogram, may better describe the range of potential impact for a given risk. Some additional distributions that are used include:

- Triangular (a linear rise from optimistic estimate to the most likely, followed by a linear decline to the pessimistic estimate)
- Normal (the Gaussian bell-shaped curve, with the most likely and expected values half-way between the extremes)
- Uniform (all values in the range are assumed equally likely, also with the most likely and expected values both at the midpoint)

There are many other more exotic distributions available, along with limitless histograms that are possible. The precise *shape* of the distribution turns out to be relatively unimportant, though, because it has only a small effect on the two parameters that matter the most for risk analysis: the mean and the standard deviation of the distribution. Assessment of risk really only requires these two parameters, and they vary little, regardless of the distribution you chose. In addition, although it is theoretically possible to carry out a detailed risk analysis mathematically, it is impractical. Project risk analysis using probability distributions is most commonly done by computer simulation or by rough manual methods to approximate the results. The choice of a precise distribution for each activity has minimal effect on quantitative assessment of risk for most projects.

For those who may be interested, some examples follow that show why the choice of a probability density function for the estimates is not terribly crucial. (If you do not need convincing of this, just note that any approach that you find easy to work with can produce useful quantitative risk data, and skip ahead to the discussion of range estimating.)

The original PERT formulation assumed that the three estimates defined a continuum shaped as a Beta distribution. The precise shape of the distribution defined by the three estimates does not have much effect on the resulting analysis. Even using only two estimates "most likely" and "worst-case," as discussed in Chapter 4, provides useful risk information. These examples all use estimates of 15 and 21 days as limits for the duration estimate ranges.

For Figure 7-6, the optimistic estimate has been assumed identical to the most likely. When values are plugged into the formula to calculate the expected duration, the PERT formula results in a t_e of 16 days.

A similar result, mathematically much simpler, can be estimated using a triangular distribution, as in Figure 7-7.

For a triangular distribution, the point at which the areas to the right and left are equal occurs slightly less than 30 percent of the way along the triangle's base. Using the same estimates as before for t_o, t_m, and t_p, the estimate for t_e is just under 16.8 days.

Symmetric distributions increase the expected estimate a bit more. Using a normal distribution (Figure 7-8) or a simple uniform distribution (Figure 7-9) for the probability distribution that lies between the range limits results in an expected value for this example of 18 days. (A symmetric triangular distribution would be equivalent to these.)

The weighted-average PERT formula for the Beta distribution in Figure 7-5 estimates t_e at 16 days, and all the other examples evaluate it to be a bit higher. For a quantitative risk assessment, some value above the mean will be selected to represent impact (a 90 percent point is common). Although these points are also not identical for the various distributions,

Figure 7-6. Two-estimate Beta distribution.

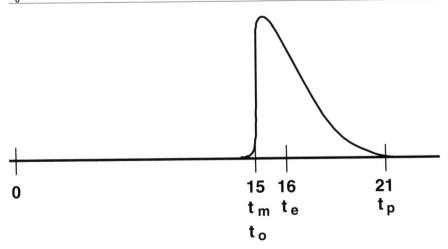

Figure 7-7. Triangular distribution.

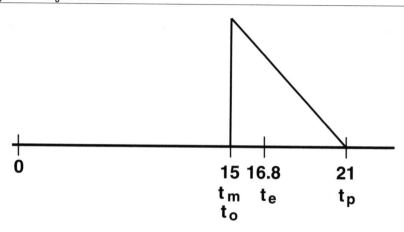

they all are quite close together, near the upper (t_p) estimate. Risk assessment is related to the *variance* for the chosen distribution, which for these examples will all be similar because in each case, the ranges are the same.

If t_p is 21 days, the 90 percent point for each of these distributions is about 20 days (rounded off to the nearest whole day), regardless of the distribution selected. There are many tools and techniques capable of calculating all of this with very high precision, displaying many (seemingly) significant digits in the results. Considering the precision and expected accuracy of the input data, though, the results are at best accurate only to the nearest whole day. Arguments over the "best" distribution to use and

Figure 7-8. Normal distribution.

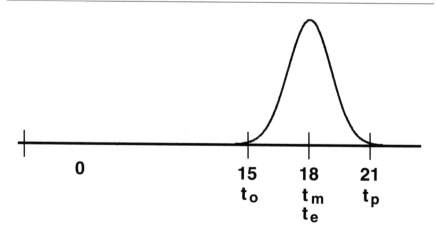

Figure 7-9. Uniform distribution.

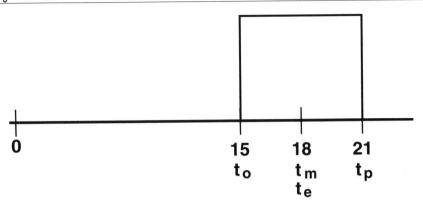

endless fretting over how to proceed are not a good investment of your time. Almost any reasonable choice of distribution will result in comparable and useful results for risk analysis, so use the choice that is easiest for you to implement.

At the project level, where PERT data for all the activities is combined, the distributions chosen for each activity become even more irrelevant. The larger the project, the more the overall analysis for project cost and duration tends to approximate a normal bell-shaped curve (more on this in Chapter 9).

Setting Estimate Ranges

What *does* matter a great deal for risk assessment is the range specified for the estimates. Setting the range to be too narrow (which is a common bias) will materially diminish the quantitative perception of risk. Risk, assessed using PERT or similar techniques, is based on the total expected variation in possible outcomes, which varies directly with the size of the estimate range.

Arriving at credible upper and lower limits for cost and duration estimates is difficult. One way to develop this data is through further analysis of potential root causes of each activity that has substantial perceived risk. As discussed in Chapter 4, seeking worst-case scenarios is the most powerful tool for estimating the upper limits. Be realistic about potential consequences; it's easy to minimize or overlook the potential impact of risks.

When there is sufficient historical information available, the limits (and possibly even the shape) of the distribution may be inferred from the data. Discussions and interviews with experts, project stakeholders, and contributors may also provide information useful in setting credible range boundaries.

In any event, quantitative assessment of risk impact depends on credible three-point (or at least expected and worst-case) project estimates. Project-level risk assessment using PERT methodology and related techniques will be explored in detail in Chapter 9.

Decision Trees

When only a small number of options or potential outcomes are possible, decision trees may also be useful for quantitative risk assessment. Decision tree analysis is a quantitative version of the process for assessing options discussed earlier in this chapter with qualitative assessment techniques. Decision trees are generally used to evaluate alternatives prior to selecting one of them to execute. The concept is applied to risk analysis in a project by using the weights and estimates to ascertain potential impact for specific alternatives.

Whenever there are points in the project where several options are possible, each can be planned and assigned a probability (the sum for all options totaling 100 percent). As with PERT, an "expected" estimate for either duration or cost may be derived by weighting the estimates for each option and summing these figures to get a "blended" result. Based on the data in Figure 7-10, a project plan containing a generic activity (that could be any of the three options) with an estimate of 16 days would result in a more realistic plan than simply using the 12-day estimate of the

Figure 7-10. Decision tree for duration.

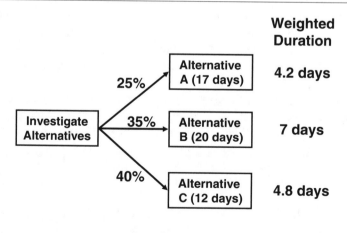

Weighted Duration

25% → Alternative A (17 days)　4.2 days

Investigate Alternatives ← 35% → Alternative B (20 days)　7 days

40% → Alternative C (12 days)　4.8 days

"Expected" Duration = 16 days

"most likely" option. The schedule exposure of the risk situation here may be estimated by noting the maximum adverse variance (an additional four days, if the activity is schedule critical) and associating this with an expected probability of 35 percent. (Another option for this case would be to assume the worst and schedule 20 days, treating the other possibilities as opportunities to be managed.)

Decision analysis may also be used to guide project choices that are based on costs. You can use decision trees to evaluate expected monetary value for various options. The analysis can explore alternatives that have the lowest expected cost and those with the lowest expected cost variance. Decision analysis can help in minimizing project risks whenever there are several alternatives, such as upgrading existing equipment versus purchasing new hardware. The analysis of costs in Figure 7-11 argues for replacement to minimize cost variance (none, instead of the $20,000 to $120,000 associated with upgrade), and for upgrade to minimize the *expected* cost. As is usual on projects, there is a trade-off between minimizing project parameters and minimizing risk—you must decide which is more important and balance the decisions with your eyes open.

Simulation and Modeling

Decision trees are useful for situations where you have discrete estimates. In more complex cases, options may be modeled or simulated using Monte Carlo or other computer techniques. If the range of possibilities for an activity's duration or cost are assumed to be a statistical distribution, the standard deviation (or variance) of the distribution is

Figure 7-11. Decision tree for cost.

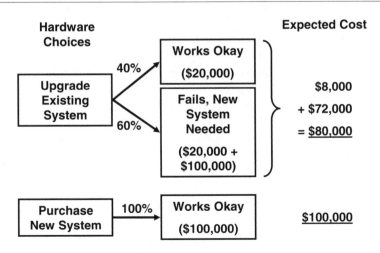

a measure of risk. The larger the range selected for the distribution, the higher the risk for that activity. For single activities, modeling with a computer is rarely necessary, but when several activities are considered together (or the project as a whole), computer-based simulations are useful and effective. Use of both software tools and manual approximations for this are key topics in Chapter 9.

Key Ideas for Activity Risk Analysis

- Assess probability and impact for each project risk.
- Use qualitative risk analysis to prioritize risks.
- Apply quantitative risk analysis techniques to significant risks.
- If you use PERT or related techniques, keep things simple.

Panama Canal: Risks (1906–1914)

As with any project of the canal's size and duration, risks were everywhere. Based on assessment of cost and probability, the most severe were diseases, mud slides, the constant use of explosives, and the technical challenges of constructing the locks.

Diseases were less of a problem on the U.S. project, but health remained a concern. Both of the first two managers cited tropical disease among their reasons for resigning from the project. Life in the tropics in the early 1900s was neither comfortable nor safe. The enormous death toll from the earlier project made this exposure a top priority.

Mud slides were common for both the French and the U.S. projects, as the soil of Panama is not stable, and earthquakes made things worse. Whenever the sloping sides of the cut collapsed, there was danger to the working crews and potential serious damage to the digging and railroad equipment. In addition to this, it was demoralizing to face the repair and rework following the each slide, and the predicted additional effort required to excavate repeatedly in the same location multiplied the cost of construction. This risk affected both schedule and budget; despite precautions, major setbacks were frequent.

Explosives were in use everywhere. In the Culebra Cut, massive boulders were common, and workers set off dynamite charges to reduce them to movable pieces. The planned transit for ships through the man-made lakes was a rain forest filled with large, old trees, and these, too, had to be removed with explosives. In the tropics especially, the dynamite of that era was not stable. It exploded in storage, in transit to the work sites, while being set in place for use, and in many other unintended situations.

The probability of premature detonation was high, and the risk to human life was extreme.

Beyond these daunting risks, the largest technical challenge on the project was the locks. They were gigantic mechanisms, among the largest and most complex construction ever attempted. Although locks had been used on canals for a long time, virtually all of them had been built for smaller boats navigating freshwater rivers and lakes. Locks had never before been constructed for large ocean-going ships. (The canal at Suez has no locks; as with the original plan for Panama, it is entirely at sea level.) The doors for the locks were to be huge, and therefore heavy. The volume of water held by the locks when filled was so great that the pressure on the doors would be immense, and the precision required for the seams where the doors closed to hold in the water was also unprecedented for manmade objects so large. The locks would be enormous boxes with sides and bottoms formed of concrete, which also was a challenge, particularly in an earthquake zone. For all this, the biggest technological hurdle was the requirement that all operations be *electric*. Because earlier canals were much smaller, usually the lock doors were cranked open and shut and the boats were pulled in and out by animals. (To this day, the trains used to guide ships into and out of the locks at Panama are called "electric mules.") The design, implementation, and control of a canal using the new technology of electric power—and the hydroelectric installations required to supply enough electricity—all involved emerging, poorly understood technology. Without the locks, the canal would be useless, and the risks associated with resolving all of these technical problems were large.

These severe risks were but a few of the many challenges faced on the canal project, but each was singled out for substantial continuing attention. In Chapter 8 on tactics for dealing with risk, we will explore what was done to manage these challenges.

8

Managing
Activity Risks

"Statistics are no substitute for judgment."
—HENRY CLAY, U.S. SENATOR

Risk assessment provides a prioritized risk register. When you use this list, it becomes clear just how much trouble your project is in. An accumulation of significant scope risks may indicate that your project is literally impossible. Too many schedule or resource risks may indicate that your project is unlikely to complete within its constraints. Project risk management can be a potent tool for transforming a seemingly doomed project into a merely challenging one.

Managing risk begins with your prioritized risks register. Based on your sorted list, you can set the boundary between the most significant and least significant risks. Risk response planning uses this boundary as a guide; all the risks above the cut-line will deserve at least some attention. In addition, though, a prudent project leader reviews the whole list, at least briefly. The most important reason for this is to reconsider all risks that have significant consequences. When the potential impact for a risk exceeds acceptable limits, a response may be in order even if the probability is estimated to be low. There may also be low-rated risks for which there are simple, cheap responses. It makes little sense to ignore risks for which there are trivial cures.

For each risk you deem significant, you can then seek root causes to determine your best management strategy. For risks where the project team has influence over the root cause, you can develop and analyze ideas to reduce or eliminate the risk, and then modify the project plans to incorporate these ideas wherever it is feasible. For risks that cannot be avoided or that remain significant, you can also develop contingency plans for recovery should the risk occur.

Root-Cause Analysis

What, if anything, can be done about a risk depends a great deal on its causes. For each identified risk that is assessed as significant, you must determine the source and type of risk that it represents.

The process for cause-and-effect analysis is not a difficult one. For risk analysis, it begins with the listed risks and their descriptions. The next step is to brainstorm possible sources for the risk. Any brainstorming process will be effective as long as it is successful in determining conditions or events that may lead to the risk. You can begin with major cause categories (such as scope, schedule, and resource) or simply think about specific factors that may lead to the risk. However you begin the analysis, complete it by organizing the information into categories of root cause. Some redundancy between items listed in the categories is common.

Cause-and-effect analysis using fishbone diagrams, so called because of their appearance, was popularized by the Japanese quality movement guru Dr. Kaoru Ishikawa. (They are also sometimes called Ishikawa diagrams.) These diagrams may be used to display root causes of risk visually, allowing deeper understanding of the source and likelihood of potential problems. Organize the possible causes into a branching diagram similar to the one in Figure 8-1. Note that some causes may themselves have multiple potential sources. Continue the root-cause analysis process for each significant risk in the project.

Categories of Risk

In dealing with risk, there are really only two options. In an advertisement some years ago, the options were demonstrated pictorially using an egg. On the left side of the picture was an egg falling toward a pillow held in a person's hand. On the right side was a broken egg oozing over the flat, hard surface it had smashed into, with a second hand swooping in holding a paper towel. The left side was titled "Prevention" and the right side "Recovery." Management of risk in projects always involves these tactics—prevention to deal with causes, and recovery to deal with effects.

The three categories of project risk are *controllable known* risks, *uncontrollable known* risks, and *unknown* risks. All the significant listed

Figure 8-1. Fishbone diagram example.

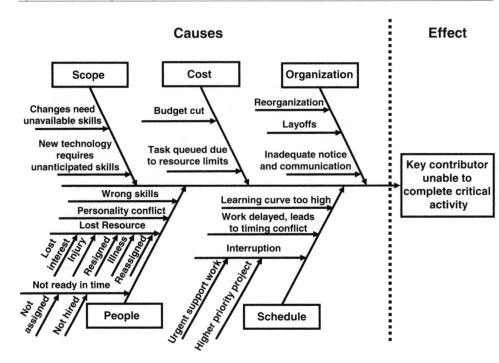

project risks are known risks and are either under your control or not. For listed risks it is possible to plan for response, at least in theory. The third category, unknown risks, is hidden, so specific planning is not generally possible. The best method for managing unknown risk involves setting project reserves, in schedule or budget (or both), based on the measured consequences of unanticipated problems on similar past projects. Keeping track of specific past problems also converts your past unknown risks into known risks. Managing unknown project risk is addressed in Chapter 10.

Root-cause analysis not only makes known project risks more understandable, it also shows you how to manage each risk. Based on the root cause or causes, you can determine whether the risk arises from factors you can control, and may therefore be preventable, or whether it is because of uncontrollable causes. When the causes are out of your control, risk can only be managed through recovery. These strategies are summarized in Figure 8-2.

Known controllable risks are at least partially under the control of the project team. Risks such as the use of a new technology, small increases in complexity or performance of a deliverable, or pressure to

Figure 8-2. Risk management strategies.

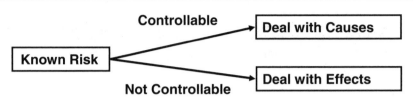

establish aggressive deadlines are examples of this. Working from an understanding of the root causes for these problems, you may be able to modify project plans to avoid or minimize the risk.

For known uncontrollable risks, the project team has essentially no influence on the source of the risk. Loss of key project staff members, business reorganizations, and external project factors such as weather are examples. For these problems, the best tactic is to deal with effects after the risk occurs, recovering with a contingency plan you prepared in advance.

It is common for a root-cause analysis to uncover some causes that you can control as well as some that you cannot for the same risk. Responding to risks with several possible sources may require both replanning and preparation for recovery.

Although the dichotomy between *controllable* and *uncontrollable* may seem simple, it often is not. The perceived root causes of a risk vary depending on the description of the risk. To take the example of the fishbone diagram in Figure 8-1, many of the root causes seem out of the control of the project team, as the risk is described as the loss of a particular person. If the exposure were redefined to be the loss of a particular skill set, which is probably more accurate, then the root causes would shift to ones that the project might influence through cross-training, negotiating for additional staff, or other actions.

Even when a risk seems to be uncontrollable, the venerable idea from quality analysis of "Ask why five times" may open up the perspective on the risk and reveal additional options for response. If weather, earthquakes, or other natural disasters are listed as risks to particular activities, probe deeper into the situation to ask why and how that particular problem would affect the project. The risk may be a consequence of a project assumption or a choice made in planning that could be changed, resulting in a better, less problematic project. Shifting the time, venue, infrastructure, or other parameters of risky activities may remove uncontrollable risks from your project, or at least diminish their potential for harm.

Risk Response Planning

Two basic options are available for risk management: dealing with *causes* and dealing with *effects*. There are, however, variations on both of these themes.

Dealing with the causes of project threats involves risk prevention—eliminating the risk (*avoidance*), lowering its probability or potential impact (*mitigation*), or making it someone else's problem (*transfer*). Avoidance of risks requires changing the project plan or approach to remove the root cause of the risk from your project. One way to avoid falling off a cliff is to avoid cliffs. Mitigating actions do not remove a risk completely, but they do serve to reduce it. Some mitigating actions reduce the probability of a risk event, such as inspecting your automobile tires before a long trip. Other mitigations reduce the risk consequences, such as wearing a seat belt to minimize injury. Neither of these actions prevents the problem, but they do serve to reduce the overall risk by lowering the "loss" or the "likelihood."

Similarly, some damaging risks may be transferred to others. Many kinds of financial risks may be transferred to insurance companies; you can purchase coverage that will compensate your losses in the event of a casualty that is covered by the policy. Again, this does not remove the risk, but it does reduce the financial impact should the risk occur. Transfer of risk can deal with causes if the impact of the risk is primarily financial, but in other cases it may be used to deal with risk effects—aiding in the recovery.

Throughout most of this chapter the term "risk" will be used to describe an uncertain event that could harm the project—a threat. Not all uncertain project events are threats, however. There may also be uncertain opportunities where risk management strives to *increase* the probability or impact. Benefiting from these project opportunities involves embracing these "positive risk" situations. Similar tactics are applied to these uncertain opportunities, analogous (though reversed) to those just outlined for prevention of threats. Where you might avoid threats by replanning to remove the potential for harm, you would replan the project to *exploit* or to capture the opportunity. You work to make it a certain part of the project. In the case mentioned in Chapter 7 of an item that might go on sale, you might investigate the planned timing for the sale and schedule the project around it. Mitigation serves to reduce the probability or impact of a threat, and the corresponding tactic is to *enhance* the plan to pursue opportunity, making the potential benefits more likely or more helpful. In the case of the sale, you might be unable to determine when (or even if) it might occur, but you could schedule the project around the dates for a sale from last year on the theory that that is when such a sale would be most likely. As with threats, sometimes the strategy involves strength in numbers. Where threats may be transferred to limit their impact, opportunities may be improved when *shared*. Cost reductions for purchased items comparable to a sale might be available if you can find others with similar needs and make purchases together to take advantage of favorable quantity pricing.

Dealing with the effect of a threat may either be done in advance (contingency planning) or after the fact (acceptance). (Uncertain opportunities generally need no particular contingency planning; those not managed are ignored, or accepted.) Some risks are too minor or too expensive to consider preventing. For minor risks, acceptance may be appropriate; simply plan to deal with the consequences of the problem if and when it occurs. For more serious problems where avoidance, mitigation, and transfer are ineffective, impractical, or impossible, contingency planning is the best option.

For some risks, one of these ideas will be sufficient; for others, it may be necessary to use several.

Timeline for Known Risks

As was discussed briefly in Chapter 6, each activity risk will have a signal, perhaps more than one, indicating that the risk has crossed over from a possibility to a certainty. This signal, or trigger event, may be in advance of the risk or coincident with it. It may be visible to everyone involved in the project, or it may be subtle and hidden. For each risk, strive to define a trigger event that provides as much advance notification of the problem as possible. Consider the risk: "A key project team member quits." One possible trigger event might be the submission of a resignation letter. This is an obvious trigger, but it is a late one. There are earlier triggers to watch for, such as a drop in motivation, erratic attendance, frequent "personal" telephone calls, or even an uncharacteristic improvement in grooming and dress. These triggers are not foolproof, and they require more attention and effort to monitor, but they may also foreshadow other problems even if the staff member does not intend to leave.

In addition to one or more trigger events, identify the portions of the project plan where the risk is most probable, being as precise as possible. For some risks there may be a single exposure related to one specific activity; more general risks (such as loss of key staff members) may occur throughout the project.

Risk management decisions and plans are made in advance of the trigger event, and they include all actions related to avoidance, mitigation, or transfer, as well as preparation for any contingent actions. Risk management responses that relate to recovery fall on the project timeline

Figure 8-3. Risk management timeline.

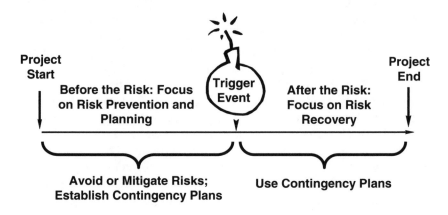

after the risk trigger, but are used only if necessary. For each significant risk that you cannot remove from the project, assign an owner to monitor for the trigger event and to be responsible for implementing the contingency plan or otherwise working toward recovery. The risk management timeline is summarized in Figure 8-3.

Dealing with Risk Causes

After each risk is categorized and you have identified those risks for which the project team could influence some or all of the causes, you are ready to begin developing response possibilities for prevention, including avoidance, mitigation, and transfer. Analyze all the options you and your team develop, examining both the cost of the idea and its potential benefits. If good, cost-effective ideas are proposed, the best of them are candidates for inclusion in your draft project plan. Prevention ideas must earn their way into the project plan. Even excellent ideas that completely remove a risk should be bypassed if their overall cost exceeds the expected "loss times likelihood" for the risk. The final process step is to integrate all accepted risk prevention ideas into your preliminary project plan and review the plan for new risks or unintended consequences as a result of the changes.

Planning for risk responses begins with generating ideas. Brainstorming with your project team is a good way to generate a range of possible choices. It is also useful to discuss risks with peers and others who may have relevant experience, and it may be worthwhile to consult experts and specialists for types for unfamiliar risks.

Few known risks are completely novel, so it is quite possible that many of the risks you face have been addressed on earlier projects. A quick review of project retrospective analyses, final reports, "lessons learned," and other archived materials may provide information on what others did in response to similar risk situations they encountered. In addition to finding things that did not work and are worth avoiding, there may be useful ideas for effectively dealing with the risks you need to manage.

There are also many ideas available in the public domain, in papers, books, and articles and on the Web. References on project management, particularly those that are tailored to projects like yours, are filled with practical advice. Life cycles and project management methodologies also provide direction and useful ideas for managing risks.

A number of possible preventative actions follow in the next several pages, including tactics for risk avoidance, mitigation, and transfer. These can be useful in seeding a brainstorming exercise or in planning for specific responses. These tactics include ideas for dealing with the worst of the risks in the PERIL database, especially those characterized as "black swans." The ideas listed here include some that may be appropriate only for particular kinds of technical projects, but many are useful for any project.

Risk Avoidance

Avoidance is the most thorough way to deal with risks, because it obliterates them. Unfortunately, avoidance is not possible for all project risks because some risks are tightly coupled to the requirements of technical projects. Avoiding risks in your project requires you to reconsider choices and decisions you made in defining and planning your project. Most of Chapters 3, 4, and 5 concerned using project planning processes to identify risks. Although some of the risks you discovered may be unavoidable, a review of the current state of your plan may turn up opportunities to replan the work in ways that remove specific serious risks. Tactics for avoiding scope risks suggested by the material in Chapter 3 include:

- Identify the minimum acceptable deliverable; avoid overdesign ("gold plating").
- Negotiate and clearly document all interface deliverables expected from other projects.
- Avoid untried, unfamiliar, or "bleeding edge" technology whenever practical.

- Plan to design using standard, modular, or well-understood methods. Look for ways to achieve project specifications using older, tried-and-true technologies.
- Buy instead of make.
- Avoid "not invented here" thinking; be willing to leverage work done by others.

Many of your schedule risks are consequences of planning. You may be able to remove sources of schedule risk using ideas covered in Chapter 4:

- Reduce the number of critical paths.
- Modify the work to have fewer activity dependencies.
- Schedule the highest uncertainty activities as early as possible.
- Avoid having the same staff members working on two successive or concurrent critical (or near-critical) activities.
- Decompose lengthy activities further.
- Reschedule work to provide greater flexibility.

Resource risks may also be a consequence of choices you made in resource planning. Explore opportunities to avoid these risks using the concepts of Chapter 5:

- Obtain names for all required project roles.
- Get explicit availability commitments from all project staff (and from their managers).
- Work to limit commitments by project staff to other projects, maintenance and support work, and other time conflicts. Explicitly document those that remain.
- Modify plans to reduce the load on fully loaded or over-committed resources.
- Use the best people available for the most critical activities.
- Educate team members to use more efficient or faster methods, and do it early in the project.
- Use mentoring to build teamwork and establish redundancy for critical skills.
- Upgrade or replace older equipment to make work more efficient, and do it in the beginning of the project.
- Automate manual work when possible.

- Locate and gain access to experts to cover all skill areas not available on the project team.
- Minimize dependence on a single individual or other resource for project work.
- When you use outside services, use the same suppliers that you (or others that you trust) have used successfully in the past.
- Establish contract terms with all suppliers that are consistent with project objectives.

Avoidance tactics are not limited to these ideas by any means. Anything that you can realistically do to eliminate the root cause of a risk has potential for risk avoidance.

Risk Mitigation

Mitigation strategies are also essential for risk management, because avoidance can never deal with every significant project risk. Mitigation strategies serve to reduce the probability and/or the impact of potential problems. Some generic ideas for risk mitigation include:

- Good communication
- Using specialists *and* generalists
- Strong sponsorship
- Continuing user involvement
- Clear decision priorities

One of the least expensive and strongest preventative actions a project leader can take is to communicate more—and more effectively. Risks and risk consequences that are visible always affect the way that people work. If all the team members are aware how painful the project will become following a risk, they are likely to work, to the best of their ability, in ways that minimize the risk. Communication can significantly reduce risk probabilities. Communicate. Communicate. Communicate.

Another broad strategy for managing risk relates to project staffing. Difficult projects benefit from having a mix of specialists and generalists. Specialists are essential on technical projects because no one can know everything, and the specialist can generally complete assigned work in his or her specialty much faster than a generalist. However, a project team composed *only* of specialists is not very robust and tends to run into frequent trouble. This is because project planning on specialist-heavy projects is often intense and detailed for work in the specialists' areas, and remarkably sketchy for other work. Also, such teams may lack broad problem-solving skills. Generalists on a project are needed to fill in the gaps and ensure that as much of the project work as possible is visible and well planned. Generalists are also best for solving cross-disciplinary problems. As the head generalist, the project manager should always reserve at least a small percentage of his or her time for problem solving, helping out on troubled activities, and general firefighting. Even when the project leader has a solid grasp of all the technical project issues, it is useful to have other generalists on the team in case several things on the project go wrong at the same time. Generalists can reduce the time to solution for problems of all kinds and minimize schedule impact.

Managing project risk is always easier with friends in high places. Establish and work to sustain strong sponsorship for your project. Although strong sponsorship does not ensure a risk-free project, weak (or no) upper-level sponsorship is a significant source of risk. Form a good working relationship with the project sponsor(s) and work to understand their expectations for project information. Reinforce the importance and value of the project regularly, and don't let sponsors forget about you. Update your management frequently on project progress and challenges, and involve them early in problems and escalations that require authority you lack. Validate project objectives with sponsors and customers and work to set realistic expectations. Using your budget and staffing plans, get commitments for adequate funding, staffing, and expertise. Strong sponsorship reduces timing problems and other risk impact and lowers the probability for many kinds of resource risks.

Project risk will increase, particularly on lengthy projects, whenever the project team is disconnected from the ultimate customers for the deliverable. Establish and maintain contact with the end users, or with people who can represent them. Seek strong user buy-in, and work with users to avoid scope gaps by validating all acceptance and testing criteria. Establish *measurable* criteria, and determine what will be required for the users to deem the project a success. Identify the individual or individuals who will have the final word on this and keep in contact with them. The probability of scope risk and the likelihood of late project schedule difficulties are both reduced by meaningful user involvement.

A final general strategy for lowering project risk is setting clear decision priorities for the project. Validate the priorities with both the sponsors and the end users, and ensure that the project priorities are well known to the project team. Base project decisions on the priorities, and know the impact of failing to meet each priority established for the project. This not only helps manage scope risks, it also permits quick decisions within the project that minimize scope creep and other change-related impact.

Mitigation Strategies for Scope Risks

Mitigating scope and technical risks involves shifts in approach and potential changes to the project objective. Ideas for mitigating scope risks include:

- Explicitly specify project scope and all intermediate deliverables, in measurable, unambiguous terms, including what *is not* in the deliverable. Eliminate "wants" early—make them part of scope or drop them.
- Gain acceptance for and use a clear and consistent specification change management process.
- Build models, prototypes, and simulations.
- Test with users, early and often.
- Deal with scope risks promptly.
- Obtain funding for any required outside services.
- Translate, competently, all project documents into relevant languages.
- Minimize external dependency risks.
- Consider the impact of external and environmental problems.
- Keep all plans and documents current.

The most significant scope risks in the PERIL database are because of changes. Minimizing change risk involves the first two tactics—scope definition and change management. Scope risk is high for projects with inadequate specifications. Although it is true that thorough, clear definition of the deliverable is often difficult on technical projects, failure to define the results adequately leads to even greater difficulty. Closely inspect the list of features to be included to verify that all the requested requirements are in fact necessary.

The second necessary tactic for reducing change risk is to uniformly apply an effective process for managing *all* changes to project scope. To manage risks on large, complex projects, the process is generally formal, using forms, committees, and extensive written reporting. For technical projects done under contract, risk management also requires that the process be described in detail in the contract signed by the two parties. On smaller projects, even if it is less formal, there still must be uniform treatment of all proposed changes, considering both their benefits and expected costs. For your project, adopt a process that rejects all changes that fail the cost-justification test. It is not enough to *have* a change management process; mitigating scope risks requires its disciplined *use*.

Scope risks are often hard to evaluate at the beginning of technical projects. One way to gain better insight is to schedule work during planning to examine feasibility and functionality questions as early as possible. Use prototypes, simulations, and models to evaluate concepts with users. Schedule early tests and investigations to verify the feasibility of untried technology. Identify potential problems and defects early through walkthroughs and scenario discussions. Also consider scale risks. Even if there are no problems during small-scale, limited tests, scope risks may still remain that will be visible only in full-scale production. Plan for at least some rudimentary tests of functionality in full-scale operation as early in the project as practical. Schedule work to uncover issues and problems near the beginning of the project, and be prepared to make changes or even to abandon the project based on what you learn.

Although it is risky to defer difficult or unknown activities until late in the project, it may be impractical to begin with them. To get started, you may need to complete some simpler activities first, and then move on to more complicated activities as you build expertise. Do your best to schedule the risk-prone activities as early in your project as you can.

Lack of skills on the project team also increases scope risk, so define exactly how you intend to acquire all needed expertise. If you intend to use outside consultants, plan to spend both time and effort in their selection, and ensure that the necessary funding to pay for them is in the project budget. If you need to develop new skills on the project team, identify the individuals involved and plan so each contributor is trained, in advance, in all the needed competencies. If the project will use new tools or equipment, schedule installation and complete any needed training as early in the project as possible.

Scope problems also arise from faulty communications. If the project depends on a distributed team that speaks several languages, identify all the languages needed for project definition and planning documents and plan for their translation and distribution. Confusion arising from project requirements that are misinterpreted or poorly translated can be expensive and damaging, so verify that the project information has been clearly understood in discussions, using interpreters if necessary. It is also critical to provide written follow-up after meetings and telephone discussions.

Scope often depends on the quality and timely delivery of things the project receives from others. Mitigating these risks requires clear, carefully constructed specifications to minimize the possibility that the things that you get are consistent with the request but are inappropriate for the project's intended use. If you have little experience with a provider, finding and using a second source in addition to the first may be prudent, even though this can increase the cost. The cost of a redundant source may be small compared to the cost of a delayed project.

External factors also lead to scope risks. Natural disasters such as floods, earthquakes, and storms, as well as not-so-natural disasters like computer viruses, may cause loss of critical information, software, or necessary components. Although there is no way to prevent the risks, provision for some redundancy, adequate frequent backups of computer systems, and less dependency on one particular location can minimize the impact for this sort of risk.

Finally, managing scope risk also requires tracking of the initial definition with any and all changes approved during the project. You can significantly lower scope risk by adopting a process that tightly couples all accepted changes to the planning process, as well as by making the consequences of scope decisions visible throughout the project.

Mitigation Strategies for Schedule Risks

Schedule risks may be minimized by making additional investments in planning and revising your project approach. Some ideas to consider include:

- Use "expected" estimates when worst cases are significant.
- Schedule highest priority work early.
- Schedule proactive notifications.
- Even if you must use new technology, explore how you *might* use older methods.
- Use parallel, redundant development.
- Send shipments early.
- Know customs requirements and use experienced services for international shipments.
- Be conservative in estimates for training and new hardware.
- Break projects with large staffs into parallel efforts.
- Partition long projects into a sequence of shorter ones.
- Schedule project reviews.
- Reschedule work coincident with known holidays and other time conflicts.
- Track progress with rigor and discipline and report status frequently.

The riskiest activities in the project tend to be the ones that have significant worst-case estimates. For any activity where the most-likely estimate is a lot lower than what could plausibly occur, calculate an "expected" duration using the Program Evaluation and Review Technique (PERT) formula. Use these estimates in project planning to provide some reserve for particularly risky work, and to reduce the schedule impact.

Project risk is lower when you schedule activities related to the highest priorities for the project as early as possible, moving activities of lower priority later in the project. For each scheduled activity, review the deliverables and specify how and when each will be used. Wherever possible, schedule the work so there is a time buffer between when each deliverable is complete and the start of the activities that require them. If there are any activities that produce deliverables that seem to be unnecessary, either validate their requirement with project stakeholders or remove the work from the project plan.

Many schedule risks are caused by delays that may be avoided through more proactive communication. Whenever decisions are needed, plan to remind the decision makers at least a week in advance and get commitment for a swift turnaround. If specialized equipment or access to limited services is required, put an activity in the plan to review your needs with the people involved somewhat before the scheduled work. If scarce equipment for some kinds of project work is a chronic problem, propose adding capacity to lower the risk on your project, as well as for all other parallel work. The preventative maintenance schedules for production systems are generally determined well in advance. Monitor availability schedules for needed services and synchronize your plans with them to reduce conflicts and delays.

New things—technology, hardware, systems, or software—are common sources of delay. Manage risk by seeking alternatives using older, known capabilities unless using the new technology is an absolute project requirement. A "lower-tech" alternative may in some cases be a better choice for the project anyway, or it could serve as a standby option if an emerging technology proves not to work. Identify what you would need to do or change in the project to complete your work without the newer technology.

One cause of significant delay is developing a specific design and then sending it out to be built or created before it can be tested. It may take weeks to get the tangible result of the design back, and if it has problems the entire cycle must be repeated, doubling the duration (or worse—it may not work the second time either). In areas such as chip design, more than one chip will be made on each wafer anyway, and it might be useful to design a number of slightly different versions that can all be fabricated at the same time. Most of the chips will be of the primary design, but other variations created at the same time can also be tested, thus increasing the chances of having a component that can be used to continue with project work. There are other cases where slightly different versions may be created in parallel, such as printed circuit boards, mechanical assemblies, and other newly designed hardware. Although this may increase the project cost, protecting the project schedule is often a much higher priority. Varying the parameters of a design and evaluating the results is also useful for quickly understanding the principles involved, which can reduce risks for future projects.

Delays due to shipping problems are significant on many projects and in many cases can be avoided simply by ordering or shipping items earlier in the project. Just because it is generally thought to take a week to ship a piece of equipment from San Jose, California, to Bangalore, India, does not mean you should wait until a week before it is needed in India to ship it. There are only two ways to get something done sooner—work faster or start earlier. With shipping, expediting may not always be effective, so it is prudent planning to request and send things that require physical transport well ahead of the need, particularly when it involves complex paperwork and international customs regulations. Use only shipping services with a good performance record, knowledge of legal requirements, and an ability to track shipments.

Similarly, delay may result from the need to have new equipment or new skills for the project. The time necessary to get new equipment installed and running or to master new skills may prove longer than you think. If you underestimate how long it will take, project work that depends on the new hardware or skills could have to wait. Planning proactively for these project requirements will remove many risks of this sort from your project (and, as mentioned earlier, it also lowers the chances that you might lose, or never get, the required funding). Estimate these activities conservatively, and schedule installations, upgrades, and training as early in your project as practical—well before they are needed.

Large projects are intrinsically risky. If a project requires more than twenty full-time staff members, explore the possibility of partitioning it into smaller projects responsible for subsystems, modules, or components that can be developed in parallel. However, when you decompose a large program into autonomous smaller projects, be sure to clearly define all interfaces between them both in terms of specifications required and timing. Although the independent projects will be easier to manage and *less* risky, the overall program could be prone to late integration problems without adequate systems-level planning and strong interface controls.

Long projects are also risky. Work to break projects longer than a year into phases that produce measurable outputs. A series of short evolutionary projects will create value sooner than a more ambitious longer project, and the shorter projects are more likely to fall within a reasonable planning horizon of less than six months. This is a central principle for evolutionary software development and agile methodologies, used to deliver intermediate results sooner and to manage risk.

If a lengthy project must be undertaken as a whole, adopt a "rolling-wave" planning philosophy. At the end of each project phase, plan the next phase in detail and adjust plans for the remainder of the work at a summary level. Make adjustments to the project plans for future phases as you proceed to reflect what has been learned in the previous phases, including changes to the project deliverable, shifts in project staffing, and other parameters of the project objective. Rolling-wave planning requires that the project team conduct a thorough project review at the end of each phase and be prepared to continue as planned, continue with changes, or abort the project.

Schedule risk also arises from time conflicts outside the project. Check the plan for critical project work that may conflict with holidays, the end of financial reporting periods, times when people are likely to take vacations, or other distractions. Verify that intermediate project objectives and milestones are consistent with the personal plans of the staff members responsible for the work. On global projects, collect data for each region to minimize problems that may arise when part of the project team will be unavailable because of local holidays. When there are known project time conflicts, minimize them by accelerating or delaying the planned work.

Finally, commit to rigorous activity tracking throughout the project, and periodically schedule time to review your entire plan: the estimates, risks, work flow, project assumptions, and other data. Publish accurate schedule status regularly.

Mitigation Strategies for Resource Risks

Mitigating resource risks includes ideas such as:

- Avoid planned overtime.
- Build teamwork and trust on the project team.
- Use "expected" cost estimates where worst-case activity costs are high.
- Obtain firm commitment for funding and staff.
- Keep customers involved.
- Anticipate staffing gaps.
- Minimize safety and health issues.

- Encourage team members to plan for their own risks.
- Delegate risky work to successful problem solvers.
- Rigorously manage outsourcing.
- Detect and address flaws in the project objective promptly.
- Rigorously track project resource use.

One of the most common avoidable resource risks on technical projects is required overtime. Starting a project with full knowledge that the deadline is not possible unless the team works overtime for much of the project's duration is a prescription for failure. Whenever the plan shows requirements for effort in excess of what is realistically available, rework the plan to eliminate it. Even on well-planned projects there are always plenty of opportunities for people to stay late, work weekends and holidays, lose sleep, and otherwise devote time to the project from their side of the "work/life" balance. Projects that require overtime from the outset face significant risks of low productivity due to poor motivation and potential turnover.

Resource risk is lower on projects whenever motivation is high. Motivation is a key factor in whether people will voluntarily work overtime, and low motivation is frequently a root cause of many resource-related risks. Technical projects are always difficult. When they succeed, it is not because they are easy; it is because the project team cares about the project. Project leaders who are good at building teamwork and getting people working on the project to trust and care about each other are much more successful than project leaders who work impersonally at a distance.

Teamwork across cross-functional project boundaries is also important. The more involvement in project planning, start-up or launch activities, and other meaningful work with others you plan early in the project, the more team cohesion you can count on. People who know and trust each other will back each other up and help to solve each other's problems. People who do not know each other well tend to mistrust each other and create conflict, arguments, and unnecessary project problems. Working together to plan and initiate project work transforms it from the "project leader's project" to "our project."

Financial risk is also significant for many projects. For activities in the project that have significant worst-case costs, estimate a realistic "expected cost" and use it to reflect the potential financial exposure and in determining the proposed project budget.

As with schedule risk, adequate sponsorship is essential to resource risk management. Get early commitment from the project's sponsor for staffing and for funding, based on planning data (a discussion of negotiating for this follows in Chapter 10). The priority of the project is also under the control of the project sponsor, so work to understand the relative priority of the project in his or her mind. Strive to obtain the highest priority that is realistic for your project (and document it in writing). If the project has more than one sponsor, determine who has the most influence on the project. In particular, it is good to know who would be able to make a decision to cancel your project, so you can take good care of them and keep them aware of your progress. It is also useful to know who in the organization above you would suffer the most serious consequences if your project does not go well, because these managers have a personal stake in your project and they will likely be useful when risk recovery requires escalation.

Too little involvement of customers and end users in definition, design, and testing is also a potential resource risk, so obtain commitments early on all activities that require it. Also, plan to provide reminders to them in advance of the project work that needs their participation.

Risks resulting from staffing gaps can be reduced or detected earlier through more effective communication. Assess the likelihood that project staff (including you) might join the project late because of ongoing responsibilities in prior projects that are delayed. Get credible status reports from these projects and determine how likely it is that the people working on them will be available to work on your project. If the earlier projects are ending with a lot of stress and overtime, reflect the need for some recovery time and less aggressive estimates in your project plans for the affected team members. Also plan to notify any contributors with part-time responsibilities on your project in advance of their scheduled work.

Loss of project staff due to safety or health problems is always possible, so a review of activities involving dangerous work is a good idea. Modify plans for any activities that you suspect may have health or safety risks to minimize the exposure. You may be able to make changes to the environment, time, or place for the work or to mitigate the risk by modifying the practices used. Also consider the experience and skills of any contributor who might be exposed to risks, and work to replace or train any team members who have insufficient relevant background.

For any activity risk where the team members involved could contribute to the risk, involve the individuals in developing a response. In addition to potentially finding more, and better, ideas for prevention, this will tend to sensitize them to the impact of the problem and may greatly reduce the likelihood of the risk.

For new, challenging, or otherwise risky activities, strive to find experienced contributors who have a reputation for effective problem solving. Although you cannot plan creativity or innovation, you can identify people who seem to be good at it.

Outsourcing is a large and growing source of resource risk on projects. The discussion in Chapter 5 includes a number of exposures, and mitigating these risks requires discipline and effort. For each contract with a service provider that your project depends upon, designate a liaison on the project team to manage the relationship. Do this also for other project teams in your own organization that you need to work with. If you plan to be the liaison, ensure that you have sufficient time allocated for this in addition to all your other responsibilities. Involve the owner of each relationship in selection, negotiation, and finalization of the agreement. Ensure that the agreement is sufficiently formal (a contract with an external supplier, a "memo of understanding" or similar document for an internal supplier) and that it is specific as to both time and technical requirements for the work, consistent with your project plan. Provide incentives and penalties in the agreement when appropriate, and whenever possible, schedule the work to complete earlier than your absolute need.

With any project work performed outside the view of the project team, schedule reviews of early drafts of required documents. Also, participate in inspections and interim tests, and examine prototypes. Identify and take full advantage of any early opportunities to verify tangible evidence of progress. Plan to collect status information regularly, and work to establish a relationship that will make it more likely that you will get credible status, including bad news, throughout your project.

A significant risk situation on fee-for-service projects is a lack of involvement of the technical staff during the proposal and selling phases. When a project is scoped and a contract commitment is made before the project team has any involvement in the project, resource risks (not to mention schedule and scope risks) can be enormous. This "price to win the business" technique is far too common in selling fee-for-solution projects, and it often leads to fixed-price contracts with large and seemingly attractive revenues that are later discovered to involve even larger and extremely unattractive costs. Some projects sold this way may even be impossible to deliver at all. Prevention of this risk would be reasonably easy using time-travel technology, by turning back the clock and involving the project team in setting the terms and conditions for any agreement. Because that is impossible, and this risk may already be a certainty when the project team gets into project and risk planning, the only recourse is to mitigate the situation insofar as possible.

Minimizing the risks associated with committed projects based on little or no analysis requires the project team to initiate the processes of basic project and risk planning as quickly as they can, doing bottom-up planning based on the committed scope. Using best-effort planning information, uncover any expectations for timing and cost that are out of line with reality. Timing expectations are visible to all, so any shifts there must be dealt with internally as well as with the customer, which may require contract modifications. Resource and cost problems can be hidden from the customer, but they still will require internal adjustment and commitment to a realistic budget for the project, even if it significantly exceeds the amount that can be recovered under the contract. If this is all done quickly enough, before everyone has mentally settled into expectations based on the price to win the contract, it may even be possible to adjust the fees in the contract. Although it may be tempting to adopt a "safe so far" attitude and hope for the miracle that would allow project delivery consistent with the flawed contract, delay will nearly always make things worse. The last, best chance to set realistic expectations for such a project is within a few days of its start. After this, the situation becomes progressively uglier and more expensive to resolve.

It is also important to document and make these price-to-win situations visible, to minimize the chances of future recurrence. Organizations that chronically pursue business like this rarely last long.

Finally, establish resource metrics for the project, and track them against realistic planning data. Track progress, effort, and funding throughout the project, and plan to act quickly when the information shows that the trends show adverse variances against the plan. Keep resource status information visible through regular reporting.

Risk Transfer

Transfer is a third option for risk prevention, along with avoidance and mitigation. It is most effective for risks where the impact is primarily financial. The best-known form of transfer is insurance; for a fee, someone else will bear the financial consequences of your risk. Transfer works to benefit both parties, because the purchaser of the insurance avoids the risk of a potentially catastrophic monetary loss in exchange for paying a small (by comparison) premium, and the seller of the insurance benefits by aggregating the fees collected to manage the risk for a large population of insurance buyers, who may be expected to have a stable and predictable "average" risk, and include only a small percentage who will generate claims. In technical projects, this sort of transfer is not extremely common, but it is used. Unlike other strategies for mitigation, transfer does not actually do anything to lower the probability or diminish the nonfinancial impact of the risk. With transfer, the risk is accepted, and it either happens or it does not. However, any budgetary impact will be borne outside the project, limiting the resource impact.

Transfer of scope and technical risk is often the justification for outsourcing, and in some cases this might work. If the project team lacks a needed skill, hiring an expert or consultant to do the work transfers the activities to people who may be in a better position to get it done. Unfortunately, though, the risk does not actually transfer to the third party; the project still belongs to you, so any risk of nonperformance is ultimately still yours. Should things not go well, the fact that a bill for services will not need to be paid will be of small consolation. Even the possibility of eventual legal action is unlikely to help the project. Using outsourcing as a risk transfer strategy is very much a judgment call. In some cases the risks accepted may significantly exceed the risks managed, no matter how well you write the contract.

Implementing Preventative Ideas

Avoidance, mitigation, and transfer nearly always have costs, sometimes significant costs. Before you adopt any ideas to avoid or reduce risks, some analysis is in order. For each risk to be managed, estimate the expected consequences in quantitative terms. For each proposed risk response, assess the incremental costs and timing impact involved. After comparing this data, consider business-justified preventative actions for inclusion in the project plan.

The expected cost of a risk, as usual, is based on "loss times likelihood." For this, you need the probability in numerical terms, as well as estimates of the risk impact in terms of financial, schedule, and possibly other factors.

For a risk that was assessed as "moderate" probability, the historical records may provide an estimated probability of about 15 percent. The impact of the risk must also be assessed quantitatively. For a risk that represents three weeks of schedule slip and $2 million in cost and a probability of 15 percent, the expected risk impact will be about one-half week (which is probably not too significant) and $300,000 (which would be, for most projects, very significant). In each case, this is 15 percent of the total impact, shown graphically in Figure 8-4.

The consequences of each idea for avoiding or mitigating the risk in time and money should be compared with the expected impact estimates to see whether they are cost-justified. If an idea only mitigates a risk—lowering the impact or probability of the problem—then the

Figure 8-4. Expected impact.

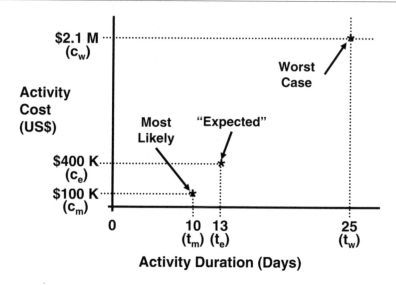

Activity Duration (Days)

comparison is generally between the cost for mitigation and difference between the "before and after" estimates for the risk.

Determining whether a preventative is justified is always a judgment call, and it may be a difficult one. It is made more so because the data is often not very precise or dependable, making comparisons fairly subjective. The exercise of comparing costs for risk prevention with the expected impact is important, though, because it is human nature to attempt to prevent problems whenever possible. Just because you *could* prevent a risk, though, does not necessarily mean that you should. Seeking a risk-free project is illogical for two reasons. First, it is impossible. All projects have some residual risk no matter how much you do to avoid it. Second, a project with every possible risk prevention idea built into the plan will be far too expensive and time consuming to ever get off the ground.

For each potential idea that reduces or removes a project risk, contrast the expected costs of the risk with the cost of prevention before pulling it into the project plan. In the case above, with the expected half week of delay and $300,000 in expense, an idea that requires a week of effort and costs $1.5 million would most likely not be adopted, as the "cure" is nearly as bad as the relatively unlikely risk. This situation would be similar to paying more for insurance than the cost of the expected loss. A preventative that costs less and requires little effort, though, may well represent a prudent plan modification.

Another consideration may enter the decision process. You may choose to respond to some risks that have high impact even though they have low assessed probabilities and "expected" consequences that position them below your "cut line" on the rank-ordered list. A decision to manage the risk outlined earlier will also need to consider whether a $2 million unanticipated expense could be tolerated. The incremental cost of the risk will never be $300,000; it will be either nothing or $2 million. If a $2 million outlay is not acceptable, a "MiniMax" strategy would lead you to invest in a risk response if you can identify one that is effective and can be accommodated in your budget.

What appears to be a simple decision, then, may not be. You may choose to develop a response for risks in your risk register for any of the following reasons:

- They are significant risks for which you have a cost-effective response.
- They are risks with high impact where a response is justified, regardless of assessed probability. (Remember, black swans do happen.)
- They are minor risks—those below the cut line—that have simple, low-cost, effective responses.

You may choose *not* to respond to risks in your risk register (to accept them) for any of the following reasons:

- They are significant risks where no response can be found.
- They are significant risks where a response is identified but thought too costly.
- They are minor risks that do not warrant attention in advance.

Even if some of the ideas you generate for risk prevention prove not to be cost-justified, the same (or similar) approaches may still have application as contingency plans.

Updating your plans is the final step in risk response planning. For each cost-justified (or otherwise approved) risk avoidance, mitigation, or transfer idea, you must update your project planning documents. Most ideas will require additional or different work, so the project work breakdown structure (WBS) may shift, and there will likely be revisions to activity effort and duration estimates. Any added work will require staffing, and so the profiles in your resource plan will also require changes. If the resulting plan has problems meeting existing project constraints, there will be additional required replanning, which may create new risks.

Before adoption, each idea for risk prevention must earn its way into the project by lowering, not increasing, project risk. Before any modifications, review the plan for unintended consequences and document the justification for all additional project work.

Contingency Planning

For some risks, your best strategy will be to deal with risk effects, not causes. Avoidance, mitigation, and transfer, when justified and added to the project, all serve to make a project less risky, but risks will inevitably remain. For some risks, you have no influence on the root causes or can find no preventative action that was cost effective. For other risks, you may have mitigation strategies that help but still leave substantial residual risk. For most of the significant risks that remain, you should develop contingency plans, although for some cases you may decide to accept the risk.

Contingency planning deals with risk effects by generating plans for recovery or "fall back." The process for contingency planning is entirely the same as for any other project planning, and it should be conducted at the same level of detail and using the same methodologies and tools as other project planning.

Each contingency plan begins with the trigger event that signals the risk has occurred. The most effective risk triggers precede the risk consequences by as much as possible. Early triggers increase the number of potential recovery options, and in some cases they may permit you to reduce the impact of the risk, so verify that the trigger event you plan to use is the best option available.

Each risk to be managed with a contingency plan also must also have an owner. The risk owner should be involved with developing the initial contingency plan and will monitor for the trigger event and be responsible for maintaining the contingency plans. If the risk should occur, the risk owner will be responsible for beginning to execute the contingency plan, working toward project recovery. The owner of a project risk will most often be the same person who owns the project activity related to the risk, but for risks with particularly severe, project-threatening consequences, the project leader may be a better choice.

General Contingency Planning Strategies

Contingency planning for risks often starts with leftover ideas. Some ideas may have been considered for schedule compression (discussed in Chapter 6), but were not used. Others could be risk prevention strategies that were not adopted in the preliminary baseline plan for cost or other reasons. Although some of these ideas may be simply adopted as contingency plans without modification, in other cases they may need to be modified for "after the fact" use. Prevention strategies such as using an alternate source for components or schedule compression strategies for expediting printing or other outsourced activities can be documented as contingency plans with no modification. Some risk avoidance ideas can serve as contingencies after minor changes. Dropping back to an older technology, for example, might require additional work to back out any dependencies on a newer technology that fails.

Contingency planning in itself is a powerful risk prevention tool, as the process of planning for recovery shows clearly how difficult and time consuming it will be to recover from problems. This provides additional incentive for the project team to work in ways that will avoid risks. Always strive to make risks and risk planning as visible as possible in project communication. Your project team can only work to avoid the potential problems that they know about.

Contingency Planning Strategies for Schedule Risks

Whenever a risk results in a significant delay, the contingency plan must seek an alternate version of the work flow that provides either a way to expedite work so you can resume the project plan at some later point or a way to complete the project on an alternate basis that minimizes impact to the project deadline.

Recovery involves the same concepts and ideas used for schedule compression, discussed in Chapter 6. The baseline plan will require revision to make effort available for recovery immediately following the risk, so other work will need to be shifted, changed, or eliminated. You may be able to delay the start of less crucial planned activities, postponing them to later in the project. Any noncritical activity work that is simultaneous to or scheduled to follow the risk event may be interrupted or postponed to allow more focus on recovery. Some activity dependencies may be revised to allow project activities to be done out of the planned sequence, freeing contributors to work on recovery. In all of these cases, necessary activities shift later in the schedule, increasing the impact of future risks and creating new failure modes and exposures as more and more project work becomes schedule critical.

It may even be possible to eliminate planned work if it is nonessential, or to devise quicker approaches for project activities that could obtain similar, but possibly less satisfactory, results. In some cases, it may be possible to defer these decisions to eliminate work or adopt "shortcuts" until later in the project, using them on an as-needed basis.

"Crashing" project activities scheduled for later in the project to decrease their duration can also help if the project has sufficient budget reserve or access to the additional staffing. Shorter durations will permit later start dates for scheduled work and potentially free up project effort for recovery. Simply adding staff to the project to work on recovery may also be an option, if you can get commitment from additional contributors. If you do plan to add people, include all training and project familiarization required as part of your baseline plan to minimize the disruption inevitable with new staff. Without adequate preparation, this tactic might delay your project even more.

It may not be possible to replan the project to protect the deadline, especially when the risk relates to work near the project deadline. In such a case, the contingency planning serves to minimize the slippage and to provide the data necessary to document a new, later completion date.

A generic schedule contingency strategy involves establishing schedule reserve for the project. Establishing schedule reserve is explored in more detail in Chapter 10.

Contingency Planning Strategies for Resource Risks

For risks that require significant additional resources, contingency planning involves revising the resource plans to protect the project budget, or at least to limit the damage. Again, the process for this parallels the discussion for dealing with resource constraints in Chapter 6.

The most common strategy is also one of the least attractive—working overtime and on weekends and holidays. This tried-and-true recovery method works adequately on most projects, providing the resource impact is minimal and project staffing is not already working significantly beyond the normal workday and workweek. If the amount of additional effort required is high, or the project team is stretched too thin when the risk occurs, this contingency strategy may backfire and actually make things worse by lowering motivation and leading to higher staff turnover.

For some projects, there may be contributors who are assigned to the project but are underused during part of it. If this is the case, shifting work around in the schedule may allow them to assist with risk recovery and still effectively meet other commitments. This tactic, like dealing with schedule risks using float, tends to increase overall project risk later in the project.

Eliminating later work or substituting other approaches than those planned may also reduce the resources needed for work later in the project, but if this is possible it is generally more appropriate to do it as part of the baseline plan. If the work is not essential, or there is a quicker way to obtain an acceptable result, these choices ought to be adopted, not viewed as potential jetsam to fling overboard if necessary.

Particularly for resource risks, it may be impossible to avoid damage to the overall resource plan and budget. All adverse variances increase the total project cost, so there may be few or no easy ways left to cut back other expenses to compensate.

Minimizing the impact of risk recovery involves contingency planning that revises resource use in ways that protect the budget as much as possible. Tactics such as assigning additional staff to later critical path activities or "borrowing" people from other, lower-priority projects may have little budget impact. Expediting external activities using incentive payments and outsourcing work planned for the project team may also be possible, but seek approval in advance for the additional cost as part of your contingency planning. If a contingency plan requires any training or other preliminary work to be effective, make these activities part of your baseline project plan.

A generic resource contingency strategy involves establishing a budget reserve for the project, similar to the schedule reserve discussed earlier. Budget reserve is discussed further in Chapter 10.

Contingency Planning Strategies for Scope Risks

Contingency planning for scope risks is not too complicated. The plans involve either protecting the specifications for the deliverable or reducing the scope requirements. Attempting to preserve the requirements is done by adding more work to the schedule (using tactics summarized previously), using additional resources, or both. In most cases it is difficult to assess in advance the magnitude of change that this may require, as the level of difficulty in fulfilling requirements for technical projects is highly variable—from relatively trivial in some cases to impossible in others. Contingency plans for scope risks usually provide for some level of recovery effort, followed by a review to determine whether to continue, modify the scope, or cancel the project.

For many technical projects, scope risks are managed by modifying the project objective, to provide most of the value of the project deliverable in a way that is consistent with schedule and resource objectives. The process for this, similar to that discussed in Chapter 6, starts with a prioritized list of specifications. It may be possible to drop some of the requirements entirely, or to defer them to a later phase or project. There may also be potential for relaxing some of the requirements, making them easier to achieve. Although this can be done effectively for some projects in advance, contingency planning for scope risks generally includes a review of project accomplishments and any shifts in assumptions, so your decisions on what to drop will be based on current data.

Risk Acceptance

For some risks, it may not be possible, or worthwhile, to plan specifically for recovery. Acceptance, as a general risk management technique, includes both transfer and contingency planning, because in both of these situations the risk causes are not influenced and the risk either happens or does not. For transfer and for contingency planning, specific responses are planned in advance to assist in recovery. For some risks, though, neither of these options may be practical. When the consequences of a risk are sufficiently unclear, as may be the case for scope and some other risks in technical projects, planning for recovery in advance may be impossible. An example of this might be a stated requirement to use new technology or hardware for the project. In such a case, many potential problems, ranging from the trivial to the insurmountable, are possible.

When a specific risk response is not an option, there are still choices available. If the risk is sufficiently serious, it may be the best course to abandon the project altogether as too risky, or consider a major change in the objective. For situations that are less damaging, you may choose to proceed with the project having no specific risk response, accepting the risks (and hoping for the best). If you adopt this alternative, it is prudent to document the risks as thoroughly as possible, discuss them with your sponsor and stakeholders, and secure project-level schedule and budget reserves to assist in managing the accepted risks.

Documenting Your Risk Plans

For risks with multiple potential consequences or particularly severe effects, you may want to generate more than one contingency plan. Before finalizing a contingency plan (or plans), review them for overall cost and probable effectiveness. If you do develop more than one response for a risk, prioritize the plans, putting first the plan you think will be most effective.

Document all contingency plans, and include the same level of detail as in the project plans: WBS, estimates, dependencies, schedule, resources required, the expected project impact, and any relevant assumptions. For each risk response plan, clearly specify the trigger event to detect that the risk has happened. Also, include the name of the owner who will monitor the risk trigger, maintain the contingency plan, and be responsible for its execution if the risk occurs.

As part of the overall project documentation, document your risk response plan and work to make the risks visible. One method for increasing risk awareness is to post a "top ten" risk list (revised periodically) either on the project Web site or with posters on the walls of project work areas. Ensure adequate distribution and storage of all risk plans, and plan to review risk management information at least quarterly.

Some projects formally maintain the risk register as part of their risk response plan. For each managed risk, the register includes:

- A detailed description of the risk
- The risk owner, plus any others with assigned roles and responsibilities
- The activities affected by the risk (including WBS codes)
- Any qualitative or quantitative risk analysis results
- A summary of risk response actions in the project plan
- The risk trigger event
- Expected residual risk exposure
- A summary of contingency and fallback plans

Add risk plans to the other project documentation and choose an appropriate location for storage that is available to all project contributors and stakeholders.

Managing a Specific Risk

Some years ago, a large multinational company initiated a year-long effort to establish a new European headquarters. Growth over the years had spread people, computers, and other hardware all over Geneva, Switzerland, and the inconvenience and expense for all of this had grown unacceptable. The goal was to consolidate all the people and infrastructure into a modern, new headquarters building. This effort involved a number of high-profile, risky projects, and I was asked to manage one of them.

One particularly risky aspect of the project involved moving two large, water-cooled mainframe computers out of the older data center where the systems had operated for some years, and into a more modern center in the new headquarters building. In the new location, the systems would be collocated with all the other headquarters computers and the telecommunications equipment that tied them to other sites in Europe and around the world. Both systems were critical to the business, so each was scheduled to be moved over a three-day holiday weekend. It was essential that each system be fully functional in the old data center at the end of the week before the move, and fully functional in the new data center before the start of business following the holiday, three days later.

Most of the risks were fairly mundane, and they were managed through thorough planning, adequate staffing, and extensive training, all committed months in advance. Other precautions, such as additional data backups, were also taken. The move itself was far from mundane, though, because the old data center, for some reason, had been established on the fifth floor of a fairly old building. The elevator in the building was small, about one meter square, and could carry no more than the weight of three or four people (who had to be on very friendly terms). When the systems were originally moved into the building, a system-sized door had been cut into the marble façade of the building, and a crane with a suspended box was used to move the systems into the data center. Over the years, upgrades and replacements had been moved in and out the same way.

Up to the time of this project, only older hardware being replaced had ever been moved out of the data center this way. In these cases, if there had been a mishap it would not have affected operations, because the older systems were only moved out once the replacement systems were successfully moved in and operational. For the relocation project, this was not the case. Both systems had to be moved out, transported, and reinstalled successfully, and any problem that started twenty meters in the air would result in a significant and expensive service interruption far longer than the allocated three days.

The new data center was, sensibly, at ground level; eliminating the need to suspend multimillion-dollar mainframes high in the air was one of the reasons the project was undertaken. Successful completion of the project would mean ground-level systems in the new data center, and far easier maintenance for all future operations.

In addition to the obvious risk of a CPU plummeting to the ground, the short timing of the project also involved other exposures such as weather, wind, traffic, injuries to workers, problems with the crane, and many other potential difficulties. The assessment of risk for most of these situations resulted either in adjustments in staffing, shifts in the plan, or acceptance, because there was sufficient experience and people were confident that most of the potential problems could be managed during the move.

The one remaining risk that concerned all of us was that one of the mainframe computers might smash into the sidewalk. The consequences of this could not be managed during the three-day weekend, so a lot of analysis went into exploring ways to manage this risk.

Risk assessment was the subject of significant debate, particularly with regard to probability. Some thought it "low," citing, "This is Switzerland; we move skiers up the mountains this way all the time."

Suspending computing in Geneva.

Others, particularly people from the United States, were less optimistic. In the end, the consensus was "moderate." There was less debate on risk impact, which in this case was literal. In addition to issues of cost and delay, there were significant other concerns such as safety, the large crater in the pavement, noise, and computer parts bouncing for blocks around.

The primary impact was in time and cost, and deemed "high," so considerable planning went into mitigating the risk. A number of ideas were explored, including disassembly of the system for movement in pieces using the elevator, building a lift along the side of the building (the two systems were to be moved a month apart, so this cost would have covered both), using padding or some sort of cushion for the ground, and a number of other even less practical ideas. The disassembly idea was considered seriously, but deemed inappropriate because of timing and the discouraging report from the vendor that "those systems do not always work right initially when we assemble them in the factory." The external lift idea was a good one, but hardware that could reach to the fifth floor was unavailable. A large net or cushion would have minimized the spread of debris, but seemed unlikely to ensure system operation. It was not until the problem was reframed that the best idea emerged. The risk was not really the loss of that particular system; it was the loss of a *usable* system.

A plan to purchase a new system and install it, in advance, in the new data center would make the swift and successful move of the existing hardware unnecessary. Once operations were transferred to the new hardware, the old system could be lowered to the street, and if successful, sold as used equipment. This was an effective plan for avoiding the risk, but it had one problem—cost. The difference between the salvage value of the current machine and the purchase price of a new one was roughly $2 million. This investment was far higher than the expected consequences of the risk, so it was rejected as part of the plan. We decided to take as many precautions as possible, and accept the risk.

All this investigation made the contingency planning easy, as the research we had done into acquiring a new system was really all that was necessary. We ordered a new system and got a commitment from the vendor to fill the order with the next machine built if there were any problems moving the existing system. (The vendor was happy to agree to this, as it was heavily involved in many aspects of the relocation.) Once the move had been competed successfully, the order could be canceled with no penalty.

The consequences documented for the contingency plan were that the system would be unavailable for about three weeks, and the cost of the replacement system would be roughly $3 million.

As it happened, the same staff and basic plan was employed for both mainframe moves, and both went without any incident. Although the contingency plan was not used, everyone felt that the risk planning had been a good investment. The process revealed clearly what we were facing, and it heightened our awareness of the overall risk. It uncovered many related smaller problems that were eliminated, which saved time and made the time-critical work required much easier. It also made all of us confident that the projects had been carefully and thoroughly planned, and that we would be successful. Even when risk management cannot eliminate all the risks, it is worthwhile to the project.

Key Ideas for Managing Activity Risks

- Determine root causes.
- Avoid, mitigate, or transfer risks when feasible.
- Develop contingency plans for remaining significant risks.
- Document risk plans and keep risk data visible.
- Thirty grams of prevention is worth half a kilogram of cure (approximately).

Panama Canal: Risk Plans (1906–1914)

Risk management represented one of the largest investments for the Panama Canal project. Of the risks mentioned in Chapter 7, most were dealt with in effective, and in several cases innovative, ways.

The risk of disease, so devastating on the earlier project, was managed through diligence, science, and sanitation. The scale and cost of this effort were significant, but so were the results. Widespread use of methods for mosquito control under the guidance of Dr. William Gorgas was effective on a scale never seen before. Specific tactics used, such as frequently applying thin films of oil on bodies of water and the disciplined dumping of standing water wherever it gathered (which in a rain forest was nearly everywhere), were so effective that their use worldwide in the tropics continues to this day. Once the program for insect control was in full effect, Panama was by far the healthiest place anywhere in the tropics. Yellow fever was eliminated. Malaria was rare, as were tuberculosis, dysentery, pneumonia, and a wide range of other diseases common at the time. Not only were the diseases spread by mosquitoes virtually eliminated, work also went much faster without the annoyance of the omnipresent insects. Although some estimates put the cost at US$10 for every mosquito killed, the success of the canal project depended heavily on Dr. Gorgas to ensure that the workers stayed healthy. This risk was managed thoroughly and well.

For the risk of frequent and sudden mud slides, there were no elegant solutions. As the work commenced, it seemed to many that "the more we dug, the more remained to be dug." Unfortunately, this was true; it proved impossible to use the original French plan for the trench in the Culebra Cut to have sides at 45 degrees (a 1:1 slope). This angle created several problems, the largest of which was the frequent mud slides. In addition, the sides of the cut pressed down on the semisolid clay the excavators were attempting to remove, which squeezed it up in the center of the trench. The deeper the digging, the more the sides would sink and the center would rise; like a fluid, it would seek its level. The contingency plan was inelegant but ultimately effective—more digging. The completed canal had an average 4:1 slope, which minimized the mud slides and partially stabilized the flowing clay. This brute-force contingency plan not only resulted in much more soil to dispose of, it represented about triple the work. Erosion, flowing clay, and occasional mud slides continue to this day, and the canal requires frequent dredging to remain operational.

Dealing with the risks involved with building the enormous locks required a number of tactics. As with the mud slides, the massive concrete sides for the locks were handled by brute force and overengineering. Cement was poured at Panama on a scale never done before. The sides of the locks are so thick and so heavily reinforced that even after close to a century of continuous operation, with thousands of ship passages and countless earthquakes, the locks still look much as they did when they were new.

The mechanical and electrical challenges were quite another matter. The locks were colossal machines with thousands of moving parts, many huge. Years of advance planning and experimentation led to ultimate success. The canal was a triumph of precision engineering and use of new steels. Vanadium alloy steels used were developed initially for automotive use, and they proved light and strong enough to serve in the construction of doors for the locks. Holding the doors tightly closed against the weight of the water in a filled lock required a lot of mass, mass that the engineers wanted to avoid moving each time the doors were opened or closed. To achieve this, the doors are *hollow*. Whenever they are closed, they are filled with water before the lock is filled, providing the necessary mass. The doors are then drained before they are opened to allow the ships raised (or lowered) to pass through.

Even with this strategy, moving doors of this size and weight required the power of modern engines. The choice of electrical operation was complicated and required much innovation (the first all-electric factory in the United States was barely a year old at the time of this decision), but electricity did provide a number of advantages. With electric controls, the entire canal system can be controlled centrally. Scale models were built to show the positions of each lock in detail. The lock systems are all controlled using valves and switches on the model, and mechanical interlocks beneath the model prevent errors in operation, such as opening the doors on the wrong end of a lock, or opening them before the filling or draining of water is complete. Complete status can be monitored for all twelve locks.

When George Goethals began to set all of this up, he realized that neither he nor anyone else had ever done anything like it. For most of the controls and the 1000+ electric motors the canal required, Goethals managed risk by bringing in outside help. He awarded a sizable contract to a rapidly growing U.S. company known for its expertise in electrical systems. Although it was still fairly small and not known internationally, the General Electric (GE) Company had started to attract worldwide attention by the time the Panama Canal opened. This was a huge contract for GE, and it was the company's first large government contract. Such a large-scale collaboration of private and public organizations was unknown prior to this project. The relationship used by Goethals and GE served as the model for the Manhattan Project during World War II and for countless other modern projects in the United States and elsewhere. For good or ill, the modern military-industrial complex began in Panama.

Despite the project's success in dealing with most risks, explosives remained a significant problem throughout construction. As in many contemporary projects, loss of life and limbs while handling explosives was common. Although stringent safety precautions helped, the single largest cause of death on the second Panama Canal project was TNT, not disease. For this risk, the builders found no solutions or viable alternatives, so throughout the project they were quite literally "playing with dynamite."

9

Quantifying and Analyzing Project Risk

"Knowledge is power."
—FRANCIS BACON

Information is central to managing projects successfully. Knowledge of the work and potential risk serves as the first and best defense against problems and project delay. The overall assessment of project risk provides concrete justification for necessary changes in the project objective, so it is one of the most powerful tools you have in transforming an impossible project into one that can be successful. Project-level risk rises steeply for projects with insufficient resources or excessively aggressive schedules, and risk assessments offer compelling evidence of the exposure this represents. Knowledge of project risk also sets expectations for the project appropriately, both for the deliverables and for the work that lies ahead. The focus of this chapter is analyzing overall project risk, building on the foundation of analysis and response planning for known *activity* risks discussed in Chapters 7 and 8.

Project-Level Risk

Considered one by one, the known risks on a project may seem relatively easy to deal with, overwhelming, or somewhere in between. Assessing risk at the activity level is necessary, but it is not sufficient; you also need to develop a sense of overall project risk. Overall project risk arises, in part, from all the aggregated activity-level risk data, but it also has a component that is more pervasive, coming from the project as a whole. High-level project risk assessment was discussed in Chapter 3, using methods that required only information available during initial project definition. Those high-level techniques—the risk framework, the risk complexity index, and the risk assessment grid—may also be reviewed and revised based on your project plans.

As the preliminary project planning process approaches completion, you have much more information available, so you can assess project risk more precisely and thoroughly. There are a number of useful tools for assessing project risk, including statistics, metrics, and modeling and simulation tools. Risk assessment using planning data may be used to support decisions, to recommend project changes, and to better control and execute the project.

Some sources of overall project risk include:

- Unrealistic deadlines: High-tech projects often have inappropriately aggressive schedules.

- No or few metrics: Measures used for estimates and risk assessment are inaccurate guesswork.

- "Accidental" project leaders: Projects are led by team members skilled in technical work but with no project management training.

- Inadequate requirements and scope creep: Poor initial definition and insufficient specification change control are far too common.

- Project size: Project risk increases with scale; the larger the project, the more likely it is to fail.

Some of these project-level risks are well represented in the PERIL database, and methods for determining overall project risk can be effective in both lowering their impact and determining a project's potential for trouble. In addition, overall risk assessment scores can:

- Build support for less risky projects and cause cancellation for some higher-risk projects

- Compare projects and help set relative priorities

- Provide data for renegotiating overconstrained project objectives

- Assist in determining required management reserve
- Facilitate effective communication and build awareness of project risk

The techniques, tools, ideas, and metrics described in this chapter address these issues.

Aggregating Risk Responses

One way to assess project risk is to add up all the expected consequences of all of the project risks. This is not just a simple sum; the total is based on the estimated cost (or time) involved multiplied by the risk probability—the "loss times likelihood" aggregated for the whole project.

One way to calculate project-level risk is by accumulating the consequences of the contingency plans. For this, sum the "expected" costs for all the plans—their estimated costs weighted by the risk probabilities. Similarly, you can calculate the total expected project duration increase required by the contingency plans using the same probability estimates. For example, if a contingency plan associated with a risk having a 10 percent probability will cost $10,000 and slip the project by ten days, the contribution to the project totals will be $1,000 and one day (assuming the activity is critical), respectively.

Another way to generate similar data is by using the differences between Program Evaluation and Review Technique (PERT)-based expected estimates and the "most likely" activity estimates. Summing these estimates of both cost and time impact for the project generates an assessment roughly equivalent to the contingency plan data.

Although these sums of expected consequences provide a baseline for overall project risk, they will tend to underestimate total risk, for a number of reasons. First, this analysis assumes that all project risks are independent, with no expected correlation. The assumption of negligible correlation is generally incorrect for real projects; most project risks become much more likely after other risks have occurred. Project activities are linked through common methodologies, staffing, and other factors. Also, projects have a limited staff, so whenever there is a problem, nearly all of the project leader's attention (and much of the project team's) will be on recovery. Distracted by problem solving, the project leader will focus much less on all the other project activities, making additional trouble elsewhere that much more likely.

Another big reason that overall project risk is underestimated using this method is that the weighted sums fail to account for project-level risk factors. Overall project-level risk factors include:

- Inexperience of project manager
- Weak sponsorship
- Reorganization, business changes
- Regulatory issues
- Lack of common practices (life cycle, planning, and so forth)
- Market window or other timing assumptions
- Insufficient risk management
- Ineffective project decomposition resulting in inefficient work flow
- Unfamiliar levels of project effort
- Low project priority
- Poor motivation and team morale
- Weak change management control
- Lack of customer interaction
- Communications issues
- Poorly defined infrastructure
- Inaccurate (or no) metrics

The first two factors on the list are particularly significant. If the project leader has little experience running similar projects successfully, or the project has low priority, or both, you can increment the overall project risk assessment from summing expected impacts by at least 10 percent, for each. Similarly, make adjustments for any of the other factors that may be significant for the project. Even after these adjustments, the risk assessment will still be somewhat conservative, because "unknown" project risk impacts are not included.

Compare the total expected project duration and cost impacts related to project risks with your preliminary baseline plan. Whenever the expected risk impact for either time or cost exceeds 20 percent of your plan, the project is very risky. This project risk data on cost and schedule impact is useful for negotiating project adjustments, justifying management reserve, or both.

Questionnaires and Surveys

Questionnaires and surveys are a well-established technique for assessing project risk. These can range from simple, multiple-response survey forms, to assessments using computer spreadsheets, Web surveys, or other computer tools. However you choose to implement a risk assessment survey, it will be most effective if you customize it for your project.

Many organizations have and use risk surveys. If there is a survey or questionnaire commonly used for projects similar to yours, there may be very little customizing required. Even if you have a format available, it is always a good idea to review the questions and fine-tune the survey before using it. If you do not have a standard survey format, the following example is a generic three-option risk survey that can be adapted for use on a wide range of technical projects.

This survey approach to risk assessment also works best when the number of total questions is kept to a minimum, so review the format you intend to use and select only the questions that are most relevant to your project risks. An effective survey may not need to probe more than about a dozen key areas—never more than about twenty. If you plan to use the following survey, read each of the questions and make changes as needed to reflect your project environment. Strike out any questions that are irrelevant, and add new questions if necessary to reflect risky aspects of your project. Effective surveys are short, so delete any questions that seem less applicable. If you develop your own survey, limit the number of responses for each question to no more than four clearly worded responses.

Once you have finalized the risk assessment questionnaire, the next step is to get input from each member of the core project team. Ask each person who participated in project planning to respond to each question, and then collect his or her data.

Risk survey data is useful in two ways. First, you can analyze all the data to produce an overall assessment of risk. This can be used to compare projects, to set expectations, and to establish risk reserves. Second, you can scan the responses question by question to find particular project-level sources of risk—questions where the responses are consistently in the high-risk category. Risk surveys can be very compelling evidence for needed changes in project infrastructure or other project factors that increase risk. For high-risk factors, ask, "Do we need to settle for this? Is there any reason we should not consider changes that will reduce project risk?" Also investigate any questions with widely divergent responses, and conduct additional discussions to establish common understanding within the project team.

Instructions for the Project Risk Questionnaire

Before using the following qualitative survey, read each one of the questions and make changes as needed to reflect your project environment. Eliminate irrelevant questions and add new ones if necessary to reflect risky aspects of your project. Effective surveys are *short*, so limit the survey to ten to twenty total questions. Section 2, "Technical Risks," normally requires the most intensive editing. The three sections focus on:

1. Project external factors (such as users, budgets, and schedule constraints)

2. Development issues (such as tools, software, and hardware)

3. Project internal factors (such as infrastructure, team cohesion, and communications)

Distribute copies to key project contributors and stakeholders and ask each person to select one of the three choices offered for each question. To interpret the information, assign values of 1 to selections in the first column, 3 to selections in the middle column, and 9 to selections in the third column. Within each section, sum up the responses, then divide each sum by the number of responses tallied. Within each section, use the following evaluation criteria:

- Low risk: 1.00 to 2.50

- Medium risk: 2.51 to 6.00

- High risk: 6.01 to 9.00

Average all questions to determine overall project risk, using the same criteria. Although the results of this kind of survey are qualitative, they can help you to identify sources of high risk in your project. For any section with medium or high risk, consider changes to the project that might lower the risk. Within each section, look for responses in the third column. Brainstorm ideas, tactics, or project changes that could shift the response, reducing overall project risk.

Risk Questionnaire

For each question below, choose the response that best describes your project. If the best response seems to lie between two choices, check the one of the pair further to the right.

Section 1. Project Parameter and Target User Risks

1-1. Scope (project deliverable specification) stability.
☐ Change is unlikely   ☐ Small change is possible   ☐ Changes are likely or definition is incomplete

1-2. Project budget/resources.
☐ Committed and realistic   ☐ Probably sufficient, with margin/reserve defined   ☐ Insufficient or unknown

1-3. Project deadline.
☐ Realistic   ☐ Possible; margin/ reserve defined   ☐ Overly aggressive or unrealistic

1-4. Total project length.
☐ Less than 3 months   ☐ 3–12 months   ☐ More than 12 months

1-5. Total effort-months estimated for the project.
☐ Less than 30   ☐ 30–150   ☐ More than 150

1-6. Peak size of core project team (key contributors critical to the project).
☐ 5 or fewer   ☐ 6–12   ☐ More than 12

1-7. Project manager experience.
☐ Finished more than one comparable project successfully   ☐ Finished a project about the same size successfully   ☐ None, or has done only smaller or shorter projects

1-8. User support for the project objective (scope, schedule, and resources).
☐ Enthusiastic   ☐ General agreement   ☐ Small or unknown

1-9. Prioritization of scope, schedule, and resources (constrained, optimized, accepted).
☐ Known and agreed upon; only one parameter constrained   ☐ Two parameters are constrained, but one is flexible   ☐ No priorities set or all parameters are constrained

1-10. Number of different types of users (market segments).
☐ 1   ☐ 2   ☐ 3 or more

1-11. Project team interaction with users during project.
☐ Frequent and easy   ☐ At project start and end only   ☐ Little or none

1-12. User need for the project deliverable.
☐ Verified as critical to user's business   ☐ Solves a problem; increases user efficiency   ☐ Not validated or unknown

1-13. User enthusiasm generated by the project deliverable at project start.

☐ High ☐ Some ☐ Little or none

1-14. User acceptance criteria for the project deliverable.

☐ Well defined ☐ Nearly complete ☐ Definition incomplete

1-15. User environment and process changes required to use the project deliverable.

☐ None ☐ Minor ☐ Significant

1-16. User interface to operate or use the project deliverable.

☐ Identical to one now in use ☐ Similar to one now in use ☐ New or represents major changes

1-17. Testing planned with actual users of the project deliverable.

☐ Early, using models or prototypes ☐ Mid-project, at least for key subdeliverables ☐ Late in project; Beta test

Section 2. Technical Risks

General

2-1. Complexity of development.

☐ Less than recent successful projects ☐ Similar to recent successful projects ☐ Unknown or beyond recent similar projects

2-2. Development methodology.

☐ Standardized ☐ Similar to other recent projects ☐ Ad hoc, little, or none

2-3. Minimum team experience with critical development technologies.

☐ More than 1 year ☐ 6 months to 1 year ☐ Little or none

2-4. Tools, workstations, and other technical resources.

☐ Established, stable, and well understood ☐ All have been used before ☐ Some new facilities or tools required

2-5. Planned reuse from earlier projects.

☐ More than 75 percent ☐ 40 percent to 75 percent ☐ Little or none

2-6. Early simulation or modeling of deliverable.

☐ Will be done with existing processes ☐ Planned, but will need new processes ☐ Not planned or not possible

2-7. Technical interfaces required (connections of this project's deliverable into a larger system or to deliverables from independent projects).

☐ None (stand-alone) and well understood ☐ Less than 5 and all are to existing systems ☐ More than 5 or more than 1 that is new (parallel development)

Hardware

2-8. Hardware technology incorporated into deliverable.

☐ All established, existing technology

☐ Existing technology in a new application

☐ New, nonexistent, or unknown technology

2-9. Testing.

☐ Will use only existing facilities and processes

☐ Will use existing facilities with new processes

☐ Unknown, or new facilities needed

2-10. Component count.

☐ Number and type similar to recent successful projects

☐ Similar number but some new parts required

☐ Unknown, larger number, or mostly unfamiliar components

2-11. Component sources.

☐ Multiple reliable, managed sources for all key components

☐ More than one identified source for all key components

☐ A single (or unknown) source for at least one key component

2-12. Component availability (lead times, relative to project duration).

☐ Short lead time for all key components

☐ One or more key components with long, but known, lead times

☐ One or more key components with unknown lead time

2-13. Mechanical requirements.

☐ All significant processes used before

☐ Some modification to existing processes required

☐ New, special, or long lead processes needed

Software

2-14. Software required for deliverable.

☐ None or off-the-shelf

☐ Mostly leveraged or reused

☐ Mostly new development

2-15. Software technology.

☐ Very high-level language only (4GL)

☐ Standard language (C++, Java, PERL, COBOL)

☐ New or low-level language (assembler)

2-16. Data structures required.

☐ Not applicable or relational database

☐ Other database or well-defined files

☐ New data files

2-17. Data conversion required.

☐ None required

☐ Minor

☐ Major or unknown

2-18. System complexity.

☐ No new control or algorithm development

☐ Little new control or algorithm development

☐ Significant new or unknown development

2-19. Processing environment of deliverable.

☐ Single system

☐ Multisystem but single site

☐ Distributed, multisite system

Section 3. Structure Risks

3-1. Project sponsorship and management commitment to project objective (scope, schedule, and resources).

☐ Enthusiastic   ☐ Supportive   ☐ Neutral or none

3-2. Project priority.

☐ High   ☐ Moderate   ☐ Low

3-3. Project manager experience.

☐ Success on recent similar project
☐ Managed part of a recent similar project
☐ Low or none on this sort of project

3-4. Project manager authority.

☐ Most project decisions made by PM
☐ Limited decision making and budget control
☐ None; all decisions escalated to others

3-5. Project manager focus.

☐ Full time on this project
☐ More than half time spent managing this project
☐ Less than half time spent managing this project

3-6. Project plan.

☐ Plan is realistic and bottom-up
☐ Plan seems possible and has defined reserve for schedule/budget
☐ Plan is unrealistic or no plan exists

3-7. Project version control and change management.

☐ Well-defined and rigorously used process
☐ Informal but effective process
☐ Little or no change control

3-8. Project life cycle.

☐ Well-defined with clear milestones and phase deliverables
☐ Defined but not rigorously used
☐ No formal life cycle

3-9. Project staffing.

☐ Available and committed
☐ All key people identified
☐ Significant staffing unknowns remain

3-10. Subprojects.

☐ This project is independent of other work
☐ All related subprojects are well defined and coordinated
☐ Related subprojects are loosely coupled or not clearly defined

3-11. Project work environment.

☐ Your site; workplace known and conducive to project progress
☐ Some work must be done in an unknown or poor work environment
☐ Mostly off-site or in a poor work environment

3-12. Staffing commitment.

☐ All key people are full-time   ☐ Mix of full-time and part-time staffing   ☐ All part-time or external staffing

3-13. Team separation.

☐ Collocated   ☐ Single site   ☐ Multisite

3-14. Team enthusiasm for the project.

☐ High   ☐ Adequate   ☐ Reluctant or unknown

3-15. Team compatibility.

☐ Most of team has worked together successfully   ☐ Some of team has worked together before   ☐ New team

3-16. Lowest common manager for members of the core project team.

☐ Project leader   ☐ Up to two levels in same organization   ☐ More than two levels up, or none

3-17. Number of outside organizations or independent projects that this project depends on for inputs, decisions, or approvals.

☐ None   ☐ One other   ☐ More than one

3-18. Project dependence on external subcontractors or suppliers.

☐ Little or none (<10 percent)   ☐ Minor (10–25 percent)   ☐ Significant (>25 percent)

3-19. Quality of subcontractors.

☐ High—with relevant experience (or no subcontractors used)   ☐ Good—solid references from trusted sources   ☐ Doubtful or unknown

3-20. Project communication.

☐ Frequent (weekly) face-to-face status gathering and written reporting   ☐ Sporadic, informal, or long-distance status and reporting   ☐ Ad hoc or none

3-21. Project tracking.

☐ Frequent (weekly) reporting of actual progress vs. plan   ☐ Project leader tracks and and deals with plan exceptions reactively   ☐ Informal or none

3-22. Project documentation.

☐ Accurate, current documents are online for project team   ☐ Current status and schedule are available to project team   ☐ Documents known only to project leader, or none

3-23. Project issue resolution.

☐ Well-defined process; issues tracked and closed promptly   ☐ Informal but effective process   ☐ Issues are not easily resolved in a timely fashion

Project Simulation and Modeling

Most project modeling methodologies may be traced back to the PERT, discussed in Chapter 4 with regard to estimating and in Chapter 7 for analysis of activity risk. Although the applications discussed earlier are useful, they were related to project activities. The original purpose of PERT was to quantify *project* risk, which is the topic of this chapter. There are several approaches to using PERT and other simulation and decision analysis techniques for project risk analysis.

PERT for Project Risk Analysis

PERT was not developed by project managers. It was developed in the late 1950s at the direction of U.S. military to deal with the increasingly common cost and schedule overruns on very large U.S. government projects. The larger the programs became, the bigger their overruns. Generals and admirals are not patient people, and they hate to be kept waiting. Even worse, the U.S. Congress got involved whenever costs exceeded the original estimates, and the generals and admirals liked that even less.

The principal objective of PERT was to use detailed risk data at the activity level to predict project outcomes. For schedule analysis, project teams were requested to provide three estimates: a "most likely" estimate that they believe would be the most common duration for work similar to the activity in question, and two additional estimates that define a range around the "most likely" estimate with a goal of including all realistic possibilities for work duration.

Shown in Figure 9-1, the three PERT time estimates are: At the low end, an "optimistic" estimate, t_o; in the middle somewhere, a "most likely" estimate, t_m; and at the high end, a "pessimistic" estimate, t_p.

Originally, PERT analysis assumed a continuous Beta distribution of outcomes defined by these three parameters, similar to the graph in Figure 9-1. This distribution was chosen because it is relatively easy to work with, and it can skew to the left (as in Figure 9-1) or to the right based on the three estimating parameters. (When the estimates are symmetric, the Beta distribution is equivalent to the normal distribution: the Gaussian, bell-shaped curve.)

Some issues with PERT were discussed in the earlier chapters, but there is an additional issue with PERT for project schedule analysis. PERT uses simple approximations for estimating expected durations and tends to underestimate project risk, especially for projects having more than one critical path. Based on the weighted averages, PERT expected durations can be used to perform standard critical path methodology

Figure 9-1. PERT estimates.

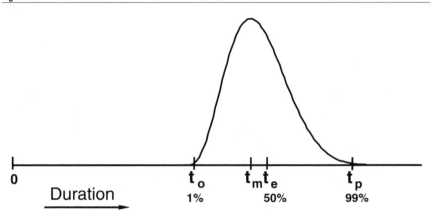

(CPM) analysis. The resulting project will have a longer expected path, but analysis using computer simulation will provide a more useful assessment of overall project schedule impact. Computer simulation uses pseudo-random number generation to calculate a duration within each activity range estimate and repeats the process over and over, each time using new activity duration estimates. CPM is used to calculate the project's critical path for each of these new schedules, and over many repetitions this simulation builds a histogram of the results.

Today's computer simulation and modeling tools for project management offer many alternatives to the Beta distribution. You may use triangular, normal, Poisson, and many other distributions, or even histograms defining discrete estimates with associated probabilities. (For example, you may expect a 50 percent probability that the activity will complete in 15 days, a 40 percent chance that it will complete in 20 days, and a 10 percent chance that it will complete in 30 days. These scenarios are generally based on probabilities associated with known risks for which "worst-case" incremental estimates are made—the five-day slip associated with a contributor who may need to take a week of leave to deal with a family situation, the fifteen-day slip associated with a problem that requires completely redoing of all the work.)

As discussed in Chapter 7, the precise choice of the distribution shape is not terribly important, even for activity-level risk analysis. At the project level, it becomes even less relevant. The reason for this is that the probability density function for the summation of randomly generated samples of most types of statistical distributions (including all the realistic ones) always resembles a normal, bell-shaped, Gaussian distribution. This is due to the central limit theorem, well established by statisticians, and it is why the analysis for a project with a single, dominant critical path always resembles a symmetric, bell-shaped curve. The normal distribution has only two defining parameters, the mean and the variance (the square of the standard deviation). For the Beta distribution the mean and standard deviation are estimated with the formulas referenced earlier:

$$t_e = (t_o + 4t_m + t_p)/6, \text{ where}$$

t_e is the "expected" duration—the mean

t_o is the "optimistic" duration

t_m is the "most likely" duration

t_p is the "pessimistic" duration

and

$$\sigma = (t_p - t_o)/6, \text{ where}$$
σ is the standard deviation

For a project with a single, dominant critical path, the expected duration for the project is the sum of all the expected (mean) durations along the critical path. The standard deviation for such a project, one measure of overall project risk, can be calculated from the estimated standard deviations for the same activities. PERT used the following formulas:

$$t_{proj} = \sum_{i=CP_{first}}^{CP_{last}} t_{e_i} \qquad \sigma_{proj} = \sqrt{\sum_{i=CP_{first}}^{CP_{last}} \sigma_i^2}$$

where:

$$t_{proj} = \text{Expected project duration}$$
$$CP_i = \text{Critical path activity } i$$
$$t_{e_i} = \text{"Expected" } CP \text{ estimate for activity } i$$
$$\sigma_{proj} = \text{Project standard deviation}$$
$$\sigma_i^2 = \text{Variance for } CP \text{ activity } i$$

These formulas work well whenever there is a single critical path, but it gets more complicated when there are additional paths that are roughly equivalent in length to the longest one. When this occurs, the PERT formulas will *underestimate* the expected project duration (it is actually slightly higher) and they will *overestimate* the standard deviation. For such projects, computer simulation will provide better results than the PERT approximations. The main reason for this inaccuracy was introduced in Chapter 4, in the discussion of multiple critical paths. There, the distinction between "Early/On time" and "Late" was a sharp one, with no allowance for degree. Simulation analysis using distributions for each activity creates a spectrum of possible outcomes for the project, but the logic is the same—more failure modes lead to lowered success rates. Because *any* of the parallel critical paths may end up being the longest for each simulated case, each contributes to potential project slippage. The simple project considered in Chapter 4 had the network diagram in Figure 9-2, with one critical path across the top ("A-D-J") and a second critical path along the bottom ("C-H-L").

CPM and PERT analysis, as should be expected, show that there is about one chance in four that the project will complete on time or earlier than the expected durations associated with each of the critical paths. The distribution of possible outcomes for the project has about one-quarter of the left tail below the expected dates, and the peak and right tail are above it, similar to Figure 9-3. The resulting distribution is still basically bell-shaped, but compared with the distributions expected for each critical path, it has a larger mean and is narrower (a smaller standard deviation).

To consider this quantitatively, imagine a project plan using "50 percent" expected estimates that has a single dominant critical path of 100 days (5 months) and a standard deviation of 5 days. (If the distribution of

Figure 9-2. Project with two critical paths.

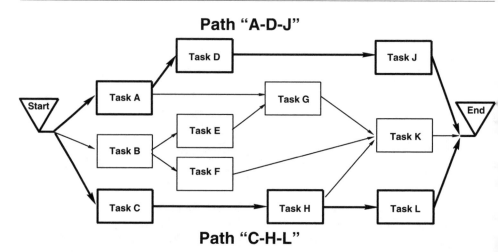

Path "A-D-J"

Path "C-H-L"

Figure 9-3. PERT results.

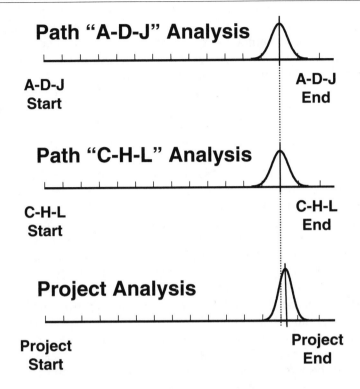

Path "A-D-J" Analysis

A-D-J
Start

A-D-J
End

Path "C-H-L" Analysis

C-H-L
Start

C-H-L
End

Project Analysis

Project
Start

Project
End

expected outcomes is assumed symmetric, the PERT optimistic and pessimistic durations—plus or minus three standard deviations—would be roughly 85 days and 115 days, respectively.) PERT analysis for the project says you should expect the project to complete in five months (or sooner) five times out of ten and in five months plus one week over eight times out of ten (about 5/6 of the time)—pretty good odds.

If a second critical path of 100 days is added to the project with similar estimated risk (a standard deviation of 5 days), the project expectation shifts to 1 chance in 4 of finishing in 5 months or sooner. (Actually, the results of the simulation based on 1,000 runs shows 25.5 percent. The results of simulation almost never exactly match the theoretical answer.) In the simulation, the average expected project duration is a little less than 103 days, and the similar "5/6" point is roughly 107 days. This is a small shift (about one-half week) for the expected project, but it is a very large shift in the probability of meeting the date that is printed on the project Gantt chart—from one chance in two to one chance in four (as expected).

Similar simulations for three and four parallel critical paths of equivalent expected duration and risk produce the results you would expect. For three paths of 100 days, the project expectation falls to one chance in eight of completing on or before 100 days (a simulation of this showed 13 percent) and an expected duration of roughly 104 days. The project with four failure modes has one chance in *sixteen* (6.3 percent in the model), and the mean for the project is a little bit more than 105 days. The resulting histogram for this case is in Figure 9-4, based on 1,000 samples from each of four independent, normally distributed parallel paths with mean of 100 days and a standard deviation of 5 days. (The jagged distribution is typical of simulation output.)

For these multiple–critical path cases, the mean for the distribution increases, and the range compresses somewhat, reducing the expected standard deviation. This is because the upper data boundary for the analysis is unchanged, while each additional critical path will tend to further limit the effective lower boundary. For the case in Figure 9-4, the project duration is always the *longest* of the four, and it becomes less and less likely that this maximum will be near the optimistic possibilities with each added path. Starting with a standard deviation for each path of five days, the resulting distribution for a project with two similar critical paths has a standard deviation of about 4.3 days. For three paths it is just under four days, and with four it falls to roughly 3.5 days, the result from the example in Figure 9-4. The resulting distributions also skew slightly to the left, for the same reasons; the data populating the histograms is being compressed, but only from the *lower* side.

Computer simulation analysis of this sort is most commonly performed for duration estimates, but effort and cost estimates may also be used. As with schedule analysis, three-point cost estimates may be used to generate expected activity costs, and sum them for the entire project. Because all costs are cumulative, the PERT cost analysis formulas analogous to those for time analysis deliver results equivalent to simulation.

Figure 9-4. PERT histogram.

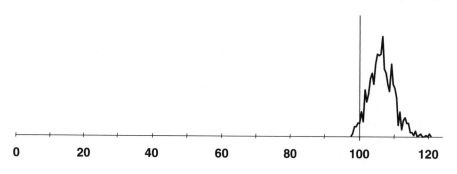

| 0 | 20 | 40 | 60 | 80 | 100 | 120 |

Using Computer Simulation

Simulation analysis uses computers, and for this reason it was impractical before the 1960s (which is why PERT depended on simplified approximations). Once computer-based analysis was practical, Monte Carlo simulation techniques began to be widely used to analyze many kinds of complex systems, including projects. Initially, this sort of analysis was very expensive (and slow), so it was undertaken only for the largest, most costly projects. This is no longer an issue with today's inexpensive desktop systems.

The issue of data quality for schedule risk analysis was also significant in early implementations, and this drawback persists. Generating range estimates remains difficult, especially when defined in terms of "percent tails" as is generally done when describing three-point estimates in the project management literature. Considering that the initial single-point "most likely" estimates are generally not very precise or reliable, the two additional upper and lower boundary estimates are likely to be even worse. Because at least some of the input data is inexact, the "garbage in/garbage out" problem is a standard concern with Monte Carlo schedule analysis.

This, added to the temptation for misuse of the "optimistic" estimates by overeager managers and project sponsors, has made widespread use of computer simulation for technical projects difficult. This is unfortunate, because even if range estimate analysis is applied to suspected critical activities using only manual approximations, it can still provide valuable insight into the level of project risk. Some effective methods require only modest additional effort, and there are a number of techniques, from manual approximations to full computer simulation. A summary of choices appears in the next few sections.

Manual approximations One way to apply these concepts was discussed earlier in this book. If you have a project scheduling tool, and project schedule information has been entered into the database, most of the necessary work is already done. The duration estimates in the database are a reasonable first approximation for the optimistic estimates, or the most likely estimates (or both). To get a sense of project risk, make a copy of the database and enter new estimates for every activity where you have a worst-case or a pessimistic estimate. The Gantt chart based on these longer estimates will display end points for the project that are further out than the original schedule. By associating a normal distribution with these points, a rough approximation of the output for a PERT analysis may be inferred.

The method used for scaling and positioning the bell-shaped curve can vary, but at least half of the distribution ought to fall between the lower "likely" boundary and the upper "pessimistic" limits defined by the end points of the two Gantt charts. Because it is very unlikely that all the things that could go wrong in the project will actually happen, the upper boundary should line up with a point several standard deviations from the mean, far out on the distribution tail. (Keep in mind, however, that this accounts for none of your unknown project risk.) The initial values in the scheduling database are probably somewhere below the mean of the distribution, though the exact placement should be a function of perceived accuracy for your estimates and how conservative or aggressive the estimates are. A histogram similar to Figure 9-5, using the initial plan as about the 20 percent point (roughly one standard deviation below the mean) and the worst-case plan to define the 99 percent point (roughly three standard deviations above the mean), is not a bad first approximation.

If the result represented by Figure 9-5 looks unrealistic, it may improve things if you calculate expected estimates, at least for the riskiest activities on or near a critical path. If you choose to do the arithmetic, a third copy of the database can be populated with expected estimates, defining the mean (the "50 percent" point) for the normal distribution. The cumulative graph of project completion probabilities equivalent to Figure 9-5 looks like Figure 9-6.

Although this sort of analysis is still subjective, the additional effort it requires is small once you generate a preliminary schedule for the project, and it provides valuable insight regarding project risk.

One of the most important things about techniques that make schedule risk visible is that they provide a very concrete, specific result. The results of this analysis will either look reasonable to you or they will seem "wrong." If the results seem realistic, they are probably useful. If they look unrealistic, it usually indicates that additional work and planning is warranted. Improbable-looking results are a good indication that your activity list is incomplete, your estimates are inaccurate, you missed some

Figure 9-5. "PERT" approximation.

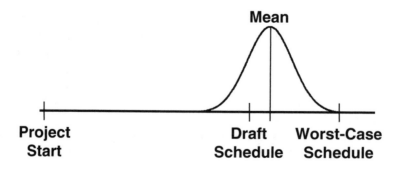

Figure 9-6. "PERT" estimates.

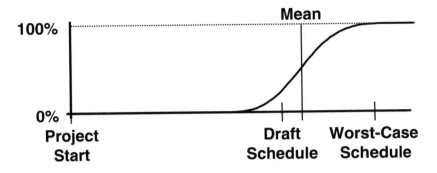

dependencies, you underestimated some risks, or your preliminary plan has some other defect.

Even this "quick and dirty" type of schedule risk approximation provides insight into the thoroughness of your project plan.

Computer spreadsheets The next step up in sophistication involves a computer spreadsheet. This is particularly useful for resource analysis, where everything is cumulative. Spreadsheets are a very easy way to quickly assess three cost (or effort) estimates to derive an overall project-level budget analysis. A list of all the activities in one column with the "most likely" and range estimates in adjacent columns can be readily used to calculate expected estimates and variances for each activity and for the project as a whole. Using the PERT formulas for cost, it is simple to accumulate and evaluate data from all the project activities (not just from the critical path). The sum of all the expected costs and the calculated variance can be used to approximate project budget risk. Assuming a normal distribution centered on the sum of the expected cost estimates with a spread defined by the calculated standard deviation shows the range that may be expected for project cost.

For the reasons outlined earlier, similar duration estimate analysis will underestimate the expected project duration and overestimate the standard deviation, but it could be useful for a simple or small project.

Computer scheduling tools True Monte Carlo simulation analysis capability is not common in most computer-based scheduling tools, and what is available to support three-point activity duration estimates tends to be implemented in quirky and mysterious ways. It is impractical to list all the available scheduling tools here, so the following discussion characterizes them generically.

There are dozens of such tools available for project scheduling, ranging from minimalist products that implement rudimentary activity analysis to high-end, Web-enabled enterprise applications. Often, families of software offering a range of capabilities are sold by the same company. Almost any of these tools may be used for determining the project critical path, but schedule risk analysis using most of these tools, even some fairly expensive ones, often requires the manual processes discussed already or purchase of additional, specialized software (more on this specialized software follows). In general, scheduling tools are set up for schedule analysis using single-point estimates to determine critical path, and three-point estimate analysis requires several copies of the project data (or a scratch pad version for "what if?" analysis) to analyze potential schedule variance. Some products do provide for entry of three-point estimates and some rudimentary analysis, but this is typically based on calculations (as with PERT), not simulation.

Some high-end project management tools, which are both more capable and more costly than the more ubiquitous midrange tools, do provide integrated Monte Carlo simulation analysis, either built-in or as optional capabilities. Even with the high-end tools, though, schedule simulation analysis requires an experienced project planner with a solid understanding of the process.

Computer simulation tools Tools that provide true Monte Carlo simulation functionality are of two types, designed either to be integrated with a computer scheduling tool or for stand-alone analysis. Again, there are many options available in both of these categories.

There are quite a few applications designed to provide simulation-based risk analysis that either integrate into high-end tools or "bolt on" to midrange scheduling packages. If such an add-on capability is available for the software you are using, simulation analysis can be done without having to reenter or convert any of your project data. With the stand-alone software, project information must be input a second time or exported. Unless you also need to do some nonproject simulation analysis, Monte Carlo simulation tools designed to interface directly with scheduling applications are generally a less expensive option.

In addition to products specifically designed for Monte Carlo schedule analysis, there are also general-purpose simulation applications that could be used, including decision support software and general-purpose statistical analysis software. For the truly masochistic, it is even possible to do Monte Carlo simulations using only a spreadsheet—Microsoft Excel includes functions for generating random samples from various distribution types as well as statistical analysis functions for interpreting the data.

Whatever option you choose, there are trade-offs. Some techniques are quick and relatively easy to implement, providing subjective but still useful insight into project risk. Other, full-function Monte Carlo methods offer very real risk management benefits, but they also carry costs, including investment in software, generation of more data, and increased effort. Before deciding to embark on an elaborate project Monte Carlo simulation analysis, especially the first time, carefully consider the costs and added complexity.

A primary benefit of any of this risk analysis is the graphic and visible contrast between the deterministic-looking schedule generated by point-estimate critical path methods, and the range of possible end points (and associated probabilities) that emerge from these methods. The illusion of certainty fostered by single-estimate Gantt charts is inconsistent with the actual risk present in technical projects. The visible variation possible in a project is a good antidote for excessive project optimism.

Also, keep in mind that precise-looking output may create an illusion of precision. The accuracy of the output generated by these methods can never be any better than that of the *least* precise inputs. Rounding the results off to whole days is about the best you can expect, yet results with many decimal places are reported, especially by Monte Carlo simulation software. This is particularly ironic considering the quality of typical project input data. Generating useful estimates and the effort of collecting, entering, and interpreting this risk information represents quite a bit of work.

In project environments that currently lack systematic project-level risk analysis, it may be prudent to begin with a modest manual approximation effort on a few projects, and expand as necessary for future projects.

Analysis of Scale

Quantitative project analysis using all the preceding techniques, with either computer tools or manual methods, is based on details of the project work—activities, worst cases, resource issues, and other planning data. It is also possible to assess risk based on the overall size of the project, because the overall level of effort is another important risk factor. Projects only 20 percent larger than previous work represent significant risk.

Analysis of project scale is based on the overall effort in the project plan. Projects fall into three categories—low risk, normal risk, and high risk—based on the anticipated effort compared with earlier, successful projects. Scale assessment begins by accumulating the data from the bottom-up project plan to determine total project effort, measured in a suitable unit such as "effort-months." The calculated project scale can then be compared with the effort actually used on several recent, similar projects. In selecting comparison projects, look for work that had similar deliverables, timing, and staffing so the comparison will be as valid as possible. If the data for the other projects is not in the form you need, do a rough estimate using staffing levels and project duration. If there were periods in the comparison projects where significant overtime was used, especially at the end, account for that effort as well. The numbers generated do not need to be precise, but they do need to fairly represent the amount of overall effort actually required to complete the comparison projects.

Using the total of planned effort-months for your project and an average from the comparison projects, determine the risk:

- Low risk: Less than 60 percent of the average
- Normal risk: Between 60 percent and 120 percent of the average
- High risk: Greater than 120 percent of the average

These ranges center on 90 percent rather than 100 percent because the comparison is between actual past project data, which includes all changes and risks that occurred, and the current project plans, which do not. Risk arises from other factors in addition to size, so consider raising the risk assessment one category if:

- The schedule is significantly compressed
- The project requires new technology
- 40 percent of the project resources are either external or unknown

Project Appraisal

Analysis of project scale can be taken a further step, both to validate the project plan and to get a more precise estimate of risk. The technique requires an "appraisal," similar to the process used whenever you need to know the value of something, such as a piece of property or jewelry, but you do not want to sell it to find out. Value appraisals are based on the recent sale of several similar items, with appropriate additions and deductions to account for small differences. If you want to know the value of your home, an appraiser examines it and finds descriptions of several comparable homes recently sold nearby. If the comparison home has an extra bathroom, a small deduction is made to its purchase price; if your house has a larger, more modern kitchen, the appraiser makes a small positive adjustment. The process continues, using at least two other homes, until all factors normally included are assessed. The average adjusted price that results is taken to be the value of your home—the current price for which you could probably sell it.

The same process can be applied to projects, because you face a similar situation. You would like to know how much effort a project will require, but you cannot wait until all the work is done to find out. The comparisons in this case are two or three recently completed similar projects, for which you can ascertain the number of effort-months that were required for each. (This starts with the same data the analysis of scale technique uses.)

From your bottom-up plan, calculate the number of effort-months your project is expected to take. The current project can be compared to the comparison projects, using a list of factors germane to your work. Factors relevant to the scope, schedule, and resources for the projects can be compared, as in Figure 9-7 (which was quickly assembled using a computer spreadsheet).

One goal of this technique is to find comparison projects that are as similar as possible, so the adjustments will be small and the appraisal

Figure 9-7. Project appraisal.

| Project : Zinfandel | | Effort-Months (Planned) | | | 100 | |

		Project A		Project B		Project C	
		Comparison	Change in Effort	Comparison	Change in Effort	Comparison	Change in Effort
Effort-Months (Actual)		110		80		107	
Scope:	Functionality	Similar	0	3%	2.4	Similar	0.0
	Usability	–3%	–3.3	Similar	0	Similar	0.0
	Reliability	Similar	0	3%	2.4	Similar	0.0
	Performance	5%	5.5	Similar	0	–3%	–3.2
	Supportability	Similar	0	Similar	0	Similar	0.0
	Technology	–5%	–5.5	5%	4	–3%	–3.2
Resources:	Maximum Staff	–3%	–3.3	3%	2.4	–5%	–5.4
	Control	Similar	0	Similar	0	Similar	0.0
	Staff Experience	3%	3.3	Similar	0	Similar	0.0
	Geographical Separation	Similar	0	5%	4	Similar	0.0
Schedule:	Total Length	–5%	–5.5	Similar	0	3%	3.2
	Net adjustments	–8%	–8.8	19%	15.2	–8%	–8.6
	Indicated effort-months		101.2		95.2		98.4

Mean effort-months   98.3

can be as accurate as possible. If a factor seems "similar," no adjustment is made. When there are differences, adjust conservatively, such as:

- Small differences: Plus or minus 2 to 5 percent
- Larger differences: Plus or minus 7 to 10 percent

The adjustments are *positive* if the current project has the higher risk and *negative* if the comparison project seems more challenging.

The first thing you can use a project appraisal for is to test whether your preliminary plan is realistic. Whenever the adjusted comparison projects average to a higher number of effort-months than your current planning shows, your plan is almost certainly missing something. Whenever the appraisal indicates a difference greater than about 10 percent compared with the bottom-up planning, work to understand why. What have you overlooked? Where are your estimates too optimistic? What activities have you not captured? Also, compare the project appraisal effort-month estimate with the resource goal in the original project objective. A project appraisal also provides early warning of potential budget problems.

One reason project appraisals will generally be larger than the corresponding plan is because of risk. The finished projects include the consequences of all risks, including those that were invisible early in the work. The current project planning includes data on only the known risks for which you have incorporated risk prevention strategies. At least part of the difference between your plan and an appraisal is due to the comparison projects' "unknown" risks, contingency plans, and other risk recovery efforts.

In addition to plan validation, project appraisals are useful in project-level risk management. Whenever there is a major difference between the parameters of the planned project and the goals stated in the project objective, the appraisal shows why convincingly and in a very concise format.

A project appraisal is also a very effective way to initiate discussion with your project sponsor of options, trade-offs, and changes required for overconstrained projects, which is addressed in Chapter 10.

Project Metrics

Project measurement is essential to risk management. It also provides the historical basis for other project planning and management processes such as estimation, scheduling, controlling, and resource planning. Metrics drive behavior, so selecting appropriate factors to measure can have a significant effect on motivation and project progress.

HP founder Bill Hewlett was fond of saying, "What gets measured gets done." Metrics provide the information needed to improve processes and to detect when it is time to modify or replace an existing process. Established metrics also are the foundation of project tracking, establishing the baseline for measuring progress. Defining, implementing, and interpreting a system of ongoing measures is not difficult, so it is unfortunate that on many projects it either is not done at all or is done poorly.

Establishing Metrics

Before deciding what to measure, carefully define the behavior you want and determine what measurements will be most likely to encourage that behavior. Next, establish a baseline by collecting enough data to determine current performance for what you plan to measure. Going forward, you can use metrics to detect changes, trigger process improvements, evaluate process modifications, and make performance and progress visible.

The process begins with defining the results or behavior you desire. For metrics in support of better project risk management, a typical goal might be "Reduce unanticipated project effort" or "Improve the accuracy of project estimates." Consider what you might be able to measure that relates to the desired outcome. For unanticipated project effort, you might measure "Total effort actually consumed by the project versus effort planned." For estimation accuracy, a possible metric might be "Cumulative difference between project estimates and project results, as measured at the project conclusion."

Metrics are of three basic types: *predictive, diagnostic,* and *retrospective.* An effective system of metrics will generally include measures of more than one type, providing for good balance.

Predictive metrics use current information to provide insight into future conditions. Because predictive metrics are based on speculative rather than empirical data, they are typically the least reliable of the three types. Predictive metrics include the initial assessment of project "return on investment," the output from the quantitative risk management tools, and most other measurements based on planning data.

Diagnostic metrics are designed to provide current information about a system. Based on the latest data, they assess the state of a running process and may detect anomalies or forecast future problems. The unanticipated effort metric suggested before is based on earned value, a project metric discussed below.

Retrospective metrics report after the fact on how the process worked. Backward-looking metrics report on the overall health of the process and are useful in tracking trends. Retrospective metrics can be used to calibrate and improve the accuracy of corresponding predictive metrics for subsequent projects.

Measuring Projects

The following section includes a number of useful project metrics. No project will need to collect all of them, but one or more measurements of each type of metric, collected and evaluated for all projects in an organization, can significantly improve the planning and risk management on future projects. These metrics relate directly to projects and project management. A discussion of additional metrics, related to financial measures, follows this section.

When implementing any set of metrics, you need to spend some time collecting data to validate a baseline for the measurements before you make any decisions or changes. Until you have a validated baseline, measurements will be hard to interpret, and you will not be able to determine the effects of process modifications that you make. There is more discussion on selecting and using metrics in Chapter 10.

Predictive project metrics Most predictive project metrics relate to factors that can be calculated using data from your project plan. These metrics are fairly easy to define and calculate, and they can be validated against corresponding actual data at the project close. Over time, the goal for each of these should be to drive the predictive measures and the retrospective results into closer and closer agreement. Measurement baselines are set using project goals and planning data.

Predictive project metrics serve as a distant early warning system for project risk. These metrics use forecast information, normally assessed in the early stages of work, to make unrealistic assumptions, significant potential problems, and other project risk sources visible. Because they are primarily based on speculative rather than empirical data, predictive metrics are generally the least precise of the three types. Predictive project measures support risk management in a number of ways:

- Determining project scale
- Identifying the need for risk mitigation and other project plan revisions
- Determining situations that require contingency planning
- Justifying schedule and budget reserves
- Supporting project portfolio decisions and validating relative project priorities

Predictive metrics are useful in helping you anticipate potential project problems. One method of doing this is to identify any of these predictive metrics that is significantly larger than typically measured for past, successful projects—a variance of 15 to 20 percent represents significant project risk. A second use for these metrics is to correlate them with other project properties. After measuring factors such as unanticipated effort, unforeseen risks, and project delays for ten or more projects, some of these factors may reveal sufficient correlation to predict future risks with fair accuracy. Predictive project metrics include:

Scope and Scale Risk

- Project complexity (interfaces, algorithmic assessments, technical or architecture analysis)
- Volume of expected changes
- Size-based deliverable analysis (component counts, number of major deliverables, lines of noncommented code, blocks on system diagrams)
- Number of planned activities

Schedule Risk

- Project duration (elapsed calendar time)
- Total length (sum of all activity durations if executed sequentially)
- Logical length (maximum number of activities on a single network path)
- Logical width (maximum number of parallel paths)
- Activity duration estimates compared with worst-case duration estimates
- Number of critical (or near-critical) paths in project network
- Logical project complexity (the ratio of activity dependencies to activities)
- Maximum number of predecessors for any milestone
- Total number of external predecessor dependencies
- Project independence (ratio of internal dependencies to all dependencies)
- Total float (sum of total project activity float)
- Project density (ratio of total length to total length plus total float)

Resource Risk

- Total effort (sum of all activity effort estimates)
- Total cost (budget at completion)
- Staff size (full-time equivalent and/or total individuals)
- Activity cost (or effort) estimates compared with worst-case resource estimates
- Number of unidentified activity owners
- Number of staff not yet assigned or hired
- Number of activity owners with no identified backup
- Expected staff turnover
- Number of geographically separate sites

Financial Risk—Expected Return on Investment (ROI)

- Payback analysis
- Net present value
- Internal rate of return

General Risk

- Number of identified risks in the risk register
- Quantitative (and qualitative) risk assessments
- Adjusted total effort (project appraisal: comparing baseline plan with completed similar projects, adjusting for significant differences)
- Survey-based risk assessment (summarized risk data collected from project staff, using selected assessment questions)
- Aggregated overall schedule risk (or aggregated worst-case duration estimates)
- Aggregated resource risk (or aggregated worst-case cost estimates)

Diagnostic project metrics Diagnostic metrics are based on measurements taken throughout the project, and they are used to detect adverse project variances and project problems either in advance or as soon as is practical. Measurement baselines are generally set using a combination of stated goals and historical data from earlier projects. Diagnostic metrics are comparative measures, either trend-oriented (comparing the current measure with earlier measures) or prediction-oriented (comparing measurements with corresponding predictions, generally based on planning).

Based on project status information, diagnostic project metrics assess the current state of an ongoing project. Risk-related uses include:

- Triggering risk responses and other adaptive actions
- Assessing the impact of project changes
- Providing early warning for potential future problems
- Determining the need to update contingency plans or develop new ones
- Deciding when to modify (or cancel) projects

A number of diagnostic project metrics relate to the concept of earned value management (EVM). These metrics are listed with resource metrics below and described following this list of typical diagnostic project metrics:

Scope Risk
- Results of tests, inspections, reviews, and walkthroughs
- Number and magnitude of approved scope changes

Schedule Risk
- Key milestones missed
- Critical path activity slippage
- Cumulative project slippage
- Number of added activities
- Early activity completions
- Activity closure index: the ratio of activities closed in the project so far to the number expected

Resource Risk
- Excess consumption of effort or funds
- Amount of unplanned overtime
- Earned value (EV): a running accumulation of the costs that were planned for every project activity that is currently complete
- Actual cost (AC): a running accumulation of the actual costs for every project activity that is currently complete
- Planned value (PV): a running accumulation of the planned costs for every project activity that was expected to be complete up to the current time

- Cost performance index (CPI): the ratio of earned value to actual cost
- Schedule performance index (SPI): the ratio of earned value to planned value
- Cost variance (CV): the difference between earned value and actual cost, a measurement of how much the project is over or under budget
- Schedule variance (SV): the difference between earned value and planned value

Overall Risk

- Risks added after project baseline setting
- Issues opened and closed
- Communication metrics, such as volumes of e-mail and voicemail
- The number of unanticipated project meetings
- Impact on other projects
- Risk closure index (ratio of risks closed in a project divided by an expected number based on history)

Many of the metrics listed here are self-explanatory, and many routinely emerge from status reporting. Exceptions include the EVM metrics—EV, AC, PV, CV, SV, CPI, SPI, and the rest of the EVM alphabet soup. The definitions make them seem complex, but they really are not that complicated. EVM is about determining whether the project is progressing as planned, and it begins with allocating a portion of the project budget to each planned project activity. The sum of all these allocated bits of funding must exactly equal 100 percent of the project staffing budget. As the project executes, EVM collects data on actual costs and actual timing for all completed activities so that the various metrics, ratios, and differences may be calculated. The definitions for these diagnostic metrics are all stated in financial terms here, but mathematics of EVM are identical for equivalent metrics that are based on effort data, and a parallel set of metrics defined this may be substituted. The terminology for EVM has changed periodically, but the basic concepts have not.

The basic principle of EVM is that every project has two budgets and two schedules. It starts with one of each, making up the baseline plan. As the project executes, another schedule and another budget emerge from actual project progress data.

The combination of planned funding and timing may be graphed as a curve starting at zero and meandering up and to the right until it reaches the data point that represents the scheduled end of the project and the cumulative funding for the project. (The metric for the cumulative budget is Budget at Completion, marked as BAC in Figure 9-8.) The expected funding consumption curve describes the PV metric, also called the budgeted cost of work scheduled (BCWS). The combination of actual spending and actual activity completion may be plotted on the same graph as the AC metric, also called the actual cost of work performed (ACWP). These two metrics may be calculated at any point in the project, and if the project is exactly on schedule they may be expected to match. If they do not, something is off track. Because PV and AC are based on different schedules and budgets, you cannot really tell whether there is a timing problem, a spending problem, or some combination. To unravel this, we can use EV, also known as the budgeted cost of work performed (BCWP). As project work is completed, EV accumulates the cost estimates associated with the work, and it may also be plotted on the graph in Figure 9-8. These three basic EVM metrics are presented in the following table.

		Budgets	
		Planned Expenses	Actual Expenses
Schedules	Planned Schedule	Planned Value (PV)	
	Actual Schedule	Earned Value (EV)	Actual Cost (AC)

Figure 9-8. Selected earned value measurement metrics.

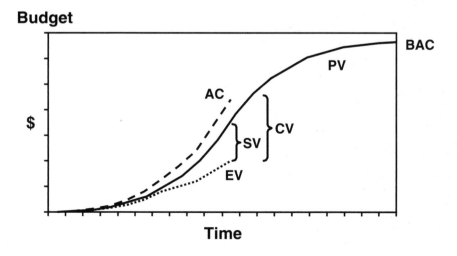

As a project progresses, both PV and AC may be compared with EV. Any difference between AC and EV—in the figure this is shown as CV, or cost variance—must be due to a spending issue, because the metrics are based on the same schedule. Similarly, any difference between PV and EV—SV, or schedule variance on the graph—has to be due to a timing problem. There are indices and other more complex derived metrics for EVM, but all are based on the fundamental three: EV, PV, and AC.

There is much discussion concerning the value of EVM for technical projects. It can represent quite a bit of overhead, and for many types of technical projects, tracking data at the level required by EVM is thought to be overkill. EVM typically can accurately predict project overrun at the point where 15 percent of the project budget is consumed.

If the metrics for EVM seem impractical for your projects, the related alternative of activity closure index (listed with the schedule metrics) provides similar diagnostic information based on the higher granularity of whole activities. This metric provides similar information with a lot less effort. Activity closure rate is less precise, but even it will accurately spot an overrun trend well before the project halfway point.

Retrospective project metrics Retrospective metrics determine how well a process worked after it completes. They are the project environment's rear-view mirror. Measurement baselines are based on history, and these metrics are most useful for longer-term process improvement. Use retrospective project metrics to:

- Track trends
- Validate methods used for predictive metrics
- Identify recurring sources of risk
- Set standards for reserves (schedule and/or budget)
- Determine empirical expectations for "unknown" project risk
- Decide when to improve or replace current project processes

Retrospective project metrics include:

Scope Risk
- Number of accepted changes
- Number of defects (number, severity)
- Actual "size" of project deliverable analysis (components, lines of noncommented code, system interfaces)
- Performance of deliverables compared to project objectives

Schedule Risk

- Actual project duration compared to planned schedule
- Number of new unplanned activities
- Number of missed major milestones
- Assessment of duration estimation accuracy

Resource Risk

- Actual project budget compared to planned budget
- Total project effort
- Cumulative overtime
- Assessment of effort estimation accuracy
- Life-cycle effort percentages by project phase
- Added staff
- Staff turnover
- Performance to standard estimates for standardized project activities
- Variances in travel, communications, equipment, outsourcing, or other expense subcategories

Overall Risk

- Late project defect correction effort as a percentage of total effort
- Number of project risks encountered
- Project issues tracked and closed
- Actual measured ROI

Financial Metrics

Project risk extends beyond the normal limits of project management, and project teams must consider and do what they can to manage risks that are not strictly "project management." There are a number of methods and principles used to develop predictive metrics that relate to the broad concept of ROI, and an understanding of these is essential to many types of technical projects. As discussed in Chapter 3 with market risks, ROI analysis falls only partially within project management's traditional boundaries. Each of the several ways to measure ROI comes with benefits, drawbacks, and challenges.

The time value of money The foundation of most ROI metrics is the concept of the time value of money. This is the idea that a quantity of money today is worth more than the same quantity of money at some time in the future. How much more depends on a rate of interest (or discount rate) and the amount of time. The formula for this is:

$$PV = FV/(1 + i)^n, \text{ where}$$
PV is present value
FV is future value
i is the periodic interest rate
n is the number of periods

If the interest rate is 5 percent per year (.05) and the time is one year, $1 today is equivalent to $1.05 in the future.

Payback analysis Even armed with the time value of money formula, it is rarely easy to determine the worth of any complex investment with precision, and this is especially true for investments in projects. Project analysis involves many (perhaps hundreds) of parameters and values, multiple periods, and possibly several interest rates. Estimating all of this data, particularly the value of the project deliverable after the completion of the project, can be very difficult.

The most basic ROI model for projects is simple payback analysis, which assumes no time value for money (equivalent to an interest rate of zero). This type of ROI metric has many names, including breakeven time, payback period, or the "return map." Payback analysis adds up all expected project expenses and then proceeds to add expected revenues, profits, or accrued benefits, period by period, until the value of the benefits balances the costs. As projects rarely generate benefits before completion, the cumulative financials swing heavily negative, and it takes many periods after the revenues and benefits begin to reach "break-even."

The project in the graph in Figure 9-9 runs for about five months, with a budget of almost $500,000. It takes another six months, roughly, to generate returns equal to the project's expenses. Simple payback analysis works fairly well for comparing similar-length projects to find the one (or ones) that recovers its costs most rapidly. It has the advantage of simplicity, using predictive project cost metrics for the expense data and sales or other revenue forecasts for the rest.

Refining simple payback analysis to incorporate interest (or discount) rates is not difficult. The first step is to determine an appropriate interest rate. Some analyses use the prevailing cost of borrowing money, others use a rate of interest available from external investments, and still others use rates based on business targets. The rate of interest selected can make a significant difference when evaluating ROI metrics.

Figure 9-9. Simple payback analysis.

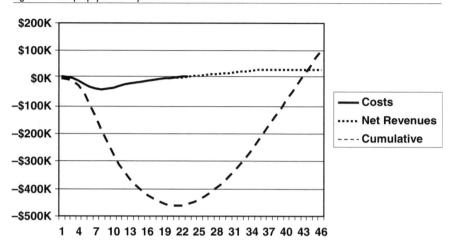

Once an appropriate interest rate is selected, each of the expense and revenue estimates can be discounted back to an equivalent present value before it is summed. The discounted payback or break-even point again occurs when the sum, in this case the cumulative present value, reaches zero. For a nonzero interest rate, the amount of time required for payback will be significantly longer than with the simple analysis, since the farther in the future the revenues are generated, the less they contribute because of the time value of money. Discounted payback analysis is still relatively easy to evaluate, and it is more suitable for comparing projects that have different durations.

Payback analysis, with and without consideration of the time value of money, is often criticized for being too short-term. These metrics determine only the time required to recover the initial investment. They do not consider any benefits that might occur following the break-even point, so a project that breaks even quickly and then generates no further benefits would rank higher than a project that takes longer to return the investment but represents a much longer, larger stream of subsequent revenues or benefits.

Net present value Total net present value (NPV) is another method to measure project ROI. NPV follows the same process as the discounted payback analysis, but it does not stop at the break-even point. NPV includes all the costs and all the anticipated benefits throughout the expected life of the project deliverable. Once all the project costs and returns have been estimated and discounted to the present, the sum represents the total present value for the project. This total NPV can be used to compare possible projects, even projects with very different financial profiles and time scales, based on all expected project benefits.

Total NPV effectively determines the overall expected return for a project, but it tends to favor large projects over smaller ones, without regard to other factors. A related idea for comparing projects normalizes their financial magnitudes by calculating a profitability index (PI). The PI is a ratio, the sum of all the discounted revenues divided by the sum of all the discounted costs. PI is always greater than one for projects that have a positive NPV, and the higher the PI is above one, the more profitable the project is expected to be.

Even though these metrics require additional data—estimates of the revenues or benefits throughout the useful life of the deliverable—they are still relatively easy to evaluate.

Internal rate of return Another way to contrast projects of different sizes is to calculate an internal rate of return (IRR). IRR uses the same estimates for costs and returns required to calculate total net present value, but instead of assuming an interest rate and calculating the present value for the project, IRR sets the present value equal to zero and then solves for the required interest rate. Mathematically, IRR is the most complex ROI metric, as it must be determined using iteration and "trial and error." For sufficiently complicated cash flows, there may even be several values possible for IRR (this occurs only if there are several reversals of sign in the cash flows, so it rarely happens in project analysis). These days, using a computer (or even a financial calculator) makes determining IRR fairly straightforward, if good estimates for costs and revenues are available. For each project, the interest rate you calculate shows how effective the project is expected to be as an investment.

ROI estimates All of these ROI methods are attempts to determine the "goodness" of financial investments, in this case, projects. Theoretically, any of these methods is an effective way to select a few promising projects out of many possibilities, or to compare projects with other investment opportunities.

Because of their differing assumptions, these methods may generate inconsistent ranking results for a list of potential projects, but this is rarely the biggest issue with ROI metrics. In most cases the more fundamental problem is with input data. Each of these methods generates a precise numeric result for a given project, based on the input data. For many projects, this information comes from two sources that are historically not very reliable: project planning data and sales forecasts. Project planning data can be made more accurate over time using metrics and adjustments for risk, at least in theory. Unfortunately, project ROI calculations are generally made before much planning is done, when the project cost data is still based on vague information or guesswork, or the estimates come from top-down budget goals that are not correlated with planning at all.

Estimates of financial return are an even larger problem. These estimates are not only usually very uncertain (based on sales projections or other speculative forecasts), they are also much larger numbers, so they are more significant in the calculations. For product development projects, in many cases revenue estimates are higher than costs by an order of magnitude or more, so even small estimating errors can result in large ROI variances.

ROI metrics can be very accurate and useful when calculated retrospectively using historical data, long after projects have completed. The predictive value of ROI measures calculated in advance of projects can never be any more trustworthy than the input data, so a great deal of variation can occur.

Key Ideas for Project Risk Analysis

- Survey contributors and stakeholders for risk assessments.
- Use worst-case estimates, contingency plan data, or Monte Carlo simulation analysis to determine project uncertainty.
- Estimate project scale in effort-months.
- Establish and use project metrics.

Panama Canal: Overall Risks (1907)

When John Stevens first arrived in Panama, he found a lack of progress and an even greater lack of enthusiasm. He commented, "There are three diseases in Panama. They are yellow fever, malaria, and cold feet; and the greatest of these is cold feet." For the first two, he set Dr. William Gorgas to work, and these risks were soon all but eliminated from the project.

For the "cold feet," Stevens himself provided the cure. His intense planning effort and thorough analysis converted the seemingly impossible into small, realistic steps that showed that the work was feasible; the ways and means for getting the work done were documented and credible. Even though there were still many specific problems and risks on the project, Stevens had demonstrated that the overall project was truly possible. This was quite a turnaround from John Wallace's belief that the canal venture was a huge mistake.

With Stevens's plan, nearly every part of the job relied on techniques that were in use elsewhere, and almost all the work required had been done somewhere before. Project funding was guaranteed by the U.S. government. There were thousands of people able, and very willing, to work on the project, so labor was never an issue. The rights and other legal needs were not a problem, especially after Theodore Roosevelt had manipulated the politics in both the United States and in Panama to secure them. What continued to make the canal project exceptional was its enormous scale. As Stevens said, "There is no element of mystery involved, the problem is one of magnitude and not miracles."

Planning and a credible understanding of overall project risk are what convert the need for magic and miracles (which no one can confidently promise to deliver) into the merely difficult. Projects that are seen as difficult but *possible* are the ones that succeed; a belief that a project can be completed is an important factor in how hard and how well people work. When it looks as though miracles will be necessary, people tend to give up, and their skepticism may very well make the project impossible.

10

Managing Project Risk

"Let us never negotiate out of fear, but let us never fear to negotiate."
—JOHN F. KENNEDY

It is rare to encounter a project where everyone involved feels things are adequately under control. There never seems to be enough time, funding and staffing seem too low, and there are generally a few technical challenges yet to figure out. Managing project-level risk involves understanding all of this well enough early in your work to set realistic project expectations and, if necessary, to negotiate at least minor changes to the project. Although *completely* dealing with project risks and issues is never possible, shifting things to minimize the worst problems may be sufficient. Once a project is seen to be feasible, hard work, with a bit of inspiration, cleverness, and luck, will often be enough to let you close the rest of the gap.

Managing project risk begins with the risk assessments and plans of the preceding chapters. This chapter builds on that foundation, discussing how to effectively use risk and project data to influence necessary changes, to clearly communicate project risks, and to adopt ongoing risk management practices that detect new risks promptly and minimize problems throughout the project.

Project Documentation Requirements

One of the only things less interesting than assembling project documentation is reading a lengthy description of what it "must" include. Because technical projects come in all sizes, shapes, durations, and complexities, the requirements for project documentation—the written descriptions for project deliverables, plans, and other relevant information—vary a great deal. Whether the documentation is lengthy and elaborate or fairly informal, it serves as your basis for project execution and control. Project teams that fail to put adequate documentation in place know too little about their projects and they carry more risk. In addition, when you lack data, you have a much lower chance of influencing necessary changes to your project, because your proposals and negotiations will not have enough facts supporting them. Although it is certainly possible to overinvest in project documentation, it is far more common on technical projects to do too little. Prudent project risk management tends to err on the side of capturing more, rather than less, data.

Project documentation is most effective when it is available in "layers." At the most detailed level, there is the thorough, everything-including-the-kitchen-sink version of the project plan, needed by the project team. For others, such lengthy detail is neither necessary nor appropriate. You also need clear, summary-level documentation that can be used in discussions with sponsors, stakeholders, and others who are less involved with the project but will take part in project discussions, negotiations, decisions, escalations, problem solving, and other project communication.

Thorough project documentation created during your planning and risk assessment gives you a foundation for validating your project plan. It also provides the leverage you need to negotiate project modifications when it is necessary to transform an overconstrained project into one that is more realistic. The ultimate goal of this process is to set your project plan of record consistent with both the project objective and a realistic plan. Ongoing project risk management also requires periodic plan reviews and an effective change management process, and these also rely on thorough documentation.

Project Documents

Project documents fall into three categories: definition documents, planning documents, and periodic project communications.

Definition documents are generally assembled earliest. They include:

- A high-level project overview
- A scope statement and a summary of the project objective
- The project proposal (or "data sheet," project charter, or whatever the overall description of the project may be called)

- Project stakeholder and sponsor analysis
- Project staffing and organization information
- Significant assumptions and project constraints
- Methodologies or life cycles to be used
- Risk management plans
- Process documentation for managing specification changes

Additional necessary documentation may include detailed specification documents, a high-level project financial analysis, the project budget, detailed release or acceptance specifications, any market research reports or user investigations, and any other specific project data required by your organization.

Planning documentation is also assembled in the earliest project stages, but it may be modified and augmented throughout the project as a result of approved changes or new information. Typical project planning documents are:

- The project work breakdown structure (WBS) and activity list
- The project schedule
- The project resource plan
- Functional plans (for quality, support, test, and other aspects)
- The risk register and management plan
- Planning assumptions and constraints

Periodic project communications accumulate throughout the project. They will include:

- Status reports
- Meeting minutes
- Specification change notices
- Project review
- Phase transition or stage-gate reports
- Interim and final project retrospective reports and "lessons learned"

Project documents are most useful when they have a consistent, easy-to-read format, so you should adopt an appropriate existing format (or define one) and stick with it. Especially for lengthy documents, use a format that begins with a high-level summary or abstract that is no longer than half a page of text. It is always risky to bury important information on page 43 of a project report. For each project document, identify an owner (often the project leader) who will be responsible for creation, maintenance, and distribution. Define how and when document changes can or should be made. When there are approved changes, you need to assign responsibility for providing up-to-date documents and for marking old versions obsolete.

Documents have value only if the people who need them have ready access to them. Storing documents online (with appropriate access security) is an effective way to ensure that all team members will have access to and will be working from the same information. Establish a centralized location for any paper documents (or several, for geographically separated teams) that is well known and easily accessed. Whether your project documents are in a notebook, in a file cabinet, or on a server, keep them available and current.

Project Start-Up

One of the most significant problems on technical projects is lack of team cohesion, particularly for projects that have geographically separated teams. Completing a difficult project requires teamwork, trust, and a willingness to look out for and help the others on the project. Under tension, chains tend to break at the weakest link; projects staffed by "virtual" teams have nothing but weak links.

One method for countering this problem and minimizing the risks that result when projects must be staffed by people who do not know each other is to hold a project start-up workshop. A start-up workshop (sometimes referred to as a project launch, a "kickoff" meeting, a planning workshop, or a project initiation meeting) is an event intended to initiate the project processes and to build teamwork. A well-run start-up will achieve a common understanding of the project goals and priorities and avoid wasted time and redundant efforts. It also builds a more cohesive team that will get a fast, efficient start on the project.

Typically, you will want to hold these workshops early in the planning process, at the start of project execution, and before each major new phase of the project. The precise objectives will vary somewhat for workshops held at these different times, but all start-ups focus on team-building and on common project understanding. Achieving these objectives will substantially reduce many types of project risk.

Justifying and Preparing for the Workshop

One reason given for not holding start-up workshops is cost. Particularly for global teams who must travel to take part in a face-to-face workshop, costs and travel time can be significant. But the cost of *not* doing a project start-up is also high; serious problems and loss of productivity can result whenever people are uncooperative or misunderstand information in complex projects. For technical projects, it is not a choice between the expense of a project start-up workshop and saving money; it is between investing a relatively small amount of time and money early or spending a lot more time and money later in the project. Establishing common objectives and language for the project and building relationships among the project team members minimizes risk and creates the environment needed for a successful project.

Work to justify a face-to-face start-up workshop at the beginning of the project. If the timing or cost aspects of a project start-up genuinely make an in-person meeting impossible, at least plan and hold a meeting, or a series of meetings, using videoconferencing or other teleconferencing technology. Such a meeting is less effective at building relationships and trust, but it will be much better than doing nothing.

Productive project start-up workshops need a well-planned agenda and sufficient time to accomplish the activities listed. It's difficult to participate fully while leading a start-up workshop, so consider enlisting a workshop facilitator. Determine the people you need to participate in the workshop and get their commitment. Prepare and distribute all the information that participants will need to review in advance, and have all needed project information available throughout the workshop.

Holding the Workshop and Following Up

Begin the meeting with personal introductions, especially for contributors who don't know each other. Open the start-up workshop with a review of the meeting agenda, project objectives, ground rules, and other necessary background information.

Throughout the workshop, have someone capture issues, questions, action items, and other data produced by the team. As the workshop progresses, work together with the attendees to review, develop, and improve the project definition and planning documents.

Toward the end of the workshop, review the issues and assumptions captured and assess them for project risks. Risk identification is a significant byproduct of start-up workshops, so explicitly add any newly uncovered risks and significant issues to your risk list for further analysis and follow-up. Wrap up the workshop by identifying all assignments, due dates, and owners for all action items and other required additional work. Close the meeting by thanking the participants for their contributions.

After the workshop, integrate the work done during the workshop into the appropriate project documents, and put the updated documentation where it can be referenced and used. Follow up on all action items and other assignments made during the workshop, by either bringing them to closure or adding them to your project plan.

Selecting and Implementing Project Metrics

Project metrics are fundamental to project risk management. Some metrics relate to risk triggers, and others may provide trend data that foreshadows future project problems. The value of project metrics depends on what, and how much, is measured. A project is a complex system, so you will need a number of metrics to adequately monitor process. Defining too many metrics also causes problems, starting with the excessive cost and effort required to collect them. Strive to define a minimum set of project metrics that you need to give a balanced view. There are examples of many useful metrics in Chapter 9.

Selecting Metrics

Useful metrics are objective; if they are evaluated by several people, each person will get the same result. Good metrics are also easy to understand and to collect. Clarify how and what you need to measure, and verify through discussion that everyone involved understands the process consistently. Define the units and precision to be used for the measurements, and use the same units for all collection, evaluation, and reporting. For example, you might decide that all measurements for duration estimates be rounded to the nearest full workday. Also, determine how often to measure. You need to collect data frequently enough to support the results you desire, but not so often that it represents higher overhead than necessary. Capturing data too often will also display "noise," variations in the data that have little or no meaning.

Prioritize any metrics you are considering, using criteria such as criticality, contribution to potential process improvement, linkage to desired behaviors, or availability of data. Collect only metrics that will make a meaningful difference; never collect data just because you can. An effective set of metrics also provides tension—improvement of one measure may diminish another one. Opposing a metric measuring speed of execution with another measuring defects or quality will result in more appropriate behavior than either measurement by itself. Work to minimize "gaming" of the metrics by eliminating factors that might improve the measurement without achieving any desired results. It is possible to subvert almost any metric, so define them in terms that minimize differing interpretations and loopholes.

Finally, work to ensure that any metrics collected are used primarily for process monitoring and improvement, not as a basis for punishment. Metrics are powerful tools for identifying opportunities for beneficial change and determining trends, but the quality of the data that people provide will be less useful if they know that it will also be used to evaluate their performance. Once metrics are identified with processes used to rank and cancel projects, the reliability of future data deteriorates substantially. Use metrics for process control and improvement, not to generate criticism of the project team. If any personal information is involved, ensure that the measurements are kept confidential.

Implementing Metrics and Collecting Data

Before you start to use a project metric, work to get consensus from all members of the project team on the definition, the planned collection and use of the data, and the meaning of the results. Get commitment from everyone who will collect or supply data in advance, and seek agreement not to "game" the metrics.

After defining a set of metrics, the next step is to define an acceptable or desirable normal range. For well-established metrics, baselines may already be documented. For new measures, or for metrics used in a new application, you need to establish a "normal" data range. Although you can begin with an educated guess as a provisional baseline, you should use the first several cycles of data collected to confirm it. Until you have established the baseline using measurements, resist the temptation to make decisions and process changes.

Document each metric and its parameters, and provide this data to everyone affected. Include information such as the name of the metric, the intended objective, data required, measurement units, measurement frequency, the method for data collection, any formulas used, the target acceptable range, and who is responsible for making the measurement.

After setting a measurement baseline, collect project data as planned, and use the information to guide your project decisions. Set baselines for diagnostic metrics early in projects, using current data or data from similar earlier projects. For retrospective metrics, set baselines using existing data from earlier projects, or wait until several completed projects have collected the data required. For predictive metrics, establish corresponding retrospective metrics (for example, validate financial return on investment predictions against actual performance), and establish norms that plausibly connect to the desired results. With all metrics, you should remain skeptical; review the data, and confront any suspected "gaming" of the measurements. Periodically reevaluate all metrics, especially after significant organizational or process changes. Following changes, review the baseline and acceptable range for each metric. Validate any necessary adjustments with new baseline measurements before considering additional system changes.

Throughout the process, make the measurements visible. Report the status of measured factors as planned, to all project stakeholders who need the measurements or are affected by them. Be prompt in evaluating and reporting the data to ensure timely feedback and early detection of significant variances.

Management Reserve

Imagine a large target with a big, red, circular bull's eye in the center. If you stand two meters away from the target and aim a target rifle right at the center, you should have no difficulty hitting the middle of the bull's eye. If you were to repeat the shot, but this time from two *hundred* meters away, the situation changes. For the second shot, aiming at the bull's eye will no longer be effective, because you can no longer rely on the projectile to fly in a straight line. If you aim at the center of the target, you will hit below its center. The parabolic arc that controls the flight of the bullet was described with precision hundreds of years ago by Sir Isaac Newton, and the principle is so well understood that even the average middle manager would not be tempted to hike out and give the bullet a lecture on "flying smarter, not harder." Everyone knows that you need to aim higher than the point you wish to hit, to compensate for the effects of gravity.

Simple, short projects are analogous to the first shot. Setting a date and planning to hit it will work more often than not, because the time window is brief, the work is fairly obvious, and the risks are small. For most technical projects, though, the analogy of the second shot is better. The longer duration, with substantial unknowns and risks, is a different situation. As with gravity for the flying bullet, risk has an effect on the trajectory of a project. Project plans that set deadlines to line up *exactly* with the final planned activities, even if the plans are based on reasonable, realistic estimates, have little chance of completing on time. The "force" of risk makes this sort of schedule unreliable.

Management reserve is a general tactic for dealing with project risk that helps to compensate for uncertainty. Reserve—in time, in budget, or in both—based on *expected* risk may be used to develop credible schedules. Establishing reserves is not about padding estimates or making scheduling choices to accommodate sloppiness or team sloth; it is about using risk assessment information to set appropriate buffers at the project level to allow the project to deliver on commitments. In effect, management reserve is about setting project objectives with ranges, with the size of the range, or reserve, defined by project-level risk assessment.

Management reserve is based on two factors: known risks, with contingency plans, or worst-case scenarios (this includes any known risks you may have elected to accept—that you have decided *not* to manage), and unknown risk. The first factor, discussed in detail in earlier chapters, comes from planning data. Unknown risk, by definition, is risk you are unable to anticipate and describe. Explicit planning for unknown risks is not possible, but metrics from earlier projects can provide guidance on the magnitude of exposure. Using project risk assessment data and metrics, you can estimate appropriate schedule and budget reserves. In effect, management reserve is a generic contingency plan for your overall project. Reserve is *never* allocated to the activity level, and it is managed by the project leader, not by activity owners.

Schedule Reserve

Management reserve for schedules may be implemented in several ways. The simplest method is to estimate the amount of expected schedule exposure, and then develop a plan that supports completion of the project earlier than the required completion date by that amount. In dealing with problems, project slip that stays within the reserve will still permit you to meet the project commitment. The published project schedule either could show only the more aggressive, target completion date, or it could show the target date as a milestone followed by a dummy activity, and then the committed deadline. The dummy activity can have a name such as "allowance for risk," and it has a duration estimate equal to the schedule reserve.

For known risks, the amount of reserve needed for a given project can be estimated using methods that have been described in earlier chapters of this book. From Chapter 4, the idea of worst-case estimates provides one source. Using the "most likely" duration estimates establishes one possible project end date. Schedule analysis based on the worst-case estimates calculates a second end date for the project further out. The difference between these two dates can be used to determine the required reserve. How you do this depends on your confidence in the data, but it is common to set up half of the difference as a reserve—managing the work using the "most likely" schedule, but setting the project deadline to be a date midway between that schedule and the worst-case end date.

A second method for determining schedule reserve is based on data from contingency plans. This process uses the method discussed in Chapter 9 to aggregate activity risk data. In this case, you would track and manage your project using the project plan as a target, but your committed deadline would be later by a duration defined by the cumulative *expected* consequences of having to use your contingency plans.

A third way to assess schedule reserve using data from known risks, also discussed in Chapter 9, relies on Program Evaluation and Review Technique (PERT) analysis or Monte Carlo simulation. The histograms or expected distributions can also be used to estimate required reserve, by determining the duration between the "most likely" (30 to 50 percent likelihood) date and some higher probability point farther out that is consistent with your project's risk tolerance. Again, your plan supporting the "most likely" dates will be used to manage the work and define the early point of a range window of acceptable dates. The upper boundary of the window will be the project commitment.

Estimating schedule reserve using any of these ideas will still necessarily be incomplete. These calculated allowances for reserve are based only on known risks, so without some consideration of the magnitude of your unknown risk, the reserve allowance will be too small. If you have metrics that measure typical schedule impact from unanticipated problems, incorporate this into your estimate of required reserve.

One common example of reserve for unknown risk is explicit in many kinds of project plans. At the end of many construction and relocation projects there is an activity scheduled called a "punch list," or something similar. The purpose of this activity is to fix and close out all the defects, problems, omissions, or other issues that will accumulate on a list during the project. At the start of the project, a duration estimate based only on the list would logically be zero—there is no work yet identified. Because a duration estimate cannot be based on explicit knowledge of the work, it is based on the history of dozens, or hundreds, of similar projects. Experience from earlier work tells you how much time and effort, on average, you can expect between completion of the final scheduled activity and customer sign-off. Metrics that measure unscheduled effort, the number of activities added during projects, underestimated activities, and other indicators of plan incompleteness are all useful for estimating typical "unknown" risk.

An alternative method for estimating the schedule consequences of unknown risk is the project appraisal idea discussed in Chapter 9. The comparison projects include the effects of unknown risk, where your planned current project does not. Part of any difference shown in an assessment is due to unknown risk.

The amount of required schedule reserve varies greatly depending on the type of project. A reserve of only a few days may be appropriate for short, routine projects. For complicated, aggressive projects, target dates may need to be established weeks, or even months, before the committed deadline to deal with the many possible problems and potential sources of slippage. Whether the reserve is short or long, remember that it, like schedule float, belongs to the project as a whole. It is available only for problem solving, not for personal convenience. Using reserve established to manage project risk for other purposes (especially for scope creep) will *increase* project risk.

How schedule reserve is best handled will vary. On some projects, reserve is discussed and managed in the open. Schedules posted and distributed reflect its existence, and the status of remaining schedule reserve is discussed in status meetings with other topics. On other projects, the management of reserve is more covert. As far as the teams on these projects know, the deadline for the project is the date that follows the final activity in the plan. Although this has the desired effect of focusing attention on getting the work done as promptly as possible, it is inconsistent with open and honest project communications. The alternative of managing the reserve openly is usually the better method, but it may be undermined unless you effectively guard against two potential issues: scope creep and Parkinson's Law.

Scope creep is always an issue on technical projects; the more time the team spends thinking about and doing the work, the more ways they come up with to make it "better." In projects that possess a time buffer for risk management, the temptation may become overwhelming to add and modify the project scope, because "we have the time available." On all projects, risk management depends on disciplined and thorough control of changes, and this is particularly true of projects that have visible schedule reserve. Schedule reserve should be used only to accommodate project changes that are a direct result of project problem solving and issue resolution. Schedule reserve is not a tool for project "improvement."

The second issue, Parkinson's Law—work expands to fill the time available—also presents a significant challenge. Misuse of schedule reserve, particularly unused reserve still available late in the project, is a constant temptation. One method for guarding against this is to establish the available window of time for project completion, and to set up rewards for the team proportionate to any *unused* reserve at the end of the project. Incentives for avoiding misuse of the reserve can be effective, but they need to be developed carefully so that they are effective in discouraging misuse and scope creep.

The best methods for reserve management ensure that all decisions are ultimately in the hands of a project leader who will apply the available reserve only to deal with real-time problems, issues, and conflicts. This way, the established reserve operates to counteract the effect of risk and helps aggressively scheduled projects complete on or before their committed deadline.

Budget Reserve

Reserve for resources uses resource analysis and risk data to establish a budget reserve at the project level to expedite work, add additional resources, or take other necessary actions to stay on schedule.

The amount of reserve needed is estimated similarly to the schedule reserve discussed earlier, from analysis of known risk using worst cases, contingency plans, or budget analysis. For unknown risk, estimate reserve using metrics derived from earlier projects. Base your determination of required budget reserve on the best data you have available.

Again, it can be a challenge to be aware of the budget reserve while resisting the temptation to use it for project modifications that have nothing to do with risk. It is usually somewhat easier on technical projects to manage budget reserve than schedule reserve, because decisions concerning money and resources are generally made by the project leader, and sometimes even higher in the organization.

Using Management Reserve

Although determining a prudent allowance for schedule and/or budget reserve is the first step, setting it up requires discussion, negotiation, and approval from project sponsors and stakeholders. You will need all the planning and other data you used to calculate required reserves, but this is not sufficient. You also need to identify and factor in your project constraints. Requesting schedule reserve that is not consistent with a hard completion date for the project probably makes no sense, nor would a proposed budget reserve that exceeds the expected benefit for the project. Work to keep your analysis consistent with the goals and objectives for the project, and understand that when your estimate for reserve exceeds what is logical for the project, project risk is high, and it may be an indication that your project cannot be completed successfully. Abandoning such a project in favor of better alternatives could be the best decision.

Project Baseline Negotiation

Managing project risk nearly always involves some shift in the project objective. In the unlikely event that your bottom-up plans and risk assessment are wholly consistent with the project objective, no negotiation is necessary; validating the plan and documenting the baseline is all that you need to do. For most projects, however, there are issues to confront, often significant ones.

Project negotiation serves a number of purposes. The most obvious one is to shift an overconstrained project enough to bring it in line with a realistic plan. Other reasons for negotiation include securing sponsor support, setting limits on project scope, and managing expectations.

Strong Sponsorship

Risky projects need all the help they can muster, so work to get and retain high priority and visible support for your project. Projects that have substantial risk are generally undertaken because there are large potential benefits expected, and you should make sure that all discussions of the project emphasize the positive results that will come from the project, not just the risks, problems, and challenges. Build awareness of your project, early and often, so that your management will continue to support the project in its words and actions. Particularly on risky projects, you need commitment for quick resolution of escalated issues, protection of the project team from conflicts and nonproject commitments, and approval for any requested management reserve. You may also need sponsor approval for training to acquire new skills and to streamline or change processes. The sponsor can also lower risk for the project by aggressively removing organizational barriers and administrative overhead, and by dealing with organizational and business factors that may inhibit fast execution of the project. Conversely, management can exacerbate risk by contributing to these factors and initiating new work that requires people currently assigned to your project. Strong, continuing sponsorship is one of the key factors that separates risky projects that succeed from those that crash and burn.

Setting Limits on Project Scope

Another goal of project negotiation is to set boundaries for the project. A great deal of risk for technical projects, as was discussed in Chapter 3, arises from the fact that there may be any number of different conceptions for what, exactly, your project is supposed to produce. Even though you and your project team probably have a fairly clear definition as the planning and risk analysis come to closure, there still may be residual "fuzziness" in other quarters. The project scope must be just as clear as the deadline, to everyone involved.

For discussions with sponsors, prepare project documentation that is unambiguous about what the project will include and specific in outlining what it will *not* include. Setting limits on scope early, using "is/is not" scope descriptions that are clear to all, will either validate the project team's conceptions or trigger discussions and necessary adjustments.

Either way, doing this early in the project is the best course; it lowers risk and results in consistent expectations for all parties.

Fact-Based Negotiation

Project baseline negotiation requires your definition and planning documents. Initial discussions will focus on summaries, so writing clear, informative summaries is essential. In preparing project information for discussion, include a high-level objective summary, a milestone project schedule, a high-level WBS, a project appraisal, and a summary of major assumptions and risks. If your planning shows a major mismatch between the current project plan and the requested project objective, you should also have several high-level proposals describing project alternatives.

With this data in hand, your next step is to set up a meeting with the project sponsor to discuss the project, the results of your planning, and, if necessary, the alternatives. Begin the discussion with a presentation of your planning results. Whenever your project plan is inconsistent with the originally requested project objective, you need to negotiate changes. Changes to consider include requesting additional resources, extending the deadline, getting contributors with more experience or more training for the people you have, reducing project scope, or any number of other options.

Having data is critical for your success, because the balance of power in such negotiations is not in your favor. Although it is relatively easy for sponsors and managers to brush aside concerns and opinions, it is much more difficult for them to dismiss hard facts. When there is a significant difference between project expectations for timing and resources as seen by the project team and their management, a half-page project appraisal (described in Chapter 9) can be a good starting place for the discussion, showing why the requested project is not likely to be done as quickly or inexpensively as desired. ("Remember this project? That's the one we had to do in two months and it ended up taking six.") When the issue is a request to do a project much faster than is possible, your project Gantt chart, showing all the activities and durations, is an effective tool. When the deadline requested is far too short to accommodate the work, hold up the chart and say that you can only do it on schedule if the sponsor will select which activities to delete. Most sponsors will quickly back down and begin a productive discussion of alternatives, rather than randomly removing work they probably do not understand. Any project information backed up by historical, documented data can be a good starting point for a fact-based, not emotion-based, negotiation.

Reducing project risk through negotiation is best done with the ideas outlined by Roger Fisher, William Ury, and Bruce Patton of the

Harvard Negotiation Project in their book *Getting to Yes*. Their process of principled negotiation is effective for "win-win" negotiations, where all parties get at least some of what they seek. In project negotiations where only the sponsor "wins," everyone has actually lost. It does no one any good to force a commitment to an impossible project. The team and project leader lose because they are stuck on a doomed project. The sponsors, managers, and customers lose too, because they do not get what they expect and need. Principled negotiation, done early, is essential for dealing with impossible projects.

Some useful ideas for project negotiations include separating the people from the issues and focusing on interests, not positions. By sticking to facts and mutually understood needs, you raise the discussion beyond "This project is *hard*" on the project side and "You are the best project leader we have" on the other. Although both of the statements may be true, neither one actually addresses the real issue—that the project objective, as stated, is not possible. As you prepare for negotiation, develop project alternatives that provide for mutual gain, such as exploring opportunities that could extend beyond the original project request, or segmenting the project into a sequence of smaller projects capable of delivering value earlier. In your negotiations, base decisions and analyses on objective criteria. Brainstorm, problem solve, and get everyone involved in seeking better options. Ask lots of questions, and focus on resolving the issues, not just arguing about the project.

Your biggest asset in all of this is your knowledge. As a result of your project planning, no one alive knows more about the project than you do. You also have a track record and credibility, built up over a body of prior work. The managers and project sponsors are aware of this; that is why they requested that you lead the project. Proceed with negotiations using your technical and planning expertise, and the experience of your project team.

Lay out the consequences of accepting a commitment to a project with excessive residual risk in clear, fact-based terms. By using conservative assumptions to support the analysis of the potential project problems, you will end up with one of three possible results. The most desirable outcome is shifting the project objective in line with, or at least closer to, your plan. For other projects, realistic analysis of the work and risks may lead to the conclusion that the project is not a good idea, and it is taken no further. Either of these outcomes will avoid a failed project.

The third possibility is that your data may not be sufficiently compelling or that your sponsors will pay no attention to it. In this case, you may end up forced to commit to an infeasible project, with no realistic plan to support it. Should this happen, document the situation for future reference, to make it less likely to recur. Then you can try your best and hope for miracles (or work on updating your résumé).

Project Plan Validation

Following discussion and negotiation, validate that you have consensus on the project. Verify that you have a plan supporting the project objective that is acceptable to the project sponsor and other stakeholders as well as to you and your project team.

Use the project documents from the planning processes, with any negotiated modifications, to establish the project baseline plan of record. Before finalizing the plan, review it to ensure that it includes periodic risk reassessment activities throughout (at least at major phase milestones). During these reviews, additional risks not apparent at project start will be identified, and your contingency plans can be updated.

Publish the final versions of the project documents and distribute them so that the project team can access and use them to manage progress throughout the project. Put your project documents online if possible so that everyone has access at any time to current versions. If a computer scheduling tool is to be used for project tracking, save the project schedule as a baseline and begin tracking activity status in the database.

When you set the project baseline, freeze all specifications. Set both the project scope definition and your baseline plan at the same time, and change neither one without using your established process for making changes. Freezing the schedule and resources on a project while allowing the scope to continue to meander is a massive source of project risk.

For risk visibility, create a "top ten list" of the most significant known risks for the current phase of your project, and post it where the project team will be aware of it—in the team workplace, on the project Web site, or in another prominent location. Commit to periodically reviewing and updating the list throughout the project.

Specification Change Management

Once the project plan is accepted and you have frozen the specifications, adopt a process to carefully consider all changes before accepting them. After the project documents are signed off by all appropriate decision makers—the project sponsor, customers, stakeholders, and others—it is risky to allow unexamined changes in the project. Although new information flows around technical projects continuously, maintaining specification stability is crucial for project success. Unmanaged change leads to slipped schedules, budget problems, and other consequences, as seen in the PERIL database.

Having a process for submission, analysis, and disposition for each proposed change lowers the risks, especially if "reject" is the default decision for submitted change requests. An effective change management process puts the burden of proof on each change request; all changes are considered *unnecessary* until proven otherwise.

Another requirement for effective change control is giving the people responsible for the change process the authority to enforce their decisions. Change approvers need the power to say "no" (or at least "not yet") and make it stick. For reasons of efficiency, some change processes establish change screeners, who initially examine any proposed change and determine when (or even if) a change deserves further consideration.

Change Process

Change control processes should be documented, in writing. The formality of the actual process adopted varies a great deal with project type, but at a minimum, it should include:

- Logging and tracking of all change requests
- A defined process for analyzing all proposed changes
- Documented criteria for accepting, rejecting, or deferring changes
- Communication of decisions and status

Change submissions Ideas for change generally begin in problem solving or from recognition of an opportunity. Submissions should include information such as:

- Why the change is necessary
- An estimate of expected benefits from the change
- The estimated impact of the change on schedule, cost, and other factors
- Specific resources needed for the change

Log all changes submitted, and maintain an up-to-date list of submitted change proposals throughout the project. Following submission, examine each submitted change, and if the information is unclear or key data is missing, return the request to the submitter for correction.

Change analysis Analyze all changes for both impact and cost/ benefits. Impact assessment parallels the processes used for impact analysis of risks. It begins with high-level categorization of change impact:

- Small (minor effect on the deliverable or project plan)
- Medium (functional change to the deliverable but little project impact)
- Large (major change to project object and the deliverable)

Also evaluate the costs and benefits of the change. Each change presumably has some benefits, or it would not have been submitted. The expected benefits need to be estimated and verified so they can be compared with the expected costs and other consequences.

Changes generally fall into one of several categories. Many proposed changes resolve problems encountered on the project or fix something that is not functioning as required. The benefits of these changes relate to the avoided expense or time slippage that will persist on the project until the problem is solved. Other changes arise from external factors such as new regulatory or safety requirements, the need to comply with evolving standards, or actions by competitors. These types of change, which are solving real problems, complying with firm requirements, and reacting to adverse shifts in the environment, are often unavoidable. Your project deliverable will lose much, if not all, of its value unless the changes are made. The benefits of both kinds of changes are usually sufficient to justify their serious consideration.

Other project changes are intended to make the project "better" and are on less solid ground—changes that add something to the deliverable, alter something about the deliverable to improve it, or introduce new processes or methods to be used for project work. The benefits of these changes are more speculative, and thus more difficult to analyze. Credible estimates for increased sales, revenue, or usefulness as a result of the change are difficult, and they tend to be optimistic. Although some opportunities for change may result in significant benefits, many changes intended to improve technical projects generate unintended consequences and lead to benefits that are far smaller than expected. The impact to the project may also be difficult to estimate, particularly if the change involves adopting a new approach to the work. Effective change management systems are highly skeptical of these discretionary modifications and tend to reject them. When outright rejection is not possible, the system should at least be adept at saying "not yet," allowing the project to complete as planned and then embarking on a follow-on effort to pursue the new ideas.

In all cases, a rational consideration of the net benefit of the change—the reasonably expected benefits less the estimated costs and other consequences—is the basis for a decision. This analysis should apply to *all* submitted changes, regardless of their origin. If customers submit changes, the specific consequences in terms of timing and cost must be visible to them, and generally borne by them as well. If a project contributor submits a change, he or she should provide ample documentation for it and expect to fight hard to get it approved. Politically, the most difficult situation on technical projects arises from the changes requested by sponsors and management. Although it is never easy to say "no" to the people you work for, the existence of a documented process that has been approved to manage project change is a vital initial step, and clear, data-supported descriptions of the consequences of requested changes are also necessary. As with risk management generally, managing change risk effectively relies on thorough, credible project planning data.

Disposition For each potential change, you have four options: approval, approval with modification, rejection, and deferral. The process for making a decision on each change request uses the results from the analysis and documented information on project objectives and priorities to make a business decision. The primary criterion for the decision will generally be the assessment of benefits versus costs, weighing the relative advantages and disadvantages of each change. The level of formality will scale with the project, but two aspects of the decision process are universal. The first requirement is to make decisions promptly. Change requests, particularly those that address problems, need quick attention. The value of a change can diminish significantly as it sits, so ensure that all changes are considered and closed without undue delay, generally within a week. The second need is for consistent adherence to agreed-upon requirements for decisions. Some change systems are based on approval by a majority of those involved; some require unanimity; and still others grant veto powers to some approvers who have greater authority. Effective change systems avoid having too many approvers to minimize scheduling problems and shorten debate, and they provide for alternate approvers whenever a designated approver is not available.

An effective change management process always starts with the presumption that changes are unnecessary, and rejects all changes that lack a compelling, credible business basis. Even for changes that have some benefits, carefully examine them to determine whether some parts of the change are not needed, or whether the change might be deferred to a later project, especially if the impact significantly interferes with project objectives. Seek substantial credible net benefits even for changes you decide to approve with modifications or to defer. Approval and acceptance of changes should be relatively rare, and reserved for the most compelling requirements for problem solving or other significant business needs. The more change a project is subject to, the higher the risk. Whatever the decision, close out all requests quickly, within the documented time goals established for the process. Also, promptly escalate any issues or conflicts that cannot be resolved at the project level.

Communicating the decision As each decision is made, document it in writing. Include the rationale for the decision and a brief description of any project impact. Prepare and distribute a summary of the pending, accepted, and rejected change proposals to project stakeholders and to your project team members.

Whenever a change is not approved, respond to the submitter with an explanation, including the rationale for the decision. If there is a specific process for appeal and reconsideration, provide this information to the submitter as well.

For any accepted changes, update all relevant project documents—the WBS, estimates, schedules, specifications and other scope documents, the project plan, charts, or any other project documents that an approved change affects.

Even for rejected changes, retain the proposals in the project archives. The "good ideas" may be worthy of consideration in follow-on projects or in parallel projects. When your project is over, you can use the change history to reduce risk on future projects by carefully reviewing the process and the decisions made.

Key Ideas for Managing Project Risk

- Hold a project start-up workshop.
- Select and use several project metrics.
- Determine required project reserve.
- Negotiate and validate possible project objectives.
- Freeze scope and manage specification changes.

Panama Canal: Adjusting the Objective (1907)

Setting a concrete objective for a project is not necessarily a quick, easy process. In the case of the Panama Canal, although Theodore Roosevelt made the decision to build the canal and the Senate approved the commitment in early 1904, the specifics of exactly what sort of canal would be built were still not settled nearly two years later. All the data accumulated by John Stevens led him to the same conclusion ultimately determined by the French engineers—building a sea-level canal at Panama was not feasible. He estimated that a lock-and-dam canal could be completed in nine years, possibly eight. A sea-level canal could not be built in less than eighteen years, if at all. He convinced Theodore Roosevelt of this, and he thought the matter was settled.

This, however, was not the case. In spite of the French experience, the lock-and-dam versus sea-level debate was still going strong in the U.S. Senate in 1906. Showing much of the same diligence and intelligence one might expect of today's Senate, they took a vote on how to build the canal. By one vote, they approved a sea-level canal. One unavoidable observation from study of past projects is that things change little over time, and politics is rarely driven by logic.

John Stevens had just returned to Panama from Washington in 1906, and although he was quite busy with the project, he turned around and sailed back to the United States. He met extensively with members of both the U.S. House of Representatives and the Senate. He patiently explained the challenges of a sea-level canal in a rain forest with flooding rivers. He developed data, drew maps, and generally described to anyone who would listen all the reasons why the canal could not be built at sea level. As was true earlier for the French, the main obstacle was the flooding of the Chagres River, which flows north into the Gulf of Mexico parallel to the proposed canal for nearly half of its route.

Stevens spent a lot of time with one ally, Senator Philander Knox. Senator Knox was from Pennsylvania—specifically, he was from Pittsburgh, Pennsylvania. Stevens worked with Knox on a speech in which the senator described in detail why the canal must be constructed with dams and locks. By all reports, it was an excellent speech, delivered with great eloquence and vigor. (It was probably not entirely a coincidence that a sea-level canal required none of the locks, steel doors, and other hardware that would come from Senator Knox's friends in the foremost steel-producing city in the Americas.)

Despite of all this, there were *still* thirty-one senators who voted for a sea-level canal. Fortunately for the project and for Stevens, there were thirty-seven senators who were paying attention, and the design Stevens recommended was approved.

It had taken him more than a year, but finally John Stevens had his plan completed and approved. Defending the feasible plan required all of his data, principled negotiation, and a great deal of perseverance, but he ultimately avoided the costly disaster of a second impossible canal project at Panama.

11

Monitoring and Controlling Risky Projects

"Adding manpower to a late software project makes it later."
—FRED BROOKS, AUTHOR OF *THE MYTHICAL MAN-MONTH*

Apart from phrasing (the very 1970s *manpower* would be replaced by the more politically correct *people* or *staff*), it's hard to quibble with Fred Brooks's statement. In fact, the effect described by Brooks applies to projects of almost any type, not just software projects. Adding contributors to a late project never seems to help very much, because the first thing that new people on a project need is information, so they ask blizzards of questions. These questions are directed to the overworked people already on the project, which further slows their progress. There are other reasons adding staff late in a project can be counterproductive, such as the need to build trust and to move through the team-building stages of "forming, storming, and norming." It is not the additional staff that is the real problem, though. It is additional staff *too late*. Monitoring and control of the work is essential to detecting problems such as insufficient staffing early enough to avoid the need for chaotic, and seldom successful, heroic measures. Disciplined monitoring and control finds and fixes problems while they are still small, so the project avoids serious trouble in the first place.

Risk management cannot end with the initial planning. Your project starts with its plan, just as a lengthy automobile trip begins with an itinerary based on maps and other information. But what trip ever goes exactly as planned? As the driver continues on the trip, small adjustments based on events and conditions are necessary. More serious issues such as vehicle problems or automobile accidents may result in major modifications to the itinerary. Throughout the trip, the driver must remain alert and reasonably flexible. Managing risk in projects is about detecting things that are not proceeding as planned in your project. Like the driver who must remain alert and responsive to things that happen on the road, the project leader uses tracking, reviews, and reapplication of the planning concepts discussed in the preceding chapters to adjust to the prevailing project conditions, seeking to bring it to successful to closure.

Effective management of project risk relies on frequent and disciplined reassessment of new information and status as the project proceeds. Particularly on longer projects, you cannot know everything about the work at the beginning. Periodic project reviews are necessary to keep the project moving and productive.

Don't Panic

The main focus of this chapter is ongoing execution of a project with as few detours and aggravation as possible. Risk planning helps to reveal what might go wrong, and responds to much of it. However, project work is unpredictable, so things will happen. Effective project leaders strive to remain calm when problems arise. Risk management depends on level-headed analysis and prompt action, so work to remain composed. Recovery from problems not only depends on a prompt and appropriate response, it also depends on competent execution. You will stay on track more successfully by heeding Rudyard Kipling: "If you can keep your head when all about you/Are losing theirs and blaming it on you. . . ."

This is much easier to say than to do, but minimizing emotions and chaos in a crisis is the fastest route to problem recovery. Stress causes inefficiency and mistakes, and raises the likelihood of future risks, so do your best to keep things running smoothly throughout your project—even when things seem to be falling apart. Panic will only make things worse.

Applying the Plan

Predictable project progress depends on your baseline project plan. The plan is now the road map for your work, and you can begin tracking status and updating your project database with actual results. Status information is primarily useful in assessing progress, but it also provides early warnings for risks. Status data also supports longer-term risk management through process improvement during periodic project reviews and postproject retrospective analysis.

Risk management relies on systematic project tracking to provide the information necessary for proactive detection of project problems while they are still small and easily solved. Project tracking helps you anticipate potential problems, allowing the project to avoid at least some of them. Disciplined tracking makes it difficult to ignore early warning signals, and it provides the data you need for effective response. Without accurate, timely information, project problems remain hidden, so they will occur without warning, inflicting serious damage to your plans.

Credible status data also can reduce the project worries and team stress that arises from a lack of good information. Even when the project status reveals bad news, the true situation viewed with credible information is nearly always less dire than the alternatives that people dream up when they lack data. In addition, detailed status often provides the information you need for recovery. Factual information also helps minimize both excessive optimism and pessimism, neither of which is helpful to a project.

Dogmatic collection of project status and routine comparison to the plan guards against a common project risk—"safe so far" project reporting. As long as the project deadline is still way out in the future, the project is not officially late. Even without any data, project reporting continues to say that the project is doing fine. Only at the deadline, or perhaps a little before it, does the project leader publicly admit that the project will not meet its schedule commitment. This is analogous to a man who falls off a ten-story building and reports as he passes by each row of windows, "Safe so far!"

Projects become late *one day at a time*. Failure to detect this as soon as possible allows schedule and other risks to remain undetected, grow, and ultimately overwhelm the project.

Project Monitoring

Project monitoring can begin as soon as there is a clear, validated baseline plan that has been approved by the project sponsor and accepted by the project leader and team. Other prerequisites for effective project tracking are a functioning communications infrastructure, functioning tracking methods, and thorough project planning data available to all team members and stakeholders.

Decisions Related to Monitoring

Specifics concerning project status collection and storage are basic decisions that you need to make as part of the initial project infrastructure for your project.

You need to commit to an appropriate frequency and method for status collection. Tracking on technical projects is usually done weekly, but for very short or very urgent projects more frequent data collection may be warranted. For long projects, less frequent data collection may be appropriate, but a cycle longer than two weeks is inconsistent with good risk management. Online or e-mail status collection is most common, but any method that is effective and in writing can work.

On large, complex, multiteam programs, consistent data collection is essential, and the volume of status information can become quite a burden. One way to manage this is through a centralized project office, responsible for assembling, summarizing, and analyzing the data consistently for all the project teams. This ensures current, consistent data, and also permits use of more complex scheduling tools without the cost of so many copies and the considerable effort that would be required for all the project leaders to master the tool.

Project status meetings are also usually weekly. When face-to-face meetings are not possible, use the best available telecommunications methods. The frequency and methods used vary from project to project, but risks rise steeply when reports, meetings, and other communication are more than two weeks apart.

Decisions on how and where to store the project status information are also important. Online storage of project data is best, because it provides the project team access at any time. Determine the tools and systems to be used for collecting and storing the data, and set up appropriate security so that only team members who should be updating project information will be able to modify it.

The precise details for these decisions related to project monitoring will affect your ability to manage risk, so commit to methods and frequencies that will best serve your project.

Project Status

Project status information is of two types: hard data (facts and figures) and soft data (anecdotal information, rumors, and less specific information). Both types of data are useful for risk management. Hard data includes the project metrics discussed in Chapter 9, and most of them are diagnostic metrics—telling you how the project is proceeding. Some of the hard data collected will relate to, or may even be, a risk event trigger, and other data may reveal dangerous trends. Soft data can tell you the causes for your project status; it may also provide early warnings of future problems and risk situations.

Hard data Hard project data includes metrics that assess progress, including revised start and completion estimates for future work. Hard data collection should be routine, easy, and not too time consuming. On most technical projects, people are so busy that if collecting hard status information is not simple, it will not get done. At a minimum, collect:

- Schedule data, such as activities completed and activities scheduled but not completed, milestones completed or missed, actual activity start and finish dates, and duration remaining for incomplete activities
- Resource data, including actual effort consumed, cost data, remaining effort for incomplete work, and missing resources
- Data regarding issues, problems, and specification changes

Soft data Additional information of a less tangible nature also permeates your project. Information about the project contributors may alert you to potential threats to needed resources, individual productivity, and other potential sources of project risk. Changes in the work environment, a rumored reorganization, or individual team members having personal problems may also adversely affect upcoming project work. Soft data may also provide information on opportunities to help the project. Soft project data includes issues such as:

- Conflicts arising from expected new projects or other work
- Falling productivity of individual team members
- Suspected changes to the project environment
- Changes needed by your project that seem threatened
- Potential problem situations with a common, persistent root cause
- Frequent situations requiring more authority than you have
- Long delays getting resolution of escalated issues and decisions

The Status Cycle

Project monitoring depends on a four-stage cycle that repeats periodically (generally weekly) throughout the project. The first stage is inbound communication, collecting of project status information. The second stage of the cycle compares the status to the plan, evaluates the metrics, and analyzes any variances. The third stage responds to any issues or problems detected. The fourth and final stage is outbound communication, keeping people aware of what has happened in the project.

The monitoring cycle provides for analysis and planning after collecting project status information, but before project reporting. This lets you include your responses to any issues or problems in your project status report. Any bad news you report will be received better if it is accompanied by credible plans for recovery.

Collecting Project Status

Collecting project status is primarily your responsibility as the project leader. Status data is your "dashboard" for the overall health of your project. Whatever data you decide to collect, be dogmatic in collecting it. Project risk management requires data, so do what you must to keep it flowing.

There are a number of factors that can impede status collection. One pitfall is to collect project status only "when there is time." As typical technical projects proceed, the work intensifies and problems, distractions, and chaos build. It may be tempting in times of stress to skip a status collection cycle. Especially during significant problems, it is very risky to lose information. You may even find it necessary to *intensify* data collection during problems or near project completion.

Other things to guard against are collecting data and then not using the information, or misusing it. After you collect status, at least incorporate a summary of it into your overall project status report. When you fail to use what you collect, your team members will either stop sending it or will put no effort into supplying meaningful data. Misuse of status information can also be a major problem. When the status you receive is bad news, your first temptation may be to grab a chair and break it over the head of the person who sent it, or at least to yell a lot. One of the hardest things a project leader has to learn is not to shoot the messenger. You need to respond positively, even to bad news. Thanking people for bad news is never easy, but if you routinely punish team members for providing honest data, you will quickly stop hearing what you need to know and project risks will escalate. It is much better to mentally count to ten, and then offer a response such as, "Well, I wish you had better news, but I appreciate you raising this issue promptly. What will help get you back on schedule?" The sooner everyone begins to focus on recovery, the earlier things can get back on track.

Metrics and Trend Analysis

After collecting status, look for project problems by analyzing variances. Variance analysis involves comparing the status information you collected with the project baseline plan to identify any differences.

Variances, both positive and negative, need to be analyzed for impact; positive variances may provide opportunities for improved execution of future work, and negative variances need attention so that they do not send the project spiraling out of control. Trend analysis on the metrics may also reveal potential future risks and disruptions.

Diagnostic Metrics

After contrasting the status data with the plan, the first thing to do is to validate the differences, particularly large ones. Before spending time on impact analysis, check with the people who provided the data to make certain that the problems (or for positive variances, any apparent opportunities) are real. For each difference, determine the root cause of the variance, not just the symptoms. (Root-cause analysis is explored in Chapter 8.) Work with both hard and soft project data to understand why each variance occurred. Metrics seldom slip out of expected ranges in isolation; the project schedule, resources, and scope are all interrelated, so problems with one of these parameters will probably affect the others.

Armed with the underlying cause of each variance, you can best decide how to respond. Dealing with the root cause of a problem also prepares you for similar problems later in the project. In variance analysis, focus on understanding the data; never just look for someone to blame.

Schedule metrics Schedule variances are generally examined first, whether positive or negative. If there are positive variances—work completed early—there may be an opportunity to pull in the start date of other work. It is also worthwhile to discuss the early finish with the activity owner to see whether it is the result of an approach or method that could be applied to similar work scheduled later in the project, or whether you could shorten any duration estimates.

The more common situation is an adverse variance, which for critical activities will impact the start of at least one scheduled project activity. Unless an activity following the slip can be compressed, it will affect all of the activities and milestones later in the project, including the final deadline. Even for noncritical activities, adverse variances are worth investigating; the slip may exceed the flexibility in the schedule, or it might reveal an analysis error that could invalidate duration estimates for later project activities.

Finally, schedule variances may be due to root causes that were not detected during risk analysis. If the root cause of a slip suggests new risks and project failure modes, note the risks and set a time for additional risk analysis and response planning.

Resource metrics Resource variances are also significant. Metrics related to the concept earned value management (EVM) are particularly useful in examining resource use throughout the project. EVM metrics, such as the cost performance index (CPI), measure the effort or money consumed by the project in relation to the plan. If the consumption is low (CPI less than one) but the schedule progress is adequate, there may be an opportunity to complete the project under budget. If it is too low and the schedule is also slipping, the root cause is likely to be inadequate staffing or too little of some other resource available. Whenever project progress is too slow because of insufficient resources, escalate the situation to higher management promptly, especially if your project is being denied access to committed resources.

Whenever resources are being used in excess of what is expected—that is, when CPI is higher than one or another metric shows your "burn rate" is too high—the variance is almost certainly a serious problem. The likelihood is strong that the project will ultimately require more resources to complete than the plan indicates, because it is very difficult to reverse resource overconsumption. Even as early as 20 percent through the project schedule, a project with an adverse CPI variance has essentially *no chance* of finishing within budget. Using more resources than planned may cause your project to hit a limit on staff, money, or some other hard constraint, and halt the project well before it is completed. Publicly admitting to this sort of problem is never easy, but if you wait it will be worse. Problems like this increase with time, and the options for recovery diminish later in the project. Sympathy from your project sponsors and stakeholders will drop from little to none at all if you wait too late to deliver bad news.

Some resource issues are acute, having impact on only a short portion of the project; others are chronic and will recur throughout the work. Chronic situations not only create project budget problems, they also may lead to frequent overtime and constant stress on project staff. Risk probabilities rise with increased stress and lowered motivation. Chronic resource problems may also have an impact on your ability to execute existing contingency plans.

Scope metrics Although schedule and resource data provide the most common status variances, at least some of the data relates to the project deliverables. The results of tests, integration attempts, feasibility studies, and other work will either support the expectations set out in the project requirements, or they will not. Significant variances related to scope may indicate a need to propose project changes. Major variances may even foreshadow ultimate project failure.

If a scope-related metric exceeds the result expected, you should explore whether there might be an opportunity for the project to deliver a superior result within the same time frame and budget. It may even be possible to deliver the stated result sooner or less expensively. Although this situation is relatively rare, it does happen, and how best to exploit such opportunities may not be obvious. Discuss them with your project sponsors, customers, and other stakeholders before adding something to the project scope "just because you can." Use your change management process to assess the value and utility of any additional product feature before incorporating it into the project.

When scope-related data indicates a problem that can be resolved with additional work, the impact may be to the project schedule, resources, or both. Consider various alternatives by analyzing what realistically can be delivered consistent with the project budget and deadline. Determine the most palatable option (or options) based on relative project priorities, and propose required changes to the project objective.

If you cannot resolve a scope problem with extra work, your only options are to modify the deliverable or to abandon the project. As with recognition of a resource overconsumption problem, scope underdelivery issues are always difficult to deal with. Some projects choose to hide the problems, hoping that someone comes up with a brilliant idea to close the gap between what is desired and what can credibly be delivered. This is a very high-risk strategy that seldom works. The best course is to raise the issues as soon as you have validated the data. If you do this early, project options are more numerous, the total investment in the project is still relatively small, and expectations are less "locked in." Although still painful and unpleasant, this is a lot easier than dealing with it later. When a project deliverable proves to be demonstrably impossible, the best time to change (or kill) it is early, not late.

In addition to the impact on the current project, scope problems may affect other projects. Inform the leaders of projects depending on your deliverable (or who may be using similar flawed assumptions), so that they can develop alternate strategies or work-arounds.

Once you have completed the variance analysis, document the impact. List the consequences of each variance in terms of:

- Predicted schedule slip
- Budget or other resource requirements
- The effect on the project deliverable
- Impact on other projects

Once you have determined the source and magnitude of the problem, you have a basis for response.

Trend Analysis

Trend analysis does not necessarily need to be part of each monitoring cycle, but periodically it is a good idea to examine the trends in the status data. When the resource consumption rates or cumulative slip for the project moves in a dangerous direction, the trend data will make it clear. The earlier you are able to detect and analyze an adverse trend, the easier it will be to deal with it. Trend data may reveal a need to adjust the project end date, raise the budget, negotiate for more resources, renegotiate contracts, or modify the project deliverables. If so, the earlier you start, the better your chances for success.

Unfavorable trends detected early in the project can show the need for change when there is much more tolerance for it. Near the start of a project the objectives remain somewhat flexible in the minds of the project sponsors, stakeholders, and contributors. Ignoring or failing to detect adverse trends in the status data is very risky. If trend information indicates a problem and no action is taken, the trend is likely to continue and grow. Ultimately, something *will* have to be done. As it gets later in the project, the options diminish and the changes required to reverse the trend become more extreme and less likely to help. These actions may create additional problems and even lead to project failure.

Detecting and dealing with adverse project trends early enough avoids the late project changes and cancellations that are so demotivating for technical project teams. After having worked for months, or even years, on a project, even small changes to the deliverable can be devastating to the team. Allowing everyone to identify with a very aggressive, high-tech, bleeding-edge objective for the bulk of the project and then having to chop the heart out of it at the last minute so you can ship *something* on time is demoralizing and embarrassing. People identify with the work they do, so late project changes are taken very personally. Team building and motivation on subsequent projects become very difficult. If this happens often, project staff members are trained not to care about the projects and not to trust the people who lead and sponsor them. Technical projects are successful not because they are easy; they succeed because people care about them. Anything that interferes with this raises project risk to insurmountable levels.

Responding to Issues

At this point in the status cycle, any significant differences between the plan and actual project performance are visible. Treating plan variances as issues and resolving them soon after they occur, when they are still small, allows project recovery with minimum disruption. Responding to project issues resembles risk response planning, discussed in Chapter 8. In fact, for issues that you anticipated as risks, the response could be as simple as implementing a contingency plan. Base your response plan on the specifics of the problem. If the variance is small, it may be sufficient to delegate the response to the team members responsible for the work affected. Other possible responses range from very minor staffing shifts or resequencing of project activities to major changes to the project objective, or even to project cancellation. The process for issue response closely resembles the "Plan-Do-Check-Act" cycle from quality management. In planning problem responses, work quickly, but seek good solutions.

When you have captured ideas for response, analyze how each will affect project schedule, resources, and scope. Probe for possible unintended consequences, both in your project and for other related work. The best of the options developed may not present any obvious problems or require any significant project changes (sometimes the "brute force" option of just working some additional overtime is the path of least resistance).

Larger problems may require major changes. If so, submit each option you are considering to the change management process for review. For even more significant changes, analysis process could also involve fundamental replanning. If so, get buy-in from the project team and stakeholders for the revised plan. When necessary, revalidate the objective and baseline with the project sponsor, and update all affected documents.

Once a response plan is accepted, implement it. Communicate the plan and the information on required project changes to the project team and any other people involved. After taking the actions in the response plan, monitor to see whether you have solved the problem. If the actions are ineffective, plan for additional responses, looking for a better solution.

The situation is similar to the way a fire department treats a fire. Initially a new fire is "one alarm," and one fire crew is sent out. When the fire is too large, or it spreads, the fire department escalates to two alarms, and then, if needed, to three or more. The escalation continues until the fire is brought under control. Ongoing project risk management requires the same diligence, escalation, and persistence. Significant project changes often lead to unintended consequences. During the status cycles that follow big changes, be particularly thorough in your data analysis and look for unexpected results.

Communication

The final step in the status cycle is to let people know how the project is doing. This includes project status reports and status meetings, as well as less formal communication. Successful projects depend on a solid foundation of clear, frequent communication. Without effective communication, project risks may not be detected, let alone managed.

Communication on projects presents a number of growing challenges. Distance is a well-known barrier to communication. It restricts both the type and amount of communication possible, and reduces informal interaction to almost none. As project teams become increasingly global, time differences also interfere with communication. Even phoning people on global projects can be difficult; whenever you need to talk, it is the middle of the night for them. Different languages and cultures are another growing communication challenge for technical projects. Global work involves people who speak different languages and who have different ways of working and communicating. Sharing complicated technical project information in this sort of environment is never easy, and omissions and misunderstandings are common. Cultural and linguistic diversity in technical work is becoming the norm, not the exception, for all types of projects. Finally, few technical projects are *only* technical. Cross-functional project teams involve people from very different educational and work backgrounds. It may be easier for an engineer in Ohio to communicate with an engineer in Japan than it is for them to communicate with the marketing manager down the corridor.

As the project leader, you are the person primarily responsible for project communication. You need to rise to these challenges and minimize project communication risk. In today's projects, this requires discipline and effort.

Project Status Reports

The most visible communication for most projects is the written status report. Ongoing risk management depends on clear, credible project information that is understood by everyone on the project. Status reporting that is too cursory increases risk because no one has enough information about the project to know what is happening—leading to chaos. This may occur because the project leader is busy or distracted and provides too little data. It also may be the result of "need to know" project reporting, where the project leader sends out very brief notes to each team member containing only data on the portion of the project that he or she is involved with. It can even happen because the project leader dislikes writing reports. Whatever the source, projects with too little information become very prone to risks, particularly risks related to dependencies and interfaces.

On the other hand, status reporting that rambles on and on is no better. No one has time to read it all, and although the information everyone needs is probably there, somewhere, finding it is impossible. One common reason for long reports is a project leader who solicits individual reports from the whole team and concatenates them into a compendium running to dozens of pages. Time pressure can be a factor in this; there is much truth in the old saying, "I didn't have time to write a short report, so I wrote a long one." Whatever the reason, the result of rambling reports is increased project risk, because no one will have the patience or time to digest the entire report.

The best reports start with a short, clear summary, including current risks. Regardless of who you are sending a status report to, begin with a brief (twenty lines or fewer) summary. Be aware that sometimes the summary is all that will actually be read, and that some of the people who receive your report will not need or want any more detail than this.

Follow the summary with additional needed information that is concise, honest, and clear. If you commit to weekly reporting on a specific day, do it. Understand what your stakeholders need to know and provide it in your reports, in a consistent place and format. Any important data that people notice is missing will probably result in unnecessary and time-consuming telephone calls or other interruptions.

Following your high-level summary, your project status report may include:

- A short description of each major accomplishment since the last report. This portion of the report is an excellent place to "name names" and to recognize individual and team accomplishments.
- Activities planned during the next status period.
- Significant risks, issues, and problems with your planned responses.
- A schedule summary, with planned, actual, and expected future dates.
- A resource summary, with planned, actual, and expected future resource requirements.
- Project analysis, including an explanation of any variances, issues, and plans for resolution.
- Risk analysis, including the known risks in the near project future and the status of any ongoing risk recovery efforts.
- Additional detail, charts, and other information as needed.

In written reports, include only status information that is substantiated, and use soft status data sparingly, if at all.

Other Reporting

In addition to the project status report, other reporting may be required, including various other periodic reports to support organizational needs. Other reporting also provides occasional opportunities for higher-level reporting and presentations. Such cases are an excellent opportunity to reinforce the importance of your project, to be positive about what the team has done, and to share your plans for the future. Presentations are a particularly effective way to renew strong project sponsorship, motivate your team, and renew enthusiasm for the project. On longer projects, all of these factors can assist in avoiding future problems and risks.

Project Status Meetings

Project status meetings for technical projects are viewed by many as a necessary evil, and by everyone else even less positively. Technical people, for the most part, hate meetings, especially long ones. Considering the increase in project risk that results from inadequate communication, this is unfortunate. The discussions and exchanges that occur during project status meetings are essential for avoiding risks, and many potential problems never occur because they are discussed during status meetings. Holding regular status meetings, even via teleconferencing, is a potent tool for keeping difficult projects on track and risks under control.

One key to improving attendance at and participation in status meetings is to keep them short. Meetings are more interesting and energized if they focus only on important project information—what has been accomplished and what issues are pending. Problem solving and issue resolution are unquestionably important, but they rarely require the entire project staff to be involved, so delegate problem solving and extended discussions to smaller groups, and keep your meetings brief.

Effective meetings are well structured, sticking to an established meeting agenda. They also start on time, set time limits for the agenda items, and end early whenever possible. Face-to-face communication minimizes misunderstandings and reinforces teamwork, but may not always be possible. For teleconference meetings, minimize communication risks by:

- Using the best meeting technologies available
- Ensuring that the technologies used are familiar to all participants
- Verifying that the technologies to be used are compatible and functioning, and retesting them following any changes or upgrades

However you conduct your meetings, record what was discussed and distribute meeting minutes promptly to all project contributors (and to others as appropriate). File meeting minutes in your project archives.

Informal Project Communications

Never limit project communications to scheduled meetings. Some of the most important communication on technical projects takes place at coffee machines, in hallways, and during casual conversations. Project risks may surface far earlier in these discussions than in formal analysis.

Successful project leaders create opportunities for these frequent, unstructured conversations. The idea of "management by wandering around," popularized by Dave Packard and Bill Hewlett, is a particularly effective way to reinforce trust and build relationships within a project team. Even when teams are distributed and you are unable to talk frequently with people in person, there will be opportunities to do it once in a while, and you can rely on the telephone in between. A great deal of "soft data" and valuable project information on project risks surfaces during casual exchanges. Effective project leaders also work to encourage interactions among project team members. Team cohesion, which correlates strongly with the amount of informal communication, is one of your best defenses against project risk.

Project Archive

In addition to distributing project documents and reports to your stakeholders and contributors, you also need to retain copies as part of your project management information system (PMIS). This archive not only serves as an ongoing reference during the project, it is essential for capturing the lessons learned during postproject analysis, and it contains data that can improve risk management on future projects.

A typical project archive contains:

- Project definition documents
- All project planning documents
- Each project status report
- Other periodic project reports and communications
- A change control history

When the project is completed, the final addition will be the post-project retrospective analysis and lessons learned.

Project Reviews and Risk Reassessment

When you operate a complex piece of machinery such as an automobile, you frequently need to add fuel, check the oil and the air pressure in the tires, and make other minor adjustments. This is sufficient in the short run, but if you never do anything more, the car will soon break down. Periodically, you also must perform scheduled maintenance, to change the oil, replace worn out or poorly functioning components, check the brakes and other systems, and generally bring the vehicle back into good operational condition.

A project is also a complex system. The activities in the status cycle are necessary, like adding fuel to a car, but unless the project is very short, they are not sufficient. Most projects also require periodic maintenance, in the form of a project review. The planning horizon for some technical projects may be as short as two to three months, or it may stretch to most of a year, but no project can plan with adequate detail beyond its planning limit, whatever it may be. Project reviews allow you to take a longer view, beyond the next status cycle, to revalidate the project objectives, plans, and assumptions. Successful project and risk management require cycles of review and regular reassessment to keep the project on track.

The limited planning horizon and technical complexity also contribute to the greater project risk of lengthy projects, and project reviews are an effective way to better manage these factors. During a project review, one of three scenarios will arise. Some reviews find few issues and the project will proceed as planned. Other reviews will reveal changes or additional planning that is necessary, and the project will continue, but only after modifications. The third possible outcome of a project review is a recommendation to cancel future project work. Although this is not pleasant, it is ultimately better for everyone to cancel a project that will eventually fail before spending even more time and money.

Whatever other agenda items you set for your project review, plan to explicitly reassess your risks and analyze your reserves. Discuss the problems and risks you have encountered in the project so far, and brainstorm methods for avoiding similar trouble as the project proceeds. Also, review your existing risk list, and identify additional scope, schedule, resource, or other risks that are now visible in the project. Add the new risks to your risk register and reassess all of them, rank-ordering the risks based on current information. Develop appropriate risk responses for any significant risks that have none.

As you review your risks, also reassess the overall risk profile for the project. As projects proceed, things change and overall risk changes with them—either increasing or decreasing. As the work proceeds and more is known, project-level risk should decrease, but every project is different and it is prudent to reassess. In particular, review the usage of any reserves established for the project. If contingency funds have been depleted faster than anticipated, determine what might be done to replenish them. If you have used most (or all) of your schedule reserve, consider options for increased staffing, revision of the deadline, or other alternatives.

After your review, document what you discussed and learned. If changes to the project objective or reserves are necessary, discuss your recommendations with your project sponsor and use your change processes to implement them.

A project review is also a good opportunity for recognition and celebration. Prepare a presentation to summarize the project's progress to date, and your plans going forward. Use the presentation to report significant accomplishments and to publicly thank specific people and teams. Accentuate the positive, emphasizing the value and importance of the project. Use the presentation to renew enthusiasm for the project and motivate the project team. Project reviews are also a good time to celebrate your accomplishments. Long projects, especially, need more parties.

Taking Over a Troubled Project

This chapter ends by exploring one additional project execution risk. As the PERIL database shows, staff turnover is a significant problem. It can be an especially personal one if the turnover results in your being asked to lead a failing project. This unfortunate situation is one of a project leader's worst nightmares. Even if you inherit a project that appears to be in pretty good shape, it's best to respond to such a request with, "I'll take a look at it and let you know as quickly as possible if any changes or adjustments might be needed."

Your first order of business is to find out whatever you can about the project and get to know the team. Although it may be interesting to dig into why the prior project leader is no longer in the picture, this can probably be left for later unless the information will contribute to project recovery.

Learning about the project can begin with a review of project documents and other information in the project archive and elsewhere. If there is a well-maintained archive of project information in a PMIS, it will be invaluable. A new project leader who has access to such data still faces a daunting task but will be light-years ahead of where he or she would otherwise be. On a troubled project, though, there may be little useful information. You may need to do the best you can to quickly fill in the gaps.

For current information, spend time reviewing recent status reports. Be skeptical and verify any information in them that is inconsistent with what you see. Discuss the project with each project contributor, and use these conversations to solicit suggestions for change, to build your understanding of where things are, and to start establishing relationships and trust. Avoid making predictions or firm commitments while you investigate, but do communicate openly and let people know when you expect to have better answers.

If there is little concrete (or credible) information, you will need to initiate a very fast planning effort to develop some. Even if there is data, at least do a quick project planning review to validate it. Someone else's plan can be a good starting point, but it won't serve as a credible foundation for project execution until it's yours. An "express" planning exercise should include, at minimum, detailed examination of all current and pending activities, verification of the project's committed scope, timing, staffing and funding, and documentation of all currently identified issues and problems.

There are a number of reasons that projects may be viewed as failing, so determine what the main problem (or problems) are. Some typical issues include:

- Schedule delays
- Excessive resource consumption
- Insufficient staff or other resources
- Scope not achievable using available technologies and capabilities
- Low priority
- Conflicts with other projects
- Weak sponsorship

Recovery requires prompt action, and the best strategy for this comes from the medical field: triage. Once you have determined what is not going well and listed all the project activities and issues needing attention, sort them into three categories. Some things need immediate attention and will result in permanent damage to the project if not addressed immediately. Identify and staff this work, stopping other activities with lower urgency where necessary. Other matters on your list need attention but not right now, so put them aside for the present and plan to address them soon. Other matters listed may be hopeless. Note these and move on.

This last category is potentially very revealing, because these legitimate project problems may provide evidence that the project cannot be completed. Even the issues that you are able to manage and resolve may require more resources, time, or both than can be justified. Schedule time with the project sponsor to review your response actions and the overall project. Plan to discuss modifications to the project or even cancellation. Not all troubled projects can be fixed, and it's better to pull the plug on a doomed project sooner rather than later.

If the project is recoverable, your next steps after resolving the short-term problems will be to schedule an in-depth project review, as described above. Your goals for this are to understand the project and engage the project team in developing current and realistic project planning information, including updated risk data. Once you have the truck back on the highway, invest the time it takes to ensure that you can keep it there and out of the ditch. Tools for this are found throughout this book.

Key Ideas for Risk Monitoring and Control

- Collect status dogmatically.
- Monitor variances and trends frequently throughout your project.
- Respond to issues and problems promptly.
- Communicate clearly and often.
- On long projects, conduct periodic risk and project reviews.

Panama Canal: Risk-Based Replanning (1908)

Project monitoring and prompt responses when necessary were among the main differences between the first effort to construct the Panama Canal and the second one. No project proceeds exactly as planned, and the U.S. canal project was no exception. It was ultimately successful because the managers and workers revised their plans to effectively deal with problems as they emerged.

As the work at Panama continued, for example, it seemed that the more they dug, the more there was to dig. Mud slides were frequent, and between 1906 and 1913 the total estimates for excavation more than doubled. The response to this problem was not terribly elegant, but it was effective. Following the report of a particularly enormous mud slide in the Culebra Cut, George Goethals remarked, "Hell, dig it out again." They had to, many times. Some risks are managed primarily through persistence and perseverance.

As time passed, a number of factors not known at the start of the project came into focus. By 1908, it became clear that new materials, including the steels to be used on the canal, were making possible the construction of much larger ships. Goethals made two significant design changes as a result of this. The first was to commit to a wider excavation of the Culebra Cut, increasing it to nearly 100 meters (from 200 feet to 300 feet) to accommodate ships wider than 30 meters sailing in each direction. Although this represented much additional digging, it also made the tasks of ongoing maintenance and dredging a little easier.

The second change was to the size of the locks. Based on Goethals's estimates of the size of future ocean-going ships, the locks were enlarged to be 110 feet wide and 1,000 feet long. Although conversion to metric units of these dimensions is simple, few do it, as this somewhat arbitrary choice of dimensions became the single most important factor in twentieth-century ship building. These dimensions are the exact size of the rectangular-hulled PANAMAX ships, the largest ships that can transit the canal. Apart from oil supertankers (which are generally designed for use on a single-ocean, point-to-point route), very few ships are built any bigger than a Panama Canal lock.

In addition to making the locks larger, Goethals made another change to them. All the water used to operate the canal flows by gravity. Locks are filled from the man-made lakes above them and then emptied into the ocean. During the rainy season, this works well. In the drier parts of the year, the depth of the lakes falls, and the water level in the cut connecting them could fall too low to permit ocean-going ships to pass. To save water, Goethals redesigned each of the twelve locks with multiple sets of doors, enabling smaller ships to lock through using a much smaller volume of water.

One additional significant change was adopted midproject, primarily for security reasons. At the start of the twentieth century, the global political situation, particularly in Europe, was increasingly unstable. The geography of Panama has a long, gradual slope from the central ridge north on the Atlantic side, and a much shorter, steeper slope on the south, facing the Pacific. On the steeper Pacific slopes, the locks in the original plan were visible from the water, and Goethals, a military man, feared that the canal might be closed down by projectiles fired from an offshore warship. To avoid this, he moved the Pacific locks further inland. The change actually made the engineering somewhat easier, as the new plan took better advantage of the more level land farther up the slope.

George Goethals minimized risk through scrupulous management of all changes, insisting throughout his tenure that "everything must be written down." Once the plan was set, the debating stopped, and all the effort went to execution.

12

Closing Projects

> *"History repeats itself. That's one of the*
> *things wrong with history."*
> —CLARENCE DARROW

Reviewing the records of technical projects, it is striking how many consecutive projects fall victim to the same problems. Common issues such as inadequate staffing, top-down imposed deadlines that have nothing to do with the work, fixed commitments based on little or no analysis, and many other issues listed in the PERIL database plague project after project. One definition of insanity is repeating the same actions over and over, hoping for a different result. More than a little risk in most projects is a direct result of using the same methods for projects that have caused problems in the past.

Getting better results requires process improvement. Using a continuous cycle of measurement, small modifications, new measurement, and comparative analysis, you can discover ways to improve any process. You can, as part of project closure, examine the results you obtained from the processes that were used for each project. Achieving consistently better results and minimizing future risks requires you to identify what worked well, ensuring that these processes are repeated on subsequent projects, and it also requires you to isolate the processes that do not work and investigate changing them. Any process change you come up with is probably a better bet than repeating something that does not work. After the changes, if the performance of your next project is still not good enough, you can always change it again. Postproject analysis is a powerful and effective tool for longer-term project risk management.

Project Closure

There are a number of closure activities common to most technical projects, but the specifics vary a great deal with the type of project. Project close-out generally involves:

- Formal acceptance of the project deliverables (for successful projects)
- The final written report
- Close-out of all contracts, documents, and agreements for the project
- Acknowledgment of contributions
- A postproject retrospective analysis to capture the lessons learned
- A celebration or other event to commemorate the project

The most relevant of these to risk management is the retrospective analysis, which is covered in detail later in this chapter.

Formal Acceptance

One of the greatest potential risks any project leader faces is finishing the work only to be asked, on delivery, "What's this?" Scope risk management seeks to avoid this situation through validation of the initial specifications and scrupulous management of changes. Defining all final acceptance testing, aligned with the initial specifications, should be one of the first activities undertaken in technical projects, as part of scope definition and planning. Testing and acceptance requirements must also be modified as needed throughout the project in response to authorized changes. If final tests and acceptance criteria are defined late in the project, it is only through happenstance that the project deliverables will meet the requirements.

Managing this risk involves thorough specification of the deliverable and frequent communication throughout the project with the people who will evaluate and accept it. You can also minimize the risk greatly by engaging them in discussions and evaluations of any prototypes, models, incremental results or other interim project deliverables. Detailed, validated scope definition is the best way to minimize late project surprises.

When your project is successful, get formal acknowledgment of this from the project sponsor, and as appropriate from the customer or other stakeholders. For technical projects undertaken on a fee-for-service basis, generate the final billing information and ensure that the customer is properly and promptly billed. Even for projects that end in cancellation or fail to deliver on all of their objectives, you should obtain written acknowledgment whenever possible of the partial results or other accomplishments that you did successfully complete.

Final Project Report

The main purpose of a final report is to acknowledge what has been done and to communicate to everyone involved that the project is over. Every final project report should also thank the contributors.

Contract and Document Close-Out

For all internal agreements and external contracts that are specific to your project, complete any final paperwork required. Following final payments of all invoices, summarize the financial information and terminate the agreements. If there are issues or problems relating to any contracts, escalate and resolve them as soon as practical. If you have had difficulties with any outside service providers, document them and make the information available to other project leaders to avoid similar risks in the future.

As part of project closure, add all final project documentation to your project information archive.

Acknowledging Contributions

It is a small world. When you work with people once, the chances are fairly good that you will work with them again. Managing risk in a continuing stream of projects depends on developing and maintaining trust, relationships, and teamwork. Recognizing the accomplishments and contributions that people have made is fundamental to this.

On technical projects, expertise and hard work are frequently taken for granted. When technical people finish difficult activities, often the only feedback they get is an assignment to another, even more difficult activity. Especially at the end of a project, you need to *thank* people, both in person and in writing. For people who work for other managers, acknowledge their contributions to their management also. Keep your remarks truthful, but focus on positive contributions. If it is culturally appropriate, praise people and teams publicly as well. If there are programs in place for specific rewards, such as stock options or other tangible compensation for extra effort, submit recommendations for deserving project contributors to reward them for their work.

Celebration

Whatever the atmosphere has been in the closing days of your project, bring the project to a positive conclusion. Celebrate the success of the project with some sort of event. Even if the project was not a success, it is good to get people together and acknowledge what was accomplished. Celebrations need not be lavish to be effective; even in businesses that may not currently be doing well financially, project teams can get together and share food and beverages that they provide for themselves. Moving on to the next project or another assignment is much easier when people have a chance to bring the last project to a friendly conclusion. If your project has a global or distributed team, arrange a similar event for each location at roughly the same time.

Project Retrospective Analysis

Managing project risk on an ongoing basis requires continuing process improvement. Whether you call this effort a retrospective meeting, lessons learned, a postmortem, a postproject analysis, or something else, the objective is always the same: improving future projects and minimizing their risks. If the people who led the projects before yours had done this more effectively, your project would have had fewer risks. Help the next project leader out—it could be you.

The overall process for a project retrospective analysis is similar to the project review process discussed in Chapter 11, but the focus is broader. Project reviews are primarily concerned with the remainder of the current project, using the experiences of the project so far to do "course corrections." A retrospective analysis is backward-looking and more comprehensive, mining the history of your whole project for ideas to keep and processes to change in projects generally.

Before you schedule and conduct a project retrospective, get organizational commitment to act on at least one of the resulting change recommendations. Performing postproject analyses time after time that always discover the same process defects is worse than useless. It wastes the time of the meeting participants and is demotivating. Decide how you will use the resulting information before you commit resources to the analysis.

Preparing for and Scheduling the Project Retrospective

Thorough postproject analysis requires you to have accurate, completed project data. As the final project documents are added to the archive, determine what information is necessary, and ensure that it will be available for review during your project retrospective meeting. Schedule the retrospective analysis soon after the project, but not immediately after it. If it is too soon, final documents will be incomplete and events from the last, chaotic days of work will dominate the analysis. Don't wait more than about two to three weeks after the project, though, or important memories, particularly the less pleasant ones, will begin to fade.

Allocate sufficient time. Even shorter projects can generate enough data to justify an hour or so to look backward. Set an agenda providing time for all contributors to comment and to collect both positive results and proposals for process change. Encourage participants to come prepared with specific examples of what went well and what changes they would recommend.

Retrospective Surveys

If your business has a standard retrospective survey form, plan to use it. A retrospective survey typically includes questions about project definition, planning, defect and issue management, decision making, teamwork, leadership, process management, managing dependencies and deliverables, testing, logistics, and general recommendations. Standard formats usually have lists of statements to be rated on a scale from "strongly agree" on one extreme to "strongly disagree" on the other, and spaces for written comments.

If there is no survey form or the one you have does not include much in the way of risk information, the following survey form may be useful.

Postproject Risk Survey

Please evaluate each of the following statements using the scale:

1—Strongly disagree, 2—Disagree, 3—No opinion, 4—Agree, 5—Strongly agree

1 2 3 4 5	The project developed and used a risk plan.
1 2 3 4 5	Project problems were dealt with quickly and were escalated promptly when necessary.
1 2 3 4 5	Schedule problems were dealt with effectively.
1 2 3 4 5	Resource problems were dealt with effectively.
1 2 3 4 5	Project specifications were modified only through an effective change control process.
1 2 3 4 5	Detailed project reviews were done on an appropriate basis.
1 2 3 4 5	Project communication was frequent enough.
1 2 3 4 5	Project communication was thorough and complete.
1 2 3 4 5	Project documentation was self-consistent and available when needed.
1 2 3 4 5	Project status was reported honestly throughout the project.
1 2 3 4 5	Reporting of project difficulties resulted primarily in problem solving.
1 2 3 4 5	The project had adequate sponsorship and support throughout.

Plan to use the survey in addition to the discussion of processes during the meeting. You can also use it to collect inputs from any project contributors who are unable to participate.

Conducting the Meeting

Start a retrospective meeting with a statement of objectives, and review the meeting agenda and ground rules for the meeting. At a minimum, establish a rule to maintain a focus on the processes and to avoid attacking individuals and "blamestorming."

Capture ideas generated in the meeting, starting with "Positives" before moving to "Needed changes" (*not* "Negatives"). Collecting positives about the project first reminds people of all the aspects that went well. Probe for specific opinions on project aspects that led to success. Capture what went particularly well on your project; identify new practices that you should repeat or extensions to existing processes that were valuable.

When most of the positives have been cataloged, focus on desirable changes. Identify process areas that need improvement and practices that should be simplified or eliminated. Consider project issues and problems that you had to deal with, and develop process recommendations to avoid them on future projects. Seek the root causes of disappointments or failures on your project and brainstorm possible ideas for mitigating them.

Throughout the meeting, work to hear from everyone, not just a vocal minority. As the allotted time winds down, summarize the recommendations, and ask each participant to nominate one recommendation that he or she believes would make the most significant difference on future projects. Work as a group to develop consensus, if possible, on the most important change, or at least generate support from the group for one or two that top the list.

Close the meeting with reflections on the process and encourage people to share what they learned from the project personally and how they plan to work differently in the future.

Documenting the Results and Taking Action

Document the meeting results in a concise format with the top recommendation (or recommendations) and key findings in a clear, short summary at the beginning. Distribute the project retrospective report to the participants for review and comment. When completed, put a copy of the results in the project archive, and share the findings with others who could benefit from the information, including the leaders of similar projects.

Take the principal recommendations to your management and request support for making necessary changes. Small changes can be fairly trivial to implement, but more significant ones may trigger new projects and require significant data, planning, and resources to initiate. If your recommendation is rejected, discuss alternatives with the project team and investigate whether there might be other ways to mitigate the problem that, although less effective, would be under your control.

In any case, take at least one issue emerging from every project and resolve to do something different in your next project to address the problem. Effective risk management requires your firm commitment to continuous process improvement.

Process improvement rests on the "Plan-Do-Check-Act" cycle, and requires persistence. Managing project risk means reusing what has worked before on your projects and fixing or replacing what has failed. *Every* project offers beneficial lessons learned.

Key Ideas for Project Closure

- Thoroughly and accurately document the project results.
- Recognize accomplishments and thank contributors.
- Conduct a project retrospective and *use the recommendations*.

Panama Canal: Completion (1914)

On August 15, 1914, the first sea-going vessel crossed Panama, and the Panama Canal opened all the way through. This huge accomplishment was reported far and wide as the biggest news of the day. The attention lasted only a short time, though, as soon World War I broke out in Europe and quickly overshadowed the canal story.

In retrospect: The eighty-kilometer (fifty-mile) lock-and-dam canal was completed, slightly more than ten years after the congressional act that initiated the work. About 5,000 additional lives were lost finishing the U.S. project. Some died from disease, with most of the loss of life due to handling explosives (making the total death toll as high as 30,000, including those who died in the 1800s). The canal opened six months *ahead* of the schedule set earlier by John Stevens, despite all the difficulties and changes. Even more remarkable, it finished at a cost US$23 million *less* than the budget (US$352 million had been approved). The total cost for construction was over US$600 million, including the cost of the French project. If this is not the only U.S. government project ever to finish both early and under budget, it is certainly the largest one to do so.

Most of the credit goes to George Washington Goethals. Although he acknowledged his debt to John Stevens, nearly all the work was accomplished while Goethals was chief engineer. After the opening of the canal, Goethals remained in Panama as governor of the Canal Zone, to oversee its early operation and deal with any problems. His thoughts on completion of the work at Panama, delivered in March of 1915, were:

> We are gathered here tonight, not in the hope of something to be accomplished, but of actual accomplishment: the two oceans have been united. The [mud]slides hinder and prevent navigation for a few days, but in time they will be removed. The construction of the Canal means but little in comparison with its coming usefulness to the world and what it will bring about. Its completion is due to the brain and brawn of the men who are gathered here—men who have served loyally and well; and no commander in the world ever had a more faithful force than that which worked with me in building the Panama Canal.

If you were asked to name a famous engineer, Goethals would be an excellent choice. Although there are other engineers who have become famous as astronauts, politicians, and multimillionaires, Goethals is famous for *engineering*. His accomplishments in addition to the canal are substantial, and he remains a significant influence in civil engineering to this day. The lessons learned from this project are thoroughly documented (as with all projects undertaken by the U.S. Army Corps of Engineers). They serve as the foundation not only for the subsequent civil engineering projects of the twentieth century but also for much of what is now recognized as modern project management.

13

Program, Portfolio, and Enterprise Risk Management

"There are risks and costs to a program of action.
But they are far less than the long-range risks
and costs of comfortable inaction."
—JOHN F. KENNEDY

The future, for any organization, requires action and entails risk. The subject of this book, project risk management, is a useful starting point for managing risk, but it will rarely be sufficient. Projects are always part of something larger. Programs are made up of projects, so program risk management relies on project risk management, among other things. Project portfolios are made up of projects and may also include programs, so portfolio risk management also depends on project risk management. Enterprise risk management includes all of these types of risk management, along with additional considerations. This chapter explores the relationship of project risk management to each of these higher-level perspectives.

Project Risk Management in Context

Project success or failure is generally measured against the triple constraint of scope, time, and cost, and the risks listed in the PERIL database reflect these categories. The success of programs and portfolios, not to mention the health of the enterprise as a whole, depends on successful projects—those that meet the objectives that they commit to. However, at each level above the project, the connection with project risk management becomes more abstract. The focus shifts, and these managers are not necessarily measured and evaluated based on the fate of any particular single project. Risk management in these other arenas goes beyond the concerns that keep project leaders awake at night.

The Focus of Program Risk Management

"Program" is a term that means different things in different contexts, but the Project Management Institute defines a program as "a group of related projects managed in a coordinated way." This chapter explores this type of program, where the main objective for program management is better overall control of interconnected projects than would be possible if they were managed autonomously. Programs include projects that are executed in parallel, in sequence, or both. Projects are time limited, with a specific start and finish. Programs may also have deadlines, but some are open ended—only the component projects have well-defined closure objectives. Programs may contain a few projects, hundreds of projects, or any number in between.

Program risk management closely resembles project risk management. For small programs, there may be no difference at all. Risk management for the program can be little more than aggregation of the risk plans and strategies for the included projects. For larger programs, however, there is an increasing focus on the successful delivery of benefits and value, which may require risk trade-offs among the constituent projects.

The Focus of Portfolio Risk Management

When projects are aggregated into portfolios, the overall focus shifts even further from the results of a particular project or program. Portfolios, whether made up of stocks, junk bonds, subprime mortgages, or projects, are primarily focused on delivering an expected return. For portfolios of projects, risk in the aggregate depends more on the average project performance than on the success or failure of each particular project.

The Focus of Enterprise Risk Management

In the abstract, an enterprise can be thought of as a bundle of projects and other activities that increases in value over time though successful execution of those undertakings. Ideally the appreciation in value will be more attractive to the investors and owners than alternatives such as stuffing money into mattresses. From this perspective, enterprise risk management is little different from portfolio risk management, and again the main objectives tend to be financial. At the enterprise level, though, there are other risks that must be managed. Some relate to the survival and ongoing health of the organization. Laws and regulations must be obeyed, and principles need to be established and followed to ensure the trust of owners, customers, employees, and others in the future. In addition, corporate officers of public corporations in the United States and elsewhere are now faced with significant new personal penalties and potential legal prosecution. The relationship between enterprise risk management and project risk management is bidirectional. The financial success and overall well-being of an enterprise depends on effective project risk management, especially for large and high-visibility projects. In addition, enterprise risk management, particularly since 2000, has been a particularly fertile source of projects.

Program Risk Management

The line between project and program management is not exactly precise. An endeavor with ten people that delivers a result in six months is a project, and an undertaking with hundreds of people working globally in a dozen independently managed teams to deliver periodic deployments over the course of five years is a program. Between these extremes, you will find both very large projects and modest programs, and the difference between the two can be fuzzy. From the perspective of risk, though, program risk management depends heavily on the project risk management principles outlined in the earlier chapters of this book, with a few added considerations.

The main purpose of program management is dealing effectively with the potentially overwhelming detail; work that entails thousands of activities and large numbers of contributors is unwieldy to plan, and it's impossible to monitor as a single effort. Program managers have daunting responsibilities. They are accountable for the overall program objective, managing the efforts of the individual project leaders, and often a dedicated program staff or a program office as well. Breaking large undertakings into chunks of work that can be effectively delegated and managed as (largely) independent projects is done for the same reason that projects are decomposed using a work breakdown structure—it reduces the complexity by converting the large and complicated into parts that are easier to deal with. Managing risks at the program level begins with ensuring adequate planning and risk management at the component project level. Although doing this is an effective start on program risk management, it is insufficient.

It is never possible to break up a large piece of work into a set of totally disconnected pieces; interrelationships remain that represent program-level risks. At a minimum, program scope connects the included projects, along with the overall business justification for the work. From a scheduling perspective, there are always cross dependencies connecting the projects within the program. None of the interconnections is entirely contained within any of the component projects, so they need to be tracked and managed at the program level. These program interconnections showed up in the PERIL database both as scope defect risks due to integration issues and as schedule dependency risks arising from project timing difficulties. Also, because programs are generally bigger and often longer than projects, they represent larger risk because of their scale.

For all these reasons, programs usually have a risk profile that exceeds the sum of their parts. A collection of modest-risk component projects may well aggregate into a high-risk program because of positive probability correlations for project risks in the interconnected projects. There are also cascade effects. When a risk occurs in one project, it can trigger additional problems in several other projects—quickly spinning things out of control. Managing project risks is necessary but program risk management requires additional work.

Planning Program Risk Management

Chapter 2 discussed the topic of planning for project risk management, observing that for small undertakings informal risk planning is generally sufficient. For a program, informal planning is not good enough. Formal program risk planning is a part of program initiation. To get started, map out how much effort this will require and verify support for the work with your program sponsor (and with your other stakeholders, as appropriate). Program risk management is often integrated with other ongoing responsibilities of the program staff, but if you plan to use a separate staff with a separate budget, secure approvals and funding for this. For the program, document:

- The risk tolerance of your sponsor and key stakeholders
- The owner for program risk management (if not the program leader) and other program staff who will participate, with their roles
- The process you will use for program risk management, including the format for the program risk register
- The planned frequency for program risk reviews
- The location where program risk information will be stored and how you will track and communicate program risks
- Any metrics to be used in monitoring program risks

As an example, for several years I was responsible for planning and risk management for a large program that started at Hewlett-Packard in 2002. This program was responsible for consolidating global oversight for all current fee-for-service projects under a single, consistent set of processes and information technology applications. The program had direct responsibility for a budget of several million dollars per year and had a shifting roster of about 200 contributors working on more than a dozen project teams that were either geographically based or responsible for delivery of key functions. The program implemented roughly four countries per quarter, and by 2006 the system was in operation in more than fifty countries worldwide.

Risk management was an important success factor for the program. The processes used for this were well defined and documented. I used them throughout the program to conduct monthly program risk reviews with the rest of the program staff. In our meetings, we reviewed the risks already listed in the program risk register, retired any that were no longer of concern, and added new risks based on evolving program plans and external changes. During each meeting we reprioritized the significant risks and then outlined risk prevention strategies. Where necessary, we also developed contingency plans for recovery. Following each monthly meeting, I distributed the updated risk register to the project leaders, and I made the current version available to everyone working on the program on the program's Web-based knowledge management system. By periodically considering the risks and keeping them visible, we avoided quite a few problems and kept the program on track.

Identifying Program Risks

Program risk identification begins with planning each component project and identifying the risks at that level. Across the entire program there may be hundreds or even thousands of identified risks. Nonetheless, the program risk manager should review all of them and provide feedback on the analysis and response strategies, especially where the assessments appear inconsistent or flawed.

Generally, project-level risks are best managed at the project level. However, you do want to add any project-level risks to the program risk register that are:

- Significant enough to be program "showstoppers"
- Associated with technical complexity (architecture, systems engineering, and the like) that could result in integration problems or defects

- Potential conflicts involving individuals or other resources needed by two or more of the projects
- Related to cross-project dependencies

In addition to these risks, you should list program exposures that relate to the overall scale and staffing, especially if project teams are geographically distributed or managed through outsourcing. Also consider risks related to turnover, queuing for key program resources, program communications, and ongoing motivation (particularly for long duration programs).

Build a program risk register similar to that used at the project level, adding program-level risks as appropriate through brainstorming, review of lessons learned from earlier similar programs, and scenario analysis. The risk register for the HP program discussed earlier in this section started with about twenty-five items and averaged roughly thirty throughout the program. (Risks that were managed at the project level were typically about an order of magnitude more numerous.)

Assessing Program Risks

Program risk assessment does not really depart much from the principles of project risk assessment described in Chapter 7. Use qualitative assessment methods based on categories to prioritize program risks. For significant risks, use quantitative analysis to refine your understanding and drive response strategies. Because the information for risk may come from remote or second-hand sources, be especially wary of data-quality issues and skeptical about impact and probability estimates that seem excessively optimistic. If risk consequences are expected to be within a wide range, be conservative and use the worst case for your assessment. For probability, probe connections between the risks, and increase probability assessments for related risks.

Sort the risk list and select the most significant ones, focusing on:

- Interdependencies and interfaces between projects
- Complexity and potential deliverable defects
- Staffing difficulties, motivation issues, and funding commitments

Responses for Program Risks and Interface Management

As with assessment, program risk responses primarily depend on tactics similar to those effective for project risks. For each selected program risk, consider options for avoidance, mitigation, or transfer. If you can find no appropriate response for any of the significant risks, develop contingency plans for recovery. Ensure that the individual project plans include the specifics necessary for managing the important risks, and determine how you plan to monitor for key risk triggers at the program level.

Cross-project dependencies, or interfaces, are one of the biggest sources of program-level risk. An effective process for dealing with these connections is central to managing these interconnections. Although project interdependencies may be identified during basic project planning, it is the program manager who is ultimately responsible for managing these relationships and their related risks. Initial planning for these predecessor/successor relationships is done at the project level; managing them may require trade-offs and decisions that cannot be made by individual project leaders. Even when interfaces appear to be under control at the project level, each still represents potentially significant program risk to be managed.

Responding to these risks involves reliable, well-documented cross-project commitments. The relationship depicted in Figure 13-1 shows a typical interface. Each interface is partly within a project contained in the program, but it is also partly in "no man's land" where neither of the involved projects has full control.

The terminology of suppliers and customers is useful in analyzing program interconnections. The interface linkages initiate in the supplier project, and they terminate in the customer project.

Within a program, external predecessor dependencies are inevitable, so they will surface as part of project schedule development, as discussed in Chapter 4. Managing these interfaces begins with the planning for the customer project. Each external input for a "customer" project is a risk both for that project and for the program. Project planning processes will also uncover external successor dependencies, where

Figure 13-1. Program interface connecting two related projects.

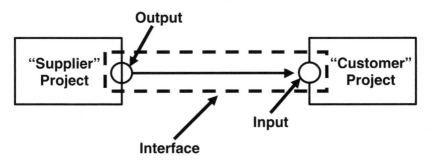

the projects supply deliverables as *outputs* to other projects within the program.

Once identified, each interface in the program needs a formal written description—documenting all the inputs and outputs identified by the connected projects. At the program level, each input must be sorted out and matched with an equal and opposite output. Program interface management requires that all identified interfaces be resolved and support the overall program plan. To begin the process, the project leader of the customer project documents all inputs required, listing specifications and requested timing. Ideally, each documented input is quickly associated with an output planned by a supplier project, and there is quick agreement by the corresponding project leader to supply it. When there are no issues with requirements or timing, the two project leaders formally agree on the terms of the interface, treating it as a binding contractual commitment.

For many situations, though, it won't be that simple. There may be required inputs for which there are no planned outputs. For some of these, additional planning by a plausible supplier project may be needed to ensure that the need is met. For others, a change of scope may be necessary, or the customer project may need to plan to meet the need internally. Even when the inputs and outputs align there may be issues. When there are differences between the input specifications needed and the output specifications planned, the program manager may need to participate in negotiations between the project leaders and guide the process to a resolution that serves the program.

Interface timing issues also are common, where inputs are needed earlier than the corresponding outputs are planned. This situation resulted in an average of seven weeks of slip in the PERIL database, one of the largest types of schedule risk and representing an abnormally large number of "black swan" risks. Significant program timing exposure results from these problems, due to the sort of project schedule gaps shown in Figure 13-2. The program manager must coordinate reconciliation and work to resolve these conflicts.

If there are identified program outputs that are unclaimed, it may reveal a planning gap in one or more projects. For necessary outputs, the program manager must locate the project that has corresponding missing inputs and work with the project leader to integrate them into the plans. Some identified outputs may prove to be unnecessary, in which case the program manager will work with the leader of the supplier project to eliminate them, along with their related activities.

All interfaces should be visible at the program level, formally documented, and agreed to in writing by each of the customer and supplier project leaders. Even when interfaces are thoroughly planned and managed, they remain program risks and belong on the program risk register, usually close to the top.

Figure 13-2. Interface timing connections within a program.

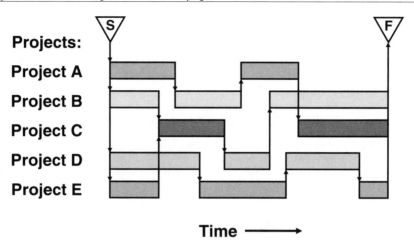

Time ⟶

The process for managing interfaces also helps with another common source of program risk. Programs regularly get into difficulty because they are quickly chopped up into projects, with little consideration of the project cross-connections that will result. The more autonomous each project is, the easier it will be for the project leader to manage. It also means fewer "white space" issues for the program manager to deal with. Integration problems, a substantial source of scope defect risk in the PERIL database, are often the result of excessive organizational complexity for the program. If there are ten projects in a program and 150 interfaces, there is almost certainly a less complicated decomposition of the program into projects where more of the dependencies lie wholly within the component projects. Excessive interfaces connecting project teams, particularly geographically distributed teams, leads to more program failure modes and higher risk. As project plans evolve and are integrated within the program, monitor the number of interfaces and keep your eyes open for a more straightforward program breakdown.

As with risks in projects, visibility is a powerful program risk mitigation strategy. When the consequences of program risks are apparent, people work to avoid them. Even when risks do occur, response to the ones that people are aware of is faster, minimizing the impact.

One final differentiator for risk response planning at the program level is the need to have an effective and well-established process for rapid escalation for when a significant risk occurs. Quick response also depends on a pre-established program-level budget reserve for use in dealing with contingencies. Where possible, also set up adequate program-level schedule reserve to protect your schedule.

Monitoring and Controlling Program Risks

Because risks at the program level are larger and generally more distant and they tend to become major disasters quickly, disciplined monitoring is essential. Frequent effective communication is central to this, and it's one of the main responsibilities of the program manager and staff.

For the Hewlett-Packard IT program mentioned earlier, our monthly risk management review meetings were a large part of our communication and risk monitoring. We also discussed major risks regularly at our weekly program staff meetings, and scheduled time during our semiannual face-to-face program review meetings to plan for risks in the next phases of work with a larger than normal number of participants. In addition, we made discussion of important upcoming risks part of our monthly "all hands" conference calls. These were "virtual" program team meetings where the program leadership team presented current program status. All of the presentation materials to be discussed on these calls were distributed in advance to the roughly 200 program contributors, and the information was also archived on the program Web site for review by those who missed the calls.

The size of the program risk register changed over time. Although it did not drop significantly, the list of program risks we were managing also did not expand, as seen in Figure 13-3. The overall severity profile of our managed risks also remained stable over time.

Program control and effective risk management also depends on strict control of changes. For large, complex programs, any change, regardless of how innocent it appears, can create a major problem. Com-

Figure 13-3. Program risks over time, categorized by severity.

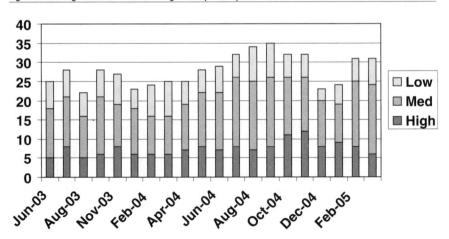

plexity also requires a hard limit on how late changes can be made; when changes are attempted too late they often are not successful in test and need to be backed out at the last minute. This creates unnecessary work both to attempt the change and then to remove it, effort that could have been applied productively elsewhere in the program and may have been effective in avoiding serious risks.

Another control strategy for programs is ongoing commitment to process review and improvement. Doing a "lessons learned" session after a project is complete is useful, but for lengthy programs there are frequent opportunities to find and deal with recurring program problems.

Particularly for lengthy programs, decreasing interest and motivation can be a big risk. Work to keep people engaged by periodic program reviews, frequent implementations and delivery of incremental value, training, and opportunities for advancement (or at least movement into new responsibilities).

Finally, programs with large numbers of contributors rarely achieve the status of a "high-performing" team, because there are just too many people involved for the necessary interpersonal connections to develop. Large programs can, however, build a high-performing program staff or program office team among the smaller number of people who are responsible for planning and managing the work over the long haul.

When I look back on the HP IT program discussed here, our biggest success factor was the investment we made, early and often, in building strong relationships and trust among the program staff. As a group, we all placed the needs of the program well above the specific details of our individual roles. There were never issues of coverage when people were absent from the program. Each individual had broad knowledge of the overall program and could fill in during times of stress (which were frequent). It mattered little what our formal roles were; we all pitched in and got things done. The atmosphere of "one for all and all for one" was our most effective tactic for managing risk and ensuring a successful program.

Portfolio Risk Management

As you move up the food chain in an organization, risk management moves from the "micro" to the "macro," as discussed in Chapter 1. Where project and program risk management focus on the specific, portfolio risk management focuses more on the aggregate. The details continue to matter, though, because one important objective of portfolio risk management is selecting projects and programs that have risks that are independent. When the risks in population of items offset, the overall risk—the expected variability of the combined outcomes—falls. Portfolio risk management tends to focus primarily on financial returns, and selecting the right mix of projects can substantially lower the variability.

Portfolio Risks: Specific and Overall

Portfolio risk management does not exclusively focus on the aggregate; obtaining the best overall return also requires working to achieve good results in each of the projects and programs that make up the portfolio. Managing projects well depends on the techniques outlined throughout this book. People responsible for managing portfolio risk tend to delegate the risk management for a particular project (or program—for the purposes of this section, the term "project" includes programs) along with all the other management responsibilities.

Managing overall portfolio risk starts with the understanding that there can be safety in numbers. Ideally, if enough projects are in plan and the organization is reasonably competent at managing the work, the few projects that fail will be offset by the small number that achieve success beyond their objectives. The theory of large numbers takes over, and the details become less important. The performance of such a portfolio is equivalent to that of the "average project." Portfolio risk management primarily depends on this.

Some projects in the project portfolio may be exceptions to the idea that only averages matter, though. These are the projects that could fail with severe consequences to the organization beyond the merely financial. Because this level of exposure could threaten the organization as a whole, managing these risks goes beyond the topic of portfolio risk management. This type of enterprise risk management will be explored in the final section of this chapter.

Planning Portfolio Risk Management

Project portfolio management is primarily concerned with categorizing, prioritizing, and selecting projects. Best-in-class organizations have a well-documented plan for portfolio management, including a strategy for ongoing portfolio process assessment and improvement. Some organizations make portfolio decisions annually and some do it more frequently, but the process is generally periodic, not continuous. During the times when decisions are being made, managing portfolio risk requires a good deal of interaction with project management processes.

Planning for portfolio management begins with a number of project management factors, including the target mix of projects by type for the organization. The portfolio selection and decision criteria also rely heavily on project risk management and planning data that will be used to assess

Figure 13-4. Portfolio and project management linkages.

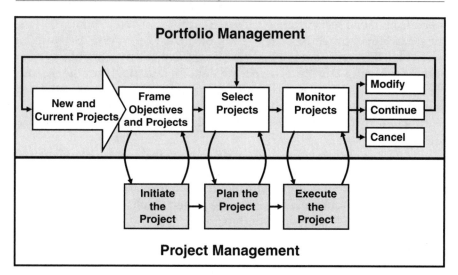

and prioritize each project opportunity. The overall relationship between an effective portfolio management process and project management is depicted in Figure 13-4.

The project portfolio management process relies on feedback from projects at several stages. The list of projects to be considered for the portfolio feeds into project initiation activities, and it depends on information obtained from them. The portfolio selection process relies on project data developed in planning, especially estimates for cost, duration, and risk. As projects execute, their status provides feedback for midcourse portfolio corrections, and it also feeds into the next portfolio decision cycle.

At all stages, project risk analysis is central to a robust portfolio management process. Deciding which projects to initiate (or to continue) relies on project risk assessments to ensure that exposures are within the organization's risk tolerances. For a start-up company there will be a high tolerance for risky projects, so the portfolio process will permit projects with considerable uncertainty. In contrast, organizations that provide custom solutions for fixed fees will tend to exclude risky projects, to protect their reputation and to avoid financial penalties. Risk information is essential to avoiding inappropriate projects.

For all these reasons, project risk data should always be a key input for portfolio selection decisions. Because these decisions are often made well in advance of any detailed planning, it is a good idea to revisit the portfolio decisions as projects develop realistic plans and can provide better data.

Planning for portfolio management also requires setting decision criteria. Because the primary performance measurement for most portfolios is financial return, some version of return on investment (ROI) estimate is inevitably at or near the top of the list of criteria. Because all types of ROI assessment depend on two estimates—the cost of a project and the worth of a project—accurate data for both is desirable. As discussed in Chapter 9, precision for ROI can be poor; premature estimates of cost are generally unrealistically low and initial estimates of value can be ridiculously optimistic. Using unreliable ROI estimates increases portfolio risk.

Other criteria derived from project management include overall effort, the project risk profile (often based on a survey, such as a shortened version of the example in Chapter 9), information based on planning, and other input collected from the project teams. Portfolio decision criteria also include data unrelated to project management, such as alignment with stated business goals and strategies, assessment of markets and potential competition, and availability of needed expertise. Selecting appropriate criteria and clearly defining how each will be evaluated contributes to minimizing portfolio risk.

Once listed, each criteria needs a weight. How the criteria are weighted also affects portfolio risk, so ensure that sufficient importance is given to risk assessment and credible project information.

Not all decision criteria are created equal. Some project selection criteria tend to bypass the portfolio process altogether. One example is a project's ability to keep you out of jail. Projects undertaken to meet industry standards or regulatory, environmental, or legal requirements generally do not require portfolio analysis; such projects are selected and funded without much debate. In your process planning, though, limit the projects that can be automatically fast-tracked into plan to those that are legitimately mandatory. Bypassing the process to accept the "pet projects" of executive decision makers without adequate analysis entails a lot of risk. Although saying "no" to such project proposals can be also risky, if you can turn them down based on objective analysis it's better for the organization, the project team, and, ultimately, even for the sponsor.

Another key consideration for portfolio planning is the mix of projects. In any organization, options vary from mundane, incremental projects to high-risk efforts that may well be impossible. Typical project category types include:

- New basic research and development
- Revolutionary products, processes, or new markets
- Next generation/new platform to replace an old offering

- Evolutionary improvements to an existing product or service
- Maintenance, support, or infrastructure

Viewed from the perspective of financial return, the highest-potential projects are usually found on the bleeding-edge end of the spectrum. If you seek to minimize risk, however, the most desirable projects are found on the end of the list with the more routine projects. For a given set of decision criteria, projects in a rank-ordered list will tend to cluster based on their category. This may result in a portfolio that is skewed, composed mostly of only one type of project. Because the balance of projects also matters, it is useful to define a target mix of project types that best supports the organizational strategy, with percentages for each project category.

These relative proportions will vary over time and from organization to organization, but the target mix should consistently reflect current tactical and strategic plans. The mix should also reflect a balance between projects that achieve results in the short term and longer-range projects that will best serve the organization's future needs. Managing this requires ongoing discipline. It is all too easy for a portfolio to become overloaded with projects of a given type—for example, too many maintenance projects or an unhealthy number of projects dependent on speculative technology. When the project load deviates from the overall business objectives, it increases business risk for the organization as a whole. Define a portfolio process that strives for a focused portfolio of good projects with risk and benefit profiles consistent with business objectives.

Identifying Portfolio Risks

Project portfolio risk identification relies heavily on the project risk identification processes described in the first half of this book.

For projects that are still embryonic, detailed analysis may not be available. In these cases, at least develop a sense of potential risks by reviewing problems encountered on earlier, similar projects. Brainstorming and scenario analysis involving people with subject matter expertise is also effective, and provides a starting point for subsequent more detailed planning and risk management.

Assessing Portfolio Risks

Although the focus of project risk management is on "loss times likelihood" for an individual project, assessment for a portfolio involves risk in aggregate. Portfolio risk assessment involves both analysis of which projects to include and exclude and an understanding of how the individual projects relate to each other.

Because most organizations always have many more promising project concepts than can be staffed and successfully executed, project portfolio management is a winnowing process. Determining how far down you can go in a sorted list of project opportunities begins with a realistic appraisal of capability. Determining overall capacity available for projects appears to be surprisingly difficult; most organizations have an exaggerated notion of how much they can accomplish. They also make matters worse by failing to account for commitments that must be staffed for support, maintenance, operations, production, and other ongoing required activities. It's not uncommon in high-tech organizations to initiate double or even triple the number of projects that can realistically be staffed. Skepticism is warranted when reviewing available capacity; the "too many projects" problem is a common and systemic portfolio risk.

The next step in the assessment process involves collecting and evaluating information on the predefined decision criteria applied to each project. As discussed earlier, relying too heavily on just estimates of ROI is problematic. Sorting a list of projects based primarily on ROI is not necessarily much better than arranging it randomly. In fact, it might even be worse, because portfolio analysis contrasts existing, ongoing projects with new project proposals. Both the cost and the value data about current projects are likely to be at least somewhat realistic, putting them at a decided disadvantage against the speculative estimates for the alternatives using data based on optimistic guesswork. Similar standards need to apply for all projects, with clear-eyed examination of potential return. New projects often appear to be straightforward, low risk, and high return prior to any detailed planning. Failure to account for this bias can lead to portfolio thrash, in which projects are regularly replaced in the portfolio by "better" opportunities, and many projects never complete.

ROI assessment for projects should also consider uncertainty. For each project, estimate the upside potential for gain (often this is equivalent to the overall ROI assessment for new projects, since it's not likely anyone has considered things that might go wrong). Also probe to realistically understand the downside potential for loss for each opportunity. Be skeptical of sales, value, profit, or other benefits assessments, especially those with suspiciously round numbers. Ask about the assumptions used to estimate the benefits, and find out how they were made. Inquire about threats, competition, or other factors that could invalidate the estimates. If there is a wide potential range, make it visible.

Ensure that decision criteria related to risk are included, and that they use input from the project team, or at least from qualified subject matter experts. Include consideration of project risks that are particularly severe, especially the potential for black swan risks. Include an assessment of risk related to the expected scale of the project, and use the project framework or one of the other high-level risk assessment ideas included in Chapter 3.

In determining the evaluations for all of the criteria, confront any known organizational biases (such as a tendency to underestimate the effort on enticing novel projects and to overestimate boring, routine ones). Work to achieve consistent, comparable results for all the projects under consideration.

After collecting and validating the project evaluation information, use it to rank-order the list of opportunities. The first few items listed will be easy to decide on: good opportunities that can be staffed are selected and put into plan. However, the deeper in the list you go, the more complex selection becomes.

One selection strategy creates a provisional list by determining the cumulative cost of projects listed starting from the top of the sorted list and drawing a cut line below the last project that can be staffed and funded using about 90 percent of available capacity. Portfolio risk management requires that some capacity be left uncommitted, primarily to deal with project risk but also to manage organizational emergencies and to provide capacity to exploit unforeseen opportunities. The list resulting from this process is provisional because it is unlikely to conform to the target mix of project types, and it also may involve unnecessary portfolio risk.

Adjusting the relative overall investments dedicated to projects in different categories is straightforward. You exclude the lowest items on the list that lie above the cut line in categories that are oversubscribed, dropping projects until the aggregate investment is in line with your target. Similarly, you include projects that are below the line to your provisional portfolio to raise the cumulative budget represented in the categories that are too small. Further adjustments may be warranted to deal with limitations on expertise, facilities, or other organizational constraints. Additional changes may be required to ensure that related projects are either all in plan or all out of plan; if projects that are cross-dependent are not executed in sync, the value they deliver can be diminished or even evaporate.

One additional factor to consider is size. The relative scale of projects also makes portfolio management challenging. To illustrate, consider this exchange:

> A university professor asked her students how many of her collected rocks she could fit into a big jar she had sitting on the desk during her lecture. Examining the pile of rocks, the class reached a consensus of perhaps six or seven. Sure enough, when she started placing the rocks into the jar, she reached the top with rock number

seven. No amount of jiggling or pressing would permit her to cram rock number eight into the jar. She then asked the class if they thought the jar was full. The students looked at the jar, looked back at the rocks, and decided that the jar looked full.

At that point the professor reached underneath the desk and pulled out a bowl filled with gravel. Since these stones were smaller than the original rocks, she was easily able to pour most of the gravel into the jar. The students watched them tumble down, filling in the open spaces between the larger rocks. She asked the class again, "Now is the jar full?"

By this time the students were starting to catch on, so most answered, "Probably not."

The professor again reached under her desk, and this time pulled out a bag of sand. She was able to dump about half of it in before reaching the top of the jar. She asked again, "Now is the jar full?"

Most students thought it was, but suspiciously they replied, "Not yet."

She reached down again, lifting a bucket of water. She proceeded to pour a good portion of it into the jar. After a moment the professor looked at the jar filled with soaking wet sand, gravel, and rocks. She looked back at the class, and asked, "What's the lesson here?"

One student bravely suggested, "A vessel is not necessarily full, even when it looks like it is?"

The professor admitted that that was not a bad lesson, but not what she had in mind. From her desk, she picked up one of the remaining larger rocks that she had initially used to fill the jar. She held it over the jar and said, "If you don't put these big ones in first, you'll never get them in at all."

In a project portfolio, there will always be some way to accommodate an additional small project. Failing to consider the large, often strategic, projects at the outset of the portfolio process, however, can result in a portfolio filled to capacity with mostly smaller projects. This may leave insufficient resources to properly support the major project opportunities, so consider putting "large rocks" in first.

It may be tempting to allocate 100 percent of your available capacity when accepting projects into the portfolio. This is risky, because putting too many projects in plan can result in problems for all projects.

The final step necessary for managing portfolio risk is to assess overall risk for the proposed portfolio as a whole. This involves estimating risk correlations for the selected projects. One of the main objectives for portfolio management is exploiting negative correlations and using them to lower the overall risk. This is the reason that some people invest in mutual funds instead of individual stocks. Although the possible gains for a mutual fund are always lower than those for a single stock, so are the potential losses. The return for the "basket of stocks" in the mutual fund more is more predictable and has lower risk. This is generally true, though it isn't always. If all the stocks in a fund are in a single industry and subject to similar exposures and threats, they will positively correlate. When any stock drops they will all probably follow, so the fund losses will mirror the losses of each stock. When project risks are related, the same will happen in a portfolio of projects.

One tactic already discussed helps in managing this—enforcing the proportions of the portfolio that will be devoted to projects in different categories. In addition to this, the portfolio manager needs to consider the projects in the provisional portfolio, examining them for, among other factors:

- Reliance on similar new technologies or applications
- Dependence on the same resources, especially outsourced or specialized staffing
- Significant project risks listed in common by several projects
- Potential failure modes shared by the projects

The portfolio management process seeks to select an optimal, or at least acceptable, mix of projects to undertake. Although risk is only one of the criteria applied to the decision process, it is a central one because the portfolio process is an important tactic for minimizing risks to the organization.

For each newly proposed or continuing project in a proposed portfolio, there are three possible outcomes.

1. The project is accepted into the portfolio, becoming or remaining an active project.
2. The project is accepted, but only after making changes (to scope, schedule, or resources) before accommodating it in the portfolio. Some projects may be lowered to an acceptable level of risk through "transfer," by purchasing insurance to deal with excessive financial exposure, by converting the project to a joint venture and sharing the risks (and rewards) with a partner organization, or through other adjustments.
3. The project is rejected. Some (perhaps most) project ideas should be turned down or postponed for reconsideration at a later time.

Before finalizing a list of projects as the "in plan" portfolio, ensure that both the individual project risks and the overall cumulative risks have been thoroughly evaluated and the candidate list is consistent with the organization's risk tolerance. Identify any particularly risky projects that are accepted into the portfolio, and ensure that the executives responsible for the portfolio will have adequate visibility of their progress and will be monitoring them at least monthly.

Portfolio decisions are never permanent; successful portfolio management must periodically revisit the selection process, including risk assessment. Portfolio reviews are typically conducted about once per quarter, and may also be necessary following the completion of a particularly large project. Portfolio reviews revisit the portfolio assumptions and criteria and manage portfolio risk by considering project status information, especially data on troubled projects.

The portfolio review process is essentially the selection process described earlier, but one of the key risk objectives in a review is detecting and weeding out inappropriate projects early. This ensures that the mix of ongoing projects will continue to encompass the best available project opportunities. Best-in-class high-technology companies find and cancel questionable projects early, before too much investment is made.

Other goals for the portfolio review are maintaining a balance of projects and keeping the project portfolio requirements within the capacity limits of the organization. Immediately after a portfolio is determined, additional good project ideas will surface. One reason for maintaining some unused capacity is to permit the organization to exploit new, unexpected opportunities, so adding some of these ideas to the portfolio is not necessarily a problem. However, there is frequently little discipline used in selecting and starting new projects, and the standards used for putting them in plan are not always as rigorous as those used for the initial portfolio decisions. This can quickly lead to a list of in-plan projects that have inadequate resources; progress will falter and stall for many of them. The "if some is good, more must be better" philosophy creates both excessive project and portfolio risk. It is not uncommon for the projects undertaken by high-tech organizations to require resources that are double, or even triple, what is actually available. Resource underestimation is a common project problem, as demonstrated by the data in the PERIL database. Making matters worse, the extra projects crammed into plan are often "urgent," which tends to shift the mix toward short-term projects. This zero-sum game will result in inadequate resources being devoted to strategic projects that are more important to the organization, increasing future risk. Portfolio reviews manage risk by rectifying inappropriate balance and trimming the project list back to what can be adequately staffed and managed.

Monitoring and Controlling Portfolio Risks

The portfolio management process is not usually something that requires a lot of day-to-day attention. Portfolio risk is mostly managed in the selection and review processes. There are several matters, however, that do need ongoing attention.

Monitor high-level status for all the projects in your portfolio at least monthly. The portfolio monitoring process operates in parallel and depends upon the project execution and control processes, as illustrated in Figure 13-4. For each project, define and track a few diagnostic project metrics such as those described in Chapter 9. There are a number of software tools available for monitoring a collection of projects that can be used to implement a "project dashboard" for the portfolio. Dashboards can be quite useful, and for larger project portfolios may be necessary. For modest project portfolios, though, ongoing oversight using a handful of key measures does not usually need to be quite so complicated—a spreadsheet or a deck of presentation slides for tracking and reporting will likely suffice.

Most project portfolios have a small number of high-risk projects, and these need particular attention. At least monthly, conduct an in-depth review of progress. Work to detect issues early that might develop into major problems. For all projects in the portfolio that are currently in trouble, focus on what is necessary to bring them back under control. Allocate additional resources, revise expectations, or make other changes. Use the available reserved resource capacity to resolve the issues, and deal promptly with any problems that are escalated from the projects needing management attention.

Managing bad news at the portfolio level, as at the project level, requires a single-minded focus on problem solving and resolution. Responding to unfavorable status information with criticism, punishment, or even disapproval can take a situation from bad to worse. Motivation on risky projects is often tenuous, and you need a motivated, enthusiastic project team to solve tough problems. A troubled project staffed by disillusioned, depressed contributors will never recover.

If, after a sincere effort, there appears to be no plausible recovery scenario for a project, cancel it and get it out of the portfolio. A key job of the portfolio manager is to limit the losses when a project is headed irretrievably toward failure.

It is also necessary to monitor overall resource use, and to detect when projects are competing for the same resources. When there are resource contention issues, adjust the portfolio to deal with them, shutting projects down temporarily (or even permanently) when necessary. When projects are delayed while queuing for scarce resources, consider acquiring more capacity, or at least ensure that the queuing is based on project priority, not just "first come, first served."

One additional wrinkle at the portfolio level comes from the essentially financial basis used to measure success or failure. Assumptions made for projects are often overtaken by events, especially on long duration projects. Also, as projects progress, the estimates for cost and value are likely to change. Changes inside your organization or even outside can significantly alter the overall evaluation for any given project, and some of these changes may substantially decrease a project's expected value. As new information becomes available, re-evaluate the affected projects to determine whether they still deserve to be in the portfolio.

Overall, managing risk in a project portfolio involves ongoing dedication to ensuring that needed resources are available, risks are anticipated and managed, decisions and other required management actions are timely, barriers to progress are removed, and problems are solved. A portfolio filled with understaffed, poorly funded, trouble-ridden projects represents unacceptable risk in any organization.

Enterprise Risk Management

The final section of this chapter climbs one level higher in the organization. Enterprise risk management encompasses all the project, program, and portfolio risk management concepts, and more. One type of enterprise risk management takes a traditional view of risk, as an uncertainty with a potential for harm, in this case to the organization as a whole. There's also a more narrowly defined concept for enterprise risk management that has emerged recently, with government regulation and industry standards as its foundation. We explore the relationship between project risk management and both of these types of enterprise risk in the remainder of this chapter, beginning with the more conventional perspective.

Organizational Threats in General

Enterprise risk relates to project risk management because projects both contribute to enterprise risk and are employed to manage it. Projects create organizational risk for all the reasons discussed throughout this book. Managing enterprise risk that arises from individual projects is generally delegated to lower levels of the organization. Risk management of this type relies on the techniques for project risk management outlined in Chapters 8 and 10 for projects, and the ideas for managing program and portfolio risks explored earlier in this chapter. With the exception of the most major black swan risks that could materially damage the entire organization, few risks associated with projects are actively managed at the enterprise level.

Although project risk is not generally a big concern to the enterprise risk manager, the converse is not true. The impact of enterprise risk management on projects is quite substantial. The purpose of enterprise risk management is to ensure the ongoing viability of an organization. There are a number of specific areas where enterprise risk managers focus their attention that may affect projects, including:

- Safety and security
- Fraud and financial liability
- Casualty loss and disaster preparedness
- Organizational reputation and brand protection
- Intellectual property management

This is only a partial list, of course. There may be many other specific concerns representing potential for loss or damage to a given enterprise. One line of defense used to manage enterprise risk is defining and enforcing processes for the organization that are designed to minimize exposure. For example, legal contracts templates and review processes limit financial risks. They also include mandatory provisions intended to limit other types of risk to the organization, such as nondisclosure terms protecting intellectual property. Mandatory training for well-defined, documented standards for business ethics, enterprise controls, and other business processes are also essential to managing enterprise risk. Worker safety is also important to the enterprise. Reflecting the origins of the company manufacturing gunpowder two centuries ago, DuPont still requires stringent processes for safety in all locations and mandates periodic safety meetings for all employees, including people who are based in offices at headquarters where the safety risks tend toward paper cuts.

These and other actions at the enterprise level aimed at managing risk relate to project risk management because they influence the risks faced by each individual project. Conformance to risk-related policies set by the organization is intended to reduce project risk, and they provide leverage for enforcing risk management methods that a project leader may otherwise lack. In addition to the policies and procedures a project is subject to, each deliverable created by a project must also meet the established standards for protection of confidential information, security, reliability, and other organizational mandates. Staying within the bounds of accepted organizational expectations is good risk management.

For some projects, the link to enterprise risk management is even more fundamental. In any given year, some fraction of the projects undertaken in an organization will be primarily to manage enterprise risk. Some of these projects will implement new safety procedures or replace faulty equipment. Others will develop techniques or algorithms that limit threats to security, eliminate fraud, or deal with other sources of potential loss. Enterprise risk management is a fertile source for projects.

The Millennium or Y2K bug is a good example of this from the recent past that affected companies worldwide. As the end of the twentieth century approached, the consequences of decades of software developed and implemented using only the last two digits in dates to represent the year began to loom ominously. Most organizations trace their recognition of this as a real and immanent threat to a 1993 article in *ComputerWorld* written by Peter de Jager. In his piece titled "Doomsday 2000," he spelled out in some detail what would occur as the world's clocks ticked over from December 31, 1999, to January 1, 2000. Despite the title, the article was less about the "end of the world as we know it," and more about the breadth of the problem and the magnitude of the effort it would require to deal with it. To quote from de Jager's article:

> One IS person I know of performed an internal survey and came up with the following results: of 104 systems, 18 would fail in the year 2000. These 18 mission-critical systems were made up of 8,174 programs and data-entry screens as well as some 3,313 databases. With less than seven years to go, someone is going to be working overtime. By the way, this initial survey required 10 weeks of effort. Ten weeks just to identify the problem areas.

This article raised a lot of concern, because by the early 1990s computers were incorporated in all conceivable applications, from defense systems and automated factory control to determining the moisture in clothes dryers and the color of toasted bread. The article also provided some good advice for separating the important from the not so important. The main point was to separate the real risks, those that represented significant, permanent potential harm, from the rest. Not all computers were necessarily at risk. What mattered was whether a date function was employed, and how it was used. For some situations the problems were transitory, such as for real-time applications that rely on information for only a few days or hours. For other cases the harm would be only temporary because it could be easily detected and corrected after the fact (often manually and at substantial cost, but without much external publicity). Once the problem was publicized, programmers all over the world began to consider the possible consequences of disregarding a key portion of each stored date in their applications. There was a great deal of attention to financial and payroll systems, to ensure that paychecks would be correct and savings accounts would not be wiped out.

There were, however, situations where the impact would not be temporary or easily fixed, as well as cases where the risks might have enormous consequences that were not easily diagnosed. There were legitimate questions concerning missiles erroneously being launched, critical-care hospital equipment going haywire, and airplanes falling from the sky. Most of the extreme scenarios were low probability propositions, and this was known at the time. In a recent conversation, de Jager recalled responding with incredulity to a prediction that Y2K might result in "losing power in the United States forever." Again, the point of the article was not that we were facing the end of civilization. As de Jager stated in 1993, "It is very difficult for us to acknowledge that we made a 'little' error that will cost companies millions of dollars. . . . We must start addressing the problem today or there won't be enough time to solve it."

As with any risk, analysis of Y2K came down to "loss times likelihood." Overall assessment of the Y2K risk was fairly straightforward. The probability of malfunction of some sort on January 1, 2000, for many software applications was high, essentially certain. Impact was not difficult to estimate for most cases either. For many situations it was also high. Even for situations where the estimated economic impact appeared to be modest, there could be other enterprise-level considerations. Given the publicity, especially near the end of 1999, few organizations were willing to appear unprepared. Having difficulties related to such a highly publicized problem would make companies look incompetent and do damage to their reputations. Even though the measurable impact in such cases might have been hard to estimate with precision, it was nonetheless quite real. As was discussed in Chapter 7, this kind of qualitative risk impact often represents the most significant consequence of a risk, particularly as viewed from the enterprise level.

I saw the evolution of Y2K response at the project level firsthand, as an internal engineering and project management consultant with Hewlett-Packard. At HP, the risks were unquestionably real, and there was universal recognition that timely action was necessary. Hundreds of projects at HP were initiated to deal with Y2K. As at many companies, a lot of legacy software at HP was carefully inspected. Some projects rewrote or replaced applications. Other projects upgraded computer hardware to eliminate the potential for problems.

Estimates for such project work and infrastructure changes for all companies, governments, and other organizations worldwide range into the hundreds of billions of dollars, a massive amount of money invested in risk management.

At the project level, the impact of Y2K was mostly limited to technical projects of this sort. Risk exposure at the enterprise level, though, for some organizations extended well beyond this. Companies involved in providing IT products and services had the additional risk of potential lawsuits and damage to their corporate reputations. The threats went well beyond expense; there was a real potential for loss of customers and a fundamental threat to the business as a whole.

Managing this at HP initiated still more Y2K-related projects and work. In 1998, Ted Slater was involved in managing a business crisis communications program as part of his responsibilities in marketing in the Americas. The program was not initially related to Y2K, but as 2000 approached, it was expanded to cover corporate-level Y2K response for the entire company, worldwide. The focus was dealing effectively with any and all customer problems, especially any that had the potential for generating public relations or legal problems. The primary goal was to "do the right thing for the customer," and to do it fast. The effort involved:

- Establishing well-defined, rapid escalation processes, particularly for cases where there were any potential safety or health consequences
- Quickly involving all people who would play a role
- Maintaining effective and visible communication with all parties
- Identifying one individual responsible for all external communications and management of a consistent single message for each situation

The primary objective was to protect the reputation and brand identity by acting swiftly to solve problems and "make the customer whole." Preparations for Y2K involved simulations that tested the processes required. These tests ensured that they would function as planned. The scenarios resulted in improvements to training materials and shifts in preparation in the lead-up to Y2K, for which HP was well prepared.

Slater reports that a small number of HP customer situations arose with the beginning of January 2000, but only a tiny fraction of the worst-case estimates and none that was significant. This particular enterprise risk at HP was well managed.

As at HP, Y2K risk management everywhere proved to be successful. As 1999 ended, there were many problems—mostly small and quickly fixed—but few disasters. Although the consequences of Y2K were apparently minimal, the actual consequences did include a good deal of "clean-up" work that was neither publicly reported nor visible, particularly in areas where the threat was not taken seriously. There were, however, some significant problems that did surface despite all the publicity and preparation, including one case involving an application used in the United Kingdom to screen pregnant women. The software tragically provided faulty reports for months before its date-related defect was diagnosed and could be repaired.

The absence of massive fallout from Y2K is seen as a satisfactory result made possible by skillful application of risk management. Nevertheless, this lack of fallout has also been characterized by some as evidence that Y2K was much ado about nothing. There seems little doubt to me that the risks were real, and that doing nothing would have been ugly.

The very existence of this debate, however, raises a fundamental issue about risk management in general, and not just at the enterprise level. Managing risks is never free, and for Y2K the costs were quite large. For any risk we choose to manage, we must invest real time and money, which are easily measured, right now. We generally make a choice to act when the potential costs and consequences of inaction appear to be even higher, as John F. Kennedy stated in the quote at the start of this chapter.

Choosing to act, however, changes everything. A response that removes or mitigates a risk makes it impossible to know what would have happened without that action. Because of this, it's rarely possible to "prove" conclusively that managing a risk was worthwhile. If, as was common for Y2K, you mitigate the risk by examining and fixing deficient software or avoid the risk by dumping older systems and applications and replacing them, the cost of inaction can never be determined with certainty. Estimates of the avoided impact will forever remain an uncertain forecast, open to conjecture. You can't measure something if it doesn't happen. Particularly in retrospect, there are often people who criticize the expense of managing risk, either because they do not understand (or don't care about) the potential consequences or because they don't believe the impact or probability for the risk. Especially in the current climate of short-term organizational thinking, making investments right now to manage risks that may or may not occur in the future is becoming harder and harder to sell.

Enterprise Risk Management Based on Standards

Enterprise risk management has also come to also mean something much more specific, especially in the United States. There are a number of organizations that have codified practices for managing enterprise risk using this label. One of them is the Committee of Sponsoring Organizations of the Treadway Commission, or COSO, a U.S. government–initiated organization. COSO and other groups have defined frameworks and standards for managing enterprise risk that have had substantial influence on organizationwide risk management.

COSO is the current incarnation of a commission initiated by the U.S. Congress in the 1980s that was formed to address issues concerning inaccurate financial reporting, particularly by companies on the brink of failure that nevertheless managed to publish healthy-looking financials. It was led by James Treadway, a former head of the U.S. Securities and Exchange Commission, and comprised five U.S.–based financial standards organizations, each involved with some aspect of financial accounting or auditing. In 1992, COSO published the *COSO Internal Control—Internal Framework*, which defined tightened standards for financial reporting. The framework addressed enterprise risk assessment, but not in much detail. It called for determining risk significance (impact) and likelihood or frequency, but it did not specify how this was to be carried out. It also outlined the need to determine how to manage the risks and what actions to take, but it left the details on this to the management of each enterprise. In the wake of additional reporting irregularities, including the now well-documented shenanigans of Enron, WorldCom, Tyco, and others, COSO expanded the control framework to include enterprise risk management. COSO initiated this project in 2001, engaging Pricewaterhouse-Coopers. The project culminated in 2004 with the publication of the *COSO Enterprise Risk Management—Integrated Framework*.

One of the main reasons that this framework has had such wide-ranging influence is its relationship in the United States with the Sarbanes-Oxley Act of 2002 (SOX), and increasingly with regulatory legislation around the world similar to SOX. To meet the requirements set out by SOX and equivalent laws in other countries, companies must establish and follow well-defined and controlled processes for their public reporting, and risk management has become a central aspect of this.

This book is not primarily about enterprise risk management in general or COSO in particular, but the practice and discipline of project risk management has been influenced extensively by COSO and similar standards organizations. It is useful to understand the broad outlines of the COSO enterprise risk management framework to ensure that your projects are aligned and conducted consistently with enterprise requirements.

The COSO enterprise risk management framework includes eight interrelated components that are to be defined consistently at all levels of the organization, from the board of directors all the way down to the trenches where projects are managed:

- *Internal environment*: Includes standards, processes, codes of ethics and conduct, and much of what was discussed in Chapter 2 regarding risk management planning. Risk tolerance here is referred to as "risk appetite."

- *Objective setting*: The "what?" question. At the enterprise level, this starts with setting strategy and includes tactics, goals, and current projects. The process for this overlaps with and includes the project portfolio process explored earlier in this chapter. This is also where measures are defined that will be used throughout the organization.

- *Event identification*: Risk identification for the enterprise, including (but not limited to) project risk identification as covered in Chapters 3 through 5.

- *Risk assessment*: Both qualitative and quantitative analysis of overall enterprise risk, using techniques consistent with those discussed in Chapters 7 and 9.

- *Risk response*: This component defines precisely the same responses as Chapters 8 and 10: avoid, mitigate (here called "reduce"), transfer (here called "share"), and accept.

- *Control activities*: This and the last two COSO enterprise risk management framework items align with the practices outlined in Chapter 11 on risk monitoring and control. Emphasis is on ownership of the risk responses and on the use of retrospective analysis for feedback (as described in Chapter 12).

- *Information and communication*: Communication is always fundamental to good management at all levels. Emphasis here is on credible, frequent reporting and retention of information.

- *Monitoring*: Tightly coupled with control activities, with particular prominence for metrics. Concepts such as Robert Kaplan's "balanced scorecard" are commonly part of this at the enterprise level.

Overall, the road map outlined by COSO enterprise risk management is highly compatible with what is found in the Project Management Institute *Guide to the Project Management Body of Knowledge*, in this book, and in most other useful guidance on managing business risk.

COSO is not alone in the field of enterprise risk management standards. The Risk and Insurance Management Society is aligned with the global insurance industry and has a similar defined set of guidelines. The International Organization for Standardization (ISO) is in the process of developing an international risk management standard, ISO 31000. There are others as well, and the future will doubtless bring still more standards for managing risk. Regardless, the basic content is not likely to change materially—the fundamental ideas for risk management that have worked in the past are quite durable. No matter what, though, there will continue to be a stream of new projects created as a direct consequence of enterprise risk management. The program that I was responsible for planning at Hewlett-Packard described in the program risk management section of this chapter was largely a consequence of the regulatory changes in the United States and elsewhere. In particular, the requirements outlined in Section 404 of SOX call for a top-down risk assessment and impose standards for reporting. This has led to a tightening of processes for companies throughout the United States. At HP it also involved replacing disparate tracking and management methods in the fee-for-service project businesses worldwide to ensure consistency. The trend toward better internal controls, more audits, and improved process testing appears here to stay.

Key Ideas for Program, Portfolio, and Enterprise Risk Management

- Manage risk well in every project.
- Understand and manage program-level risks, particularly those that involve cross-project dependencies, resource contention, or program "showstoppers."
- Minimize portfolio risk through use of appropriate criteria, including risk, and unbiased assessment of project opportunities.
- Determine relative risks for projects and programs, and use risk correlation analysis to lower project portfolio risk.
- Manage enterprise risk through dogmatic monitoring and periodic maintenance of the project portfolio.
- Understand and comply with your organization's policies and standards for enterprise risk management.

Panama Canal: Over the Years

When the project finishes, the project team moves on. The deliverable remains, however, and things are rarely static. The success of the Panama Canal was as predicted, which was both good and bad. The growing traffic through the canal in its first years of operation required increasingly frequent filling and draining of the locks. The locks were filled from above using water from Gatun Lake and drained to the sea, so the water required depended on the volume of traffic. The more ships that passed through the locks, the more water had to be drained out of the lake. Even a tropical rain forest has dry seasons, so it was not uncommon for the water level to drop periodically. When the water was too shallow in the roughly 13-kilometer Gaillard Cut that sliced through the continental divide in central Panama, the canal shut down.

This enterprise risk was increasingly troublesome as the years passed. It interfered with the operation of a two-ocean U.S. Navy, which was one of the main reasons for the U.S. canal project in the first place. After several decades of periodic difficulty keeping the canal operational year-round, a sizable follow-on project was initiated to ensure a more reliable supply of water. This project constructed yet another dam, this one further up Chagres River above Gatun Lake. In 1935, the Madden Dam was completed, creating Alajuela Lake and the supply of additional water that the canal depends upon to this day.

Chapter

14

Conclusion

"Whether you think you can do a thing, or not,
you are probably right."
—HENRY FORD

Risk management processes provide a way to learn whether your project is feasible—whether you *should* think you can do it. A feeling of confidence, based on credible information, is a powerful determinant of success, and project risk information is a key source of the data that people need. When the verdict of the risk assessment is poor, it leads you to better alternatives.

This book contains a wide range of ideas and techniques for project risk management. It is fair to ask if all of these are always necessary, and the answer is simple: No. Each is essential to *some* projects at *some* times, but it is hard to imagine any project that would benefit sufficiently from everything discussed in this book to justify doing all of it. Besides, some of the concepts covered represent alternative approaches to similar ends, and would be redundant.

So, how much *is* appropriate? The answer to this, like the answer to every other good question relating to project management, is: it depends. Technical projects vary so widely that there can be no "one size fits all" answer. The trade-off between the value of risk information developed and the effort and cost associated with obtaining it always makes deciding how much project risk management to do a judgment call.

That said, there is at least one useful guideline. Do enough planning and risk management to convince yourself that the project is, in fact, possible. The quote from Henry Ford is applicable to projects of all kinds. People successfully deliver on ridiculously difficult objectives with amazing regularity, when they *believe* that they can. When people are confident that they will be successful, they persist until they find a way to get things done. Conversely, even the most trivial projects fail when the people working on them lack confidence. Their belief in failure becomes self-fulfilling; no one puts in much effort—why bother?

Demonstrating to all concerned that your project is at least plausible defines the minimum investment in project planning and risk assessment that is prudent. If you can do this with informal discussions and capture the necessary information on index cards or yellow sticky notes, do it that way and get to work. If your project warrants more formality, and most technical projects probably do, determine what you need to do to provide confidence to the project team and establish a baseline for status tracking and change management. But remain practical. Getting more involved than necessary in computer tools and complex assessment techniques is just as inappropriate to project and risk management as doing too little.

The most successful strategy for making permanent process improvements is to define your objective clearly, in measurable terms, and then to make small process additions and adjustments over time, assessing whether they are effective and helpful. Continuing this strategy over a sequence of projects will result in good control of risk at an acceptably modest cost in time and effort. Adding a lot of new overhead to a project environment all at once is not only expensive but also distracts at least the project leader from other project issues, often creating more problems than it solves.

Think about all the ideas and techniques in this book in the same way that a craftsperson views his or her tools. In the tool set there are tools that are used every day, tools that are used only once in a while, and even a few tools that have never been used, at least so far. The entire set of tools is important because even the unused tools have applications, and the craftsperson knows that when the need arises, the right tool will be available.

Choosing to Act

Charles Bosler, chairman of the PMI Risk Management Specific Interest Group (RiskSIG) and noted authority on project risk management, says, "Risk is simple. It is anything that requires you to make choices about the future." If you are currently doing little to manage risk, consider some of the following choices for your future. If your project success rate improves, this may be enough. If problems persist, add a few more ideas, and keep trying. Although risk can never be eliminated from projects completely, it can always be reduced, often with relatively minor incremental effort. The following are suggestions for getting started managing project risk.

Scope Risks

Minimize risk by thorough definition of project scope. Every aspect of the project deliverable that remains fuzzy, ill defined, or "flexible" represents a real failure mode. If you do not know enough to define everything, convert the project into a sequence of smaller efforts that you can define, one after the other, and perform reviews and testing as the interim subprojects complete. As you proceed, refine the scope definition and the next steps. If actually breaking the project into incremental pieces is not feasible, use a straw-man specification to document as much specific detail as you can and invite criticism. Always validate the scope definition with project sponsors, customers, and key stakeholders, and set the expectation that every scope change will require significant justification.

Schedule Risks

Project planning is the foundation for managing schedule risk, and planning for the immediate short-term activities (at minimum) is never optional. Based on the profile for the work, identify all the project activities that are similar to past work that has caused trouble. For every project estimate, set a range based on your confidence, or better yet, probe for the worst cases and document their consequences. For projects that carry significant risk, negotiate some schedule reserve, but establish a credible plan that could complete at a date prior to the committed deadline.

Resource Risks

Most resource risks relate to bottlenecks and constraints. Past project resource problems are likely to recur unless you develop plans to avoid similar situations. Perform sufficient resource analysis to reconcile your requirements and skill needs with the project budget and available staff. For particularly risky projects, negotiate a budget reserve.

General Risks

Examine your plan and brainstorm probable risks with the project team. List known risks and determine probability and impact for each risk using at least "high/moderate/low" assessments. Prioritize and distribute a list of significant risks, even if you only use the list to make the project exposures visible. Develop prevention or recovery strategies, as necessary, for substantial risks.

Paying Attention

The remaining minimum requirements for risk management relate to tracking and change control. Dwight Eisenhower said, "In preparing for battle I have always found that plans are useless, but planning is indispensable." Eisenhower recognized the fact that few things ever go exactly as planned, which is especially true for projects. The exercise of planning never predicts the future precisely, but it does provide what you need to measure progress and quickly detect problems. For risk management, tracking progress at least once a week for all current project activities is prudent. Failure to do this periodic monitoring allows project slippage and other problems to quickly expand and cascade, and they can soon become insurmountable. Dogmatic, frequent tracking of project work is crucial to ongoing risk management. Through disciplined tracking, many risk situations can be detected while they are small. Small problems can be resolved quickly, preserving the project plans and objectives; large problems can easily take a project down.

Project control is also central to risk management. During a running project there are many things going on that a project leader cannot control. Use the controls you do have to your best advantage. One of the most important controls the leader does have is the process for managing project changes. Projects with no ability to control specification changes are almost certainly impossible. Another thing leaders control is the flow of information. Use project reports, meetings, and discussions to communicate risks and to keep project issues and progress visible.

Long-term improvement of project risk management relies on postproject analysis. Through this, you can assess project results and make recommendations for more (or different) processes devoted to risk management and project planning, execution, and control.

Succeeding with failure-prone projects requires three things. The first, thorough planning based on stable specifications, is the primary subject of this book. The second is diligent tracking and control of changes, covered in Chapter 11. The third requirement, which is project specific and beyond the scope of this (or any single) book, is technical expertise.

Risk management is much easier when you are lucky, and this third element of success, expertise, represents the most obvious way to boost your luck. To the best of your ability, staff the project with a range of skills, including specialists in each field that the project is likely to need. Projects with experienced practitioners are much better equipped to deal with the twists and turns in a typical project trajectory. Recovery from risks is quick and effective when there are a few battle-scarred veterans who know what needs to be done and what has worked in the past. It never hurts to recruit at least some people for the project who have reputations as generalists known for their problem-solving talents. Once your team is together, you can boost your luck further by rehearsing contingency plans for significant potential problems, so if you need to use them, you will be competent and efficient.

Through all of this, never lose sight of the main objective: to manage your project to successful completion. The project management ideas presented here are components of the *means* to this end. Treat the ideas and concepts of this book as your risk management toolbox. When it makes sense, use the processes just as they are described. You may need to tailor other ideas to make them work in your environment. If a risk management idea promises you little current value, hold it in reserve. Above all, persevere. Inside every impossible project lies a perfectly credible one, waiting for you to break it free. Also remember that a little risk is not a bad thing; as Ferengi Rule of Acquisition 62 points out, "The riskier the road, the greater the profit."

Panama Canal: The Next Project

Projects have a beginning and an end, but there is nearly always a next project. These have included many over the years, such as widening of the Gaillard Cut, and the new dam built upstream in the 1930s to ensure continuous operation through the drier seasons described at the end of Chapter 13. The largest operational issue for the canal that has yet to be successfully addressed has been the limit on ship size imposed by the lock dimensions chosen by George Goethals.

To accommodate larger ships, excavation began in the late 1930s for a set of larger locks for both sides of the canal. This work was interrupted by World War II and has remained uncompleted until recently. Various alternatives for permitting transit by larger ships have been investigated over the years. Planning for this even included a proposal that was seriously considered in the 1950s to create Ferdinand de Lesseps's imagined sea-level canal using thermonuclear bombs, a project estimated to require about 300 detonations. Enterprise risk management might have been a good reason to pass up this project, but the main reason appears to have been cost.

As the twenty-first century began, so did a new era for the canal. Following the 1999 turnover by the United States, the canal is now operated by Panama. It remains a vital link in world shipping, but to ensure this into the future, the first major operational change in the nearly ninety-year life of the canal is now in the planning stages—adding a third transit through the isthmus. After a seventy-year interruption, a new set of locks is now under construction. These new locks will be parallel to the existing locks on the Atlantic and Pacific sides of the canal and are to be nearly twice as wide, 40 percent longer, and 25 percent deeper. This new route will permit transit of larger ships in addition to quicker transit for the PANAMAX freighters currently using the canal, though with a single set, transit will be in only one direction at a time. The new locks will hold nearly four times the volume of water required to operate the current locks, and elaborate and clever plumbing is planned to conserve and reuse water, allowing the existing lakes to supply enough water.

Current plans call for a budget of just over 5 billion Panamanian balboas (or U.S. dollars; the balboa has been pegged to the dollar since 1903), including a contingency of about 20 percent. The target for completion is in 2014, with traffic through the new locks commencing no later than 2015. The magnitude of this project is comparable to the original work, so it will be interesting to see which of the earlier projects the new endeavor will most resemble.

Selected Detail from the PERIL Database

The following information is excerpted from the Project Experience Risk Information Library (PERIL) database. (These risks are an illustrative subset selected from the database, representing less than three months of schedule slippage. The 20 percent of the risks that resulted in more than three months of impact are discussed in Chapters 3, 4, and 5.)

Scope Risks

- New product features were added at every weekly meeting and stage review.
- Project was based on standards still in draft form. Several options are possible, but project is staffed to pursue only one.
- Conversion from legacy system caused unanticipated problems leading to delays of three to ten days per module to fix.
- Data conversion problems made the implementation of a new system dependent on manual data reentry.
- Functionality for e-mail added late to a document retrieval project.
- Processes were changed and made more complex late in the project.
- A solution project was "priced to win" with few details on the work.
- The sponsor demanded specification changes late in the project.

- User interface requirements for a new database system were not specific enough.
- A key telecommunications requirement was detected late.
- Component failure required finding a replacement and redoing all tests.
- A 1,000-hour test was required at project end. Failure halfway required repairs and a complete test rerun.
- A critical component broke because the packaging for it was too flimsy to withstand the stress of standard shipping.
- Test hardware did not work, so all tests had to be conducted manually.
- A complex system was designed in pieces. When integration failed, redesign was required.
- Two related projects failed to synchronize, missing their release.
- A poorly implemented Web tool caused ongoing support issues.
- A problem solution was developed based on assumed root cause. The cause was actually something else and resulted in a major slip.
- A purchased electronic component failed. It was necessary to design a new one late in the project.
- The delivery of the content started before the requirements were finalized.
- An application was found to need its own server, causing delay for installation.
- In a large system conversion, new applications were not able to work with existing data as expected.
- Mid-project, scope was expanded to include the accounts receivable process.
- The database designed into the system was changed, requiring more resources and causing delay.
- An expected operating system release was canceled; the project forced to use a prior version.
- A new CPU chip to be used in the product was assumed same as old version, but required an additional heat sink and mechanical design work.
- Original scope missed supply chain issues and could not be used without changes.

- Scoping was documented and estimated based on data from only one customer.
- The product was developed for multiple platforms, but worked on only two. The project was delayed to fix some, but others were dropped.
- Market research and competitive analysis information was faulty but not discovered until late in the project.
- New technology was used, hoping for faster performance. It did not work well and resulted in redesign and rework.
- An instrument system built for a customer had been designed using the current model of PC. A new version was released that was incompatible and project completion required finding and using an older salvaged PC.
- A system using new components failed in final tests. Obtaining replacement older components proved to be difficult.
- All the individual components passed their tests, but the assembled system failed.
- A problem with transaction volumes that was not detected in test showed up in production.
- Purchased software was limited and inflexible, which necessitated workarounds and additional software.
- Late design changes required manufacturing retooling at the last minute.
- "Minor" changes were added and accepted late in the project. This doubled the work in the final phase and delayed the project.
- A database set up for the client did not have sufficient free space for all the growing accounts.
- The development team misinterpreted a number of requirements.
- Documentation was provided in only one of the two required languages, causing a delay for translation.
- Network configuration sometimes caused backups to fail, but only intermittently; troubleshooting was hard.
- PC board failure required redesign and fabrication.
- An upgrade to software was required. The planning and training for this caused delays.
- New software was installed by IT. It didn't work, and fixing it caused delay.

- Metrics from many sites were required. When collected, the data was inconsistent, causing unanticipated additional work.
- The online badge printing requirement was completely missing from the scope definition.
- Proprietary data was needed, which the owners were unwilling to provide. After some delay, they finally shared partial information.
- Expected release of a new operating system expected slipped. This forced the project team to use the prior version, which was missing needed functionality.
- Although the system functions well in Germany, it had no German documentation. Translation resulted in delay.
- A solution project elected to integrate a new, untried technology.
- Software modules in the system did not work together as planned.
- A major bug could be fixed only by moving to a later software version.
- The system move was delayed by last-minute system changes that made backups take too long.
- Scope was changed after the writers had completed their initial draft.
- A large print run of materials was scrapped and redone because of late changes required by legal.
- After the project was "complete," significant rework was required before customer approval.
- The design team failed to collect the details on what was to be displayed to users.
- The project deliverable eventually collapsed because of vibration in transit that caused nuts and bolts to work loose.
- Bugs were reported in user test that should have been caught earlier by QA.

Schedule Risks

- The quantity of CPU processor chips needed was not available.
- There were too few disc drives and insufficient physical space for the needed number.
- Conversion normally requires six months from the date a contract is signed, but project goal was four months.

- Software development was underestimated by a factor of three.
- None of the project staff knew the technology.
- Training for a new tool took more time than planned.
- Because the water supply available to complete project was inadequate, water had to be trucked in.
- Expert opinion estimated two weeks, but the work took eight.
- Needed components were delayed because of an internal supplier problem.
- Work estimated displayed chronic optimism on completion dates.
- Multiple phase rollout was delayed near the end because the systems needed were temporarily out of stock.
- Decisions were delayed without apparent reason.
- International leased line order was delayed while awaiting management approval.
- The systems required were on back order for six months, so the project was forced to use a competitor's system.
- The business counterparts were not in agreement on which option to choose.
- A special peripheral needed for the project deliverable was discontinued.
- Compilers and open source libraries needed were not available.
- Partner organizations were late with promised work, and even then their deliverables did not work as expected.
- Field engineers experienced long learning curves.
- The customer insisted on a deadline shorter than the plan.
- Development scheduled in parallel led to frequent rework.
- Needed skilled resources were unavailable.
- A three-week test took seven because of learning curves and ramping time.
- New hires used for critical work, which required time for training.
- Senior management approval for software licenses was delayed.
- The system needed was delivered to wrong building, and was lost for weeks.
- The shipping requirements changed. Some shipments bounced, others got stuck in customs.

- Metrics required by a process improvement project were collected and delivered late.
- With a twelve-hour time difference and heavy dependence on e-mail, even simple questions take two to four days to resolve.
- International shipment of parts is estimated to take six weeks, but it actually averages nine.
- Some parts were damaged in shipping and had to be reordered.
- Space was unavailable, so the project was forced to implement in the old space.
- Infrastructure changes caused last-minute problems.
- A sole-source chip supplier was reliable for low volume, but at high volume (and lower cost) it had quality problems that created delays.
- Components that could have been purchased were developed by the team, which took longer than expected.
- The system integration task was not broken down to small manageable pieces in the project plan.
- There were chronic problems getting timely management decisions.
- Disaster recovery tests were delayed at project end because the hardware required was tied up solving another customer's problem.
- Some critical equipment needed for the project came from a pool of hardware in another country, which was delayed in customs.
- Parts of the development team have a twelve-hour time difference.
- Bugs took an average of two to three days longer to fix.
- Defective parts were received, and reordering doubled the time required.
- There were frequent delivery problems on international shipment with customs and paperwork.
- Firewall changes typically had taken twenty-five days, but the estimates were capped at fifteen.
- Estimates for cabling were too optimistic.
- The deliverable expected from a related project arrived on time, but the project could not use it.
- A flood shut down the data center, resulting in delay to restore power and for clean up.

- "Customer supplied" hardware does not work, and replacements were needed.
- A system was taken down for scheduled maintenance when needed by the project.
- There was no coordinated shipment of system components, so the last part to arrive delayed installation.
- A dependency on another project was not discovered until project end.

Resource Risks

- Project needed $150,000 per month in supplies but had a limit of $100,000.
- The senior system analyst who was fully trained on the application resigned.
- The travel budget for the project was cut, which led to inefficient long-distance collaborations.
- A key subcontractor went out of business and it took two months to find a replacement.
- Midway in design stage, an important engineer had a family emergency and had to leave the country for a month.
- Two technicians were reassigned to a more "business critical" project midway through system development.
- The government contract required that the staff have only U.S.–born nationals, but there were too few.
- The only experienced programmer gave notice and left the company.
- Halfway through the project, three of the engineers had to return to China because of visa issues.
- A key engineer was pulled off the team to work on another project.
- The project manager was unavailable because of jury duty.
- Money for needed software was not in the current budget, so the project was delayed to push the expense into next quarter.
- Contract negotiations delayed the start of work.
- The project leader resigned and was not promptly replaced.
- Outsourcing the order entry process delayed all U.S.–based customers.
- Legacy systems were not retired as planned and the project team got tied up with unplanned support work.

- Critical skills unique in the head of a programmer were lost when he had a heart attack.
- Critical training had to be postponed because of last-minute emergency leave by the lead designer.
- For cost reasons, an Asian supplier was chosen, but qualification and paperwork caused delays.
- Initial stages of the project were outsourced to a professor who started late and lacked needed information.
- Last project tied up and exhausted the staff; so the following project started late and slowly.
- A key contributor was lost while solving problems related to a previous project.
- An engineer critical to the project left the company.
- Team members were reassigned to other, higher priority projects.
- Only one employee had both the COBOL and relational database data conversion experience needed and she had other conflicting commitments.
- A valuable resource was pulled off of project to work on a higher profile project.
- Team members were lost to a customer hot site.
- A consultant broke both arms three weeks before project end.
- Two projects depended on one resource for completion and the other project had higher priority.
- The system architect who knew how to integrate all the components fell sick and was hospitalized.
- An earthquake in Taiwan made part of the project team unavailable.
- There was a lack of money for needed equipment.
- Pricing negotiations stalled project work until they could be resolved.
- Slow renewal of the contract for a consultant caused a work interruption.
- The contract had no penalties for missing deadlines and a one-week task took three weeks.
- Outsourced tasks were slipping, but this was not known until too late.
- At a critical stage of the project the medical director left the company.

- Late in project, the budget and staff were cut. This resulted in delays, forced overtime, and team demotivation.
- Key people resigned, leaving too few to complete project on time.
- On a very long project, enthusiasm and motivation fell, and task execution stretched out.
- Key work in flu season was delayed when most of the staff was out ill.
- The team was frequently diverted from project to do support.
- A key resource was pulled off the project twice to fix bugs in a previous product.
- The lead engineer was stuck in Japan for two weeks longer than expected because of a visa problem.
- A packaging engineer was working on another high-priority project when needed.
- Key welding staff members were out with the flu.
- Manufacturing volumes spiked, which diverted several project contributors.
- An unannounced audit mid-project caused delay to participate and respond.
- An important team member was grounded in the Middle East during a regional war.

Index

BLOOD SECRETS

BLOOD SECRETS

By Craig Jones

HARPER & ROW, PUBLISHERS

New York, Hagerstown, San Francisco, London

FIRST EDITION

Designed by C. Linda Dingler

Library of Congress Cataloging in Publication Data

Jones, Craig.
  Blood Secrets.

  I. Title.
PZ4.J749B [PS3560.466]   813'.5'4   78-4743
ISBN 0-06-012264-1

78 79 80 81 82 10 9 8 7 6 5 4 3 2 1

BLOOD SECRETS

You never think this kind of thing really happens to people who've been to college. A strange consideration perhaps, but after the murder this was one of the first thoughts to strike me. And all through the trial I sensed that same thought hovering behind the faces of the jurors. In the beginning they seemed almost pleased, titillated by the fact I am an "educated, professional" woman, a teacher; each day their eyes would greet me with renewed astonishment. But as we progressed to the final stages they began to look embarrassed, and in the end, weary. In a trial as long as mine was, particularly a murder trial, there develops a bond between defendant and jury, at least on the defendant's part. After a while, you know instinctively what words, what phraseology, will make this one chuckle, that one wince. From their glances at each other you see where alliances have been formed and hostilities upheld. You recognize the leaders and the followers, and when you receive an occasional furtive look of sympathy, you end up measuring its worth by which face it comes from. Does that sound cold-blooded? It is, and so were the proceedings—cold-bloodedly civilized. Just the facts. My uncivilized crime ended up in a civilized trial: hecklers were promptly removed from the courtroom; "hate mail" was intercepted by my lawyer and burned; the first and only time the prosecuting attorney raised his voice to a shout, he sensed the inappropriateness, and he lowered it in midsentence. The courtroom experience produces many revelations, and the strangest one occurred on the last day. After all the torture I thought *I* had gone through—all the testimonies being weeded, repeated, reweeded—I stood up to hear the verdict and found myself feeling

1

sorry for the jury. They looked more beaten than I was. Even though it was my life hanging in the balance, it had been, after all, *my* crime, and they had been dragged through every detail of it. Who can say to what degree the whole ordeal of sitting in judgment taxed, perhaps even changed, their lives? One murder, yet who knows how far the reverberations can reach? However, I'm not going to tell you much about the trial. I'm going to tell you about the murder itself and the circumstances leading up to it. Not surprisingly, those circumstances were defined and determined by love, my own and my victim's. Since love is neither static nor isolated from everyday events, it journeys through a number of stages, from one place to another. And for some, love's last stop is a public courtroom. The newspaper implied as much when it printed my wedding picture next to a later photograph of my husband, my daughter and myself, our smiling faces looming above copy that detailed the grim events surrounding the murder. This juxtaposition was calculated to dramatize not only the death of a person but also the death of a marriage, the disintegration of a once happy family—and, of course, calculated to strike suspicion and fear in the hearts of the complacent.

I hope I am as objective and detached as I sound. During the trial, I had plenty of time to become that way, and I'll try to remain so as I tell you the story. If at any point I feel I'm losing that detachment, I'll do my best to let you know it so you can be on your guard. After all, you have your own powers of judgment to rely upon; *mine* only got me to where I am now. . . .

Detachment. It was the very thing that first attracted me to Frank. I was working on my master's degree at the state university and was quite content with being the fair-haired favorite in the English Department. As an undergraduate, I had made the dean's list every term and had been admitted to the Honors College, a distinction which carried all sorts of practical advantages, including a private room in an overcrowded dormitory. I stayed on at State for my master's even though I was courted by fellowship offerings from five more prestigious universities. I was secure, comfortable and smugly superior. At the time I met Frank, I wasn't consciously aware that I was tiring of my niche. Had I been as satisfied as I thought I was, I probably would have dismissed him at our first encounter.

I had only one girlfriend, Gloria Davidson, who lived in an apartment off campus. There were many reasons for my liking Gloria. Being number four scholastically in the English Department, she never begrudged my being number one, and she never competed. She was forthright and witty, more glamorous but less vain than I, and uncommonly loyal. Despite the fact that we were the same age, I called her "the kid," an endearment she would smile at and one that succinctly defined our relationship. I had no sister, only two younger brothers; she had one older sister, whom she disliked, and so the chosen roles in our friendship were perfectly suited to each of us. Whenever we double-dated, she had a childlike and charming way of showing off our friendship by directing most of her attention to me while her date was drooling over her. She enjoyed my mock cynicism and was dazzled by the impression I gave of being totally self-sufficient. Whenever possible, she signed up for the same classes I did. Sitting next to me, she would take copious notes while I slouched in my seat, lost in a crossword puzzle or a newspaper bridge column. Now and then, when there was a lull in the lecture, she would glance at me, amused, and yet admiring my "rebelliousness." I helped her shop for clothes and passed judgment on the men she went out with. Secretly, I reveled in the knowledge that I was the rock and she the tide. However, the self-serving incompleteness of this metaphor escaped me at the time: for it is the movement of the tide which shapes the rock. Later, Gloria was to become a major influence in my life—and a witness to the murder.

Frank lived in Gloria's building, and we met at a party given by another tenant. After my first glimpse of him standing in the middle of the room, I turned to Gloria and said, "Where did they dig up Abe Lincoln?" I assumed immediately, and correctly, that he was a history major, since that department had a reputation for corraling the oddest-looking people on campus. He had the uniform black-frame glasses and the pipe filled with

3

Cherry Blend, the requisite tattered turtleneck (although it was the middle of May) and the worn trousers shiny in the seat. His stiltlike legs seemed to compose more than half his height of well over six feet. Actually, he didn't look at all like Abe Lincoln; his face wasn't that dramatic. I remember thinking his features were actually recessive, because there was nothing distinctive or imposing about them. His eyes were simply oval, his nose short and straight, his mouth neither too thin nor too ample. Viewed full face, he was average; in profile, forgettable. For 1958, his hair was rebelliously long, the color of mud, the texture of straw. He was nothing the movies were looking for and not what *I* would have looked for—had I been looking.

The party was quite successful. Most of the people were serious students who on the weekends became serious drinkers. Long before midnight, most of us were drunk and playing a vicious game called Speculation, wherein each of us matched up two unpopular faculty members, created an unlikely dialogue between them, then speculated on what they could possibly find to do with each other in bed. I loved this game (I played only those games I was good at) because my speculations usually made me the center of attention. At these parties, I was the rock, with all kinds of crosscurrents caressing me. This party was no exception—until I went into the kitchen to freshen my drink. Just before I reached the doorway, I heard Frank say inside: "It's the purest form of love there is."

I rounded the corner in time to see the other man responding with a smirk. "What is?" I asked.

Frank blushed at my intrusion. "It's too involved," he replied. "Don't you history people ever *relax?*"

He smiled indulgently, and his silence indicated the conversation would continue only after I left. I took my time mixing my drink. They waited. Not a word. At parties, there were damned few conversations I was not welcome in. *I* was the one who did the picking and choosing. Just where did this recessive Abe Lincoln get off being a snob?

The more I drank, the larger the slight became, and I grew sullenly discontent with the attention the others were paying

4

me. The next time I went to the kitchen, I stood on the other side of the doorway and eavesdropped.

"A good historian is never completely objective," Frank was saying to his companion. "Without subjectivity, you might as well let those computers write the textbooks."

This was my cue. I stepped in and said, "We *could* use those computers to replace some of the dialogue that goes on at parties. Really, boys, didn't you get your fill of profundities back in your sophomore year?"

"Maybe not," said Frank, "but long before then I learned eavesdropping is rude."

I had always appreciated a good rejoinder, but Frank's voice did not carry the typical *touché*. His smile remained polite and unchastising. I withdrew again, but when I returned to the group in the living room I took up a new position on the floor, which gave me a partial view of the kitchen door. The game of Speculation continued, but I bowed out so as not to have my attention divided.

Finally, Frank and the other man came out of the kitchen and stood next to our seated circle. I was drunk, so drunk I could feel the tiny contortions my face was going through trying to find the smirk I wanted. The effort was pointless. Frank said goodnight without singling me out by word or gesture. And off he went.

He was, I told myself, too tall, too skinny, too humorless, too *forgettable* (and gap-toothed, besides), to get away with that condescending attitude. I hadn't had a challenge in a long time, and as petty as this one was, I decided to finish the evening with it: I turned to Gloria and asked which apartment he lived in. She looked at me in amazement.

"Him? You don't know the first thing about him," she said, implying *she* did.

With my opening line decided upon, I left the party and knocked on his door. It took three knocks before he answered. He was wearing a bathrobe that was meant to reach the shins but only made it as far as his knees.

"What *is* the purest form of love there is?" I asked.

5

His smile was tight and tolerant, enough to push my courage back into reserve. "Right now," he said, "the purest form would be the consideration we give our neighbors when they want to sleep. Good night."

Well, I thought, not bad. Not bad at all. It could be he was not half so dreary as I imagined. And different, much different from the other men I'd met at these parties.

As always when I had drunk this much, I stayed at Gloria's. She rolled her eyes when I came in. "My God"—she laughed—"you must really be smashed."

"Why?"

"Going up to the weirdo's."

"The weirdo?"

"That's what they call him."

"They who?"

"People in the building." She cocked her head, her smile now puzzled. "Why *did* you go up there?"

"To"—thinking quickly—"apologize."

"Apologize! For what?"

"I was rude to him in the kitchen. How is he weird?"

"The girls come and go at all hours. He ought to put up a revolving door."

"Him? Come on! He's not the type."

"No, he's not the type—for anything *conventional.* And you ought to get a load of the girls."

"Cheap?"

"No. But pathetic. Homely and kind of lost-looking. And very young. Some of them must still be in high school."

"Maybe he's a counselor or something."

"Yeah, and I'm Greta Garbo going to college. Listen, Tom Kennard's apartment is right next to his and he hears everything through the wall. He says there's always a lot of crying."

"Crying?"

"I'm telling you, he is *weird.* Even the guys in this building think so."

I laughed. "Oh, well, then, that should settle it!"

I didn't see him again for over a month. I had six dates with a basketball player who at any other time would have been just the nourishment my ego delighted in. He was considerate, affectionate, very sexually interested, but gentleman enough to take no for an answer and still keep calling, and he wanted to read some of the authors I said were my favorites so we could discuss them. He even wanted to take me home with him over Memorial Day weekend to meet his parents. For a while, he balanced the scales of my indecisiveness perfectly. On the one hand, he was kind and sensitive; on the other, dull and persistent. The only way my conscience would let me unload him was by lying. I told him I had rekindled an old flame and there was no future in our continuing to see each other. He took it with the kind of graciousness that made me want to slug myself.

Spring term ended, and I signed up for two classes over the summer. I moved out of the dormitory and in with Gloria. She was short on money and took a part-time job in a travel agency, so that three days a week I had the apartment to myself. During the first week I saw nothing of Frank, and I thought maybe he had gone away for the summer even though his name remained on the mailbox. With too much time on my hands, I became friendly with Tom Kennard, a likable bore, and his girlfriend, Janet, a harmless twit whose most memorable features were a sorority pin and a lisp. The three of us spent several afternoons drinking beer in Tom's apartment, and I sometimes turned the topic of conversation to "the weirdo" living next door to him.

Frank, they said, was something of a prodigy, having finished his master's at twenty-one and now, at twenty-five, nearly through with his doctoral dissertation. His area of concentration was Asian-African Studies ("Very faddish," affirmed Janet, puckering the f), which probably accounted for the sparseness of his living conditions. Tom had been in Frank's apartment only once, and according to him, once was enough. Old cushions and pillows substituted for furniture, the walls were absolutely barren, and except for one study lamp and the fluorescent tubes in the kitchen and bathroom, the entire place was lighted by candles. The living room, said Tom, looked more like a hut than a home.

"What about those girls who come to see him?" I asked.

7

"God only knows what they do in there," said Janet. "I wouldn't be surprised if he practices voodoo."

When I finally saw him again, it wasn't in our apartment building but in the student union grill. Sitting alone in a booth, he had a book in front of him, from which he read only bits at a time. He would lift his eyes from the page and squint pensively, giving the impression he was not about to accept anything until he had taken it apart for himself. While I stood in the cafeteria line waiting for my cheeseburger, I stared at him, but I was analyzing myself. Why in hell did he interest me? There had been other guys, much more appealing in every respect, whom I had found unattainable, and I had never compromised myself by pursuing them. Here I was a student of Literature and therefore, I figured, a student of human motives and emotions; still, I could not put a finger on the motives behind my own behavior. I wasn't out husband-hunting, I didn't suffer from nymphomania, I had no penchant for tall men, I wasn't a masochist who enjoyed rejection, I had little interest in history or politics or anything else he was likely to talk about, I was unimpressed by his bohemian appearance, and I *certainly* wasn't one of those lost little girls who need a man to tell them who they are.

"Hi. Remember me?"

He looked up and blinked. He was still absorbed in his book and his own thoughts. I felt like the violator of some intimate connection.

"Yes," he said, "I remember. The eavesdropper."

I sensed I wouldn't be invited, so I sat down immediately.

"Well, eavesdropping is one way of finding out things. Another thing I've found out is that you make your girlfriends cry."

His mouth tightened. "Let's put it another way: I *let* them cry."

"Oh? And what do they have to cry about?"

"Things you probably wouldn't understand." Said oh, so politely, but it was a definite swipe. An emotional snob, I thought.

"Do you run ads in the paper? 'Strong shoulder seeks tears'? Or 'Have compassion, will travel'?"

He inhaled deeply and looked away.

"Well," I continued, "how *do* you meet them?"

"You don't strike me as the type who goes in for small talk. Why are you doing it with me?"

"I wouldn't classify this as small talk. Unless you consider your personal life small."

"You're very good at passing the ball. If you'll excuse me, I—"

"No. Please. I don't like eating alone."

"You came in here alone."

"But now I'm not. Please stay."

"I'm too uncomfortable," he said.

"I make you uncomfortable?"

"Yes."

"Why?"

"Because . . ." His face reddened, his tone hardened. "I don't know what you're up to. But whatever it is, it's not attractive, and I'm not amused."

"You mean I'm not your type?"

He winced at this, picked up his book and left.

I sulked the entire evening. Gloria and I played Scrabble. I drew nothing but vowels, cursed my luck, snapped at Gloria, smoked one cigarette after another, criticized Rita Hayworth's acting on the midnight movie, and went to bed with a headache.

When I woke up on Saturday, I resolved to pull myself out of this slump. But the very fact that I did not understand the slump irritated me all the more. I began working on a paper due on Tuesday, but Ugo Betti and his "emblematic themes" could not compete with Frank's words going round and round in my head: "Things you probably wouldn't understand" and "I'm not amused." How dare he! If I considered myself to be anything, it was bright and amusing. I was the "star" of the dormitory I had lived in, always the center of attention when I wanted it. I was also famous for whipping up a paper in five or six hours, and I had often been propositioned by the other girls to write theirs for them. I wanted to tell *him* about the time a girl from Shaker Heights laid a hundred dollars on my desk (tempted, I still declined it) and begged me to write something on Sinclair Lewis so she could spend the weekend shacked up

9

with the mechanic who had replaced the spark plugs in her Corvette.

But *this* paper I was working on did not come together. By Sunday night it was still disjointed and lacking focus. I pushed it aside and asked Gloria if she wanted to go out for a beer. Although she had to get up for work the next morning, she sprang from her chair and got to the door before I did. All weekend she had been watching me the way I imagine doctors watch a terminal case; obviously, she equated my suggestion with improved health.

Just as we reached the parking lot, Frank and a girl were getting out of his car, each with a bag of groceries. Instantly, I consoled myself with the fact that the girl was pale and mousy. But as Frank looked at me and quickly turned away, I was struck by something else: because the girl was so puny, she could easily have been seventeen or eighteen, but she could also have been as young as fourteen. What really got to me were the groceries; somehow, they seemed just as suggestive as a toothbrush and pajamas.

"What a sorry-looking little thing she is," I muttered as we drove away.

"That's exactly what I told you about," said Gloria. "And she'll probably be sorrier for getting mixed up with him."

I didn't answer. I waited until we got to the Campus Keg and had a beer in front of us, then told her what had happened in the union grill. She looked at me in surprise.

"You mean *you* went over to *him?*"

"You don't have to say it like that," I protested.

"Oh, brother!" she said, rolling her eyes. "Are you suddenly developing a taste for strange excitement?"

It was bad enough being angry at *him,* but Gloria's criticism of me tempted me into playing devil's advocate.

"Don't get dramatic," I said. "What is he—Jack the Ripper?"

"Meet him in the fog sometime and find out." She lifted her glass of beer and was about to sip, when suddenly her face turned sly. "Waaaait a minute. Is that why . . ." She leaned forward.

10

"Is that little incident with *him* the reason you've been obnoxious all weekend?"

"Of course not," I answered irritably. "I just don't see why you're so critical of him."

"Me critical! Look who's talking—Irene Rutledge, verbal lampoonist *par excellence.* Compared to you, I'm Little Nell."

"All right, Nell, let's drop it."

As we drove back home, I was fully aware of the subtle side glances she was giving me. When we pulled into the parking lot, Frank's car was gone. Gloria looked at the empty spot and said, "Well, that must have been a quick meal."

"Maybe the girl took off with his car," I said sullenly.

"I hope you're not going to knock on his door to find out."

"Let's just forget it."

"Exactly my sentiments."

For the next two weeks I busied myself with reading, working on a tan at the campus swimming pool, and deliberating over which classes to take in the fall, when I would enter the Ph.D. program. Gloria had a party and conspicuously left Frank uninvited; if she expected a reaction from me, she didn't get it. I was regaining the old grip on myself, the rock reassuming its comfortable firmness.

Then came the incident with Larry.

One morning in July, I saw a group of fraternity boys, identifiable by the pins on their sport shirts, running around blindfolded in the grassy area between the auditorium and the river which cut through the center of the campus. The mysterious game turned out to be Blindfolded Football, wherein the *un*blindfolded quarterback of each team called the signals and yelled out directions to the other team players. I thought it thoroughly ridiculous but just comic enough to watch a few minutes before moving on to my class. Standing on the dirt footpath about three feet from the river, I was soon noticed by one of the quarterbacks. He smiled and before the next play he shouted to his team, "All right, you guys, there's a gorgeous redhead standing over here who's waiting to see what you can do!"

11

Coming toward me on the footpath, but a good distance away, was a blind boy. In one hand was a briefcase, in the other the white stick he used as a "sweep" in front of him. Even farther in the distance, but approaching in the same direction, was Frank. Although I pretended to watch the players, I kept Frank in my sights, and I noticed quite plainly that the second he saw me, he turned abruptly and began to cut across the grass toward the auditorium. He kept his eyes on the ground and quickened his step until it was almost a sprint.

God! I fumed. What does he think I am—poison?

"To the left! To the left! The *left*, Donovan, you dumb jerk!"

I turned in time to see a wave of players heading toward the river—and the blind boy. The boy stopped immediately, his head making the same back-and-forth sweeping motion his stick had made.

"Look out!" I yelled. "Look out for—" It was too late.

Some of the players did halt, but three crashed into the boy and sent him tumbling right into the river. For a few seconds, my legs wouldn't move, and when they did, I found myself converging on the scene simultaneously with Frank. The boy was flailing the water, and the others, blindfolds removed, were shouting, "This way! Swim *this* way!" Fortunately, there was a good-sized stick right at my feet. I picked it up and called, "Use this—get him to grab hold of this!" (The reason we were all unwilling to jump in unless the boy went under was that the river was practically stagnant and notoriously filthy, not so much a river as an elongated cesspool. Upstream from where we stood there were patches of green slime beneath an overhang of trees.) The boy stretched out his hand, but a few inches remained between him and the stick. One of the quarterbacks surrendered it to Frank, whose long and lanky arm filled in the needed inches. The boy was pulled out, and Frank sat him down on the ground. The smell of the river on his clothes was atrocious; the players backed away from it.

"My briefcase! Where's my briefcase!"

I turned and saw the last corner of it sinking into the water.

Frank said, "I'm afraid it's gone."

12

"It can't be! Everything's in it! My notes, my . . ." He was almost crying.

My panic gone, I was quickly filled with anger. Eying the quarterback, I said, "I hope you're satisfied, you stupid ass!"

"Me? *I* didn't run into him."

"You were calling the directions! You know there's a footpath here, you know people use it, you saw *me* here, you certainly saw *him!*"

"I didn't. I—"

"And the rest of you, running around like five-year-olds—blindfolded, for God's sake!" Their blindfolds were off; they could walk away as freely as they pleased. But the boy couldn't. The grim irony of the situation made me furious. "He could have drowned!"

"Look, we're sorry."

"Sorry isn't going to rescue his briefcase."

Satisfied that Frank was looking after the boy, the players retreated, mumbling to each other. I heard one of them say, "Man, what a bitch *she* is."

I bent down in front of the boy. "You know, you'll have to have a tetanus shot."

"My notes, everything . . ." He bit his lip.

"His stick went into the river," I said to Frank. "I'd take him to the health center, but I have to get to class. I have a test. Could you take him?"

"Sure," he said, actually smiling at me.

I was in the middle of supper and telling Gloria about the incident when the doorbell rang. It was Frank.

"Come in. Did he get his shot?"

"Yes, he's okay. I spoke to three of his professors this afternoon and told them what happened. They'll arrange to have someone dictate the notes he lost. By the way, I invited him over for dinner tomorrow night. I wondered if you wanted to come too."

The invitation came too unexpectedly for me to be anything but direct. "Sure. Why don't you sit down and have some coffee? We were just finishing."

"Thanks, but I have company." He looked past me and said, "You're invited too, Gloria."

13

The double invitation annoyed me. And "I have company" con-
jured up a picture of that mousy girl with the groceries.

"And what are *you* looking at?" I challenged Gloria after he
left.

"The willing fly about to enter the web."

"You mean you're not going?"

Her only answer was a smirk.

Frank made spaghetti and clam sauce and presented Larry
with a new briefcase. After dinner we sat on cushions and drank
wine. My face was as placid as Buddha's, but my insides were
roiling, first with anticipation, then with resentment. Frank
turned the whole conversation over to Larry, asking about things
like the Braille facilities in the library and the note-taking device
blind students use. Larry needed little encouragement. He rattled
on about his childhood, and the two of them tossed around the
subject of who were more fortunate—those who had never seen
or those who had lost their sight. I contributed nothing, even
though Frank tried to rope me in by asking my opinion here
and there. I kept pouring wine from the half-gallon jug and staring at Frank's bare legs. They were so skinny that the thighs
were barely wider than the knees. Why, I asked myself, would
someone with those legs wear shorts? But then, why should I
be staring at them? Why did I want to reach out and run my
hands down them? Up to this time, I had slept with only two
guys. Both of them had been handsome, nearly perfect specimens,
but even so, I never became aroused simply by looking at them.
Maybe because this new attraction was so alien to me, I was
able to get hold of myself and switch from wine to coffee. The
coffee kept my eyes off his legs, but watching his face and listening
to his voice didn't help my resistance. He listened to Larry with
the same facial expression he had had while reading that book
in the union grill: he wasn't being merely polite, he was *interested*.
Sullenly, I told myself he'd listen to a grasshopper if it could
talk.

Finally, Larry said he had to be getting back to the dorm.
Boldly, I told Frank I wanted to go along for the ride. He nodded

and smiled, but even in the candlelight I could see him coloring.

Before he got out of the car, Larry asked if he could feel our faces. He did Frank's first. When it came my turn, I expected his hands to be as clammy as his eyes looked. They weren't. As a matter of fact, there was something comforting in the touch, as though I were being examined by an old family doctor. When he finished, he said we made a nice-looking couple. Frank was clearly embarrassed, and I was ashamed at having said practically nothing to Larry all evening.

Riding back home, I tried to think of anything except where we were heading. Inviting myself along to the dorm was one thing; I could not suggest that he invite me back up to his apartment. I looked over at his white, white legs as we passed under a streetlamp.

"Do you ever go out in the sun?" I asked.

"You mean lie in it?"

"Yes."

"I don't have the patience for it."

"Really? You strike me as the very essence of patience."

No response.

"Besides the sun," I said, "what else are you impatient with?"

He smiled. "Other people's impatience, I guess."

"Ohhh, impatient with impatience. Very Philosophy 101. Shall we go on to falling in love with love and I hate to hate? Anything else you're impatient with?"

"I'll have to think about it."

"What about . . . aggressive girls?"

"They make me nervous."

"Why is that?"

"They usually have too many expectations. They want soft bells and sirens and violins and calliopes all at the same time."

"I see. Tone deaf emotionally. Your, uh, little girlfriend with the groceries—she's very retiring, I suppose."

"Yes." It was a "yes" that meant "Back Off: Dead End."

"The aggressive girls—how do you handle them?"

"Would you like to get some ice cream?"

The thought of taking it back to his apartment squelched my

15

objection to the evasion. "Anything but strawberry."

For the first time, he took his eyes off the road and looked at me. *"That's* how I handle aggressive girls." He smiled.

"Very cute. You *are* smug."

"Oh, no." He chuckled. "When it comes to smugness, you've got the market cornered."

We pulled up to a small grocery store, and he went in.

I was not aware of any hidden chord in me aching to be plucked. Yet as I sat there staring through double glass—the windshield and the store window—I was determined to make him want me. He stood at the counter talking to the clerk, a middle-aged man whose face and manner were so thoroughly bland that his conversation just had to match. The man propped his arms on top of the cash register as if his listener were going to stay for a while. Frank smiled, then laughed. I saw him laugh, but I had never *heard* him laugh—not in the open, forthright way he seemed to be doing it now. A storekeeper, not clever Irene Rutledge, caused him to laugh. It didn't make sense.

We took the ice cream back to his apartment. Coming up the steps, we met Gloria on her way to the incinerator. The look she gave me would have wilted a nun, but nothing short of an earthquake could have altered my course.

He spooned my ice cream into a dish and ate his from the container. Gospel music was playing on his transistor radio, and the flame of the candle seemed to flicker with the voices. The barrenness of the room, which I had found unpleasant earlier, now seemed comforting.

"How did you happen to go into Asian-African Studies?"

He shrugged. "I guess because so much of their history has yet to be made. Right now they're the world's underdogs, and underdogs are always interesting to watch, if just to see which way they'll go— Look, I don't want to bore you."

"You're safe until I yawn."

He laughed. Out loud. Very good, I thought. You're making *some* progress. What he didn't know was that he could have read me the Betty Crocker cookbook, for all I cared. At least he was talking.

There was a storytelling lilt to his voice as he enumerated

historical examples of underdogs turned top dogs. He talked about turnabouts in national identities, the role of chance in determining world powers. What really impressed me was that he did not sound academic or pedantic. History, it seemed, was a very *personal* matter to him.

"History," he said, "has always proven one cliché: After you get what you want, you don't want it. It'll be interesting to see what Asia and Africa *give* up as they try to *catch* up—what they give up willingly and what they give up unknowingly. Look at Japan. Someday they'll put all their chopsticks in museums and pick up the plastic fork." He pressed his palms together and bowed. "Ah so. End of honorable and pompous lecture."

"What inspired this interest in the underdog?"

He hesitated, scraping the bottom of the ice cream container. "I guess most of my life *I* was pretty much the underdog."

"In what way?"

"I was raised in a small town, where your name sums you up. There were two rock-bottom families, us and the Hooples. Old Man Hoople was a drunk and eventually went to prison. None of the Hoople kids except one made it beyond the tenth grade. But we were considered respectably poor because my father always worked. Most people pitied us, but they had contempt for the Hooples. Even my mother. If any of us complained about something we didn't have, she'd say, 'Just be glad you ain't a Hoople.' She spent half the day reading the Bible, but she pulled rank on the Hooples every chance she got. She was too ignorant to see that what she was doing to them, everyone else was doing to us: clustering us under one name as if we'd all been stamped out of some inferior mold. She didn't know there was one Hoople she could never pull rank on." He stared wistfully into the flame of the candle between us. "Wanda Hoople," he said softly, as though caressing the name. "I haven't thought about her in years. Not until yesterday. It hit me when I was holding that stick out for Larry to grab. Suddenly I wished I'd done the same for Wanda."

I began to picture Wanda Hoople as the girl with the groceries. "She drowned?" I asked.

"In a way," he said, still looking at the candle. "Every year

17

the high school put on a Holly Hop, a dressy Christmas dance where the girls asked the boys. I had never had a date in high school and I sure wasn't planning on being asked. But Wanda asked me. Three days in a row she stood on this street corner in the morning when I came to school and then again in the afternoon when I went home. She lived in the opposite direction, so there was no reason for her being there. The third day we saw her, my friend and I started joking about it. I said maybe she was trying to get picked up. Her sisters were all whores, so it was easy to figure she would follow the same path. Since it had been drilled into me that the Hooples were below us, I didn't want to admit even one of them could be different from the rest. But Wanda *was* different. Her skirts were always safety-pinned in the back and her ankle socks were so limp they kept sliding down into her shoes, but her face and hair—shiny as glass. The other girls in school were experimenting with make-up, but she never wore it. Her *sisters* wore it in layers, but she didn't. Her face and hair were sort of a badge, something that would show everyone she was *clean.* Her sisters were loud too, always egging on the boys to prove they could talk dirtier. But Wanda was a mouse. That third afternoon we passed her, she called out my name. Her eyes looked terrified when she asked me to step over to the curb. There was this pause and when she finally asked me to go to the dance she didn't look at me, she looked at the fire hydrant. For a minute I thought it was a joke, or maybe I was hoping it was. I didn't answer her; I just stared at the rip in her coat and felt my face getting hot. Then she began to back away, very slowly. I stood there, she stopped for a second, then backed up some more. I heard my friend snickering and I felt the heat in my face, but I didn't say a word. She gave me one last look, like I was going to kill her or something, and she ran off down the street. I could have called out to her, but I didn't."

"Did you ever speak to her after that?"

He shook his head. "My friend spread the word and it became a big joke for a while. I wanted to hate her for embarrassing me, but . . . I couldn't get past that look on her face. Or those socks that went down in her shoes. Whenever we saw each other in school, we both looked the other way. I didn't want to admit to myself I was ashamed. When she asked me that day, it must have taken every ounce of courage she had, and all she got for it was humiliation. She quit school in the middle of the twelfth grade and got married to a much older man who was a farmer. That was just about the time I was looking forward to getting out of that town and going to college."

He lit his pipe and blew smoke rings, staring at each one as it drifted upward to build a hazy scaffolding of gray. When he spoke again, he continued in that soft, storytelling tone. But his face appeared cautious, as if he were veering away from an emotion that would interrupt him.

"The PTA gave me a one-year scholarship, something they'd never have given a Hoople. I got my picture in the paper and then I got a letter from Wanda. It said: 'Dear Frank, I'm sorry about that day. Good luck in college and in the future. Sincerely, Wanda Lowell—parentheses Hoople. You know what got me? The parentheses. Reminding me as if she were *forgettable*. No one should ever have to feel that way." Then in the next breath, but out of nowhere, he said: "I hate it when people just *breed.*"

The mixture of sadness and repugnance startled me, but I had no time to respond. He looked at me full face and said, "Why have you been showing an interest in me?"

"Because I've never gone out with a history major." It was a stupid cover-up, far beneath my talents, and that tolerant smile of his made me feel more ridiculous. "I don't know," I mumbled.

"Well," he said, "it's not because I look like Clark Gable and it's not because you've seen me driving around in a Cadillac. I'm not one of the campus lovers." He smirked. "It must be my reputation as the life of the party."

"Don't toy with me."

"Don't *you* toy with *me.*"

"What are you talking about?"

"I don't enjoy being a diverting amusement. Although in your case . . ."

"You haven't given me a chance to. I'm surprised you even bothered to find out my name!"

19

"I found out a lot this morning. Your name is Irene Abigail Rutledge. Student number: 111314. Hometown: Cedar Run. Major: English. Birth date: June 1, 1936. Two younger brothers. B.A., summa cum laude. The English Department's model student and secretly—or semisecretly—leched after by two esteemed members of same department."

"What!"

"You're very confident, probably too bright for your own good, susceptible to alcohol, aggressiveness and sarcasm, charming when made to feel secure, intolerant of carelessness (yesterday's incident), and lovely to look at in *any* mood." He paused, lowering his voice. "And perversely fond of shaking up scarecrows."

There seemed to be tiny fish swimming through my blood: my hands felt twitchy although they were perfectly limp in my lap. "How did you find out all that?"

"I never reveal my sources."

"You're not a scarecrow," I said, "but I'd like to hear how I shook you up."

"I'm sure you would. But you have a capful of feathers already. I'll tell you about it later—when I'm over it."

"Maybe I don't want you to be over it."

He got up and brought over the wine. We drank and stared at each other. He gave in and lowered his eyes.

"I guess," he said, "this is where I'm supposed to take you in my arms."

"Why don't you?"

He shook his head. "I'd rather wait. If you don't mind."

"Until when?"

"Next time."

"Tomorrow night?"

"No; I'll have quizzes to grade tomorrow night."

"Are you backing off now?"

"Can you meet me for lunch day after tomorrow?"

We set the time and place, and I got up to leave. Before he opened the door, I stood on my toes and put my hands behind his neck.

"How about a down payment?" I said.

20

His body trembled and his lips quivered against mine. It was the tenderest and most awkward kiss I had ever gotten, and I hung on until he pulled away.

For the next few weeks, Wanda Hoople took up daily residence in my thoughts simply because Frank's description of her also applied to him. Around me, he was hesitant and timid. *I* had to reach for *his* hand when we walked together or take him in *my* arms when I wanted a kiss. He always waited for me to let him know when I was "free" to see him. And the first time we slept together it was at my insistence.

"I'm not very experienced," he said, looking away. It was a Saturday afternoon in August, pouring rain. He had just taken off his wet socks, and I was drying my hair with a towel.

"I don't want experience. I want you."

We sat down on the cushions; I leaned over and kissed the arch of his foot.

"We don't have to do anything," I said. "We can just lie naked together."

I stood up and undressed. The look on Frank's face was almost reverential; for a second, I felt like Botticelli's Venus on the half shell. When I sat down next to him, he gently pushed my knees up under my chin, held all of me in his arms, and kissed my hair and eyes. Then he released me and stood up. He tried to hide his apprehension as he pulled off the shirt and trousers. When he stuck his thumbs into the waistband of his boxer shorts, he paused and said, "I'm not circumcised." He said it as though this were equivalent to being a hermaphrodite.

"That's all right," I said. "Neither am I."

It worked. He laughed out loud and pulled off the shorts.

"Why does it bother you?" I asked.

"I've heard a lot of women don't like it. They find it repulsive."

"I don't see why." I reached down and slowly pulled the foreskin back. "Look, it's like watching something being born."

"In more ways than one." He was becoming erect.

The first time we made love, there on the floor, it was awkward but not embarrassingly so. We were both intent upon pleasing

21

each other, but he was too large and I was too tight.

"Can we stop for a while?" I said. "It hurts."

"Sure. It hurts me too."

This surprised and pleased me. I had thought anything that hard must be invincible. Knowing that he hurt too made the pain almost pleasurable. We lay back on the cushions and had several glasses of wine.

By the time we went to sleep that night, we had made love six times. It would have been five, but just as we were drifting off, he suggested we make it an even half dozen. The whole afternoon and evening I experienced a new and wonderful feeling of abandonment: he was like a starving man, and my body was the banquet.

I returned to my apartment Sunday night riding on a balloon even Gloria couldn't puncture.

"Well, well, look who's back from the stud farm."

"Is there anything to eat?"

"Why? Didn't you have time for that?"

"No, as a matter of fact."

She looked me up and down, as if overnight I had become defective. I made a sandwich and sat down opposite her while she lacquered her nails. Her intense concentration was an obvious ploy to irritate me.

"And what's wrong with you?" I said.

"There's nothing wrong with *me*. I don't understand it. I've known you four years and I'm just finding out I don't know you at all."

"Why? Because I spent two days with a man?"

"With *that* man."

"What exactly is wrong with him?"

"That's just it—*you* don't see it. That's what's so crazy!"

"Suppose you spell it out for me."

"Spell it! All right, he's w-e-i-r-d. You're way out of his c-l-a-s-s. He can't function socially, he has no friends except those pathetic creatures he drags in, he's always got his nose in a book, he looks like he's never seen sunlight or decent food, or soap and water for that matter."

"Now wait a minute—"

22

"His hands are filthy, or didn't you notice?"

"That is grease on his hands because he works on his car instead of paying some half-wit mechanic to do it."

"Well, hooray for the handyman. What gets me is you don't mind being one of *that* harem."

"There is no harem. You're being awfully presumptuous."

"I suppose those girls are phantoms. And the one we saw in the parking lot—I suppose that's his sister."

"He's discussed all that with me. He just happens to feel sorry for them. That girl we saw is a freshman in the class he teaches. She's from a small town and she's having trouble adjusting. She has two horrendous roommates who—"

"Spare me the details. All I'm going to say is I thought you had better sense. I thought it would take only a few dates for the novelty to wear off. And now"—she shivered—"you've slept with him."

"You bet I did," I said to get even for her shiver. "Slept and slept and slept."

"Irene, there's something wrong with him. I can *sense* it."

"That analysis is medieval."

"You listen to me. 'The kid' has something to say."

" 'The kid' has had plenty to say."

"Be quiet, for a change. I thought you, of all people, would keep your eyes open when you met someone. A good relationship has to be equal, one where both parties bring something valuable to share. The scales have to balance or else someone gets cheated. And it's always the one who had the *most* to offer."

"Thank you, Ann Landers."

"I've watched it happen. It happened to my mother."

"Yes, you've told me." Her father was an inveterate lecher, her mother now an alcoholic. "But I don't plan to go down the same path. Now can we drop the subject? No one has said I'm going to marry the guy."

"Famous last words."

Gloria's appraisal of Frank did not soften. Whenever he came into the apartment she managed to be civil, *too* civil; then she would retreat to the bedroom and stay there until he left. Even on the nights I had him in for dinner, she refused to join us and often went out to eat; sometimes she would call from a public phone to make sure he was gone before she got back. Aside from Gloria's behavior, I was angered by Frank's complacent acceptance of it.

"She loves you very much," he said. "I never had a friend like that. You're very lucky. I think it's better if I don't come down here anymore."

"I'm not going to let her rule my life."

"Irene, it's her apartment, it's her name on the lease. We can see each other at my place."

"We can at least come here when she's out."

"Honey, what's the point? She'd find out. Doing it behind her back would insult her."

"Frank, why are you giving in to her like this?"

"Because she's upset and hurt and I'm not."

So far as he was concerned, it was that simple. Before he got carried away with this consideration for her, I was itching to tell him some of the things she had said behind his back. But I didn't. No matter how magnanimous he might be, there was still room for hurt. Besides, I didn't have to wait long for him to admit she was way out of bounds. He admitted it the day my parents paid a surprise visit.

I had spent Saturday night at Frank's. We were just finishing a late breakfast when the bell rang. Fortunately, I had brought my own robe and had it on when Frank opened the door to my mother and father. My first emotion was murderous: their sheepish smiles told me immediately that Gloria had engineered this intrusion.

"We went to your apartment first," was my mother's weak excuse, "but we didn't know how long it would take you to come down."

"Frank has a telephone," I said. "And so do I. Why didn't you let me know you were coming?"

They had visited me only three times during my college career, and always reluctantly. They preferred my coming home to visit them.

24

"Well, your father and I thought we'd start doing a few things on the spur of the moment."

"Did you bring Neil and Barry?"

"No. Neil had a date to go bowling with his girlfriend. Barry went camping this weekend."

What she said was plausible but not very probable. Neil loved the campus and would go off on his own to explore whenever he came. I couldn't imagine him passing up this opportunity, especially if he had a girlfriend to show it to. And Barry, who ranked me even higher in his affections than he did his catcher's mitt and hockey stick, was not likely to let a camping trip interfere with visiting me. Unless he hadn't been told.

"Would you like some breakfast?" said Frank.

"Oh, no," said my mother. "We stopped on the way."

"Coffee, then?"

"That would be nice."

My father's eyes were crawling all over the place, until they found my brassiere draped over the desk chair.

"Quite a place you've got here," he said to Frank. "It's really . . . different."

"Different from what?" I said.

Frank flashed me a look which meant "Be gracious," and my mother jumped in to steer the conversation.

"Those big cushions there look comfortable," she said. "And they're so practical too."

Frank brought the coffee, and we all sat down to a grating silence. I broke it with the suggestion that we invite Gloria up too.

"Oh, no," my mother said, flustered. "She was just going out when we came in."

"How convenient for her."

"You'll stay for dinner, won't you?" asked Frank.

"We don't want to impose."

"You're not imposing. I was just going out to the store for vegetables. Any particular kind you like?"

"No, really—"

"They both like green beans," I said.

25

As soon as Frank was dressed and gone, I put on another pot of coffee and took the chicken from the refrigerator to prepare it for the oven. I wanted them to see that I was familiar with everything in the apartment.

"Are you ready to tell me the truth?" I said casually.

"How long have you been living here?" My father's tone was too nonchalant, the tone people sometimes use when they find they have been shifted from offense to defense.

"I don't live here. And you didn't answer my question."

"We just hadn't heard from you. . . ." My mother was too unpracticed in lies to complete this one.

"Frank will be back soon," I said, "and I'm not going to discuss this in front of him. Let's not waste time beating around the bush."

"We thought you might be in some kind of trouble," said my father.

"Where did you get that idea?" Neither of them answered. "I know it had to be Gloria. She called you, didn't she?"

"Yes."

"Kenneth!" My mother winced. "You promised you wouldn't—"

"Because she was concerned. It sounds as though you're in a situation you're not aware of," he said.

"Is that so? What did Gloria use for evidence?"

"Now just hold on. We'd like some explanation from *you*. What do you know about this guy? How come there's no furniture in this place? And just what in hell is your brassiere doing over there?"

"Obviously I spent the night here."

"Obviously. And quite a few other nights, it seems."

"That's right."

"I'm glad you're so proud of it!" he snapped. "Maybe you wouldn't mind your brothers knowing about this, either."

"Kenneth!"

"That's up to you," I said. "I didn't ask you to come spying. I'm twenty-two years old. If you care to remember, you got married at twenty and Mom was eighteen."

26

"That's right. Married. Not shacking up!"

I knew what I was about to say would hurt my mother more than him, but I couldn't resist. "Married January second. I was born June first. And I wasn't premature."

"Irene! We were engaged!" said my mother.

"You don't have to justify anything to her, Millie. She's just trying to turn the tables." He lit a cigarette and took a deep drag. I had seen this gesture often enough to know he was shifting to his imperious pose. "You know, young lady, you think just because this college hands you some honors you've got the world by the tail. You've got all the answers—past, present and future. Your parents don't know anything and you've got nothing left to learn. You're so clever that everything will go your way, doors will fly open at the mention of your name. Let me tell you something, Miss Honor Student: the world is not holding its breath for you. You may be big stuff on campus, but a university is not reality. Nowhere near it. But you won't find that out until someone knocks you on your smug little butt."

"And you'd like a ringside seat for that event, wouldn't you?"

"Yes, I would." Pause. "And I'll probably end up hating whoever does it."

His frown, as always, was irresistible. I went over and tousled his hair. "You won't have to hate anyone. I've got a pretty good punch of my own."

"That's your trouble," he said, slipping his arm around my waist. "You've always been more independent than the boys. Maybe because you're the oldest. Sometimes you make me feel I have three sons."

"I'm glad Frank doesn't see me that way."

"And how do *you* see *him?*"

"I love him."

"You're sure?"

"As sure as I can be."

"And he feels the same?"

I nodded and felt my face shining. "You can't possibly know him from just one visit. If only you could see him—even the way he reads a newspaper."

27

He smirked. "He reads it upside down?"

"He *feels* what he reads. The expressions on his face—it's more than just gathering information. He gets involved with what's going on in the world, and that's good for me, it really is." I went on like a mute who has just found a voice. I told them about Frank's shyness, his insecurities, how I had had to go after him. I told them about the incident with Larry, about Frank's childhood of poverty, even about Wanda Hoople.

"So that explains why he hasn't had a haircut since he was ten."

"Oh, Dad, that doesn't matter. It bothered me at first too. But there are other things."

"There must be. He's a rather . . . unlikely-looking man. And a little undernourished. You might lose him to the first strong wind that comes along."

"I don't know what I'd do if that happened. I wouldn't ever want another man to touch me."

This embarrassed them both. They didn't completely look away, but their eyes shifted just slightly to avoid mine. My father rescued himself by joking. "Your mother was crazy about me that way. She was so anxious and nervous the first time I kissed her that the second we touched lips, she farted."

"Kenneth Rutledge, you are a liar!" She reddened, and her mouth puckered to stifle a smile.

"Pop! Just like bubble gum."

"Oh, what a liar you are!"

The telephone rang. It was Frank.

"I'm outside the store," he said. "Should I get some ice cream for the pie?"

"Sure. And hurry back."

He smacked a kiss into the phone.

My father lit another cigarette, imperious once again. "Irene, you've always enjoyed playing devil's advocate. That wouldn't have anything to do with your taking up with Frank, would it?"

"I don't know what you mean."

"I think you do." He looked me squarely in the eye. "He's not exactly what anyone would expect you to choose. It would be cruel to let him fall for you if he's only a novelty to you."

"Novelty—you sound like Gloria. You make me out as some kind of prize going to waste. Did it ever occur to you I might consider Frank the prize?"

"It's just that Gloria made it sound—well, we pictured Frank as the local Lothario making a conquest of our daughter. And now here I am, looking out for *his* welfare. Just promise us one thing: Keep your head and go slowly. Because, like it or not, you're *our* prize. You're our only daughter and that's the way it is."

"That makes us even, since you're my only parents."

He shook his head and sighed. "I can't remember when you didn't have an answer for everything."

The afternoon proved to be a victory over Gloria and her scheme. At first, Frank and my father had little to say to one another. Then they landed on the subject of cars, and my father explained the trouble he was having with his transmission. Together, they went down to the parking lot to look at it. When they returned, we spent the rest of the day playing bridge. Frank and my mother established an easy rapport because they discussed *me*. My mother got a little tipsy on the wine, and by evening the two of them jokingly exchanged suggestions for improving my humility, and ended up assigning me the title Irene the Arrogant.

I lived up to that title the very next night, when I returned to Gloria's apartment to confront her. Initially, she wouldn't even deign to justify what she had done, but by the time I finished packing the first suitcase, she was well into a defensive oration on friendship. In the bathroom, where I scooped my toiletries into a box and snatched up my bath mat and toilet-seat cover, she finally apologized by saying she didn't know what had come over her. Back in the bedroom, she grabbed my wrist as I unplugged my clock-radio.

"Don't, Irene. Please. I was wrong, I'm sorry. I'll apologize to Frank, too, if you want me to. You don't have to do this."

"Let go," I said calmly. She released my wrist.

"I've made a mistake. Nothing like it will happen again, believe me. This is all so ridiculous."

"It *has* been ridiculous." Matter-of-factly, I wrapped the cord around the clock-radio.

"Friends make mistakes; you don't walk out on them because of that. Let's at least talk about it!"

In perfect deadpan, I said, "Consider yourself lucky I *won't* talk about it."

Frank and I settled into a comfortable routine. Since I had more free time than he did (as a graduate assistant, he taught two classes and was adding the finishing touches to his thesis), I took almost full command of running the apartment. To my surprise, I actually enjoyed those menial tasks I had always hated. Growing up at home, I had sneered at cookbooks and dirty dishes and had complained about having to iron blouses and clean my room. All the while I had known Frank, I was amazed at the enthusiasm he had for working on his car. It didn't mesh with his intellectual pursuits, but he explained that working with his hands on a motor gave his mind a much needed change of activity. Quickly, it dawned on me that I had no hobbies at all except reading, going to movies and honing my tongue on some poor, amazed soul at a party. I turned up my nose at Frank's suggestion that I buy some plants. To my mind, plants were something old ladies fussed over after their children left home. Then one day he walked in with a philodendron and told me it was one of the easiest plants to care for. I set it in the window and doused it with water each day until it began to droop, then shrivel. I easily dismissed it as an insignificant failure. But it was the source of my first real argument with Frank.

"You're giving it too much water," he said.

"If I don't water it every day, I'll forget about it completely and never water it."

"That's ridiculous. You have to take a plant on its terms, not yours."

"I'm not going to be a slave to a plant."

"No one's asking you to be a slave. Just considerate."

"For God's sake, it's not a pet."

"It's alive. And you're letting it die."

"What do you want me to do—call in an undertaker?"

"If you can't take care of it properly, just leave it alone."

"With pleasure. It's dead anyway," I said, pulling off a leaf. "Just don't touch it."

"All right! You don't have to make it sound like I'm the Dutch elm disease." I pulled off another withered leaf. He got up and carried it from the living room into the bedroom and placed it on the window sill near his side of the bed.

I was furious.

"Maybe you'd like me to give it a 2 A.M. feeding with an eyedropper."

"I said leave it alone."

"Oh, who the hell wants to touch the damned thing!" He sat back down at his desk and opened a book. "I'll bet your little girl with the grocery bags has green thumbs."

Silence.

"I'll bet whole greenhouses burst into bloom when she passes through. She's probably an absolute Flora. I can see tulips sprouting in her footsteps, breaking right through concrete. What an enviable talent—to be able to bend your wrist just right as you tip the watering can."

"Don't belittle something you can't do. And someone you don't know." He didn't bother to look up.

"I don't think I can bear going through life now being responsible for the death of a philodendron."

He smiled incredulously. "You're unbelievable. Unbelievable."

"And you're being redundant. Redundant."

"If Irene Rutledge can't do something, then it's not worth doing. It's much more comfortable to look down your nose at it."

"Don't lecture me. I'm not one of your students."

"And don't bother to listen, either, because there's not the slightest chance someone else knows something you don't. Or if they do, it can't be very important. Besides, if it's not in a book, it's not worth knowing."

"Oh, go play with your jumper cables."

"Right now, they'd be better company."

31

I turned and walked out. I flounced down the steps and threw open the door to the parking lot, only to run smack into Gloria.

"Jesus!" she gasped, staggering backward.

This was all I needed, to have her see me angry at Frank. "I'm sorry. Are you all right?" She had dropped a folder full of travel fliers from the agency she worked at. I stooped and picked them up. "I left a book in the library; now I have to go all the way over and pick it up."

"It's after ten," she said. "The library's closed."

She was right. During the summer term the library closed early. It was a stupid lie. Still, I couldn't go back upstairs. I thrust the folder into her hand and said I'd call her sometime.

I walked ten blocks to the student union, but in the grill the custodian was already putting the chairs on top of the tables. There was still time for a quick cup of coffee, but I didn't feel much like sitting in a place that was closing up around me.

The campus was quiet, dismally so, and that was fine with me. One strolling couple, hand in hand, passed by. I muttered some obscenity under my breath, but apparently loud enough to turn their heads.

I ended up at the botanical gardens, sitting on a bench and smoking one cigarette after another. The lamppost globes lit up only the first few rows of flowers. The rest of the garden was a shadowy arrangement of spikes and clumps. What I couldn't see didn't matter. I didn't know a peony from a petunia. I had never bothered to learn flowers, since I had no plans for becoming a gardener or a Southern writer.

If it's not in a book, it's not worth knowing.

That remark kept crawling around in my mind. I couldn't dismiss it in my usual fashion because I couldn't dismiss the certainty in his voice, the authority on his face. I couldn't even keep a grip on my self-righteous anger, my only source of protection.

He was right. Since high school, I had been so wrapped up in myself that I dismissed anyone or anything that didn't in some way profit or amuse me. That night Larry had come to dinner, I could have taken an interest, but I hadn't because a blind boy didn't serve *my* interest. Looking further back, it occurred to me that when Neil was in Little League, I hadn't gone to a single game. Of course he had asked me, but I figured if my parents put in an appearance, that was sufficient. Not one game. He had been on the team three years, and I didn't know what position he played. I couldn't even remember the name of the team. And there was Barry, little Barry, who had written me letters my first two years of college, letters which went unanswered because I was much too busy.

Suddenly, I began to cry. Over Neil and Barry, over being a fool about the plant and a bitch to Frank. And to Gloria. And I kept crying because Frank saw through me before I did, because our relationship was going to require an honesty I wasn't sure I was capable of.

I thought I had finished crying when I got up and started back to the apartment. But shame was not a familiar feeling to me, and I had no way of fighting the swelling in my throat and the recurring tears. I kept wiping my eyes as I took side streets to avoid the main avenue. I was still wiping them when I reached our building and opened the door at the parking lot entrance. Not since I was twelve had I let anyone see me cry. All right, so he would see me cry; wasn't that something lovers did in front of each other? I would apologize, slip into his arms, and the whole silly mess would be over. I started up the stairs.

I was halfway up when I saw her coming down. The grocery girl. Her eyes were still red and moist from crying. A cold, dull tremor passed through me as the look of recognition was exchanged. She ran down the rest of the way and out the door.

I didn't ring. I opened the door with my key.

He was lying there on one of the cushions, and he jumped up before I got the door closed. His eyes were wild and fearful, but he said nothing. We stood staring at each other.

"Where . . . did you go?" he said at last. Voice shaky. Face flushed. My eyes slid around the room for evidence.

"I just walked. To the campus." I could hear the chill in my voice.

"Do you—do you feel better now?"

"I'm not sure," I said, letting my eyes drill into his. I went into the kitchen and poured a double shot of bourbon. When I turned around he was standing in the doorway, looking imploringly at me. I sensed he wanted to come closer but wouldn't. Or couldn't.

"Are you still angry?"

"I'm not sure about that, either."

He attempted a smile, but it faded in the silence.

"Do you want to talk about it?" He almost whispered.

"Do you?"

"I'll do whatever you want."

I couldn't even manage a smirk. I was too hurt and angry. "Why the sudden compliance, Frank?"

"I just don't think we should let an argument come between us."

"Why are you so nervous?"

Another attempted smile. "Honey, I don't like arguing. It depresses me."

"And what do you do for consolation when you're . . . 'depressed'?" He cocked his head questioningly. "Do you call someone up for a little reassurance?"

"What do you mean?"

"Since you're not going to tell me, I'll tell you. I just passed your little friend on the stairs. It was pretty obvious she'd been crying. From hearing *your* side of things, no doubt."

"Irene!"

"One argument, and she's back in the picture."

"It's not that way! She just dropped by—"

"Out of the sky."

"Honey, please! She came by about two minutes after you left. She was upset and so was I. I guess I was a little abrupt with her. She had a problem with one of her roommates again—I've told you about that. I was too distracted because of *us;* I really couldn't concern myself with someone else. I didn't tell her we'd had an argument, but I did tell her about you. I kind of wanted her to meet you but not under tonight's circumstances, so I guess I rushed her out of here."

34

"Quite a rush to make her cry."

"She wasn't crying when she left."

"And *quite* a coincidence."

"But it was a coincidence." He made a fist and held it between his head and the doorjamb. "It was a coincidence."

I started to slip past him, but he spread his arm to block me. "Don't, Irene."

"Let me past."

"Don't keep running out on me." I nudged against his arm. "Can't you be angry and *stay?*"

"Let me past."

"No." He put his arms around me and pulled me to his chest.

"Don't, Frank." I tried to wriggle free, but his arms tightened.

"Honey, please, how can you think—"

"Let me go."

"I have to tell you something. I'm a . . . freak." That's all he said for a moment. His chest quivered, then his whole body trembled, but his arms grew even tighter around me. I couldn't believe it: he was crying. "I—I love you much too much, I know that. I love you more than it's healthy to love someone. I try to hold it back so I won't smother you and— Jesus! I know it's my fault if I'm so afraid of losing you, but I never thought I'd meet anyone like you who would . . . want me too. I'm guilty of that and probably a lot of other things, but don't accuse me of even *thinking* of someone else. That's not fair, Irene, it really isn't."

He went on stroking my back and my hair. Finally, my arms went around him.

"Maybe I'm the freak," I said. "I don't *want* to be selfish, Frank. Help me not to be."

He picked me up and held me so I was looking down into his face. He smiled, but his cheeks were still wet. "You give me more than you know."

"Including a little grief now and then."

"Yes, indeed, but I'll take it." His smile widened. "You really *were* jealous for a few minutes there?"

"Frank, I don't want to—"

"Come on, were you?"

"Well, what did it look like?"

He was beaming. "No one was ever jealous over me in my life. It's a nice feeling."

"Don't plan on any repetitions, mister."

"And no more running out?"

"No more running out."

The next day, I dropped the philodendron in the trash and bought another one. Its longevity has been remarkable. For years it flourished on the window sill in the bedroom of our house. In fact, it was the last thing I looked at in that room the night I picked up the gun and slipped it into my purse.

Fearing that time and opportunity would allow me to retreat into my emotional armor, I made it a point to visit Gloria while my mood would make it easier for me to apologize. Her disapproval of Frank did not have to become an insurmountable problem; the simple solution was to keep them apart and to see her alone.

"Irene, you don't have to apologize." She was embarrassed.

"I'm not excusing what you did. But there's no excuse for what I did, either. You've been good to me; you're the best friend I've ever had. What I did was mean and—well, shabby."

This made her squirm. "Did Frank suggest this apology?"

"I may love him, but I still have a mind of my own."

"I hope so. It's too good a mind to give up. To anyone."

Fall term began, and I carried a full load of classes. For the first time, Gloria did not choose any of the ones I took. We established a routine of having dinner together one night a week, followed by a movie or a concert on campus. Too often, I caught her looking at me with that sidelong glance of hers, but I refused to confront it. I was determined to keep the friendship running smoothly, even if that meant sacrificing it to superficiality. After my argument with Frank over the plant, I was on my guard against being glib and overcritical. On a few occasions, Gloria and I went out for a drink, but I no longer scanned the bar in search of material for snide remarks. She viewed me then the way I imagine historians view great civilizations in decline. But it was pointless for me to explain my new contentment. I would just have to wait until she herself found someone who would make the same difference in her life as Frank did in mine.

She met him at midterm, but it seemed she made more of a difference to his life than he did to hers. His name was Patrick Malone. A veterinarian who had moved up here from Indianapolis, he had the kind of appeal women rarely find outside their fantasies. Though he was close to Frank's height, he had twenty more pounds distributed among his chest, arms and legs. From a distance, his face was as symmetrical as a mechanical drawing, but with sharp green eyes which pierced that distance. Up close, a slight hump on the bridge of his nose added character, and his cheeks were dotted with tiny indentations, the rugged remains of teen-age acne. His smile was quick and boyish, his laugh full-bellied and richly masculine. His conversation, his gestures, everything about him, was affirmative yet gentle. My conversations with him flowed easily, sliding comfortably now and then into friendly gibes at one another. He loved the title my mother and Frank had given me—Irene the Arrogant—and he used it every chance he got. He liked to kid me about having had skin surgery: no one, he said, could have hair as naturally red as mine without having freckles as well. In return, I nicknamed him Craterface and told him he probably hadn't had acne at all, but purposely poked those little holes in his cheeks because he was too pretty. Gloria loved our repartee and looked happiest when she could sit back, sip on a drink and just listen to us.

Unfortunately, the happy threesome became a tense foursome whenever Frank entered the picture. I saw the guardedness in Pat's manner the first time he met Frank, and I could well imagine the source of it. But I felt mildly victorious as Pat and Frank began to relax around each other. Pat loved to talk and Frank was a probing listener, always asking questions and pursuing explanations. Gloria's icy civility toward Frank had mellowed to become an artificial and awkward friendliness, and we all felt the strain. Whenever she had a few drinks in her and her defenses were down, she would slip into staring at him, watching his every movement and judging it. Frank's reaction was to avoid conversation with her; when he did address her, he never looked her in the eye.

The foursome was short-lived. Frank bowed out gradually, at first with excuses of having to work. Later, excuses weren't necessary. Measured against Frank's "exile," Pat's presence made me resentful, and I soon went back to seeing Gloria alone.

Frank and I spent an increasing amount of time alone together. We were both working very hard; sometimes during the week our only amusement was reading to each other the papers we had written. Up to the time I met Frank, I had always mailed my papers home for my father to read. He taught English at Cedar Run High School, and he was more than a little proud of his influence in getting me interested in the same field. I knew my working on a Ph.D. would complete the dream he once had for himself. Naturally, he wanted to keep tabs on that dream. When I forgot to send the papers home after reading them to Frank, I soon received a one-line note from my father which read: "Ph.D. candidates don't write papers anymore?" Chuckling, I showed the note to Frank, but he was not amused.

"You shouldn't forget your father like that," he said seriously.

"I hadn't meant to."

He reached into his desk drawer and pulled out a large envelope. "Here, get your papers together in this and mail it tonight."

I sat down on a cushion and arranged the papers in the envelope, then wrote a short note of apology.

"Do you ever send your papers home?" I asked.

"No."

"Why not?"

"No one to send them to."

"What about your parents?"

"They're dead." It was a simple statement, and he flipped a page of his book as he said it.

"Frank, you never told me!"

"Didn't I?"

"No, you didn't! I can't believe you never mentioned it."

38

"I would have gotten around to it."

"When?"

"I don't know. It's not a subject I particularly enjoy."

"But you'll tell me about it *sometime*, won't you?"

"Sometime."

I always did my studying at the kitchen table so we would be out of each other's way. But that night I couldn't concentrate. I could hear him flipping pages in the other room, and I tried to imagine what I would be like if both my parents were dead. Then I realized something else. Frank had told me he was the youngest of nine kids, yet so far as I knew, he had never got a phone call or a letter from any of them during the three months we had been living together. I sat staring at the flecks in the Formica tabletop and wondered how I could have been so blind— and selfish. Although he had chosen to say nothing about his family, why hadn't it occurred to me to ask about them?

I went to bed and lay there waiting for him. I kept telling myself it was ridiculous to be jealous over something I didn't know. Yes, I was jealous of withheld information. I wanted to know everything that had ever happened to him. After all, the death of one's parents was not a casual scrap of information.

I didn't move when he got into bed. With a short groan he stretched out on his back. We had lived together long enough to have established communication in the dark; I knew that still as I was, he knew I was wide awake and waiting.

"My father was killed in a bar when I was eighteen. My mother died of pneumonia four years ago." He said it quickly, dispassionately, then sighed heavily to signal me he wanted to sleep.

"Killed? How?"

"He was shot."

"Why?"

"It was a holdup. When the bartender wouldn't surrender the money, they shot up the place. My father was hit by accident, along with two other men."

I was about to say "How did you feel?" but realized how ridiculous it would sound. Instead, I asked how often he saw his brothers and sisters.

"I don't see them at all. Not since my mother died."

"Why not?"

"Our house was so small, we spent half our time trying to get away from each other."

"But now that you all live apart, surely you can see each other once in a while."

"I don't care to see any of them," he said flatly.

"But weren't any of you close to each other?"

"Too close; privacy was at a premium. When you're scraping elbows at the dinner table and using the bathroom three at a time, you don't want to spend your free time exchanging intimacies. You want to spend it alone."

"Not all large families are like that, are they?"

"I guess not. But I'm not going to have a large family to find out."

I remembered him saying: *I hate it when people just breed.* In a way, he was making the same statement again.

I said, "Are you sure my living with you isn't disturbing your privacy?"

"You're living here because I want you here. You're my family now."

"Am I?" I moved over and put my head on his shoulder. We lay still, saying nothing for several minutes. His chest rose, and he held his breath.

"Irene, would you marry me?"

I didn't intend to keep him in suspense, but I wanted the words to linger.

"I mean," he said, "would you think about marrying me?"

"No, I won't *think* about it." I pressed my mouth against his ear. "Just promise me we'll make it soon."

Gloria took the news standing up and with a look on her face that said: "I knew this would happen." But all she said was "Congratulations": from past experience, she had learned not to verbalize her thoughts about Frank and me.

We went to Cedar Run for Christmas and told my parents. My mother seemed genuinely pleased, while my father made a pretense of being pleased. From my recent experiences with Gloria, I was sensitive to being watched, and I felt my father watching me the more he pretended not to. I suspected he knew he had not been told everything, and I was not looking forward to the task. The night before Frank and I were to leave, I stayed up late and alone with my father to confess the rest.

"I'm taking a leave from the Ph.D. program," I began.

"You mean you're *leaving* the program."

"I'm going to take education courses next term and practice-teach in the spring so I can get a job in the fall. In a couple of years, I'll go back and get the degree."

He was sitting in his recliner. He laid his head back and sighed. "I might have expected this."

I bristled. Gloria had done her best to suggest my life was taking a downhill slide; I did not need the suggestion reinforced by my father. "It's my life. Don't you think I have the right to make a few decisions about what I want to do with it?"

"You have every right. I suppose *I* have no right to be disappointed. But I am. Was this Frank's idea?"

"No, it wasn't. In fact, he was against it at first."

"But he's going along with it?"

"It's what I want to do. Dad, do you remember what you said that day you and Mom came down to Frank's—about college being removed from reality? I've thought about that a lot, the way I've been living in a shell. I've lived away from home, but I've never really been on my own. The English Department has been my guardian and I've been its good little girl."

"So now you're Frank's little girl. I wouldn't call that being on your own, either."

"Yes, it is. Since I've known Frank, I've been on my own in a very painful way. I've had to admit things about myself that aren't very pleasant."

"Like what?"

"Just the *way* I've been, the way I never paid any attention to Neil and Barry."

"That's natural. You're the girl, you're older, you've had different interests."

41

"I've never had a job, not even a summer one, and before I met Frank I never had to consider anyone else or even meet them halfway. I've never allowed myself to be challenged. Do you remember in tenth grade how I hated gym and we got Dr. Patterson to write that phony letter so I could get excused? I've been doing that kind of thing all my life. When I got to college, if I didn't like a class the first two weeks, I dropped it. If I didn't bowl or play tennis well the first few times out, I quit doing it. I could always run back to the books and get my A's."

"You're blowing this way out of proportion. Studying is hard work. Dedicating yourself to a goal demands discipline, and you've always had perfect discipline, the kind most people never have. I won't let you minimize that. As for bowling or tennis, no one can excel in everything."

"I know that. But it's easy to hide yourself away in a niche and pat yourself on the back and never try anything else for the simple reason you might fall flat on your face."

"Honey, not having a niche is what makes people miserable. Be thankful you've got one."

I kept quiet for a few minutes until I found another argument. "When you fell in love with Mom, what did it feel like?"

"What do you mean?" He was wary of being sidetracked.

"How did you feel?"

"I was happy, of course. I guess I was flattered too, when I realized how she felt about me. There were a couple of others who wanted very much to be in my shoes. But I don't see what—"

"Then it's natural to feel happy when you love someone?"

"Certainly. What's your point, Irene?"

"Just this. When I first knew Frank I was miserable. Can you imagine why?"

"Because he bowls and plays tennis better than you do."

"Don't be cute. It was because for once in my life I was doing something I couldn't do well—loving someone."

"What makes you think you can't love well?"

"*Couldn't*. I think I'm learning."

"Well, then, what are you learning?"

"That I'm not as terrific as I thought I was and . . . that I can be better than I am. That loving someone requires making allowances."

He frowned. "What kind of allowances?"

"I didn't know until a few weeks ago that both his parents are dead. When I found out, I was insulted he hadn't told me, and I was so busy stewing in the insult that I didn't stop to consider *why* he hadn't talked about them. It was just too painful for him. I couldn't understand it because I've never had that kind of pain. Frank's been anything but sheltered and I'm tired of being sheltered. I'm sick of being so damned comfortable. I guess I'm sick of myself. I want to take those education courses and then teach for a while. I want to get out there and *do* something."

"Those who can't do, teach."

"Stop it. You of all people know better than that. I've had plenty of professors who aren't half the teacher you are."

"How would you know? You were never in a class of mine."

"I had friends who were."

He spread his fingers out on the arms of his chair. "I should know better than to try to change your mind. But let me exercise the ancient parental prerogative and give you some advice. I know I told you academic life was not reality—whatever that battered term means. And maybe it is a niche, but it's one that gives you plenty of spare time, and time is freedom. If you teach in a high school, you'd better be prepared for some intellectual shrinkage and a drastic trimming of your ideals. And don't think that your enthusiasm for your subject is going to spill out and saturate all your students. There *are* rewards, but they're quite different from what you're used to. I liked it the first few years, but then when you kids began to grow up, somehow it got stale. Maybe it'll be different for you. At least you won't be starting out as a parent."

"Maybe not."

"For God's sake, you can at least wait for *that!* Don't build your fence on all four sides."

"Do you think I'll make a good mother?"

"If your kids are like Frank, yes. God help you if you have

43

just one who turns out as headstrong as you are."

I said good night by pressing his shoulder and kissing his hair. I knew he was disappointed, but that the disappointment would pass. As I climbed the stairs to my old room, I was confident that he, like myself, would be more than pleased with everything I did.

It was true Frank opposed my leaving the Ph.D. program and joining the masses in the small auditorium of the Education Building. Dr. Denning, the chairman of the English Department, greeted my decision with absolute repugnance. I had to pedal very softly with him for two reasons. During the past four years he had assumed a regard for me that was as paternal as it was academic. And in addition to hitting him with this decision of mine, I had to ask him to use his influence in getting the Education Department to allow me to take their three sequence courses all in one term. At first, he countered by offering me an instructor's position for the spring term and practically promised me a job after I got my degree. When he saw I would not be swayed, he granted my request, but not before telling me that given the odds, my leaving the program would most likely be "terminal." As I put on my coat to leave, he stood up and, actually misty-eyed, offered his hand; he assured me his door was always open if I ever needed him.

Naturally, I was hungry for encouragement, yet I was not going to stumble over the disappointment of my father, Dr. Denning, or even Frank. Emotionally, I felt like a pioneer heading west; if the going got rough I could always turn back.

Denning carried through, and I got the three education courses concurrently. I also got a dose of boredom more excruciating than I had expected. There was nothing "entertaining" in the reading or in the papers I had to write. By the third week I was keeping a countdown calendar aimed at the end of the term. Three weeks before finals, I got the notice that my student-teaching assignment for the spring was in Elkton, thirty miles from campus. I hadn't looked forward to living away from Frank for even one term, but fortunately Elkton was close enough for me to commute.

That spring term went smoothly enough to convince me I had made the right decision. My supervising teacher was impressed enough with my scholastic record to give me her senior class— her "plum," as she called it—instead of one of her sophomore classes. The class and I took to each other beautifully, and my "shrunken expectations" were revitalized when I discovered how enthusiastic and verbal many of the kids were. I worked them as hard as I worked myself, and the results were gratifying. I came home every evening bubbling with stories and anecdotes about my day. Even Frank began to concede that my decision had been a good one, that this change was what I needed.

"Since you're adapting so well to change," he said, "when are we going to make the big one?"

"Which is?"

"Change of name. From Rutledge to Mattison."

"What comes with it?"

"Oh, nothing much. Just a man who can't live without you."

"In that case, I accept. I never could resist a worthy cause."

"Bitch." He grinned.

Before the wedding, we moved out of the apartment and into a house trailer. It was owned by a student in the History Department, who offered to let us live in it rent-free while he went off to study in Mexico. I was thrilled about the move, regarding it as another installment in the continuing adventure of changing my life. Since Frank had next to no furniture, there was very little to pack for making such a move. The first day after being set free for the summer, I decided I would take over the packing and organizing; Frank was preoccupied with the upcoming meeting where he would have to defend his thesis and with the preparation of materials and reading lists for the summer classes he would be teaching.

He was off at the library when I began the chore of packing boxes and crates and labeling them. My adrenaline was running high, so high that by midafternoon everything was squared away and ready to go, everything but the bed and the contents of Frank's desk. I took a break with a cup of coffee and a few cigarettes and debated with myself whether or not I should go ahead and clean out the desk. Frank was extremely well organized, so there wouldn't be any problem transferring his material. It was simple: each drawer would be assigned to a separate box. Still, I hesitated. The desk was Frank's only private turf in the apartment, and I had never invaded it. I sat looking at it for quite a while, until I convinced myself it was silly to put him through the task while I had time on my hands.

Everything in the four side drawers was neatly filed in folders and big envelopes and clearly labeled. The top middle drawer contained personal items. Although I promised myself not to look through anything as I packed, I broke the promise almost immediately when I saw the paper with my name and "statistics" on it—the exact information about me that he had recited our first night together. He had obviously had a connection with someone in the registrar's office. I smiled at the fact that he had gone to the trouble of checking up on me. Had I really appeared *that* forbidding?

The next thing I came across was a yellowed newspaper clipping that included a picture of Frank and five other scholarship winners in his high school. I stood there staring at it because it was so poignant: compared to the others, Frank was conspicuously ill-dressed. Instead of a sport coat he wore a snowflake-patterned sweater far too small for him; the sleeves ended a good four inches from the wrists, that remaining space taken up by a clashing checkered shirt. My God, I thought, he really was *that* poor. Looking at him in that outfit, I immediately flashed back to my high school senior prom. No dress in Cedar Run or in any of the neighboring towns was good enough for me. I had made my mother drive over a hundred miles to go shopping for something better. Even when I settled on something better, it was the style I wanted but not exactly the color and I complained about it right up to the minute my date rang our doorbell.

I took a large envelope and put the clipping in it so it wouldn't yellow or wrinkle any more than it had. Someday, I thought, if our children ever complained about what they didn't have, I could pull the clipping out and show them how far their father had come on next to nothing.

I removed the last layer of memorabilia—some concert and play programs from university productions—and found one remaining item in the corner of the drawer. It was a photograph of Frank and a girl, taken when he was probably fifteen or sixteen, both of them dressed raggedly and sitting under a tree. The girl's face was turned and smiling up at Frank. She was a pretty thing, but her sagging shoulders coupled with her low brow line gave the impression she was somewhat "slow." In striking contrast to the girl's smile was the smoldering expression on Frank's face: his jaw was clenched so hard it looked as if it had been wired shut, and his eyes were two slits behind his eyeglasses. I had never seen him look at anyone in that way; I knew if *I* had been the one holding the camera to take that picture, Frank's face would have withered me on the spot.

I had finished filling the box for this drawerful, and I laid the picture down on top of everything else. A couple of times later in the afternoon, I stopped to glance at it again, although that face was already imprinted on my mind. It was not just an angry face. It was livid.

I was in the shower when Frank came home. By the time I dried off, combed my hair and got dressed, he was loading up the car with the boxes.

"What's the rush?" I said. "Don't you want to go have dinner first?"

"I want to do this now before I eat and get drowsy."

He had worked so quickly that by the time we were ready to go, I only had to carry one shopping bag down to the car. When we arrived at the trailer, he did the unloading while I cleaned the toilet and washbowl. As we were tossing around suggestions about where to go for dinner, I happened to glance at the box that had the top desk drawer things in it.

"Hey, what happened to that picture that was sitting on top of this stuff?"

"What picture?"

"The one of you and a girl. It was right here on top of everything."

"Maybe it slipped down in. Come on, let's get going."

"Just a minute." I lifted everything from the box, but the picture was gone. "Oh, damn it! Didn't you see it, Frank? It was right on top."

"No, I didn't."

"It was you and this girl; you were sitting under a tree. I found it in your top desk drawer while I was packing."

"We'll find it later. And if we don't, it's not important."

"It certainly *is* important if you kept it all these years."

"No, it's not, really."

"Who is she?"

"Just a girl I knew once."

"A girlfriend?"

"Not in that way."

"She looked—well, a little retarded. Was she?"

"Mildly, yes."

"And you looked like you were going to bite someone's head off. Who *took* the picture?"

"I don't remember. Some relative or neighbor. Now will you come on—I'm starving."

The next day I went through all the boxes I had packed, looking for that picture. But I never found it. And Frank was blandly unconcerned over its disappearance.

At the time, it didn't occur to me to think anything of it. . . .

We were married in July in the Cedar Run Presbyterian Church. Frank had his hair cut for the wedding although I told him not to do it on my account. But he insisted, knowing it would please my parents. It did. My father must have mentioned a hundred times what "an improvement" it was. Frank merely smiled and said nothing.

The day of the wedding and the day before it were eventful, to say the least. Since Frank had no really close friends, he had asked Bernie Golden, another graduate instructor in history, to be his best man. During the rehearsal, Bernie walked around

48

telling everyone, "I don't know how Frank got her. He ought to write a book about it. Send his secret in to *Playboy*." My annoyance with him was fast approaching verbalization, but every now and then Frank would squeeze my hand and whisper, "Patience. You can afford it."

I had had a real debate with myself over asking Gloria to be my maid of honor. It was Frank who talked me into making the offer. Her acceptance was pointedly unenthusiastic, but I chose to write it off as a cover-up. When she arrived in Cedar Run, she had given up her subtle sullenness and replaced it with a look of stoic resignation. And so between Gloria and Bernie and my father (whose disappointment in me I felt was still potent), there was enough friction in the air to keep me on edge.

But there was more.

Frank and I had come close to having several arguments over his refusal to invite any of his family to the wedding. His only guests would be two professors and their wives and nine students.

"I don't see why you can't invite a few of your brothers and sisters."

"I know you don't see why," he said. "But take my word for it, it's better this way."

"Imagine how strange it's going to look in the church with your side almost empty."

"I know how it's going to look, honey, and I'm sorry. But I'll be more comfortable this way."

"Do you really hate them that much?"

The blood rushed to his face. "I just don't have anything in common with them."

"What does that matter for one afternoon?"

"It matters a great deal. To me."

"I can't understand this hostility of yours."

"Irene, considering the family you come from, I know it's hard for you to understand. It would kill something in you to give your family up. But it'll kill something in me if I *don't* give mine up. Starting now."

"But why? Why does it have to be so absolute?"

"All right," he said stiffly, "I'll tell you. My sister Doris ran

49

off with a married man fourteen years ago. When I left to go to college, his wife and kids were still waiting to hear from him. My brother Tom was a traveling salesman until he lost his license because of so many drunk-driving charges. Now he's a night custodian so he can drink on the job and get away from his wife. Jack's decided to follow in my father's footsteps. He drives a delivery truck and his wife has a baby almost every year. Terry's serving a prison term in Pennsylvania for manslaughter. He had a fight with his girlfriend one night and ran down a man at a crosswalk. Marian and her husband left town right after they were married and haven't been heard from since. Bill and Mike are as close as brothers can be—they both share Mike's wife." He was breathing like an exhausted runner. "They're not going to touch me. They're not going to touch *us*. Irene, what you come from and what I come from are worlds apart. The only way for it to work is to make one world between us. We keep your family and we drop mine."

More than his words, it was the look of repugnance and fear on his face that convinced me not to press any further. It was his family and up to him to deal with them as he saw fit. Wanda Hoople had escaped from her family and had forgone a high school diploma to do it. Frank certainly had the same right to escape at the age of twenty-six.

The evening before the wedding, we had our rehearsal, followed by a dinner for the wedding party. My spirits were dampened by my father's and Gloria's reserve; they went through the rehearsal matter-of-factly, totally bland-faced. Whatever bolstering I got came from my mother's smiling enthusiasm and Frank's caressing eyes.

My father and I were halfway down the aisle in the final run-through when I saw Frank's face go white and rigid. We continued on, but Frank kept looking past us to the rear of the church. The minister cleared his throat, then spoke Frank's name. Frank recovered himself, but when he stepped up to me I could see his eyes were wild, his hands trembling. The second we were finished I turned around and saw a man and woman sitting in the last pew. Frank didn't move. He kept his back to them and muttered, "God damn her, God damn her!"

"Frank! Who is it?"

"Vivian," he gritted.

"Who's Vivian?"

"My sister. She found out. I knew she would, I knew she would!"

"So she found out, so what? Come on, you'd better introduce me." He wouldn't budge. "Frank, what's the matter with you?"

His voice cracked. "She's the worst! And now she's here, she just walks right in!"

"And whose fault is that? I imagine she feels pretty insulted. Are you afraid she'll make a scene?"

"Yes, yes!"

"We can't just leave her sitting back there. Now come on."

By this time, everybody was staring at the couple. I took Frank's hand and started down the aisle toward them. The man's face was expressionless, but the woman was smiling, first at Frank, then at me. Although she seemed a good deal older than Frank, there was no mistaking that she was his sister. Her features were similar to his, but stronger, her eyes larger, her mouth slightly fuller. Like Frank, she was quite tall, but well built instead of gangly, and her squared shoulders contributed to her impeccably confident posture. A solitary streak of gray hair among the dark brown lent a dramatic touch to her striking appearance.

The man stood up, still expressionless, and offered his hand to Frank. Frank only glowered at him.

"Hello, I'm Vivian Snell, Frank's sister. This is my husband, Leo."

Leo turned his hand to me and I shook it. Then Vivian offered hers. There was a momentary silence. Finally, I spoke. "I really don't know what to say."

"And neither do I." Vivian smiled. "Maybe Frank has something to say."

If Frank's eyes had been bullets, Vivian would have been dead on the spot. "I have nothing to say to you. There's no reason for you to be here."

Her smile disappeared but she remained unruffled. "Frank,"

she said softly, "if you choose to walk out on your family, that's your business. But I think we all have the right to know who you're going to marry."

"You have no right. How did you find me?"

"There are other people in Ridgeway who go to the university. The word got back to us." She turned to me. "You're very pretty. Very pretty. Have you known Frank long?"

"A little more than a year."

"Oh, then it wasn't a whirlwind courtship?"

"No, it wasn't."

"I'm glad. The two of you had plenty of time to get to know each other. Are those your parents down there?"

"Yes. Come meet them. And since you're here, why don't you have dinner with us? The whole wedding party's going out."

"We'd like that very much. If Frank can put up with it."

"Don't be silly," I said, even though I saw the sick look on Frank's face.

The introductions were made. When we left the church, Frank saw to it that no one rode in the car with us on the way to the restaurant.

"Why! Why did you have to do that?" His voice was quivering with rage and his eyes were tearing. I was frightened.

"Can't you bury the hatchet for one evening?" I said timidly.

"Bury the hatchet? You think it's that simple? This isn't like one of those arguments *you* have with your father, where you make up the next day and everything's forgotten. You don't seem to understand that I hate her. I've always hated her; I'll never stop hating her; I don't want her around me! Is that clear?"

"How can you hate her so much? You never even mentioned her to me."

He swallowed hard and tightened his lips. We drove on for a few more blocks before he spoke again. "Irene, I hate her as much as I love you. Maybe you can't understand that, but please try to accept it. All my life I've watched her butt into other people's lives and twist them to her advantage. She started with my—my mother, and then the rest of us. Doris and Marian ran away because of her and so did I."

"But what did she do?"

"It's not what she did; it's what she *is*. She controls everything around her. Just watch Leo for two minutes."

"Does she have any children?"

"No."

"Maybe that's the reason she wants to hang on to the rest of you. Frank, it's just for tonight. She wants a share of her baby brother's happiness, that's all. How old is she, anyway?"

"Forty-two."

"That's sixteen years' difference. It's only natural she wants to mother you a bit—"

"After tonight, that's it. She stays away permanently."

"Whatever you say. Now how about a kiss?" I nestled up to him.

"Please, Irene, I'm trying to drive."

We were the last ones to arrive at the restaurant. The waiters had pushed three tables together to make one long one; at the head of it were two empty chairs waiting for us. I sat directly at the head, with Frank on my right, Vivian on my left. Vivian was on her second martini. Leo was nursing a club soda.

"It was nice of you to ask us," said Vivian. "We hadn't expected it."

Frank glared at her, then ordered a double Scotch. Although there were conversations all along the table, I had a feeling everyone was keeping an ear turned to Frank, Vivian and me.

"You have a nice family," said Vivian. "There's just you and the two boys?"

"Yes, Neil and Barry."

"What do your father and mother do?"

"My father teaches English at the high school. My mother's a dressmaker. She had our front porch glassed in and uses it as her shop."

"You look as if you all get along very well."

"We do. I'm quite proud of them."

"Yes, I can tell." She twirled the olive in her martini glass. "And I'm proud of Frank. We all are."

"I am too," I said.

53

"Frank's proud of himself too," she said teasingly. "He'd like to think we don't have much in common. But we do have one thing. Ambition. Leo and I started out with one lumberyard. Now we have three."

"And you have no children?"

"We couldn't have them. But I have my nieces and nephews. I'm satisfied with that. We're a very close family."

"You are?"

She picked up the surprise in my voice. "All except Frank, of course. He's always been the loner. He's more . . . private than the rest of us. It's hard to tell what's going on in that head of his. Even as a kid he was secretive."

Yes, I wanted to say, he *is* secretive. That wild anger had left Frank's face, replaced now by a look of contempt.

"Anyway," continued Vivian, "now that he's proven himself and done it all on his own, maybe he won't have to be so independent. Maybe he'll let his family do a few things for him."

Frank laid his napkin on the table, excused himself and went to the men's room. Immediately, Vivian opened her purse, pulled something from it and put it in my hand under the table.

"Don't let anybody see it," she said, "and don't say a word about it to Frank."

I drew my hand into my lap and looked down. It was a check.

"Vivian!" I whispered. "This is for a thousand dollars!"

"It's made out to you so Frank doesn't have to know anything about it. You spend it the way you see fit."

"Oh, Vivian, I can't. He didn't even invite you to the wedding and now you're giving us this—"

"In our family we look out for our own. Frank's a strange young man. I know; I watched him grow up. Maybe that's part of his charm. If he chooses to cut us off, there's nothing we can do about that. But I want you to know we're always there in case you need us."

"Why does he feel the way he does? I don't understand it."

"Don't try," she said. "I gave up a long time ago. We're a large family and every one of us is different. We were very poor

54

and we all had our share of hurt, in and out of the house. I think Frank indulges himself. I think part of him enjoys hanging on to the hurt. He never forgets, and he doesn't forgive easily. But maybe now that he's found you . . ." She leaned back in her chair, looked me over and smiled. "You really *are* a beauty. You're sure to have lovely children. You do plan to have them, don't you?"

"Of course. A little later, though. But about this check. I can't—"

"Yes, you can. And not a word to Frank."

"Then come to the wedding tomorrow. Please."

"No. The way Frank feels right now, it would be too much for him. I'm satisfied just to have met you."

I glanced at Leo, and he smiled woodenly. He appeared to have been only half listening, and he had not said a word to anyone else. It flashed through my mind what an incongruous pair they were: she was so animated and outgoing and he was such a stiff. But then, who was I to judge? Gloria, I knew, considered Frank and me incongruous.

"Here comes Frank now," said Vivian. "Remember, this is just between us."

Frank sat down and looked suspiciously at Vivian and me. So did Gloria and my father. The five of us barely spoke during the rest of the meal.

Vivian and Leo said good-bye in the parking lot and drove off. Pat Malone suggested that Frank and I come out for a drink with him and Gloria, but Frank refused before I could say a word. We got into the car and drove a few miles out of town on the highway. He turned off onto a gravel road and pulled over to the shoulder.

"Don't tell me we're going to neck," I said, trying to offset the gravity of his manner.

"There's something we have to settle right now. You know how I feel about my family. Do you or do you not intend to respect those feelings? I have to know now."

"That sounds almost like an ultimatum."

55

"I guess it does," he said firmly.

"Do you think it's fair to be handing out ultimatums the night before our wedding?"

"A lot of things are unfair, Irene. That's the way life is."

"Thank you, Philosopher Mattison!"

"Please don't take that tone."

"What tone am I supposed to take when you get sanctimonious with me? I know what brought this on. It's because I was civil to Vivian."

"You were more than civil."

"All right, I was. But I must say your behavior left a lot to be desired. Whatever resentment you have for her could be put aside for just one evening. To tell you the truth, I was shocked by you. And disappointed. You know, that first night I came to your apartment, you treated Larry like a prince and I was impressed. Then tonight you treat your own sister as if she were . . . some kind of vermin. Even when it's apparent she cares so much for you." A muted snort came through his nose. "Go ahead and shrug it off, but you might just as well shrug off the fact the earth is round. She's obliging and cautious with you and all she gets in return is the most childish rudeness. She had nothing but praise and consideration for you and she gave us—" I stopped dead, remembering too late the promise I made to her.

"Gave us what?"

"Her blessing."

"Gave us what?"

"All right, she gave us a check."

"A check? Let me see it."

"Frank—"

"Let me see it."

I took it from my purse and handed it to him. He stared at it, then calmly tore it up.

"That's just wonderful," I said. "You won't even allow her that pleasure."

"She's not going to buy her way into our lives."

"That wasn't what she was doing."

"That's exactly what she was doing. This is the kind of thing I'd expect from her."

"I don't understand it. If it's a matter of pride—"

"It's more than that. All I'm asking of you is that you respect my feelings."

"Even when you won't explain them?"

"You didn't grow up in my family, Irene, and I didn't grow up in yours. Would you like it if we moved far away from your parents and your brothers?"

"No, I wouldn't."

"All right, so we won't. I'll respect your wishes. All I ask is the same in return."

It *sounded* reasonable, yet I couldn't *feel* it was reasonable. But there was nothing I could say.

"I want nothing to do with any of them," he said. "I don't want to live near them, I don't want to hear from them—no birthdays, no Christmas cards, nothing."

"All right, all right. Let's not fight over it."

"Let's not, ever again. I don't want them to have the power to make us fight."

The next day, all my father's reservations seemed to slip away with the smile and the kiss he gave me before we started down the aisle. After the ceremony, the reception was loud and festive. My mother had two glasses of champagne and had to sit down. Lazily, she rested her head on my father's shoulder. He whispered something in her ear, she smiled, then turned and kissed him tenderly on the cheek. Frank saw it too, and he said to me: "That'll be us in twenty years."

When we were ready to make our escape through one of the rear doors, I saw Gloria sitting alone in a far corner of the room. The sight of her made me hesitate a moment. She was sagging forward, her head bowed; and in my brief glimpse I could see her hands lying in her lap, limp and curled like a pair of dead birds.

The first three years of my marriage I was recklessly happy. I wore my happiness like a badge, oversized and well polished, ostentatious in every way. And I was most ostentatious whenever I was around Gloria. For a long time, I was haunted by that single glimpse of her at the wedding reception, and I wanted to refute any unspoken predictions she might be making about my marriage. She went on being propitiously polite to Frank and guarded around me when he was present. I knew her disappointment in me struck more deeply than she let on, and that alone cast the first solid shadow on the turn my life had taken. I resented that shadow; to eliminate it, I chose to pity Gloria for her blindness.

She got her Ph.D. and married Pat Malone. Without any apparent resentment, he packed up his veterinary practice and moved it to Los Angeles because Gloria received a job offer there.

I had got a job teaching at Peck High School (the most desirable school in town because it was new and many of the students were the children of professors), and Frank was hired by the university as an assistant professor. We bought a nine-room, fifty-year-old house and the vacant lot next to it. The first few nights we were in it, we wandered through the large, empty rooms sipping on wine and making plans for the paint, wallpaper, rugs and furniture. A few times, when the second or third glass of wine had mellowed him, Frank would turn misty-eyed, slip his arm around me and assure me that *his* family was never going to be crowded. I clearly recall the urgency in his voice, as if he were saying we would never starve or perish in a flood or contract a fatal disease. *We were never going to be crowded.*

Two months later, I became pregnant. It was verified by the doctor on a Wednesday, but I waited until Friday night to tell Frank. I wanted the weekend right there with no work interruptions, so we could celebrate and play with the future. We stayed in bed talking until Saturday afternoon. That night he took me to the best restaurant in town. In candlelight and over champagne, we suggested names back and forth. By the end of the evening, we were leaning across the table, holding hands, whispering.

"Why are we whispering?" I whispered.

He smiled lazily. "Because no one else in the world has to

58

hear us. I want you always to be just a whisper away."

That weekend I fell in love all over again, but this time pain-lessly, luxuriously. Sunday night, Frank gave me a bath in that old chipped tub we would eventually replace. He washed me, oiled me, dried me off, and wouldn't let me lift a hand to any of it.

"Until the baby comes," he said, *"you're* the baby."

When we got into bed, he stroked my belly in a soft, circular motion, then laid his head there and kissed it.

"It's going to be loved," he said. "It's going to be so loved."

I finished the statement in my head: "The way you *weren't.*"

"Yes," I said, "it's going to be loved."

He kissed me there again, soft and lingering. "It's the purest form of love there is," he murmured.

I knew I had heard him say that before, but I was too drowsy to recall where and when. I went to sleep with my fingers in his hair.

She was born on June first, my birthday, and we named her Regina Frances. I had had my heart set on Mary (I was always fond of alliterative names), but Frank argued it was too common and too religious. There was really no other name I wanted, so I gave in when he insisted on Regina. At least, I thought, it sounded dignified: Regina Mattison would be quite suitable for a writer or an actress or a Pulitzer Prize winner. Naturally, I never pictured it in newspaper stories about a murder trial.

She weighed just under seven pounds and had no hair whatso-ever. The first few times she was brought to me for nursing, my joy over this tiny creation was undercut by apprehension. The veins in her head were so large, so near the surface, that I feared she was missing a necessary layer of skin. The doctor assured me she was perfectly normal. But it was really a nurse, Miss Pennington, who put my fear to rest. Whenever she brought Regina to me she would quip, "Here's Mrs. Mattison's little road map." And Frank studied Regina like a road map. He would hold her and look searchingly into that little face, then say he was sure she was going to look like me.

59

"Don't be silly," I said. "It's too soon to tell. She hasn't even got hair yet. I just hope baldness doesn't run in your family."

"It doesn't," he returned seriously.

I knew by now he did not welcome *any* reference to his family. But the day we left the hospital with Regina, he was faced with more than a reference: Vivian was waiting for us in the lobby.

Smiling, she stood up and came toward us. She had cut her hair since we saw her last, and she looked more like Frank than ever. She was still far from beautiful, but quite striking and obviously unself-conscious about her height, because she wore heels and did not slouch in the least. I was carrying Regina and Frank was carrying the two plants some of my students had brought me. As soon as he saw Vivian, he tucked one of the plants under his arm, then gripped my shoulder to steer me to the door. Vivian halted and made no attempt to follow us: that alone made me angry with Frank.

"You can't do this to her," I said, pulling away from him.

"She can't do this to *us!"* he hissed. "Come on!"

I glanced over my shoulder at her. She stood there tall and proud, yet looked at me helplessly.

"You can at least let her look at the baby."

"No."

"You're acting like a child."

"You don't know her. She's not worming her way in. You made a promise to me, Irene. Now keep it."

We continued on to the parking lot. I got into the car but Frank didn't. "I'll be right back," he said, and started for the lobby doors. Vivian came through them and met Frank on the steps. Frank spoke, then she spoke, then she reached out to touch his hand and he pulled back from her. He said something else as he backed away from her. She remained on the steps. We drove home without saying a word to each other.

A few days later, a typewritten envelope with no return address came for me. Inside was a note from Vivian explaining the accompanying check: a thousand reoffered as a wedding gift and a thousand to begin a savings account for the baby. I debated with myself over telling Frank and finally decided not to. I stuck the

60

check in my jewelry box and for a week I considered opening a secret savings account. I watched Frank carefully that week, the way he lingered at the crib staring at a miracle, the smile on his face as he sat with his arm around me while I nursed the baby.

I tore up the check and the envelope with it.

During the months that followed, I was quite naturally preoccupied with Regina. And with Frank. His energy astounded me. He hired a plumber from the university and the two of them went to work rebuilding and modernizing the kitchen and the upstairs bathroom. By the end of the summer, he was buying the materials for building a recreation room and laundry room in the basement. Yet when classes began, he assigned himself extra office hours and tutored the poorer students in our living room for midterm and final exams. Still, there was always time for the house and for the baby. He worked incessantly, sleeping only four or five hours a night, but the harsh routine he set for himself seemed to nourish rather than debilitate him. Within a year, the basement was completed, every floor in the house refinished. My initial reservations about having taken on an old house instead of a new one dwindled each time I drove up to it. The neighborhood was settled and comfortable, with fully grown oaks and maples that stood like sentinels on both sides of the street. The houses were all large and quite modest in their trimmings: standard white was the reigning preference for wood and brick alike. Ours was a dark green, but within two years we would paint it white, following suit. And within five years, our adjoining empty lot—the sunniest patch on the block—would contain a vegetable garden. Having that extra property gave us a certain prestige among the neighbors, but the feature I loved most about the house was its location at the end of the block, where the street dead-ended. I liked the feeling of being tucked away even from the minimal traffic on the rest of the street, minimal because most of our neighbors were much older, with their children already grown. However, our empty lot did attract children from neighboring streets, and I was happy that Regina would have playmates close by. Frank, in fact, encouraged kids to play in the lot by hanging old tractor tires from the oak limbs to serve as swings. "When she has friends," he would say, "I want them to feel comfortable here. I want *them* to come to *her.*" I thought at the time she would always be surrounded by friends if they came to her the way her father did. When Frank was finished preparing his lectures and reading his students' papers, when he put aside the hammer and the sandpaper and the paint, his total recreation was Regina. I was instructed to take a nap or read or go to a movie while he played with her on the living room floor. He bought a couple of dime-store wigs, a rubber nose, wax lips, and kept her entertained for hours with impersonations. He built a little stage with a cloth curtain and put on shows for her with hand puppets. I was not the entertainer Frank was. For Regina, the drawing and coloring and games I taught her were inferior substitutes for her father's performances. As soon as she heard Frank come up the front porch steps, she would scramble to her feet and toddle to the door with hand puppets dangling from her fists.

As much as I loved my daughter, my heart was not really in most of the activities we did together. While playing with her I found myself daydreaming about teaching and going back to it. The short time I taught before she was born was the happiest period of my life. When I left Peck High to have Regina, the principal, Hugh Lance, told me firmly I had damned well better plan on coming back, that he didn't want to see my talent wasted. He was not given to compliments, so I was genuinely flattered by what he said. As comfortable as I was at home, nothing in the world rivaled the sensation of being in front of a class giving my performance, which would encourage the kids to give theirs. Naturally, there were disappointments, scores of them, but somehow they were always outweighed by the accomplishments. And while I was at home with Regina, it was those accomplishments I kept thinking about. Although I said nothing, I would catch Frank every now and then giving me a knowing, sympathetic look. Finally, a few months before Regina turned four, he suggested I call Lance and ask if I could come back the following September. I wanted to leap for the phone, but I said no, another year wouldn't make any difference one way or the other. I was apprehensive about turning Regina over to a stranger before she started school. The last thing I wanted her to feel was abandonment.

I called Lance and the arrangements were made. I would start back to work when Regina started kindergarten. Frank's plan was to get Regina into the morning session and to schedule his own classes for the morning as well. That way, she would come home to him, not to a baby-sitter.

That last year alone with Regina, I managed to keep my disposition in top form: knowing I was going back to work made my patience invincible. When Regina whined and crabbed, I was stolidly serene. I didn't even mind playing chauffeur and chaperon when she and her friends wanted to go to the zoo or to the south-side swimming pool every day it didn't rain. Before that, during the winter months, I took them sledding three days a week.

Then in August came the end to my serenity. Regina began to complain of feeling cold, of aching in her ankles, arches and knees. The doctor said it was probably a summer cold or a strain of flu. I was content with that for three or four days, until she turned pale and developed dark circles under her eyes that looked as if they had been there forever.

It turned out to be rheumatic fever. Along with the prescription for the medication, the doctor handed us the news that there would be no school for Regina until January, and possibly not even then. She was to have constant rest and no excitement. That, of course, meant she had to be watched. So for me it would be good-bye to teaching for another year.

"You're going back," said Frank.

"But we'll have to hire a baby-sitter."

"No, we won't. I'll stay with her."

"But how?"

"I'll get evening classes. I'll take care of it."

And he did. He managed to get his chairman to go along with it, although he had to schedule his office hours for Tuesday and Thursday mornings. Mrs. Lorimer, a widow who lived down the street, came in for three hours on those mornings. She was a compulsive worker and very fond of Regina, two factors which made me feel lucky to have her. However, I would catch her giving me looks of disapproval as I gulped down my morning coffee and reviewed my lesson plans for the day. None too subtly, she liked to remind me that she had raised five daughters, all of whom had turned out exactly the way she wanted them to because she had stayed at home to keep her eye on them. I could have pointed out that my staying home would have put her out twenty dollars a week, but I said nothing. Yet her disapproval of me was mild compared to her disapproval of Frank. She avoided him entirely, except with her eyes: they crawled over him like hands that can't quite figure out the texture of the object they're touching. I imagined what was going through her mind: How could a man let his wife work when there was a sick child in the house? Why would a man who *is* a man shape his life around his wife's job when his own job was more important? Naturally, the answers to these questions were two of the answers to why I loved Frank. But I felt no need to explain that to Mrs. Lorimer.

That school year, 1967–1968, and the following summer proved to be a pivotal period in our lives. Trying to assess all the events and their separate impacts puts me in the position of an editor trying to decide on the right headline. First of all, I returned to Peck High in a state of ebullience that was soon diminished by an amorphous tension among the students. The summer riots in Detroit had been given tremendous publicity, and every now and then I heard "Those niggers" being mumbled in the corridors. The black population at Peck was less than ten percent, but there was already talk of redistricting to bring that figure to twenty-five percent. The majority of black students slunk around the building as if they expected the walls to open up and discharge troops against them. But there was a small group of black boys to match the group of whites who were longing for confrontation. The confrontation came in February, two days after a white woman was raped and murdered by a black man in a downtown transient hotel. It broke out in a gym class, and because the seven students involved were black and white, it was the first incident in the school's history to earn the term "racial." Hugh Lance expelled all seven and the next day called a special assembly at which he warned every student that fighting of any kind would result in automatic expulsion—girls included. The school was quiet the rest of the semester, but the fights were continued off school property, where Lance could do nothing about them.

At home I didn't think about school problems. I was too involved with Frank and Regina. Regina was crushed when she couldn't start kindergarten with her friends and crushed again when the doctor refused to let her go in January. This second blow turned her disappointment into resentment, and we had an even harder time keeping her off her feet. Television, books, games bored her. For the first two months or so, her friends were faithful in their visits—one at a time, as the doctor ordered—but as the novelty became a chore for them, they came by only when they had nothing better to do. Perhaps to punish them, Regina was petulant in their presence. She fought with each one of them so often that by the middle of the year, they stopped coming altogether.

After work and on the weekends, I took charge of her. In the rocking chair, I marked papers and wrote lesson plans to the din of the television and was interrupted constantly by her requests for juice and crackers and toys and dolls. One night while Frank was teaching, she turned to me and said:

"I have to go to the bathroom." The tone of her voice hit something in me. It was the same tone a number of my students were beginning to use, a tone that had more than an edge of command in it.

"Then go," I said.

"Carry me."

"What?"

"Carry me."

"Regina, you don't need to be carried. You can get up to do *that.*"

"Daddy carries me. He always carries me."

"I'm sure he doesn't always do it."

"Yes, he does."

65

"Well, you can walk to the bathroom and back. That little bit won't hurt you. In fact, it'll be good for you—just that little bit."

"Daddy wants me to get well."

"I want you to get well too, but you can walk to the bathroom and back. I'll come with you."

"No, I'll go alone."

I watched her from the corner of my eye. She did a dramatic wavering out of the room, and there was a long, almost ominous silence. When I heard the crash, it suddenly seemed as if I had been waiting for it.

The bottles of bath oil and cologne we kept on top of the toilet tank were scattered on the floor. Regina stood there watching one of them roll in a circle and come to a stop.

"I bumped into it," she said, without looking at me.

"It had to be bumped pretty hard."

"I fell."

The doctor's primary warning had been: "She must not become excited." "All right," I said. "From now on I'll come with you so you won't bump into things." She looked uncertain for a moment, then stooped down to pick up the bottles. "I'll pick them up," I said. "You just go to the toilet."

"I don't feel like going now."

Frank came home that night the way he always did, exhausted and pretending not to be. I couldn't hold back from approaching him with this bathroom business, so I decided to do it lightly. He said he had been carrying her to the bathroom, but he would explain to her why I couldn't.

"I don't think you should be doing it, either," I said. "The doctor says she can get up to do that."

"She can do it when I'm not here. If she likes to be carried once in a while, there's nothing wrong with that."

"She knocked over those bottles on purpose."

"Irene, she's a sick and very lonely little girl. Don't be so hard on her."

I was stung by the accusation. I looked at the philodendron on our window sill and remembered that night back in college when I had been hard and unreasonable. "You're right," I said. "Come to bed." I knew he was tired but I had to have him make love to me. I had to show him the tenderness that would prove the accusation wrong.

It may have been a few days or a few weeks later when we had our first serious argument over Regina. We were figuring the monthly bills at the kitchen table while Regina was supposed to be taking her nap. When I walked into the living room, she was off the sofa and standing at the window that faced our empty lot. Her fists were clenched against the glass, her face stony with rage. Outside, four of her friends were swinging on the tractor tires. Before I could speak, she turned to me and said: "Get them out of our yard."

"You know you're not supposed to be up."

"Tell them to get out of our yard."

"They're just playing. Now get back on the sofa."

"I don't want them there!"

"You won't know they're out there if you stay on the sofa."

"I know they're there."

Frank came in and asked what was wrong.

"She wants the kids out of the yard," I said, trying to slough it off.

"Daddy, make them get out. I don't want them there!"

"We'll just close the drape," I said, "and you won't even see them."

"Daddy, make them go," she said, ignoring me. "It's *our* yard."

"Okay, pumpkin, but you've got to get back on that sofa."

"Frank—"

He flashed me a look of angry warning, then turned and walked out the front door. I took hold of Regina's shoulder and told her to get onto the sofa. She pulled away and said she wanted to *see* Daddy tell them. I watched with her as Frank ambled up to the kids with a smile. For a minute they looked at him blankly, but one boy caught on more quickly than the others; he looked immediately toward the window where we were standing. His eyes slid from me to Regina, and his expression became fiercely identical to hers. As he walked away with the others,

67

he glanced back over his shoulder. I understood his sneer.

"How could you do that?" I asked after I motioned Frank up to the bedroom and closed the door.

"None of them come to see her anymore. It's natural for her to be angry."

"They're only kids, Frank. They don't understand."

"What about her? She doesn't understand, either."

"But she has to understand that her getting sick was . . . accidental. She can't punish everyone else for it."

"She has to understand, but they don't?"

"It's happened to *her,* not to them. I realize it's hard for her, very hard, but—"

"I would think your first loyalty would be to your daughter."

"It has nothing to do with loyalty."

"Were you ever confined to a bed?"

"That has nothing to do with what I'm saying."

"It has everything to do with what you're saying. I'd think you'd be a little more tolerant. She's sick, she deserves to be indulged a little. If it makes her upset to see those kids out there, then I don't see anything wrong with making them stay away."

"She has to learn she can't have everything her own way."

"You mean the way you have?"

That remark sliced deep. "If that's what you think, then you don't know me very well." I left him there and went down to start supper.

I breaded the pork chops, peeled the potatoes, and didn't start to cry until I got to the salad. Then I felt his arms slide around me and his lips graze my ear.

"I'm sorry," he said.

"Don't. Just leave me alone."

He held me tighter. "No, I won't leave you alone. You're going to let me say I'm sorry, because I mean it." I turned and he held me against his chest. "I do love you," he said. Then, kissing me: "I'll set the table. We'll use candles tonight."

He took down the dishes and was fishing for the silverware when Regina's voice shot in from the living room.

"Daddy, a piece of my puzzle is gone. Come find it for me."

"Coming, pumpkin." He squeezed my shoulder and said, "Be back in a minute."

I finished the salad and set the table and called them both when everything was ready.

He forgot about the candles.

The end of the school year was punctuated with the assassination of Bobby Kennedy and a massive anti-Vietnam rally at the university. Frank took part in the rally and got the expected reprimand from the university president's office. Accompanying the reprimand was a clear-cut threat that any further activity of this sort would jeopardize his position on the faculty. He was undaunted, but I was frightened and told him so. I agreed that the protest was honorable, but I didn't want him to lose his job because of it. There was a great deal of freedom in the university newspaper, but unsponsored rallies and spontaneous gatherings were prohibited on university property. Until there was a softer policy, I wanted Frank to adhere to the present one.

The day of Kennedy's funeral, Frank used our living room for a kind of wake. Bernie Golden and another professor were present, along with a dozen students. I was on tenterhooks the whole evening because I thought somehow this meeting was going to violate a university rule. And if that didn't happen, I figured a neighbor might call the police. And frankly, I was intimidated. Everyone in the group had taken up the badge of long hair—and there I was with my pageboy and bangs. One girl with hip-length friz and jungle-loop earrings looked me over suspiciously when I came down from putting Regina to bed. She eyed me several times while I sat silently at the edge of the group, and once she stared outright until I stared back. A few minutes later, she reached into her shoulder bag and pulled out three joints and held them up triumphantly.

"Can we, Frank?"

"Just let me turn up the air conditioner," he said.

"Frank," I said, "will you help me in the kitchen a minute?"

It was the most clichéd trick in the world, but it was all I could manage on the spot. The girl with the joints looked at me and smirked.

"We'll wait till you get back," she said to Frank.

As soon as we closed the door, I said to him, "I don't want that stuff in the house."

"Irene, it's harmless. It's like taking a drink."

"Except that you can go to jail for it."

"We're in our own home. Do you think the police are out setting up dragnets for a little grass?"

"The neighbors have eyes. When they see a few carloads of people with long hair pull up to our house, they're going to start wondering—"

"I've had long hair ever since you met me."

"I *like* long hair, and as for them, I don't care if their hair is green and pink. That's not the point. The point is we don't live on a desert island. We have neighbors with big eyes and bigger mouths."

"You're being paranoid."

"Stop accusing me! What about that presumptuous bitch in there bringing that stuff into our house?"

His eyes narrowed. "That presumptuous bitch, as you call her, spent half an hour in my office today, crying. And do you know why? Not because her parents forgot to send her her allowance or because some sorority rejected her. She was crying because she loved a man she never met, a man she thought was vital to her country. And even though our opinions differ, I have to respect that kind of conscience."

"Good for her. I hope her conscience keeps her company when she's sitting in a jail cell."

"Irene, this country's in big trouble. If there's going to be any change, a lot of people are going to have to take chances with their lives."

"We're off the issue. We're talking about a chance that's so foolish—"

"You like liquor, they like grass. Your preference is sanctioned, theirs isn't. That's what's bothering you."

70

"It's *my* house. That's what's bothering me."

He nodded. *"Your* house."

"I don't mean it that way."

"I think you do."

"All right," I said. "Do what you want."

His face lit up like a child's. "You come have some too."

"No; I'm going upstairs to read."

He cupped my face in his hands. "I want you to try it. With me. I want you sitting right next to me."

"Really, I don't want to."

"Please. In another hour, we'll toss them all out and go to bed."

I loved the idea of tossing them out, and I was reassured by the fact that *he* had suggested it.

"Fraaaank?" the girl called from the living room.

"In a minute," he answered.

"Let's get in there," I said. "The natives are restless."

"The natives can wait." He kissed my eyes, my cheeks, my forehead, then filled my mouth with his tongue. "I know I ask to be indulged sometimes, but I indulge you too, don't I?"

Back in the living room, Frank adjusted the lighting, a ritual which I had heard usually preceded grass-smoking. He lit the kerosene hurricane lamp on the mantelpiece and brought in the two candles from the dining room. It was apparent he had smoked before; aside from wondering how often, I wondered where and with whom. I sat on one side of Frank and the friz girl, Sylvia, sat on the other. When the joint had been smoked down to a stub, he held it for her. I didn't like the way her lips pressed his fingers as she sucked in the smoke.

For twenty minutes or so, I didn't feel a thing. But when I stood up to get the jug of wine, a flush of cold blood ran from my head to my legs, and I had to stand still before moving.

"She's *stoned,"* said Sylvia, as if I had won some kind of victory.

"Hey, Irene, how d'ya feel?" Bernie asked, laughing. The others tittered; their voices sounded hollow and metallic. Since I was the only one standing, I was the center of attention and I didn't

71

want to be. I didn't want to walk and I wasn't sure I could sit down gracefully, so I just stood where I was, in line with the blast of the air conditioner. I felt Frank's hand grip my wrist, his other hand grip my waist, and in one blurred movement I was sitting next to him again. We were all sitting in a circle and for the longest time nobody said anything. Half of them had their eyes closed, their chins lifted in the attitude of receiving a vision. I caught Bernie Golden staring at me with a bold expression I had never seen before. I stared back, dumbly, wondering if I was imagining it. When his mouth formed a crooked half smile, I quickly turned away. What I turned to was no better. Sylvia was leaning against Frank, whispering in his ear, leaning back to giggle, leaning forward to whisper again. She had on one of those muslin Indian tops and no brassiere. When she whispered to Frank, her breasts nuzzled his arm. I made another attempt to get up, but Frank caught my shoulder.

"What do you want, honey? I'll get it."

"The wine," I lied. I wanted to go upstairs.

"And some music, Frank," said Sylvia. "We need some music."

"What kind?" he asked.

Don't ask her what kind! That bitch doesn't run this house!

"Got any Jefferson Airplane?"

"No."

"Rolling Stones?"

"Uh uh. We've got Mamas and Papas."

"That's good. They're mellow."

Frank got up. Sylvia lit a cigarette, then turned to me and said, "How do you feel?"

"I feel fine."

"Good, good."

Good, good. Who do you think you are? The goddam hostess?

"Look at Tim!" she laughed. "He's spaced out!"

Everyone looked at Tim and tittered. The boy's eyes were closed, his mouth open. When he sensed everyone looking at him, he shook his hair off his shoulders onto his back and said, "Wow, am I stoned!"

The Mamas and the Papas came on with "Monday, Monday."

I thought: Good, the music will shut them up.

Frank refilled wineglasses and sat down again. Sylvia shifted her weight onto one hip, the one closest to Frank, and leaned on an arm, which touched his leg. I pretended to stare at the rug, but I had an adequate view of Sylvia. Suddenly, I thought of that girl, years ago, who had got out of Frank's car with the bag of groceries. Sylvia resembled her in that she was equally plain, almost homely. But Sylvia was not meek and retiring. Far from it. As I looked at her and at Bernie Golden, who still had that crooked smile, I wished I had Gloria next to me, someone who would see the same things I was seeing.

"All right, gang, ready for the zinger?" she said, holding up a joint the size of a small cigar.

Everyone said, "Oh, wow," "Far out" and "Too much."

When it got to me, I passed it up. I was thinking of what Frank had said about tossing them out.

"Hey!" Sylvia clapped her hands and began singing "Chicago, Chi-cago." The others joined in.

"Man, we're really gonna open their eyes," said Tim, who was not about to open his.

"Whose eyes?" I said.

"The hawks and the pigs," said the boy next to Tim. "Those capitalist killers and political money grubbers."

I turned to Frank. "The Democratic convention, honey," he said. "It's going to be one hell of a demonstration."

"What about it?"

"Well, we're all going in a kind of caravan—"

"You're going?"

Lightly, he put his hand on the back of my neck and nodded.

"When was all this decided?"

"Let's not go into it now," he whispered.

Part of me wanted to get up and out of the room immediately, but another part didn't want any of them, especially Sylvia, to see my anger. I closed my eyes, pretended to be absorbed in the music, and waited until the record ended before making my exit upstairs. My whole body felt weighted as I climbed the steps. I looked in on Regina, then went to our room, where I tried to stay awake so I could talk to Frank. It was no use. The combination of grass and wine and standing up made me want to sleep forever. And I wanted to shake the picture I had of Sylvia holding a bag of groceries.

I woke up to the sound of giggling, muffled and sporadic. It took me a few seconds to realize that it was coming from downstairs and a minute more to recognize two voices, Regina's and a woman's. Frank was lying next to me, his arm slung over his eyes and his mouth wide open, snoring. I got up and into my robe. My head was throbbing, my eyes felt puffed and raw. I wanted to get downstairs quickly, but my body wouldn't keep up with my mind.

In the living room, I found Sylvia on her elbows and knees, bent forward and shaking her head so furiously that her hair ballooned into a huge globe of fuzz. Regina, giggling, sat with her arms extended and almost lost in Sylvia's hair.

"What's going on?"

Sylvia stopped and fell back on her elbows, panting. The four buttons on her Indian top were unfastened and I could see the side of each breast. "We're playing," she said breathlessly. "I didn't think we were being that loud."

"How . . . did you get here?" For some reason, I couldn't broach the obvious.

"I passed out on the floor and woke up on the couch. Frank must have put me there." Very matter-of-fact, not a trace of apology in her voice.

"What time is it?"

"I don't know." And obviously didn't care.

"Mommy, Sylvia said you could grow your hair long if you wanted to. Will you?"

"I don't want my hair long."

"Well, I'm gonna grow *mine.*"

"It'll get in your eyes."

"I like it in my eyes. I can look through it."

"You've got pretty eyes," said Sylvia. "Just like your father."

I walked past them into the kitchen. I set up the coffeepot. While it perked, I made myself a cup of instant. Their giggling

74

started up again. I sat at the table, seething and preparing what I was going to say to Frank. I wanted a clear head, I wanted to be alone with Frank for the whole day, and more than anything I wanted the night before to be completely erased. I wanted Sylvia out of my house and I wanted to forget that bold, suggestive look on Bernie Golden's face.

The giggling stopped. Everything was too quiet. When I got to the living room, they weren't there. I knew they couldn't be outside, because Regina was still in her nightie. I didn't want to suspect what I was suspecting, but the shrill laugh—Sylvia's laugh—that shot down the stairs was a clear invitation to battle.

I found the two of them on the bed, tickling Frank. He was squirming around, wrapped up in the sheet, and he had the pillow over his head. No one noticed me, so I stood and watched. Until Sylvia's hand went *under* the sheet.

"Since everyone's awake," I said, "I think we'd better have breakfast." The announcement was for the three of them, but my eyes were on Sylvia. She looked back dumbly. *All right, bitch, let's see you start hopping.* "Sylvia, would you take Regina downstairs? Frank and I have to get dressed." She took Regina by the hand and left. Frank sat up against the pillows and smiled until he read the look on my face.

"Honey, what's wrong?"

"You haven't got the slightest idea?" He shook his head. "Well, *that's* what's wrong."

"Tell me. What is it?"

"It's so obvious! What is she doing here?"

"She passed out last night and slept on the couch."

"Yes, she told me that much."

"You don't think . . . You know better than that."

"Do I?"

"Stop it. She passed out and slept on the couch. Why make something out of that?"

"Why? Because this isn't a flophouse! Because she thinks she can do as she damn pleases here. She pulls out the grass as if she's running the place, she decides what music everyone is going to hear, she doesn't leave your side the whole night, she feels

75

perfectly free to pass out on our floor, and then she has the gall to come into our room while you're still in bed and to run her hand under the sheet. Now ask me what's wrong!"

"Come sit next to me for a minute."

"No, thanks, I'll stand. I want her out of here. She has plenty of brass and you polish it for her. Don't think she didn't enjoy the fact that you said nothing to me about going to that convention."

"I was going to tell you about it today."

"Tell me? Obviously, then, we're not going to *discuss* it. It's all been decided."

"I have to go, Irene. The bigger the number, the louder the voice. This is a chance for the people to show they won't have policy pushed onto them."

"Let's start determining a little policy around here. First of all, this is not a place for self-appointed rebels to flop. If she wants to try moving in on you, let her do it at your office, not here."

"She's not moving in on me. She's got a slight case of hero-worship, that's all. She's a little mixed up right now and she doesn't quite know how to handle her emotions."

"It's not her emotions she wants to handle."

"Will you stop being so hard on people? I told you last night what she's going through—"

"I don't want to hear any more about her 'political conscience.' She's aggressive, presumptuous and ill-mannered. And I'll tell you right now I don't like the idea of your going off to that convention with her."

"And I don't like the idea of your not trusting me. Besides, eleven of us are going. Come on now, let's not fight anymore." He rolled to the edge of the bed and put his feet on the floor. "If you don't like her, I'll make sure she doesn't come here anymore. I don't want to fight with you."

"I don't want you to give in just because you don't want to fight. I want you to *understand* what I'm saying about her."

"I understand; I just *feel* differently about it. If she makes you that uncomfortable, we won't have her here."

76

Over breakfast, Sylvia reversed her tactics. She directed all her attention to me, asked questions about teaching, about Regina's long illness and how I coped with it, then complimented me on *my* taste in fixing up the house. Frank listened to it all without a trace of "I told you so," something I both admired and resented. Relief came when he and Regina left to take Sylvia home. I needed the house to myself and I worked quickly to set it straight. I emptied ashtrays, vacuumed the rug, washed the wineglasses, and removed the candle stubs from their holders. It was the clean-up after the invasion, a grand sweep to wipe out every trace of the enemy's occupation. I sprayed Lysol until the air was thick with it.

When Frank and Regina returned, I was washing up the breakfast dishes and humming as I envisioned the three of us spending this lazy day working in the yard. Frank gave Regina a Popsicle, then went up to change into his yard clothes. She sat down at the table behind me.

"Regina, don't slurp like that."

She continued to slurp, but more quietly. "What's repressed?" she asked.

"Repressed?"

"Uh huh."

"Where did you hear that?"

"Sylvia. She told Daddy you were repressed. What's it mean?"

"It means 'quiet.' " And I told myself to keep quiet but asked her anyway: "And what did Daddy say?"

"He didn't say anything."

"What else did Sylvia say?"

"She said I could come to her apartment for a whole day and play with her cats."

Over my dead body.

I made plans to take Regina with me and stay at my parents' while Frank was in Chicago. Neil was just back from Vietnam; I thought being around him would reassure me that Frank's trip was meaningful and necessary. But the day before Frank left, Gloria called from Los Angeles to say she was flying in to

77

see her mother. (Her father had died two years earlier.) I grabbed at the opportunity of inviting her to spend a few days at our house. Pat was not coming with her, but she was bringing their three-year-old son, Brian. At first she hesitated at my offer, but when I said Frank would be gone, she readily accepted.

She timed her arrival just right; her rented car pulled into our driveway three hours after Frank pulled out of it. Instead of running out to greet her, I stood near the window, out of sight, and watched her lift Brian from the front seat and take the luggage out of the trunk. She was radiant. Her blond hair was blonder—I assumed from the sun—parted in the middle and drawn back in soft waves to form an old-fashioned bun. Instead of slacks or something else casual, she wore a cream-colored tailored suit. It was a style that seemed to be disappearing, and I was somehow proud of Gloria for hanging on to it. It made her look soft yet determined, behind the times but beyond them too. My stomach churned all the way up to my throat: I felt like a kid whose favorite grandmother was coming to visit.

I finally got myself moving to help her with the luggage. When we got it inside, I hugged her so hard that she laughed. It was good to hear her laugh, the way she used to before I met Frank.

"This is Mommy's friend," she said to Brian, who was gripping her skirt. "See, I told you her hair is red." She turned to me. "I don't think he's ever seen a real redhead. Just about everyone in California is a blond." She brushed his fleecy locks.

"Regina's taking a nap right now. Are you hungry? Do you want a shower?"

"Just some coffee." She looked around the living room and into the dining room. "This is beautiful, Irene. Really beautiful."

"It's a little too dark. We're surrounded by trees."

"I'll take this any day over that California glare."

"Stomach hurts," said Brian.

Gloria put her hand on her stomach and said, "No, it doesn't."

"Stomach *hurts.*"

"Feels fine to me," she said.

"My stomach hurts."

"Ohhh, why didn't you say so? I think you should take off

78

your shoes and lie down on that couch over there."

"You lie with me."

"No; Irene and I are going to sit at the dining room table. You'll be able to hear me."

He took off his shoes and crawled onto the couch. "I'll hear you?" he said.

"Now don't you dare go to sleep. You have to hear me."

"I won't go to sleep," he murmured, his eyes already closed. "I can close my eyes but I can hear you."

"That's right. You can close your eyes, but don't go to sleep." As we moved into the dining room, she shook her head and smiled. "Oh, the little games they teach us."

I nodded but said nothing. Already I was running a comparison: the past year with Regina had not been a light-hearted experience. She had taught us a game, all right, but it was one Frank and I reacted to differently and argued over. At the end of March, when she had recovered from the rheumatic fever, the doctor warned us to watch her carefully if she ever complained of a sore throat because it could lead to strep, which in turn could bring on a relapse of the rheumatic condition. Frank relayed this information to Regina and told her to let us know if she felt even the slightest tickle. Too many times, when she wanted to stay up late or found out she was going to spend an evening with a baby-sitter, she would begin hinting about her throat. The doctor would come, only to discover that her throat showed no trace of redness at all. Finally, one night when Frank was working, I decided this game had to come to a halt. I told Regina if her throat really did hurt, we could not take chances: she would have to have a penicillin shot to protect her. She decided her throat really didn't hurt. Frank was livid when I told him what I had done. "You've made her afraid to tell us," he said. I said I hadn't, that I had explained to her the difference between real danger and no danger. After that, her complaints did subside a bit, but when she had them, she always went to Frank.

"How's Regina?" asked Gloria.

"Fully recovered, the doctor says. Naturally, she's anxious to start school. It's been a tough year for her. Her friends sort of abandoned her and I don't think she's quite forgiven them. There's a new family on the next block and she's taken up with their little girl, so she does have someone. I must say Frank made everything a lot easier for both Regina and me." I told her how he had arranged his teaching schedule so I could go back to work. She looked a little embarrassed, then said:

"I'm happy things have turned out well for you and Frank. I think I've grown up a little since—well, since I've had Brian. And since my father died."

"How's your mother?"

She shook her head. "Hopeless. She's drunk all the time now. I was going to stay three days with her, but all I could take was one night. She won't hire a housekeeper or a gardener; the place is in a complete shambles, yet she won't sell it and move into an apartment. She won't listen to anything I say; she just wants to be left alone to drink. I'll tell you, there's no one explanation for a bad marriage, I realize that now. She was miserable when he was alive, but she's more miserable now that he's dead. I've decided she's just lazy. I know that sounds callous, but . . . happiness takes a lot of work. Misery takes no work."

"Amen."

"I've had to change my mind about a lot of things, mainly her and him. And you and Frank. Obviously you've made a go of it."

"Yes. But the differences become more sharply defined as we get older. You know he went to that demonstration. He's very political and I'm not at all."

"I'm not, either. I can't make up my mind about politics. Sometimes it all seems so complicated and other times I feel it's so damned simple-minded, just a lot of sloganeering." She smiled. "I feel the same way about Brian. Sometimes I look at him and think he's only three and therefore just a simple little soul. Then he turns around and does something that makes me say, 'No, he's already a complex little individual.' Do you ever feel that way about Regina?"

"Oh, yes. She's got her tricks and her stratagems. Not all of them pleasant, I'm afraid."

"Frightening little creatures, aren't they, when you realize they have thoughts of their own."

"Who's that?"

We both looked at Regina, standing in the archway. She was pointing to the couch, which we couldn't see. "Who's that?" she repeated.

"That's Brian," I said. "And this is Gloria."

"Hello, Regina."

"Hello. When's Daddy coming home?"

"I told you, not for a few days. Gloria and Brian are staying with us. Daddy will be back after they leave."

"Daddy's coming back when they go?"

"Yes."

"If they go now, will he come home now?"

Gloria laughed. "She's way ahead of you, Irene."

"Are they sleeping here?"

"Yes, they're sleeping here. Do you want some cookies and milk?"

"Is Sylvia going to stay with us too?"

"Sylvia's out of town."

"With Daddy?"

"Yes, they went to a convention. Now let's stop with the questions. What big plans do you have for the afternoon?"

"I want to go to Susan's."

"Fine, but be home by four-thirty. That way you can play with Brian for a little while before dinner."

She looked disdainfully in the direction of the couch. "I don't want to play with him. He's a *baby.*"

"He's small," I said, "but he's not a baby. He's three."

"I'm six. Three and three is six."

I could see Gloria was amused by this exchange, but I was growing impatient. "You can still have fun together."

"Babies aren't fun. You have to take care of them."

"That's enough, Miss Priss. You just be home by four-thirty or I'll take care of *you.* Make sure you're nearby when I call."

"Suppose I'm in Susan's house?"

"They have clocks."

"Suppose we go to the store?"

"Suppose you stay home."

That was enough to send her skipping out of the house.

"She's so tall and she looks just like Frank," said Gloria. "But she takes after you. Sharp and sassy."

"Kindergarten will smooth her corners."

She asked who Sylvia was and I poured out the story. Talking about it made me angry all over again, but this time I enjoyed the anger. Gloria's knowing smiles and nods reassured me I was talking to someone whose opinions were aligned with my own.

"So you didn't like the grass?" she asked.

"Not particularly. But then, I was drinking wine with it."

"No good. And you were with strangers too."

"Yes, I suppose that makes a difference. But I don't even drink much anymore."

"How about smoking with *me* tonight?"

"You smoke grass?"

"Once in a while. I've been dying to smoke with someone who has more to say than 'Oh, wow.' We'll smoke an official peace pipe."

I liked the idea immediately, partly because, as Gloria suggested, this was our reunion, and partly because she was the picture of propriety except for the sly grin she was giving me. She tapped her purse with her perfectly manicured painted-peach nails and said with a mock-Southern drawl: "Whah, Offi-suh, ah have no idea how six li'l ol' joints got inta this heah purse."

"Six! They could lock you up for that." Then, a little apprehensive, I asked, "How often do you smoke that stuff?"

"Once or twice a week. Just a couple of puffs to get me to sleep when I'm wound up. Purely medicinal, my dear. I never smoke with anyone; that's why I'd like to do it with you. In fact, maybe I should have a little nap now so I don't pass out on the stuff later."

"Sure, go ahead. If Brian wakes up, we'll get acquainted."

She stood up and looked around the room again. "You really have done a beautiful job with the house. It *feels* like a home."

After she went upstairs, I sat and took in the room. She was right, it did feel like a home, and I was especially proud of the dining room, with the light oak moldings around the windows and the archway, the roughly cut hutch and wine rack, the green Tiffany lamp hanging over the round, dark oak table. Spacious and uncluttered, it was a room that made you think of children getting out of wet boots and mittens and gathering around for cookies and cocoa. I was glad Gloria approved; I was glad she found Regina so amusing. And I was glad we were having this reunion. Having been involved with Regina and the house and then my job again, I had not cultivated any close friendships like the one I had once had with Gloria. Obvious as it should have been, it didn't occur to me what I had been missing until I heard her laugh again and saw her listening, really listening, to me.

I was reading a magazine in the living room when Brian woke up. He gave a big yawn, sat straight up and pressed the corners of his eyes with his fingers, then put his hands flat on his legs and said hello to me very matter-of-factly. To me, this little routine was hilariously adult, like that of an executive emerging from a stolen nap in the office. I told him his mother was sleeping upstairs; he nodded and looked out the window as if that were what he had expected me to say. After cookies and milk, he stretched out on the floor with one of Regina's coloring books. He chose a picture of Alice meeting the Queen of Hearts. Before he would touch a crayon to each item, he consulted me about the color he should use. He worked slowly, clamping his tongue between his lips and squinting his eyes when the crayon got close to the borders; when he was safely away from the borders and had more freedom of movement, his face relaxed and his hand sped up. I compared his work with Regina's on the page next to it. Her strokes jagged out of the lines and were put down with varying degrees of pressure. And like most of her pictures, this one was unfinished. I felt a twinge of jealousy as I watched Brian's steady concentration. But of course, I thought, he had not suffered a confinement to make him frustrated and impatient.

As if my silent comparison had summoned her, Regina was standing in the archway, staring at Brian.

"Aren't you the quiet one," I said. "It's only ten to four. Didn't you play with Susan?"

"Her grandma came," she mumbled, not taking her eyes off Brian. Brian looked up for only a second, and went back to his work.

"Why don't you get your other book and color with Brian?"

"Who said he could color in my book?"

"I said. He's only coloring one picture."

"I was saving that picture."

I doubted it. "I'm sorry, I didn't know. You can color one in your other book."

"I hate that other book."

"You don't hate it. You color in it all the time."

"I hate it. I was saving *that* picture and now he spoiled it!"

Brian put his crayon down and backed away to the couch.

"It's all right, Brian, you can keep coloring." He stood where he was and stared at Regina. "If you've got any notion about throwing a tantrum, young lady, you can forget it right now. I didn't know you were saving that picture and that's that. There are plenty of other pictures for you to color."

"He spoiled it! You let a baby color in my book!"

"You're acting like the baby. I don't want to hear another word about it."

"Daddy wouldn't give it to him."

"Daddy would have. Now that's enough. Brian, go ahead and finish your picture."

He started for the book but Regina shot forward and grabbed it.

"Regina, put that down!" She backed up a few steps and hung on to it. "I said to put it down." I could tell by the defiance in her eyes I was going to have to take it from her. I started out of the chair. In one quick movement, she tore the page from the book, then hurled the book to the floor. As I came to her, she crumpled the picture into a ball. I grabbed her arm and headed for the stairs. "You are going to your room and you're staying there until I tell you you can come out."

She began to cry. "I want Daddy. I want Daddy to come home!"

"Get going," I said, aiming her up the first step.

"I want Daddy," she sobbed, and slid down against the wall.

"Regina, I can't carry you, but if I have to I'll drag you up. Now get moving."

She spread herself face down on the steps and wailed, "I want Daddy. I want him *now!*"

"Get up." I tugged on her arm, but she was determined to stay where she was.

"Irene, what's wrong?" It was Gloria at the top of the stairs.

"Just the Queen of Sheba throwing a tantrum." I took hold of Regina by both wrists and started walking backward up the steps.

"Irene, don't! You'll hurt your back."

"She is going to her room—one way or the other."

"I want Daddy!"

Gloria came down. "I shouldn't butt in, but let me help you. You can't pull her like that; you'll both get hurt." She went for Regina's feet but had to pull away when Regina began to kick.

"Don't touch me! You don't live here! Go away and let my daddy come home! Don't touch me, don't touch me!"

I was furious and ashamed. I had to stand still for a minute because I was afraid I might yank Regina's arms right out of their sockets. I saw a look of sympathy, almost pity, on Gloria's face, and I hated Regina for putting it there.

When I got her into her room, I closed the door and took a few deep breaths to steady myself. She flung herself onto the bed and buried her face in the pillow.

"You can go right on crying," I said, "but you listen to me and you listen well. Gloria is my friend and she and Brian are guests in this house. When you have guests, you share things with them. So you'd better start learning how. You've had a few little taps on your butt before, but you've never had a real spanking. You're going to find out what one feels like if you dare to act the way you did just now. Do you understand?" I knew better than to wait for an answer, so I left immediately.

When I got back to the living room, Brian was uncrumpling

the picture to show to Gloria. I felt helpless, with nothing to say. If only Brian had cried or thrown a tantrum himself. But there he was accepting his mother's assurance that a few wrinkles wouldn't hurt his good coloring job. When he looked skeptical, she asked him who the prettiest woman in the world was. He said it was she. "Well," she said, "someday I'll be wrinkled just like that paper, but I'll still be pretty, won't I?" She pressed her forehead against his and said, "Won't I?"

He smiled and kissed her mouth with a loud smack. I could tell the kiss was a ritual between them and for the moment I couldn't help feeling cheated.

Regina refused to come out of her room to eat, so dinner turned out to be quite pleasant. Maybe because I was so disappointed in Regina—and myself—and because I admired the tenderness between Gloria and Brian, I set out to win the boy's attention. When I served the pudding, I gave him a side dish of whipped cream shaped like a snowman, with raisin eyes, lemon-peel mouth and a maraschino cherry cap. Once again, he showed that uncanny adult expression as he adjusted the cherry cap to his liking.

"I can see it coming," sighed Gloria as we watched him. "He's going to be a nit-picker like his father."

We had our coffee in the living room. Brian sat on my lap, running his fingers through my hair and murmuring, "Fire." Gloria watched us with the same contentment she once had when she used to listen to Pat and me kidding each other.

"Don't you think we should take something up to Regina?" she said.

"I told her if she wants to eat she can come downstairs."

"Why don't you let me take it up, as a kind of peace offering. After all, we've invaded her territory."

"All right, if you want to."

She prepared a tray with the ham and the potato salad and made a whipped cream snowman as I had done for Brian. She went upstairs, knocked and called Regina's name. There was a long silence before she came back down.

"She wouldn't answer me. I left the tray on the nightstand."

"Then let her stew." She sat down with a look of amusement. "I know. You think I'm being too hard."

She shrugged. "Not at all. I know your expectations, Irene."

"And you think they're too high?"

She cocked her head to the side. "Do you really doubt yourself that much?"

"Sometimes. Especially when it comes from all sides. Frank and I see eye to eye on all the important things except Regina. I think he's too indulgent, he thinks I'm too hard. The same thing at school. The trend now is less homework and practically no writing. Complete sentences are out of fashion, spelling is unimportant, knowing the parts of speech is considered passé. And when it comes to literature, everyone seems to be on this kick of reading what's supposed to be *relevant*—the implication being that anything written before 1950 is irrelevant. I'm not very popular with the other people in the English Department. If it weren't for the principal's support, I'd feel like a total dinosaur."

"It's no better in college. You should see the papers I had to read. But let's not talk shop."

We put Brian to bed in the same room where Gloria would sleep. We only had to promise to leave the door open and the hall light on.

"Do you want one of Regina's dolls or bears to sleep with?" I asked him.

"No," said Gloria. "He hates things in bed with him. Likes the whole place to himself. Don'tcha, kiddo?"

He smiled and stuck his arms out to the sides. "Can't fall out," he said.

"After the crib, we put him in a twin. He fell out of it six times, so now he's got a double."

I checked on Regina. She was reading comic books in bed, and the food was untouched. She would not look at me, and we said nothing to each other. I simply closed the door and went downstairs.

"How about some more coffee to go with the grass?" said Gloria. "It'll keep everything in check."

I perked a pot and we sat down at the dining room table. Gloria pulled out the joint. When we got it smoked down too far to hold, she produced a roach clip and showed me how to suck in the last of the smoke. I soon felt the mellowness come over me, and the room seemed to cool off considerably.

"How about some music? I can put on FM."

"No," she said. "No music, if you don't mind. You know what I love to do? I love to take a few puffs, settle into bed and read. But always the same stuff—S. J. Perelman or Dorothy Parker or Flannery O'Connor. I read them over and over again. I tried Waugh once but it didn't work." She giggled. "Waugh was a flop in bed."

"Doesn't Pat ever want to . . . you know?"

"Have sex? We take care of that earlier. And without grass. Then he goes to sleep and I puff and read." She smiled wistfully.

"You miss him?"

"Ummm. Every now and then I need to be away from him. But I do miss him. I learned my lesson."

"What lesson?"

"He left me once. When he found out I was having an affair."

"*You* had an affair?"

"For about two months. I was pregnant with Brian. That just about killed Pat. 'You let another man put his prick in you while you've got *my* baby in there?' 'Don't worry,' I said, 'it isn't touching the baby.' I was an out-and-out bitch."

"Who was he? How did it start?"

"He was a cashier in the supermarket, a drifter, forty-five years old. I knew I had to leave the college to have Brian and I guess I was afraid of the middle-class setup I'd be falling into. Anyway, this guy kept giving me the eye and I was dazzled by the fact he had no roots and didn't give a damn. That was before I realized half the state of California is filled with drifters and they're a dime a dozen. So one day he's ringing up my order and he says to me, 'Did you ever lie naked on pine needles?' He was so matter-of-fact, it fascinated me. We never made it to the pine needles, but I went to his house every morning for two months."

"Every morning?"

"Weekday mornings while Pat was working." She lit a cigarette. "Hal was quite violent. I had to keep warning him against leaving marks."

88

"What did he use—a rubber hose?"

She laughed. "Not violent *that* way."

"How did Pat find out?"

"The usual way. The only day I ever went out with Hal for lunch, Pat saw us and followed us back to Hal's. He didn't tell me. The next morning he drove by Hal's and saw my car in the driveway. Then he confronted me and I confessed. Then he walked out for two weeks. He wouldn't let me in his office and he hung up every time I called. I almost went crazy. I thought I was going to lose him, I thought some woman would get him and that would be the end of it. When he came back, he said if it ever happened again, he'd leave me for good and take the baby too. And I knew he meant it. You know what's crazy? I don't think I really loved him until he said that. I was very lucky. Sometimes I get the chills when I think how it could have all gone another way."

"Yes, it could have."

We sat quietly for what seemed a long time. I watched her circle the ashtray with her cigarette butt.

"It's all chance, isn't it?" she said. "Who we meet and who we don't. I know it sounds sophomoric, but when you realize it *emotionally,* it's frightening. If I'd never met you or Pat . . . Are you happy, Irene?"

"I . . ." Maybe it was the grass, maybe an echo of the past, but suddenly I suspected a trap. "Yes." Her eyes rolled up to meet mine. "I guess so. Reasonably."

She smiled. "A reasonable answer."

"Sometimes I'm afraid."

"Of what?"

"Of change. This damned war, King and the Kennedys assassinated—it's gotten Frank all worked up and involved and it scares me. And then Regina, the whole last year. And school, of course. We had so many fights last year, all that racial stuff. And some problems with drugs. And here *I* sit smoking grass with you. It's just so strange. Even a year ago I couldn't have pictured myself doing it."

"Well, you're doing it and it's all right, so relax. In fact, I think I'll send a little news item to our alumni paper: 'Irene Mattison, nee Rutledge, Queen of Sparta, renounces crown and scepter for daily dose of dope and relaxation.' "

"No one would believe it."

"That, my dear, is why it makes good copy."

She suggested we switch from coffee to Coca-Cola and have another joint. When I hesitated, she assured me we had eaten recently enough to keep us from getting too stoned. Just as she struck the match, the doorbell rang.

"Oh, my God, the cops!"

She laughed. "Very unlikely. Probably a moonlighting Avon lady. I'll get rid of her."

I watched her walk through the living room and open the door. The porch light wasn't on, so I couldn't make out the figure on the porch. "Oh, yes," I heard Gloria say, "I remember you. Come on in. Irene, you've got company."

Vivian stepped into the living room.

"Hello, Irene." She smiled meekly and looked quickly around the room. "Is Frank here?"

"As a matter of fact, he's not." *Get on your feet, you idiot!* I stood up. "He's in Chicago. On business."

"Oh? He's not teaching at the university anymore?"

"It's university business."

We stood there awkward and silent. Finally, Gloria said, "I think I'll do the dishes. If you'll excuse me . . ." She picked up the coffee cups from the dining room table—and the joint along with them.

"I know I'm not supposed to be here," said Vivian. "I just took a chance that maybe Frank has softened a little."

"I don't think he has. I'm sorry." *What are you doing standing here in the dining room while she's standing in there? Get moving!* "I really don't know what to say." I moved forward a few steps. "Would you like to sit down for a few minutes?"

"I'd better not, since Frank's not here." But she didn't move. "You never cashed that second check I sent you."

"I couldn't. I—"

"I understand, believe me." She bit her lip and looked at the floor. "Irene, I'm going to ask you a big favor. I've *got* to ask it. Can I see the baby?"

"The baby?"

"Sorry. She must be six now, going into first grade."

"Kindergarten. She was sick last year."

Her face darkened. "How sick?"

"Rheumatic fever. She was in the house for eight months."

"Is she all right?"

"Oh, yes. Spunky and sassy."

She smiled. "Could I see her. Just *see* her. I won't say a word to her. You don't have to tell her who I am. Please, you don't know what it would mean to me."

I couldn't stand hearing her beg. "If Frank ever found out . . ."

"Irene, I know it's asking a lot, but I promise you he'll never know. *No* one will know. Even Leo doesn't know I came here."

"Yes, you must promise me that."

"I do promise you."

We found Regina sprawled out on the bed, still dressed and sound asleep in a pile of comics. The food on the nightstand hadn't been touched; the raisins and lemon peel and cherry lay in a puddle of cream.

"She was being punished," I whispered in hasty explanation. "She didn't want to tare her shoys—" *Idiot!* "—I mean share her toys." God, I thought, I hope she can't smell that stuff.

She smiled and bent down closer to Regina. "Lovely, lovely. She's going to be tall like Frank."

"Yes, she looks just like Frank."

"I hope she's not going to slouch. Tall girls have a tendency to do that. I had to teach myself not to. What's her name?"

"Regina."

She looked as if she didn't believe me. "Regina?"

"Yes."

"Then Frank must have named her."

"Yes." I watched her bend even closer, until her face nearly touched Regina's. "She's a light sleeper," I lied. I was beginning to feel a vague resentment. Vivian took the hint and followed me out of the room.

"What did you mean—'Frank must have named her'?"

She looked embarrassed. "It just seemed a little coincidental. It was our sister's name."

"What sister?"

"Didn't he tell you? Our sister who died. Her name was Regina."

"When did she die?"

"She was fifteen. It was Frank who found her. In the woods."

"In the woods?"

"She was retarded. She drank a bottle of lye."

"Lye! But was it—was it by mistake?"

"No one knows. She was secretive, like Frank. They were very close and apart from the rest of us."

"Frank never mentioned her. In fact, he never mentioned you, either, until you came to the wedding rehearsal."

"Who knows what goes on in that mind of his."

"Vivian, why doesn't he like you?"

She sighed and looked away. "I don't want to give you the wrong impression, Irene. I love Frank very much. But he's always been quite committed to having his own way. We were a big family and I had to look after him a lot of the time. And discipline him. Frank does not like discipline, and he holds grudges better than anyone I know. That's why, for your sake as well as mine, I wouldn't tell him I was here."

"But I want to ask him why he never said anything about his sister."

"Don't, please. Maybe it's just too painful for him to talk about, maybe he just wants to forget about it. In time, he might tell you about it."

"In time? We've been married nine years!"

"We all have our secret torments no one knows about. There are some things people *can't* share. I shouldn't have told you."

"No, I'm glad you did."

"One more thing before I go. I know you won't accept any

money from me, but I'm going to open a savings account in my name and Regina's. By the time she's ready for college, she'll have all the money she needs. And maybe Frank will soften by then. This will be just between us."

"Vivian, I can't—"

"Yes, you can. I told you once that in our family we take care of our own. Regina shouldn't get any less than my other nieces and nephews are getting." She started for the door.

"Wait. Give me your address before you go. The least I can do is send you a Christmas card."

Smiling, she wrote it down for me. "Hide it well."

"I will."

We shook hands.

"I'm glad you came," I said. "And I'm sorry about the way the situation is between us."

"You never know, it may change. I'm extremely patient. Running a business has taught me that much. Good-bye."

"Good-bye, Vivian."

I found Gloria reading the newspaper in the kitchen.

"No bad news, I hope."

"I'm not sure."

"Let's hear it."

"Not tonight. All of a sudden, I'm exhausted. If you don't mind, I'd like to go to bed."

"Go ahead. I brought along Dorothy Parker for just such an emergency."

For a long time, I couldn't get to sleep. I kept imagining what lye would do to someone's insides. *She was retarded.* I should have been told for our daughter's sake. Never mind *his* private torment. I had a right to know. And I would find a way to make him tell me.

In the morning, we decided to take the kids on a walking tour of the campus and then to the zoo.

"I've been to the zoo," muttered Regina.

"You like the zoo. If you want, you can ask Susan to come."

"I don't want to go."

93

"All right then, you'll have to stay at Mrs. Lorimer's and I'll have to pay her. That means no money for you when the ice cream truck comes around."

"I don't want any ice cream."

"Remember that later."

"I will." Determined, as always, to have the last word.

Gloria and I packed a lunch, and after dropping Regina at Mrs. Lorimer's, drove off with Brian. The day was perfect, hot but dry, with huge clouds driven by a wind that occasionally touched ground. We parked at the edge of the campus and walked directly to Harley Hall, which housed the English Department.

"Ah, the return of the natives," said Gloria. "Let's see if Big Chief Denning's in."

The secretary told us Dr. Denning had gone to Tulane two years ago. Gloria looked at me in surprise. "Didn't you know that?"

"I never kept up with him. The only time I get out here is when Frank and I come to a lecture-concert series or a play."

"You *are* a hermit."

I suggested we have our lunch at the botanical gardens behind the Natural Science Building. Gloria warned Brian not to touch the flowers. He ran around sniffing them and giggling.

"Over nine years ago," I said, looking around us.

"Nine years ago what?"

"I sat on that bench over there and took myself apart."

"Over what?"

"I'd had a fight with Frank. I should say I'd *started* a fight with him, and I couldn't finish it. I was so damned ridiculous, so proud. I came and sat here and had this big exorcism of my pride. Oh, God, was I filled with self-pity."

"You did grow up that year. I guess I resented it because I wasn't ready to do the same. I didn't want to lose my best friend."

"Gloria, am I still your best friend?"

She chuckled. "Yes, you always will be, no matter how far apart we live. I don't click with many people."

"Same with me. What you said a few minutes ago is true. I really am a hermit. Seeing you has made me realize just how

94

much. I have no close friends at all. Oh, Frank and I play bridge with a few couples and there are a couple of people I like at work, but somehow we never manage to get together much outside of school. I guess my best friend is my husband. I don't know if that's wise, but that's the way it is. Besides him, you're the only other person I can really talk to—or *want* to talk to."

"What about your father? You used to be able to talk to him."

"There's too much disappointment and disapproval there now. On his part. He's never quite gotten over my quitting school. More than that, he's vehemently against Frank's political views, and—I hate to say it—I don't think he's as fond of Regina as a grandfather should be. She can be a terrible hellion, which you've seen, but he's not very understanding of her, the illness and all."

"And she doesn't look like you, either."

"What has that got to do with it?"

"Sometimes a great deal, unconsciously. You disappoint him by leaving school and marrying Frank and then you have a child that looks entirely like Frank, so your father feels cheated all the way around. I'll bet if you had another baby, that looked more like you, he'd treat it differently."

"I wouldn't want that."

"Of course not. Look, once you start your own family, you've got a double load. You have to manage your parents as well as your children."

And maybe your husband too, I thought. I was still thinking of what Vivian had told me, still burning over Frank's secretiveness. For some reason, Vivian's information made me think of the night Sylvia had slept over. Was Frank sleeping with her and keeping *that* a secret too?

We smoked a couple of cigarettes and watched Brian. Now and then, with an exaggerated gesture of delicacy to convince his mother, he would reach out and stroke a flower and give her a smile that said: "See, I'm not hurting them." Again, I felt a twinge of jealousy.

"I'm going to hate to see you leave," I said impulsively. "This time, let's not lose touch with each other."

"You're the hermit. If you can tear yourself away from your sanctuary, you're welcome at our place anytime. All three of you."

After an hour at the zoo, Brian got bored. When I picked him up and carried him to the car, he buried his fingers in my hair and murmured, "Fire." I thought of Regina's hands in Sylvia's hair and how I had overreacted to it. I cautioned myself about overreacting to everything Vivian had told me.

When we got home, I called Mrs. Lorimer. She said Regina was outside playing, so I told her to send her home when she came in. Brian took a nap for an hour, then went out to play in the sandbox Frank had put in the vacant lot. Around four-thirty, Gloria went up for a shower while I set up the charcoal grill in the backyard. I began making the salad in the kitchen. As I was washing the vegetables in the sink, I looked out the window and saw a patch of red move behind the tree near the sandbox. I stood still, squinting, trying to make it out. What I saw next was the point of a stick protruding from the other side of the tree. Just as I was struck by the possibility of what it was, Regina jumped out and cracked the stick over Brian's head. He went forward, face down in the sand. I opened my mouth to scream but nothing came out. Regina dropped the stick and ran. I flew out the back door yelling for her to stop, but she continued on without a backward glance. When I got to the sandbox, I saw the blood running down each side of Brian's ear. But what frightened me more was his face: his mouth was drawn back in a sob that couldn't escape and his skin was purple from the lack of air. I grabbed him up and slapped his back until his breath returned in little hitches; finally, he was able to scream. I carried him into the kitchen, where I patted his head with a wet dish towel. The profusion of blood terrified me, and I yelled for Gloria.

"My God, what happened!"

"Regina hit him with a stick." She looked at me incredulously. "I saw her. We'd better get him to the hospital. I think he's going to need stitches."

Gloria held him on her lap while I drove. His sobbing slipped into faint whimpering and he closed his eyes.

"Don't let him go to sleep," I said.

"You don't think . . ."

"I don't think anything. Just don't let him go to sleep."

The cut required six stitches, but the doctor assured us he would be all right. However, just to be safe, he told Gloria to be alert for any signs of dizziness or wavering in his walk.

When we drove into the driveway, the whole place looked disturbingly peaceful, as if nothing had happened. There was a thin line of smoke coming up from the charcoal grill; the three huge oaks blotted out the descending sun and colored the air a soft blue-gray. There was no sign of Regina. Gloria sat with Brian in the living room, cutting up an apple for him, while I searched the house. I looked under beds, opened closets and checked the basement and garage. As I was deciding my next move, the phone rang. It was Mrs. Lorimer.

"Mrs. Mattison, Regina wants to spend the night here."

"I'm sure she does. I'll be over to get her right now."

"She says she's afraid to come home."

"Just keep her inside until I get there."

I went out the back door and picked up the stick she had used on Brian and brought it into the kitchen. Then I started for Mrs. Lorimer's. When I reached the edge of her yard, Regina came barreling out the front door and went running in the other direction. I started after her, kicking off my thongs as I ran. As I rounded the corner onto the next street, my foot came down on something sharp. It was just enough to throw off my gait, and the big toe of my other foot slammed into the edge of the sidewalk. Strangely enough, the pain was more of an inspiration than a deterrent; I sped up and caught her in the next block. She had been screaming all the while I was chasing her, so there was quite an audience on hand, on lawns and porches and at windows. I got hold of the collar on her red shirt and yanked her backward so I could get a grip on her arm. Immediately, she began to pull.

"Stop pulling or so help me I'll break it!"

Mrs. Lorimer, who had been following me, arrived in time to

hear this. She scowled and took a step toward me.

"That's no way to talk to a child."

"This is none of your business," I snapped.

"It's my business when I see a child being threatened."

"Would you like to know what this *child* did?"

"I don't care what she did. It doesn't excuse—"

"There's a three-year-old in my house who has six stitches in his head because of her!"

"I didn't, I didn't!" Regina screamed.

"Don't bother lying—I saw you do it. Now start walking!" She continued to pull in the other direction. "If I have to start pulling you, you're going to be sorry."

"Mrs. Mattison, maybe it would be wise to wait until you've calmed down."

"I'm not waiting for anything." I began to pull Regina the way a cowboy might pull his horse out of mud. Mrs. Lorimer walked alongside us.

"I want Daddy!"

"Maybe she could stay at my place until her father comes home."

"She's coming home with me."

"I want Daddy! My throat hurts!"

After the distance of one block, she realized my strength was greater than hers; she gave up pulling and stumbled along hesitantly. Mrs. Lorimer walked with us as far as our yard. Her cue to stop was my emphatic good night.

As soon as we got into the kitchen, Regina pulled back at the sight of the stick. I let go of her arm and picked it up. "Do you know that that little boy had to have his head sewn up?" My hand tightened around the stick as I looked into her face: there were Frank's eyes, his high forehead, his long, thin jaw line, but there was none of his softness. That face was a wilderness to me; all my anger gathered in my throat and I had to fight not to cry. "Do you realize how badly you *hurt* that boy?"

No answer.

"Would you like to see what you did? Would you like me to show you his stitches?"

98

Gloria came in. "Irene, he doesn't know what hit him. I don't think we should even bring it up."

Regina turned and sneered at her. That was all it took. I snapped the stick in two.

"Upstairs." My tone changed both their faces. For the first time in the past two years, there was fear in Regina's eyes and I savored it. "Upstairs. Now."

"I want Dad—"

"If you say that one more time, it'll be worse. Now get moving."

She went ahead of me, looking over her shoulder as we climbed the stairs. I followed her into her room, closed the door and pulled her over my knee. When I raised my hand, I realized I still had the stick in it. I dropped it, yanked down her shorts and panties, and slapped until my hand burned. She fell back on the bed, screaming.

"You have exactly half a minute to get quiet. If you don't, you'll get more. With the stick." To prove it, I picked it up. She turned her head and cried into the pillow. "I'll tell you right now, if you *ever* do what you did today, I'll beat you until you can't stand up. And don't think for a minute your father will be able to stop me."

When I got downstairs and saw Gloria and Brian, I felt I couldn't be in the same room with them. I sat in the kitchen to gather myself, but when I saw the flies feasting on the raw steaks that were supposed to have gone onto the grill, I burst out crying. Then I felt Gloria's hands on my shoulders.

"I'm so ashamed, I don't know what to say."

"Shh, don't say anything. You just sit there while I get these steaks on." She put them under the broiler and slipped a block of frozen spinach into a saucepan.

"I don't think I can eat."

"Of course you can." She took out the plates and began setting the table.

"Oh, Gloria, don't! Yell at me—do something!"

"Yell at you for what?"

"You must be angry; you have to be!"

"I was, but not at you. And after I heard what went on upstairs,

I don't think I'm angry with *her* anymore."

"What she did is inexcusable. I'll never forgive her for it."

"Don't say that. She's had her punishment. In fact, I think our being here is her punishment. We can stay at a motel."

"I wouldn't blame you if you did. But I wish you wouldn't."

"We'll see."

In an obvious effort to lighten my mood while we ate, she got Brian to chatter about the flowers and the animals he had seen that afternoon. But the boy's readiness to be cheerful and the bandage on his head depressed me even more.

"Something has to be done about her," I said as we washed the dishes. "As soon as Frank gets home, I'm laying down some new rules."

"Don't get worked up over it again. The trouble will be over when we leave."

"No, it won't. She's got the mistaken idea she runs this house. I'm going to see to it that idea goes right out the window."

Gloria agreed to stay the night. When we took Brian upstairs, I got the cold, sick feeling that maybe Regina would attack again. I went to her room while Gloria tucked Brian in, and found her asleep clutching the Howdy Doody puppet Frank had given her. There was only contentment in her smooth brow and purring lips, but when I kissed her cheek I could smell the salty aftermath of her tears.

Downstairs, Gloria tried humoring me. I was ready for it. She widened her eyes dramatically, shook back her hair and ran her fingers through it, and said, "Whew, what a day! Mah deah, ah think we deserve some refreshment." She took out a joint and plopped down onto the couch.

"I don't think I should. Maybe I'll have a drink instead."

"You'll have some of this. You are going to relax."

I was in the mood to be told what to do. I wanted her to take me by the hand and lead me into oblivion.

She took two deep drags. "Now let's think pastel thoughts. Lightness and air, that's our need."

"Talk to me. Tell me about California," I said, taking the joint from her.

"Well"—she laughed—"that should take about two minutes. It's the epitome of contradiction and if you enjoy analyzing that sort of thing, it's rather amusing. Let's see, we have sunshine and smog, the ambitious and the idle, a richness of imagination and a poverty of style, an air of permissiveness and stringent laws, a desert kissing an ocean. Let's see, what else. . . ."

The grass was not pulling my mind away from the afternoon; it was doing just the opposite. I went on asking typical questions about California, her job at the college, where she and Pat had taken vacations. As animated as she was, I could not be distracted by the new chapters in her life or by things I'd never seen. I could barely even recall what Pat looked like.

The telephone rang. It was Frank.

"I called you earlier but there was no answer," he said. "I wanted to get through before Regina went to bed."

I wanted to tell him what Vivian had said and what Regina had done to Brian. I wanted him to know how cheated I felt, but I *didn't* want him to come running home. I needed another day or two alone with Gloria.

"Irene? Hello?"

"I'm here."

"Is anything wrong?"

"No. I was sleeping. How's your demonstration going?"

"There were some beatings and arrests. Tim's in jail. We're going to the ACLU tomorrow to see what they can do."

"You mean you might be arrested?"

"That's not what I said. Irene, you sound funny. Are you all right?"

"How do you expect me to sound when you tell me someone's been arrested?"

"I shouldn't have told you. I'm sorry."

"It's a little late for that, isn't it?"

"Honey, why are you mad at me?"

"I'm not mad. Where are you now?"

"We're at Sylvia's cousin's house."

"Who's 'we'?"

"All of us."

101

How cozy, I thought. But I said nothing.

"Is Gloria there?"

"Yes; she's sleeping." I glanced guiltily at Gloria.

"Are you having a good time?" he said.

"Wonderful."

"You don't sound it."

I heard a click on the wire.

"Is somebody listening in there?" I said.

"No, there's only one phone."

"Maybe somebody's tapping the wire."

"Daddy! Daddy! Come home, please come home! They're being mean to me!"

"Get off that phone," I said.

"Regina?"

"Daddy, please come home *now!*"

"I said to get off that phone."

"Regina? What's wrong, honey?"

"She hit me, she chased me and hit me, please come home!" She began to sob.

"Get off that phone this minute!"

"Irene, what's going on there?"

"Daddy, please come home *now,* please, please!"

"Get off that phone, young lady, before I come up and pull you off it!"

"Daddy—"

"Don't talk to her like that," he said.

"What did you say?" My voice was burning.

"I said"—his voice softened—"I just asked you not to talk to her like that."

"And how *should* I talk to her?"

"Daddy, please, before she hits me again!"

"Irene, what's *going on* there?"

"Ask your daughter." I hung up. When I turned to Gloria, I suddenly burst out laughing. "God, aren't telephones wonderful, the way you can just hang them up?"

Gloria was not amused. She looked at me apprehensively. "Don't get upset again. I shouldn't have given you the grass."

"Oh, what the hell. Let them play me for the villain. She can tell him whatever she wants. I'm not going near her. I've had enough of her for one day."

In a few minutes, the telephone rang again.

"It's me," he said. "Now tell me what's happening."

"I'm tired, Frank. Nothing's happening."

"Damn it, what are you keeping from me!"

"You're a great one to be asking that question."

A tiny pause, then slowly: "What do you mean?"

"Nothing, nothing, nothing. Look, Frank, it hasn't been a pleasant day and I'm tired. Regina hit Brian over the head with a stick. He had to have six stitches."

"Stitches?" Another pause. "Well, what did he do to her?"

"He didn't do a goddam thing to her!"

"Irene, take it easy."

"Don't tell me to take it easy! 'What did he do to her?' It seems to me your first question would be to ask how he is."

"Is he all right?"

"Yes, he's all right."

"I'm coming home. I'll take the first plane I can get."

"Fine. Exactly what *she* wants. Now she's learned the power of tears and hysteria."

"Stop it, stop making her sound so conniving. She's only a child."

"Yeah, and Hitler was a child once."

"I'm not going to argue with you. I'm coming home."

"You do that. And when you get here, I'm leaving. I'm going someplace with Gloria for a couple of days."

"I'll be there as soon as I can."

After I hung up, I made us whiskeys with soda. Gloria kept quiet, waiting for me to talk.

"I suppose I sounded like the proverbial harridan."

She shrugged. "You were angry." Then: "But you're angry at more than just Regina. Something was bothering you last night after Vivian left."

"Yes. But I don't want to talk about it until I've spoken to Frank."

103

"Of course."

"And I want you to do a big favor for me. Frank made me promise never to let Vivian come here. I'm going to tell him I ran into her downtown on the street today. I want to say you were with me."

"All right." She grinned. "Looks as if Regina wasn't the only one who was a bad girl."

We sat quietly for a while, sipping our drinks. The voice I had used on the telephone kept ringing in my head, circling round and round one figure—Sylvia. It made me squirm to admit my jealousy; verbalizing it would make it easier.

I told Gloria about the night Sylvia had stayed over and how she impressed Frank and Regina. As I continued my description of her, Gloria's face changed. She looked as if she was hearing about someone she already knew.

"I wish you could meet her sometime," I said. "I'd love to hear your appraisal."

"Frank's quite fond of her?"

"He's enamored of her social consciousness."

"In California I've seen that kind of social consciousness shoplifting in stores." She fell pensive, and I watched her.

"What are you thinking?"

"Nothing."

"Liar." I grinned. "You're thinking Sylvia's the same type he used to see before he met me."

"Is that what *you're* thinking?"

"Yes."

"And you don't like her being in Chicago with him?"

"I don't like her being with him, period. Sometimes I can't believe how naïve he is, and when I tell him he is, he just accuses me of being cynical. He has this attraction to underdogs *just because* they're underdogs. That's the way he sees Regina because of her illness."

"You certainly don't fit in that category."

"Maybe I'd have more leverage if I did."

The next morning, Frank called again.

"Is everything ironed out?" he asked almost shyly.

"She's still mad. She's not speaking to me. We had a quiet

breakfast and she went out to play. What time are you getting here?"

"That's what I called about. I'd like to stay a couple more days. I want to help straighten out this business with Tim."

I asked myself whether Sylvia had talked him into this or whether he had considered what I had said the night before about giving in to Regina's demands. I figured the least I could do was to give him the benefit of the doubt and encourage him to stay. With that settled, I still wanted to get away from the house and Regina to relax with Gloria. I called my mother and asked if I could bring Regina to Cedar Run to stay with them for a night or two. She conferred with my father and called me back to say they would come to our house because my father wanted to see an old college friend who had just been hired by the university. Regina was impassive when I announced that her grandparents would look after her for a day or two.

Gloria and I took Brian and drove eighty miles to Lake Hammond, where we got a room in a motel with a swimming pool. We had a day and a half and two nights of solid relaxation, but as we prepared to leave, a foggy depression settled over me. I knew I was going to miss her terribly and I began to resent our living so far apart.

We went directly from the motel to the airport in Detroit. We said practically nothing to each other all the way. But when we stopped for coffee in the terminal, it was Gloria who launched into resolutions for the future.

"Even hermits have telephones and stationery," she said, grinning. "Since you and Frank both have vacations at Christmas, why don't you come out and stay with us."

"Maybe we will, or maybe next summer."

When the announcement came for boarding, she gave me a firm hug and said, "Well, off to our separate lairs." I kissed Brian good-bye and he gave my hair one last stroke. Impulsively, I took out my manicuring scissors and cut off a small chunk above my ear and wrapped it in a tissue.

"There," I said. "He can have fire anytime he wants it. And before it goes gray."

"We're going to be seeing a lot of you before it goes gray."

This final assurance of hers lifted my depression. Driving home, I told myself there was no reason why Frank and I couldn't get to California once every year.

When I arrived, Regina burst out of the house, asking when her father was coming home. "Probably tomorrow," I said, and she questioned the "probably." When she asked me to call him, I realized he had forgotten to give me the number and I had forgotten to ask for it. Had he intentionally neglected to give it to me? I was too distracted by this thought to notice the coolness between Regina and my father. Then at one point, when I had answered her third demand that I call Frank, my father turned to her and said firmly: "Leave your mother alone."

"I don't have to," she shot back. "She's *my* mother."

"What did I tell you about that back talk, young lady? Do you want more of what you got yesterday?"

"Kenneth." My mother, warning him and soothing him, in the tone I knew so well.

"What did she get?" I asked.

"She got a swat on her butt."

"What for?"

"Ask her. She knows what for."

"I didn't do anything," she protested immediately. "He's just mean."

"Regina."

"He is. He's your dad, he's not mine."

"But if I were your dad, you'd be a changed little girl."

"That's enough," I said.

We were saved by Susan, who appeared at the back door to ask if Regina could come out. Regina hesitated, so I promised them both ice cream when the truck came around. They went out to play on the tractor-tire swings.

"Buying her off," muttered my father.

"Give me a break, will you? Now tell me what she did to get a spanking."

"She refused to go to bed. She said I wasn't her boss. Then when I picked her up, she tried to kick me. And when I swatted her, she said her daddy would beat me up when he got home."

106

I shrugged. "She's upset. It's the first time Frank's been away from her."

"Maybe he should be away from her more often."

"Kenneth!"

"What kind of a crack is that?"

"It's not a crack. It's advice."

"Well, I don't like it."

"I don't expect you to, but you'd better listen to it. He's spoiling her rotten and you're helping him do it."

"I'll be the judge of that."

"You know, it's usually the parents who discipline the child and the grandparents who spoil it. Not the other way around."

"Then don't discipline her."

"Someone has to. Maybe you don't mind her talking that way to you, but she's not going to do it with me."

"Kenneth, leave her alone."

"Thank you, Mother." I turned back to him. "Now let's drop it. If you have nothing to say that's pleasant—"

"That's right, something you'd *like* to hear."

"—then you can leave. You seem to forget this is my house, not yours."

" 'He's your dad, not mine,' " he said, mimicking Regina.

"Kenneth, what is the matter with you?"

"You know what it is, Mother? It's that damned male pride that can't stand a little girl talking up to it. Thank God Frank doesn't have that handicap."

"You're right, he doesn't have any pride. Maybe that's why you married him."

It was well below the belt, and I was more stunned than angry. But I quickly realized how I could zero in. "You can think that if you want. But just remember he's got one thing you don't have. He's got his Ph.D. Now go peddle your sour grapes elsewhere."

He stood up. "Maybe Regina is more like you than I thought. But at least you waited until you grew up to kick me."

My mother's consolation at the door—while my father raced the car engine in the driveway as a signal for her to hurry up—

was that he and I would make up after we had had a few days to cool off.

"Do you think I'm a bad mother?" I asked.

"Of course not. And neither does he. He's just mad at Regina, so he's taking it out on you and Frank."

"Do you think she's spoiled?"

She hesitated. "Not really spoiled, but a little high-strung. You're going to have to be both patient and firm with her and that's a hard balance to maintain." My father honked the horn. She squeezed my hand and kissed me. "Don't worry about your father. He'll brood for a few days and then he'll be ready to apologize. Give Frank our love when you talk to him."

Frank came home the next afternoon, sunburned but haggard.

"I suppose you heard about the confrontation," he said.

"What confrontation?"

"At the convention. Haven't you seen the news?"

"No."

He went into elaborate detail about the hecklings and the beatings and the arrests. They had managed to raise the bail for Tim's release and were laying plans for his lawsuit against the Chicago police. My interest and attention were half-hearted, but I managed to hear him out to the end.

"Where's Regina?"

"She's outside. Frank, there's something I want to talk to you about. And I want to discuss it calmly."

"What is it?"

"A couple of days ago Gloria and I ran into Vivian downtown."

"Vivian!"

"Yes. I didn't recognize her at first, but she recognized me." Already his eyes were blazing. "We had just a short conversation and . . . Frank, why didn't you tell me about your sister?"

"Tell you what?" His voice nearly cracked. "I told you a long time ago she was a troublemaker."

"I'm not talking about Vivian. I'm talking about Regina."

His head jerked up. "Regina?"

"Your sister Regina."

"What—what did Vivian tell you?"

"More than you've told me. I'd like to hear something from you. I'd like to know why you've kept this from me."

"She died." He looked away at the window and said it again, whispering. "She died."

"I know that. She killed herself in that horrible way. But I want to know why you didn't tell me."

"It's an ugly story. I didn't see the need."

"You didn't see the need? She was retarded, for one thing. And you named our daughter after her without my knowing it. Now I want to know why!"

"I . . . owed it to her. She was too young to die, and that way."

"Why did she do it?"

"She *was* retarded—not severely, not so you could tell it at a first or second glance. I think it was worse for her that way. And she was pretty too, except for that empty look in her eyes."

That empty look in her eyes. As soon as he said it, it hit me: the photograph I had found in his desk drawer the day I was packing everything to be moved to the trailer. His sister Regina must have been the girl in the picture—*and* the reason it had so conveniently disappeared in the moving.

"But," he continued, "the kids at school were no worse to her than her own brothers and sisters. They tormented her, and the older she got, the more they piled it on. I looked after her but it didn't do much good, because as soon as my back was turned, they were after her again."

"Where were your parents all this time?"

His voice turned venomous. "Have you ever watched parents quietly disown a child? I saw it happen. Regina had no protection except my promise to run away with her. Finally, that was all she talked about and I kept promising and promising. Then I got that scholarship, so I told her she'd have to wait a year or two. We were sitting under the dead oak in the backyard when I tried to explain it to her, but she stood up and backed away from me. . . ."

Backed away. Like Wanda Hoople.

"There was nothing more I could say to her, so I let her go. That afternoon she took the lye from under the sink and carried it into the woods where no one would hear her scream."

"Oh, God!"

He was staring at the window and I followed his gaze. We saw Regina at the edge of our vacant lot, saw her look up at Frank's car in the driveway and break into a run for the house.

"Frank, you could have told me this before. Why do you feel you have to carry something like this alone?"

"I told you once what I came from. I was raised in a cesspool and I want to keep you out of it. You and Regina."

"But, darling, you're not *them.*"

His voice broke. "I don't know what I'd do if you ever left me."

"Frank, there's no reason to leave you."

"Promise me."

"Of course I promise."

"And promise you'll help me keep Vivian and the rest of them away from us."

"They can't hurt us."

"Promise me: don't ever let them in this house or near Regina."

I nodded.

She came through the kitchen and dining room, squealing, "Daddy, Daddy," and jumped into his lap. Her hands fisted against his chest, she scowled and said, "Don't go away anymore!"

Gently, he pulled her head onto his shoulder and stroked her hair. "I won't, pumpkin, not without you."

But she was not reassured. Even as she clung to him and accepted his stroking, her scowl remained.

I think that if we could recall a nightmare in its entirety, we would find that the real horror of it lies somewhere in the middle, when you can't remember the beginning, which got you to where you are, and you can't foresee any logical end to it. Looking back now, I can only guess where our nightmare had its beginnings. I say this because it proceeded slowly and I had no feeling of momentum until very nearly the end. That momen-

110

tum became apparent when Regina entered high school at fifteen and it continued to build for two years, growing into a monstrous inevitability which I would have to face with a gun in my hand.

For me, one of the beginnings was Hugh Lance's heart attack in the school parking lot. The next day he was dead and within two years the school was in a shambles. His replacement, Jack Rand, who had connections at the board of education, neither liked nor understood kids and covered up the fact by running the school with a limp hand. Easily intimidated—I suspected he had been bullied as a child—he became a pushover for the troublemakers in the building. He never walked the halls as Lance had done, and instead of dealing with the increasingly rowdy behavior during assembly programs, he simply canceled them. When I sent a boy to his office because he had KISS MY BALLS embossed on his T-shirt (T-shirts, tank tops, shorts and halters were now standard dress in warm weather), Rand sent the boy back with a note which said that according to the constitutional dress code, the boy was allowed to wear what he pleased. My run-ins with Rand increased, as did several of the other teachers'. Fifteen students could fail your class and Rand couldn't have cared less. But if just one failed and that one contested the grade and threw a fit in his office and brought in parents and made *his* life miserable, then you were sure to be "investigated for unfairness and incompetency." Realizing he could not control the students, he turned his frustrated rage, blindly and arbitrarily, on the staff. Fortunately for me, two incidents occurred that made him keep his distance. One day during a free period, I rounded a corner in the hallway to find him just a few steps ahead, walking in the same direction. At the end of the hall, two boys obviously cutting class were loitering and preparing to light up cigarettes. Rand approached them and said timidly, "You boys had better get to class. A teacher might find you here." He gave an involuntary little jump when, right behind him, I said, "A teacher *has* found them." The boys shuffled off (no need to hurry, since tardiness was a negligible offense) and Rand squirmed under his smile before he slunk away. The second incident was even more to my advantage. At faculty meetings, we all complained about the graffiti in the halls. His response was that that was the result of faulty surveillance by the teachers. When I pointed out that there were almost no graffiti in the rooms, the teachers' territory, and that we could not be in two places at once, he resorted to his usual out: he wasn't responsible for the change in society's values and if kids didn't respect property, that wasn't his fault. The next day after school, I went to the custodian and got a wire brush and cleanser and a bucket of water and took them out to the front of the building, where we had a five-foot-high, ten-foot-long stone slab with chrome letters that spelled out AARON PECK HIGH SCHOOL. For five months, we had had to look at the spray-painted insertion of two letters, so that the name read "Pecker." I went to work with the steel brush and cleanser. A few minutes passed before a car stopped and a man got out with a camera. He was a reporter for the local paper and asked if I minded having my picture taken. His thrust-forward face and eager eyes had "muckraker" written all over them and I was more than willing to cooperate. He wanted to know how long the "er" had been there and why the custodians weren't doing this job. I told him they had their hands full *inside* the building, and besides, it was up to the principal to give the order. He asked if the principal was in the building and I said I doubted it. He asked if there were any other teachers still in the building; I said three or four. Next, he asked if Rand always left before his teachers did. I decided not to overstep myself on that one: I simply answered that I didn't keep tabs on him. Then he left me and went into the building. In the next evening's paper, there was a front-page story about Peck, accompanied by my picture. The story was continued on a back page, with photographs of the obscenities in the hallways. Rand was furious and when he called me into his office, he accused me of setting him up with the reporter. I told him exactly how it had happened, but he threatened he would have my job. I replied that he couldn't *do* my job and that if he threatened me any further or tried harassment, I would give the reporter a call. For a month after the story appeared, the whole building changed. The graffiti were eradicated; kids who were cutting classes and roaming the halls were rounded up and sent to the deans; and "inappropriate" clothing was prohibited. At the end of the month, the campaign dissolved. Rand went back to hiding out in his office and the casual chaos settled in once again.

Obscenities were no longer restricted to angry outbursts. They were implanted in the very fabric of social communication. Conversations in the hallway during passing and in the classroom before and after the bell were laced with that verb-turned-adjective "fucking," used for emphasis in both positive and negative descriptions. "Shit" was reserved for anything difficult or distasteful, as in "This book is shit"; "Don't hand me that shit"; "That's a crock of shit." "Suck" remained a verb and was generally applied to all things oppressive: school, homework, teachers and niggers all "sucked." "Prick" and "cunt," of course, were the favored ascriptions for anyone objectionable. Although there were few occasions when any of these words were said to my face, there was a lack of compunction in most of the students insofar as letting me overhear them. If I confronted a student about his/her language, the stock response was disbelief or amusement or "I didn't say it to *you.*" Once, a snappy girl told me I shouldn't be listening in. This is not to say I had no rewards in the classroom or that every day was a misery. However, the general tone of the school, fostered by Rand's permissiveness, began to take its toll on my energy and patience.

And so did Frank and Regina.

By the time Regina finished the seventh grade, she had gone through puberty and reached the height of five foot eleven. She acquired a lovely shape, which she proceeded to undermine by slouching with her shoulders curled and her pelvis thrust forward. And because her face was plain and undistinguished, she took to make-up with a vengeance. She would not step out of the house unless her face was rainbowed in iridescent color. For two years running, the arguments went on between her and Frank about her appearance. I bowed out entirely after the day she turned to me and said: "Don't tell me how I should look. *You've* always been pretty." When I assured her she would be quite attractive if she cleaned up her face and her posture, she looked as if she were tolerating a consummate liar. Then, under her breath, she growled, "I don't know why I had to look like *him.*"

And so began the rearrangement of relationships among the three of us. All those years of Regina's keeping her distance from me, of Frank's indulging her and actually reveling in her every whim, of my own abdication due to frustration and fatigue—all those years seemed to evaporate in the face of the reversals that came. Gradually, boys entered Regina's circle of friends. They gathered in our recreation room for dancing and Ping-Pong, and Frank would go down to see if they were having a good time. Regina complained bitterly about "being spied on" and told me she wouldn't mind *my* coming down to meet her friends but to keep Frank away.

"What's the difference who comes down?"

"He's out of it," she said. "He wants to know everybody's name."

"Nothing wrong with that. It's being sociable and showing good manners."

"It's being nosy. He wants to know their parents' names and where they live. He's like a cop or something."

The next time he went down, I went with him and watched. One of Regina's girlfriends had brought along a new boy. He was watching the Ping-Pong game, waiting his turn. Frank approached him, shook hands amiably, then proceeded to do just what Regina had described—asking the boy about his parents, where they lived, even where they came from.

Upstairs, I told him I thought he was being too overbearing.

"There's nothing wrong in finding out about her friends," he said. "There's a lot of drugs around and you never know who might be peddling them."

"You're not going to find out that way. You're making them uncomfortable."

"Are you faulting me for being interested? All I've heard from you about your school is 'parental apathy,' how the parents don't show up for PTA meetings and open-school conferences."

"There's such a thing as a happy medium."

114

Frank's surveillance continued until Regina announced to me that she and her friends would not be meeting in our house anymore. Instead, they would gather someplace where they would be left alone. At this point, she shut Frank out of her circle of attention almost entirely. She barely spoke to him at all, restricting her conversation to grudging answers to his questions. If she needed to be driven somewhere, she asked me to do it. When she practiced her French for oral quizzes, she would come to me even though Frank had had two more years of the language than I had and his ear for it was better than mine. I was put on the tightrope between them. It was easy to see how Regina felt suffocated by him, and a selfish part of me saw some justice in her about-face because all those years that he had won her attention and her affection cheaply, with indulgence, he had not worked at winning her respect. Of course, it was too late for that. Still, it pained me to see how deeply she was hurting him. But I sensed in him something more than hurt. I sensed panic. Not wild, hysterical panic, but the kind of panic that is kept in check. Sometimes, in the middle of the night, I would hear him get up to go to the bathroom, listen to him pause at Regina's door, open it, close it, and come back to bed. Something, something was moving in on us.

The pressures of school, the uphill battle with Rand, the friction between Frank and Regina, and perhaps the fact that Gloria now had four children made me decide to become pregnant. We had visited Pat and Gloria almost every year since that Chicago summer and I had watched her family grow. The idea of our having a second child was not new to me, but whenever I discussed it with Frank, he had always presented a firm argument for how much I would miss teaching. But that argument no longer held any ground now that the school seemed to be crumbling. Naïvely, I thought a baby would be the best thing for us all.

I got plenty of encouragement from Gloria via long distance. Her second had been another boy, and Pat had wanted her to stop there. Her third pregnancy disappointed him, but when it produced twin girls, he cut back on his office hours to spend every available minute with them. Gloria's favorite story was the one about how Pat liked to sit and watch the babies sleep. One day, he came running out of their room and hustled her back to it. "Come here—listen." She listened, then asked what the big deal was. "Don't you hear it? They're breathing together, *in unison!*" And he looked down at them as if they were the eighth wonder of the world. I could just picture Frank, Regina and myself pushing each other out of the way to take care of the baby.

But that was not to be the case. When I got the doctor's confirmation, Frank's reaction was more than disappointment. It was horror. The color left his face, he stared right through me and said, "But *how?*"

"The way it usually happens."

"But how did you let it happen?"

"I just did. My, what a wonderful reception."

"I'm sorry. But we can't. . . ."

"Can't what?"

"Regina's fifteen!"

"What difference does that make?"

"It's just so . . . ridiculous."

"I don't see what's ridiculous about it. Do you remember that day you came back from Chicago and we talked about your family?"

He winced. "What have *they* got to do with this?"

"You made me promise to help you keep them away from us and I agreed. Since then, we haven't seen hide or hair of any of them. Including Vivian. Maybe *that's* the problem. We've become so solitary. Barry's way out in Texas, Neil's up in Vancouver, my best friend lives thousands of miles away, and we see my parents twice a month at the most. What's wrong with expanding our own family? I'm sure it'll be good for Regina."

"There's nothing wrong. You're right." But there was no conviction in his voice.

Regina's reaction was not as severe, but it was far from what I wanted. She gave me a long, clinical look and said: "A baby? You're too old." After a few weeks she did warm up to the idea, but with more amusement than enthusiasm. Frank said little

116

if anything about it. I had the peculiar feeling he was watching me the same way he had been watching Regina—with panic. I kept telling myself he would change once the baby was born; the fact that the baby was *not* born showed me how wrong I was. When I lost it in the fourth month, he made a pretense of disappointment. But I could sense his relief. And after the doctor warned me against trying for another, his relief became obvious. I slipped into a quiet depression, which he tried to lift me from with candlelight dinners and little gifts. I didn't want his offerings of comfort. I began to think that if thoughts could kill, *his* thoughts had killed the baby. Within a month or so, he went back to keeping unreasonable tabs on Regina, and my feelings of menace returned.

During the next year and a half, Regina put the finishing touches on the wall that would shut out her father. In his presence, she no longer stooped to sullenness or insolence, for she had found that her most effective revenge was to ignore him. Yet he took her punishment unflinchingly, keeping her at an early curfew and insisting upon being given her exact destination (or destinations) whenever she went out with her friends.

The night she introduced us to Virgil Evans, I saw a flickering of something alien in Frank's face. Perhaps that was the beginning of the real momentum, because from then on nothing would be the same.

Regina had had exactly three dates by the time she entered her junior year of high school. Whether this was due to her intimidating height, an overeagerness to please, which hid a cache of jealousy and resentment, her unglamorous appearance next to her prettier friends, or any combination of these, I could not say for sure. (Had she gone to Peck, I might have had more ready answers. However, neither of us thought it a good idea for her to be in the school situation with me, although Frank wanted it that way. So she attended Old Central, eight blocks from our house.) What *was* obvious to me was her jealousy over her girlfriends' popularity with boys. Friday night was stag night: the girls all went out together. Saturday night was reserved for dates. It was this night that Regina sat at home, sulking and turning down every offer of consolation. Now and then, she would let slip a sour-grape criticism of her friends: they were boy-crazy or they had no taste and would go out with anyone who asked them. At these times, I saw that familiar look on her face, the one that had been there the day she sent Frank out into the vacant lot to drive the kids off the swings and the day she had begrudged Brian her coloring book. What was missing now was the gratitude, the worship, she once had for her father. Without her noticing it, I would watch her from the corner of my eye while she looked him over as though he were some kind of distasteful specimen.

"Why did you marry him?" she asked outright one day when we were alone in the car.

"What a thing to ask. I fell in love with him."

"What with?" Her voice was cool and hard.

"Of all people, it should be obvious to you. Your father's a rare man in his own way. He's intelligent and kind and conscientious and . . . humble."

"What else?"

"I think that's plenty."

"Didn't you ever go out with any handsome men?"

"Yes; I just never met a handsome man who has what your father has."

"Maybe you didn't look around long enough. Your friend Gloria found one."

"You can't always help who you fall in love with."

"If you'd married someone else, I wouldn't look like *him.*"

"If I had married someone else, you wouldn't be here."

I was well acquainted with the preoccupation teen-agers have with looks, but I was also aware of how Regina would tune out if I started in on the topic of "other qualities."

"I wonder what the baby would have looked like," she said.

I didn't answer. The baby was not a favorite topic of mine. It only rekindled feelings of resentment for Frank, feelings which would distract me from defending him to her.

"We did heredity in biology last year. It seems weird to me I didn't get anything from you. It's all *him.* If anyone looked at

118

you and me together, they wouldn't think you were my mother at all."

What she said was true and I had to think quickly. "Sure they would. You've got red highlights in your hair and you've got a very good figure. You certainly didn't get *that* from your father. In fact, sometimes you remind me of Grandma."

"Which one?" she said pointedly.

"Grandma Rutledge, of course."

"How come he hasn't got any pictures of *his* family?"

"They were very poor. They probably couldn't afford a camera."

"I'll bet they were all ugly, every last one of them."

"That's not true. Your Aunt Vivian—" A twinge of guilt stopped me.

"What about her?"

"She's a very striking woman and *she's* very tall."

"How come I've never seen her? Or any of them?"

"It's very complicated. It's the way your father wants it."

"Everything's the way he wants it."

"Never mind that. Your father is not ugly and neither are you. I wish you would get that out of your head."

"It's easy for you to say."

I waited a moment to think out my words. With Regina, they always had to be carefully chosen. "Since we're on the subject of your father, are you aware of how you've been treating him?" She rolled her eyes and put on that "Here we go" expression. "You know, he'd give up the world for you."

"I don't want him to give up anything for me," she said flatly.

"You've been shutting him out completely."

"I don't like him breathing down my neck."

"Regina, I wasn't an only child, but I was an only daughter. My father was very possessive of me too."

"He's always watching me. He gives me the creeps."

"He loves you."

"I don't want to be loved like that."

If she only knew just how much she was *my* daughter. That desire for independence, the rigid adherence to her own opinions, even the callousness—I had had them until I met Frank.

119

Her withdrawal from Frank was so complete that it included his friends as well. Bernie and Sylvia and Sylvia's husband, John, who had lavished attention on her for years, were now dismissed as "a jerk" and "a dog" and "out of it." She seemed to be shaking all identification with Frank, and although she didn't move completely into my corner, my company was always preferable to that of her father.

It was in her junior year, in late September, that she lost her appetite and sat dreamily at the dinner table. She spent most of her time in her bedroom. The eye make-up was toned down, the lipstick grew lighter, the rouge disappeared altogether. The second Thursday in October, she announced she had a date, and on Friday at seven-thirty, Virgil Evans rang the doorbell.

He was as handsome as anyone the movies or TV had to offer. Just half an inch taller than Regina, he had the solid, sinewy build of a swimmer. His sandy hair was not fashioned in the popular layered look but cut close to the scalp, with a part on the right side. His features, strong and angular, were softened by large brown eyes and full, almost overripe lips. When he smiled, he showed slightly gapped teeth, similar to Frank's. Frank shook his hand and invited him to sit down. Regina said they couldn't or they would be late for the movie. Frank said they could come back to our house for a snack afterward. Regina rolled her eyes at me with that all-too-familiar message "Get him off my back." But Virgil liked the idea. Regina's face changed. It was apparent that any idea Virgil had would be just fine with her.

It was when Frank closed the door after them that I saw that alien look on his face. He stood there gripping the door handle, his eyes squinted and his jaw pushed forward. For a moment, he appeared to be calculating something; then his lips tightened and he opened the door with a furious yank and glowered at the street as they drove away.

We both sat in the living room grading papers. Now and then, I would look up to find him staring at the floor. At ten-thirty, he began checking his watch, which he continued to do at ten-minute intervals until they walked through the door at eleven forty-five. I went into the kitchen to put the pizza in the oven. I wasn't gone five minutes when Regina burst in.

"He's starting again!"

"What?"

"Asking all those questions about Virgil's family, where they live, everything!"

"He does have the right to know a little bit about a boy who takes you out."

"Then *I'll* tell him! I don't want him asking questions. He never stops. Will you please go in and shut him up? I'll watch the pizza."

When I got to the living room, Virgil was telling Frank how he had just recently come up from Florida to live with an aunt after his father died. Right now, he was looking for a job until he entered the community college the following fall.

"Where in Florida?" said Frank.

"Fort Lauderdale."

"What was your father's name?"

"Same as mine—Evans." Virgil smiled.

"I mean his first name."

"Frank, really." I turned to Virgil. "He's writing a book about first names."

Virgil laughed. But Frank was not to be put off. "What was his name?"

"Philip."

"What kind of work did he do?"

"He was a handyman."

"Did he have a business?"

"Not really. People called him for odd jobs. But he did pretty well for himself."

"You were born in Fort Lauderdale?"

"No, in Canada in a house trailer. They were on a fishing trip."

"Are you a Canadian citizen?"

"No. They registered the birth later, in Florida."

121

The questions continued. Although Frank's tone was conversational, I felt an urgency behind the questions and I think Virgil did too. Finally, I stepped in.

"What do you plan to study in college?" I asked.

"Not history or English." He chuckled. "They've always been my worst subjects. Maybe phys ed or social work." He talked readily about his love of sports. I tried to keep my face looking interested while I observed Frank. I could see he was itching to jump back in.

"Regina said you met at a football game," Frank said.

"That's right."

"How did that happen?"

"I was sitting next to her."

"Since you don't go to that school, how did you happen to be at one of their games?"

"You know Central has been the class A state champ quite a few times. They have a big following."

"That kind of news gets all the way to Florida?"

"No, I found that out when I got up here."

"All this question and answer is making me hungry," I said. "I think we should eat."

As we moved toward the dining room, I brushed Frank's arm and whispered, "Leave him alone now."

While we ate, Virgil and Regina told us about the movie. Virgil did most of the talking and Regina hung on every word. It was both touching and amusing to see the transformation in her, all that hard brass turning to putty. Already I was drawing parallels between her and myself at the time I had met Frank.

She walked Virgil out to his car and Frank watched from the window. When she came back in, he was waiting for her.

"Did you have a good time?"

"Yes. Until we got back here."

"Honey, I'm just interested in who you see."

"You're just interested in ruining things for me! If he doesn't ask me out again, I'll—you'll be sorry!"

"If he likes you," I said, "he'll ask you out again."

122

She turned to me. "I'm not bringing him in this house again if *he's* here!"

Frank flinched. I wanted to take a crack at both of them, at Frank for his ridiculous behavior and at her for handing out orders. "No fighting," I said. "It's too late."

"Regina, I didn't mean to make you uncomfortable."

"Oh, yes, you did! You're always butting in, you're always asking questions. I'm sick of it. Just leave me alone." She ran upstairs and slammed the door.

Frank sat down with a long sigh. I knew we had to discuss this and I was anxious to get it over with.

"She's right, you know."

He looked up and looked away. He wasn't even going to challenge me.

"If you don't leave her alone, she's going to turn her back on you entirely."

No answer.

"The Frankenstein monster turned on his creator."

"I don't think that's amusing."

"It's not supposed to be. She's growing up and you had better start accepting that. You always wanted her to have everything, but now that she's found something she wants, it seems you're going out of your way to sabotage it. I don't understand it."

"I'm not sabotaging anything. I'm simply concerned."

"I'm concerned, but I'm not playing interrogator."

He said nothing. He wasn't going to talk. But I knew how to get a reaction from him.

"If we had had the baby, you might not be so preoccupied with running Regina's life."

"I'm not running her life." Then: "I'm sorry about the baby, you know that."

"No, I don't know that. Maybe losing it was a blessing. Maybe you wouldn't have had enough love to give it."

"That's a rotten thing to say."

"I can't help feeling it's the truth. But since it's not here, it doesn't matter, does it? What does matter is Regina. And you.

You're going to be very unhappy if you don't let her grow up on her own. A five-year-old or a ten-year-old may enjoy being coddled, but Regina is sixteen. She doesn't want you that way anymore."

He sat staring at the floor. There was no point in going on.

"I'm going to bed," I said. "Are you coming?"

"Later."

As I walked past him, he reached out and grabbed my wrist. "Irene, please be patient with me."

"It's not my patience you have to worry about. It's Regina's."

Within three weeks' time, Virgil Evans was bringing Regina home from school every day. He would stay for an hour, drive off, then return around nine o'clock, after Regina had finished her homework. We let them have the recreation room to themselves until ten-thirty. They went out every Friday and Saturday, and Virgil always had her home by 1 A.M., her curfew time.

There was absolutely nothing in the boy for Frank to criticize. He was bright, personable, considerate, and had a sharp, mature sense of humor. But I could see that Frank was looking for something to criticize. Quietly, he watched the boy like an apprehensive cat, and I found myself watching *him* watch.

I can't say exactly when Frank's nightmares began. I can only say when I first noticed them, between Thanksgiving and Christmas. Several times I awakened to find him thrashing and gritting his teeth. One night he fell right out of bed. When I questioned him about the nightmares, he said he didn't remember them. But the one I remember—will always remember—woke me early one Sunday morning. There was a mumbling which slowly shaped itself into words, and I heard "Regina, come back." I heard it twice. I rolled over and saw him twitch and open his eyes. In a daze, he looked right at me and said, "She's going." He then closed his eyes and went back to sleep. I got up, sat in the rocker and smoked cigarettes. He slept fitfully for another two hours.

His loss of sleep began to show. He left for work groggy and came home exhausted. He looked attentive only when Virgil was in the house. He had run out of questions for the boy, but there was always the watching, the constant watchfulness.

This change in Frank coincided with the change in Regina. Her first case of romance softened her considerably and I was delighted. Although her entire time schedule was shaped around Virgil, I didn't mind in the least. In all her sixteen years, she was the most pleasant, the least demanding she had ever been. She looked contented, and more than anything, I hoped this experience with Virgil would spawn some self-confidence in her that would remain even if he left her one day. For a while, she seemed to lay aside her resentment of Frank, but she certainly had not buried it. It exploded in my face the afternoon I came home from school to find her and Virgil waiting for me. They were sitting on the couch when I came through the door and both of them stood up immediately. That one urgent gesture spelled trouble; all I could think of was: Oh, God, they're going to tell me she's pregnant. But one glance at the rage in Regina's face told me the topic was going to be Frank.

"He's crazy! He's out of his mind!" she said.

"Take it easy," said Virgil.

"What are you talking about?"

"Him! He's spying on Virgil!"

"Regina, be quiet. Mrs. Mattison, can you sit down for a few minutes?" I sat. "A few days ago, my aunt told me she thought a man was following her. I didn't pay much attention to it because she does like to exaggerate. Yesterday, she said he drove past the house a couple of times and parked out in front for a while. The way she described him, it sounds like Mr. Mattison. She described his car too."

I sat there not saying a word, because I had nothing to say.

"I've known from the beginning he doesn't like me. I don't know why he doesn't. If I did, maybe I could do something to change it."

Only if you traded places, then he'd like you. I didn't need to say it, only think it. The dark suspicion that had taken root in the back of my mind was beginning to spread its branches.

125

"Virgil's right," said Regina. "He hasn't liked him from the beginning. But he's not going to get away with spying on him. I'll move out!"

"Don't be silly," I said. "I'll take care of this."

"You've said that before and he's still the same. He's *worse!*"

"I promise you there will be a stop to this."

"Mrs. Mattison, I don't want to make trouble, but my aunt—well . . ."

"I understand. Take my word for it, it won't happen again."

I asked him to go home and to stay away for a day or two. I let Regina go up to her room while I thought out what to say to her. I didn't want to panic her, didn't want her to see *my* panic. In the kitchen, I took a slug of brandy, then went up to her.

She was lying on her bed in her bra and panties, doing her homework. It would have been easier for me if she had had clothes on.

"I want to talk to you about something and I don't want you to be embarrassed by it. I want you to know you can trust me. Whatever we say to each other will remain strictly between us. I won't discuss it with your father and I don't want you to discuss it with Virgil."

She looked surprised, not apprehensive. That encouraged me.

"What I ask may be difficult for you to answer, but remember that it's just as difficult for me to ask." I drew breath. "You've been avoiding your father for a long time now. Even before you met Virgil. I want you to tell me why."

"You know why."

"I want you to be specific."

"He watches me. All the time. I'm sick of it. Now he's spying on Virgil."

"Let's stick to you. Has he ever said or done anything *specific* to make you . . . embarrassed or afraid?"

"He'd like to embarrass me but he can't. A few weeks ago he asked me if I was sleeping with Virgil."

"What did you tell him?"

"I told him it was none of his business."

"And *are* you sleeping with him?"

"Yes. I love him."

"Regina, have you thought about the consequences? Like getting pregnant?"

"He uses something."

"Those things aren't very reliable." God, I thought, how these kids just jump right in.

"You could get me some pills, then."

"I don't know; we'll have to talk about that later. Has your father said anything else or *done* anything to make you uncomfortable? Anything at all?"

"Just that he's always around, watching."

"From now on, if he does anything to upset you, will you come and tell me in private?"

"Sure. If you can *do* anything about it."

I wasn't certain she had understood my questions fully. But I couldn't bring myself to be more specific.

That night, I was more specific with Frank. I waited until he was in bed reading. With no preface at all, I asked him point-blank: "Why have you been spying on Virgil?" He looked up, disbelieving but guilty. "Well?"

"What do you mean?"

"You know what I mean. You drove past his house and you parked out front. I call that spying. Do you realize you've terrified his aunt?"

"I don't believe he has an aunt. At least, not in that house." He laid the book down. "Don't you see there's something about the boy that doesn't jell?"

"What, for instance?"

"Just look at him—he could have his pick of girls. Why does he want Regina?"

Soon after I had met him, *I* had been told by Gloria and my parents that I could have my pick. But it was a point I couldn't make to him. "You can't explain those things, you know that."

"It's obvious he's using her."

"It's not obvious to me. And what if he is? That's a chance everyone has to take."

127

"I don't want him using her."

"Frank, you have no say in the matter. And the crazier you act, the more appealing Regina will find him." His face was set against anything I had to say, but it changed with my next statement. "I want you to leave them alone. And I want you to see an analyst."

"What!"

"You heard me. I've had it, Frank. I've had it with your nightmares and your delusions. You want to know something? My school's gotten so awful that everyone counts the minutes, waiting for the end of the day. I don't. Because I know what I'm coming home to isn't going to be much better than work. You're making both Regina and me miserable and now you're starting in on Virgil and his aunt. You need help and I can't give it to you."

"You honestly believe that?"

"I believe it enough to tell you this: there's something terribly wrong in this protectiveness of yours. If you won't go to an analyst, I'll leave you. And I'll take Regina with me."

"Irene!"

"I mean it. You find somebody by the end of the week and you make an appointment."

When I got into bed, he turned off the light and slid toward me.

"Please don't."

He pulled away and lay on his back. "You'd really leave me?" he whispered.

"If you force me to."

I was drifting off when he spoke again. "Trust me, Irene. You know I'd never do anything to hurt you."

"But you *are* hurting me. I'll trust you when you start getting help." *And after I get some information.* I decided then that he wouldn't touch me again until I had had a talk with Vivian. And maybe not even after that.

Long-distance information gave me the number of her lumber company. I dialed twice and hung up both times before the second

128

ring. Standing there with the phone in my hand, I couldn't shake the memory of Frank's kindness to the blind boy, Larry, or the looks of adoration on the faces of those students he tutored in our living room at midterm and finals. He was still the same man and that man couldn't be capable of . . . Then I remembered the rumors about the girls, the *young* girls, coming to his apartment that summer I lived with Gloria and he lived upstairs. And I saw Sylvia's hand going under a sheet, with him accepting it. Was that another man, hidden from me all these years but forced to surface now to draw breath? One of the teachers at school had been married ten years and then discovered the two-year affair his wife had been having with another woman. And I had thought at the time: How could he have been so blind?

The third time I dialed, I let it ring through. A man answered. I asked for Mrs. Snell.

"Who's calling?"

"It's a personal call."

"She ain't here right now. She's—just a minute."

I heard some kind of rustling and the man say sniggeringly, "Says it's personal."

"Hello."

"Vivian?"

"Yes."

"This is Irene, Frank's wife."

Slight pause. "Is something wrong?"

"I was wondering if I could come and talk to you."

"What about?"

"I'd rather not say over the phone."

"Is it about Frank?"

"Yes, it is. Could I drive up tomorrow?"

Another pause. "I'll come there."

"We can't meet here."

"I assumed that," she said. "You name a place to meet where I can have a drink."

We settled on a restaurant at the edge of town near the expressway she would be coming in on.

Dinner that night was totally silent. Regina gulped down her food in five minutes and left the table. Frank picked at his and stared at the wall. When I came back from the kitchen with the coffee, there was a slip of paper near my napkin. On it was a name and telephone number.

"One of the graduate assistants goes to him. He's supposed to be good."

"Did you get an appointment yet?"

"Next Tuesday at eleven."

There was nothing more to say. Any word would have been the wrong one. I wanted him to see the analyst, knew he *had* to see one, and yet I cringed at his quick compliance. He wanted me to be pleased, but he looked more beaten and drained than I had ever seen him.

As soon as he went up to his study, Regina came down and motioned me into the kitchen.

"Well?" she said.

"It's all right. We had a talk."

"A talk? You've had talks with him before and nothing's happened."

"It's taken care of."

"What's taken care of? What did he say?"

"He knows he's been wrong."

"That's *it?*"

"What do you want—blood? I am doing the best I can. And you yourself could make things a little more pleasant by being kinder to him."

"You don't care what he does to me, do you?"

"Regina, get out of here before I slap you." A ridiculous threat. She towered five and a half inches over me. "I will handle this my way."

"You'd better."

The next day, I called school and said I was sick, but I left the house just as if I were going to work. I had three hours before I was to meet Vivian. I went to two shopping malls and browsed through the stores, rehearsing what I was going to say to her. The more I rehearsed, the more my courage began to waver, and I felt nauseous. I knew I would have to have a drink before Vivian, but I needed more than that.

I went into a phone booth and called California.

"Irene!" said Gloria. "Is anything wrong?"

"No. Why should something be wrong?"

"You've never called at seven-thirty in the morning."

"I'm sorry. I forgot all about the time difference. How is everyone?"

Brian had taken up scuba diving and was in the throes of his first romance. Ray needed glasses and was having fits over having to wear them. The twins, Amy and Amanda, were already taking a gymnastics class. And Gloria and Pat were planning a whole month in Europe. All good news. Predictable good news. When they first married, I had thought it wouldn't last a year. Now they were going to Europe for a month. Second honeymoon. Away from the kids. It wasn't what I wanted to hear. I wanted something to be wrong that I could help put right. I wanted to say, "Look, Gloria, it's not all that bad, look at it this way" or "I think you should do this, now get hold of yourself."

"Where in Europe?" I asked.

As she went through the itinerary I began to cry. We had never been to Europe. We had never been anyplace without Regina.

". . . and the college extended my leave of absence, but I don't think I'll be going back. Believe it or not, I've gotten to like it here at home. Say, aren't you supposed to be at school? . . . Irene? Hello?"

"I've got a cold."

"You sound like you've been crying."

"I think I'm getting an allergy. Anyway, I was bored and I wanted to catch up on you and Pat."

"One day away from the job and you're bored? You *are* a model of the work ethic. Anything new there?"

"Nothing much. Regina has a boyfriend and she's head over heels. That's about it. I have to run out on some errands now. I'll give you a call in a couple of weeks."

"No, it's my turn."

I got to the restaurant half an hour early and ordered a double

Scotch. Gloria's words stuck with me: *Believe it or not, I've gotten to like it here at home.* At the same time they depressed me, they made me determined to be straightforward with Vivian.

Age had been good to her: she arrived looking exactly as she had ten years before. What was more astonishing was the resemblance between her and Regina. Assessing her dignified posture and her self-assured, long-legged stride, I thought how good it might be for Regina to use this woman as an example.

"Hello, Vivian. I'm glad you could come on such short notice."

"You made it sound urgent. No one's sick, I hope."

"No, nothing like that. But I do need to talk to you. And I'd like to keep this just between us."

"That goes without saying." She eyed my drink. "I thought you were a teetotaler. Now where did I get that idea?"

I wondered if this was a digging reference to the grass I had been smoking that night she came to the house to see Regina. She settled back into the booth and ordered a martini.

"I don't know exactly how to begin," I said. "I don't know what to ask. I guess I'd like you to just start talking about Frank."

"What in particular?"

"I'd like to hear what the rest of you think of him."

"We don't all think exactly alike. Naturally, we've all been hurt by him, the way he cut us off. Let me ask *you* something. Has he cut you off too?"

"I don't know. I'm not sure. But he is alienating Regina. Lately, he's been so . . ."

"Possessive."

It wasn't a question; it was a statement. I felt a chill.

"Yes, possessive. In the most unreasonable way. Nothing I say seems to penetrate. He was always a reasonable man." She pursed her lips and lowered her eyes. "Wasn't he?"

"If he is a reasonable man, then that makes the rest of us look pretty awful—it means his reasons for cutting us off are valid. I really don't prefer to look at it that way."

"Vivian, what *are* his reasons for hating—for avoiding all of you?"

"Hate is the right word. Frank's always been good at hating."

132

I hate people who just breed.

"But what are the exact reasons? Does it have anything to do with his sister Regina?"

"Has he told you anything about her?"

"That horrible story about the lye—the one you told me—and how she was retarded and wanted him to run away with her."

"Run away with her?" Her eyes widened. "Run away with her? She wanted him to *leave her alone.*"

I knew then I should leave, that I had a sufficient glimpse of the entire picture. But I didn't move. "What do you mean—leave her alone?"

"Regina was slow, but she was sharp enough to sense something peculiar in Frank's attention. He watched her like a hawk night and day. He used to want to stay home from school to be with her. She never made any friends because she could never get away from him. Finally, I guess she couldn't stand it anymore."

"That's not enough to make a girl drink lye."

"I suppose not." She hailed the waitress and ordered another drink for each of us. Through the window I could see it was beginning to snow heavily, the wind whipping the flakes into a gauzelike curtain that obscured the highway. I wanted to jump into that wind and whiteness, have it shake me up and set me down on some new, firm ground.

"Then what *would* make her do it?" I said.

Vivian looked into her drink. "Something she never spoke of. She didn't even leave a note."

"What couldn't she speak of?"

She shrugged. "None of us ever *saw* anything. But after her death, Frank never looked any of us in the eye. And he couldn't wait to get out of town and off to college. I would like to think he hates us because he hates himself. That's what I would like to think."

"Where were your parents while all this was going on?"

"Irene, being poor is a full-time job. My father had to worry about getting food on the table and clothes on our backs. That was his main concern and everything else was just frills. He and my mother didn't have time to investigate every mood one

133

of us had. Some things they did see they probably had to turn their backs on and hope for the best."

"I'm sorry. I didn't mean to imply . . . I know a little of what you're talking about."

"Do you?"

"Regina—*my* Regina—has always been outside my grasp. And now she's turning on Frank . . ."

"Turning?"

"She doesn't want anything to do with him. And I'm getting to the point where I can't blame her. I don't know what to do anymore."

"Are you thinking of leaving him?"

"I'm trying *not* to think of it."

"Have you thought of getting him professional help?"

"He's already agreed to see an analyst."

"Then why don't you wait awhile and see how that works out? Besides, if you left and took Regina with you, it might set him off."

"Set him off?"

"I've seen his temper. If you need a little moral support now and then, you know where to reach me."

"Thank you, Vivian. I appreciate it."

She asked me questions about school and I told her I had just about reached the end of my rope there too.

"What's wrong with this country," she said, "is that there's no allegiance anymore, particularly to the family."

"I guess you're right."

"I know I'm right."

We said good-bye in the parking lot, with the blizzard blowing all around us. She repeated her offer of being available if I needed her again.

"I wish you had told me years ago what you told me today."

"Do you think you would have listened?"

"I might have."

"I doubt it. Besides, I don't know if I would have told you. Quite selfishly, I wanted Frank to be happy. Maybe that was wrong. There's no way of predicting how things are going to turn out. Take this car, for instance." She swiped the snow on the trunk of her black Lincoln. "Thirty years ago, not a single person in Ridgeway would have dreamed that a Mattison could own a car like this. Now I've got three lumberyards and the same people who used to spit at me are kissing my ass. We've had offers to join the country club, bridge clubs, every kind of organization in town. But we don't belong to anything. We belong to our family. And we take care of our own. If you're patient with Frank, maybe it'll all work out for the best."

"Maybe."

I had two hours before the time I normally arrived home. Traffic was at a crawl. I did not want to kill the time by driving around. Fortunately, the radio announced that all schools were closing early.

Heading for home, I was a little heartened by Vivian's optimism. Virgil's car was parked out front and that made me feel better too. But as I came in the back door, I was greeted by Regina's shouts from the recreation room.

"Get out! Get out of here!"

I heard Frank's voice, low and firm, then Virgil's: "Mr. Mattison, I don't know why you have it in for me. If you want me to leave—"

"No!" said Regina. "If you leave I'm going with you and I'm not coming back." Frank mumbled something and she shot back with: "Just try it and see!"

I stood still, my purse and my keys still in my hand. Frank came up the steps. He looked exhausted as usual, and he gave a start when he saw me. Whatever there was in my face, it made him lower his eyes.

"I have had it with you," I whispered, choking with rage. "Maybe you think I was joking when I said I would leave you. I'm not joking. I'm telling you right now, I don't want you to say another word to that boy. Whatever room he's in, you make sure you're not there. And I don't want you alone with Regina."

"Irene!"

"You heard me. When you see that doctor on Tuesday, you'd better be ready to level with him. I'm giving you exactly three

135

months. If you don't start making some changes during that time, I'm going to see a lawyer."

His jaw tightened and I could see his eyes misting. But I was not going to buckle under any tears. I went upstairs, closed the bedroom door, and sat down to watch the blizzard. It seemed appropriate that there was chaos outside too.

Frank kept the appointment and every one after it. Around me, he walked on eggs and avoided all direct eye contact. A hard silence settled between us. I found myself in some amorphous emotional territory where revulsion mingled with pity. During the day, pity dominated as I weighed the facts of his unfortunate childhood: poverty, passive neglect on the part of his parents, small-town and small-minded social exclusion, and finally the emotional trauma he must have suffered over his attraction to his sister and her reactionary suicide. But at night in bed with him, I huddled close to the edge and my thoughts ran from facts to suspicion. Why had he chosen the name Regina for our daughter without telling me the source of it, if not because of some dark allegiance to his sister? Had he consciously intended our daughter as a replacement for his sister *from the very beginning?* Were all those accounts he gave me of his brothers and sisters really true or had they been a ruse to gain my support in keeping away the only people who knew his secret aberration and might suspect a repetition of it? Why was he so relieved when I lost the baby—because its presence would only accentuate his strange devotion to Regina? These questions would run through my mind as I stared at the philodendron outlined against the street-lighted window shade. I clearly remembered the night we had fought over the other one and how he had regretted its being the source of our fight. Now he was seeing an analyst to try to get rid of some other source that would keep us apart. One minute, I knew I had to stand by him so long as he was willing to fight this horrible thing in him; but the next minute, I wondered if any success on his part would truly erase my revulsion, which might survive on memory alone.

For two months, silence reigned. Frank's and mine were rooted in embarrassment, but Regina's silence had a smugness to it, as though she had accomplished some private kind of victory. During meals, while Frank and I sat clenched and barely ate, she took second helpings and prolonged the ordeal by eating slowly, all the while looking perfectly content with her silence. Occasionally, when I found it intolerable to just sit there, I would ask some question about school or her friends. Sensing the desperation and awkwardness of my gesture, she would reply as briefly as possible and usually with a smirk. I could not help resenting this posture of hers, especially when I would catch a glimpse of Frank. At the table he never looked at her, and that was when I pitied him the most. There was shame and apology in his face, so obvious I was certain Regina must see it too. I had to keep reminding myself that she knew nothing of the *other* Regina and therefore could not fathom the anguish her father was going through.

At the end of February I took another day off from work, for a dental appointment. Early in the afternoon, after I returned home, the phone rang. It was the dean of girls at Old Central. She explained that due to the growing rate of truancy and forged excuses, it was now school policy to check with the parents after the fifth absence in the semester. Regina, she said, already had six, and the semester had just begun. I assured her there was some mistake, that Regina had not missed even one day of school. She then gave me the dates of absence, verified by all Regina's teachers. I said I would check with Regina and get back to her. When I hung up, I was angry, but I was also relieved that the call had not come through to Frank. This matter would have to be settled privately between Regina and me.

"I want to know where you've been on the days you haven't gone to school."

"You sound funny." She giggled. One side of my mouth was still numb from the dentist's Novocaine.

"Never mind how I sound. Answer my question."

"Just hanging around."

"Hanging around *where?*"

"I went downtown a few times. Once I went to a movie."

"You were with Virgil, weren't you?"

"Once."

"Don't lie to me. He's the only reason you'd skip school for." She sighed and rolled her eyes. "And you forged my name on those notes you took in, didn't you?"

"Yes, I forged your name."

"And that doesn't bother you?"

"So I took a few days off; what difference does it make? I'll get the same grades I always get."

"That's not the point. The point is you lied."

"They make you lie, them and their stupid notes."

"I'm not going round and round with you about this. When I call the dean, I'm going to tell her the truth."

"Oh, stop playing the teacher. I'll get two weeks' detention!"

The fact that she expected me to lie for her came as no surprise. "Well, you can tell your father and hope he'll get you off the hook—in school, at least." The scowl on her face assured me she had got the point. "You take your detention and we'll keep this between us. And no more cutting, or the next call the dean makes might be to your father."

That night, she was far from imperious at the dinner table. She sulked and ate little.

A week later, I had to give one of the teachers a ride home to the south end of town. He lived two blocks from the restaurant where I had had my meeting with Vivian. After I dropped him off, I pulled up to a stoplight right next to the restaurant. The right-of-way traffic was coming off the expressway ramp. I looked at the restaurant, recalling that day with Vivian, and I felt vaguely guilty because I hadn't talked to her since. By now, she probably thought I had simply used her to get the information I wanted. And I had.

I turned my attention back to the traffic just in time to see a familiar-looking car shooting down the ramp, racing to make the light. When it passed through the intersection I saw Virgil driving. Regina was sitting next to him.

At home, I waited an hour and a half for him to drop her off. Frank was upstairs in his study, so as soon as she came through the door, I led her into the kitchen.

"Did you serve your detention today?"

She knew something was up and wisely chose not to lie. "All right, what do you want me to tell you?"

"Where did you and Virgil go today?"

A tiny flicker of fear crossed her face before she was able to compose herself. "Go?"

"Yes, go, as in *travel*. Where did you go?"

"We went for a ride."

"The question was *where.*"

She looked me over carefully and I could almost see the wheels turning in an attempt to guess exactly how much I knew.

"We went for a ride in the country."

"Apparently you don't remember what we talked about last week. Apparently you wouldn't mind getting another two weeks of detention."

"They didn't give me detention."

"Regina . . ."

"That's the truth."

"Why didn't they give it to you?"

"I don't know."

"I can check this so easily."

"Go ahead and check."

"You didn't go to school today, did you?"

"I was supposed to go on a field trip with the natural science class. I just didn't feel like it."

"You kill me. I let you off the hook with your father, the dean doesn't give you detention, and yet you go ahead and brazenly pull the same stunt. You must *want* to be punished. You know, if I brought your father into this—"

"Go ahead. Who cares!"

I could see she *didn't* care. That frightened me.

The next day I called the dean and asked if I could see her at four o'clock. When I arrived, she stood up to shake hands and offered me a seat. Her deep, throaty voice on the telephone had led me to believe she was my age or older. I was surprised to find her a young woman not yet thirty.

139

"I don't want to take up your time," I said, "so I'll get right to the point. I want to know why Regina wasn't given the customary detention for skipping school."

"Well, we felt—*I* felt—that in Regina's case, the punishment would be redundant. She was quite ashamed of herself and in view of her scholastic average and the satisfactory appraisals from her teachers, I thought it best to give her another chance."

"Believe me, she used that chance. She skipped school yesterday."

She lowered her eyes to the pencil she was playing with. "I see. Mrs. Mattison, until this semester Regina had no record of truancy. Do you have any idea why she should suddenly begin skipping school?"

"I certainly do. She has a boyfriend."

"Yes, she's told me about him. But I don't think Virgil is the reason she's skipping school on these particular days."

Virgil. Hearing her say the name so casually, as if she knew him, bothered me.

"Regina has *discussed* the boy with you?"

"Somewhat," she said. "She's very fond of him. And the fact is she told me he doesn't like her staying out of school."

"Doesn't like . . . ! She spent yesterday with him when she was supposed to be in school!"

"I think she would have skipped school without him. I think he's the most positive factor in her life right now."

"In what way positive?"

"He seems to be giving her a certain balance, a comfort she needs right now."

"Comfort from what?"

"She seems to be under a strain."

"What kind of strain?"

"Haven't you noticed it?" she said.

"What kind of strain?"

"She feels a lack of freedom because her father doesn't like Virgil."

"Her father is opinionated and overprotective," I said quickly,

140

"but he certainly hasn't impinged upon her freedom. I don't know what you mean by this 'lack of freedom.' "

"I mean it in the psychological sense. She feels her father is watching her in a certain way."

"What way?"

She would not have had to answer. The sudden evasiveness in her manner indicated she had been told more than she was going to tell me.

"She couldn't exactly describe it to me," she said.

"Can *you* describe it?"

"I wouldn't attempt to without knowing a few more facts."

If that was my cue to provide those facts, I ignored it. "I don't want Regina to know I've been here," I said. "But I do want her to be given detention for skipping school yesterday."

"If you want. But I don't think that's going to solve the problem."

"It might be a start."

Driving home, I tried to sort out my feelings over what Regina had done. It angered me that she had taken this situation to someone else, an outsider. But I was frightened by the possibility she didn't trust me enough to tell me everything. Her unyielding harshness with Frank had seemed perverse—unless something had *already* happened.

For two days, I watched them closely. Frank was the same with her as he was with me—withdrawn, his shoulders hunched and rounded in an attitude of self-protection. Regina was self-possessed and untouchable. Around Frank she showed no fear, barely any resentment. She simply acted as if he were invisible. When Virgil came into the house, Frank dutifully hid himself in his study.

Regina got her detention and gave me smoldering, knowing looks the whole week. Suddenly, it was as if I were the one, not Frank, who was oppressing her. By the end of the week, I was so exhausted from sleeplessness, I went to the doctor and got a prescription for sleeping pills. And I decided to break the silence with Regina.

"Do you want your father to move out for a while?"

"No, not really," she answered casually, too casually, as though she had *expected* me to suggest it.

"Then he's not the reason you were skipping school?"

She sighed deeply, her usual signal that this was something she didn't care to discuss.

"Regina, what did you tell Miss McPhee about us, about your father?"

I expected an outburst, but she seemed merely indifferent. "Not much," she answered.

"She seems to have gotten the idea your father is the reason you've been skipping school."

"What does *she* know?" She shrugged.

"Did you use your father as an excuse to get out of that first detention?"

"No."

"Then why did you mention him to her at all?"

"She asked me what things were like at home."

"What did you tell her? Did you tell her anything you haven't told me?"

"I don't know what you're talking about."

For the next few weeks, I had the feeling of treading stagnant water. Frank slunk around the house and said nothing. When I asked how he was doing with the analyst, he would put on a wounded look, as if I had made the most blatant accusation—the very thing I wanted to steer clear of. Regina didn't pay much more attention to me than she did to Frank. She was animated only in the presence of Virgil. I knew she was much too wrapped up in him, but that necessarily had to be the least of my concerns. Perhaps it was this sense of treading that made me wish something—anything—would happen. Perhaps this is what sent me into Frank's study late one afternoon before he got home.

In the back of one desk drawer, tucked beneath some papers, was a gun, loaded. Under it, single pages from a Fort Lauderdale phone directory were folded in a square; all contained complete listings for the name Evans. And there was a letter from the Fort Lauderdale Health Department, which said that on the basis

142

of the information given in the request, they were unable to locate the birth certificate.

I took the gun to our room. I pulled out the bottom drawer of the dresser and put the gun on the floor, then pushed the drawer back in. I had already given Frank my ultimatum. A month and a half remained. I would wait.

The gun took up a permanent position in my mind. In the middle of teaching a lesson or pushing a shopping cart down the aisle of the supermarket, I carried a picture of its stubby barrel and deadly cylinder, and with that picture I remembered Vivian's words: "I've seen his temper."

In magazines and in the family living section of the newspapers I saw scores of articles about the increasing divorce rate and the common tendency at middle age to reassess one's marriage. I found most of the personal interviews laughable (although I was incapable of laughing) because the discussions of "changed values" and "looking for new purpose" remained abstract, nothing more than little sociological essays. But a gun was concrete. So was the letter from the Fort Lauderdale Health Department. And there was Vivian's story, and there were the circles under Frank's eyes and mine from sleeplessness. Everything pointed to the plain fact that nineteen years of marriage had not created a profound intimacy but instead left me stranded with a stranger. And to what degree was that my own doing? How many clues had I ignored over the years?

Driving to and from school, I had fantasies of running away, just stepping on the gas and aiming for Los Angeles and that Southern California sun which seemed capable of burning out your past and leaving you contentedly empty. The one thing I wanted most was to feel empty so I could sleep again.

By March, Regina had been going with Virgil six months. If one day passed without her seeing him, she was ready to jump out of her skin. I set no limits to the time she spent with him. When she was gone from the house and Frank was in his study, I could at least be alone.

The second Saturday in March, Virgil and Regina were going

143

to Detroit to see a play. Virgil came by that morning and had breakfast with us. Dressed in a steel-gray three-piece suit and sporting his wide, gap-toothed smile, he looked more handsome than ever, the archetype of America's Prince Charming. All through breakfast, Regina hung on his every word and took her eyes off him only to get the fork to her mouth. Although I found her too subservient to him, I had to admit she looked the happiest I had ever seen her. Even her coloring had changed. Her cheeks were pinker, her eyes glistened, her face looked fuller. It was saddening to realize that the most Frank and I could draw from her was a smirk or a sneer.

That morning, Frank was a little more at ease with Virgil and almost friendly. When they were ready to leave, Frank even walked them out to Virgil's car. From the dining room window, I watched him look over the car, ask questions and climb inside to inspect the dashboard. Maybe, I thought, just maybe he was beginning to get a grip on himself. This thought, however, was whittled down to wishful thinking by the end of the day. He refused lunch, went through two stop signs on our way to the supermarket, ate only a few mouthfuls at dinner, then planted himself in the living room to wait for their return.

"Maybe they'll want something to eat when they get back," he said. "What time was that play supposed to be over?"

"Four-thirty, five."

"It's seven o'clock now. They'll probably be hungry."

"I doubt it. They'll probably have dinner along the way."

"They didn't say anything about stopping for dinner. Did they say anything to you?"

"No."

"Maybe they'll be a little hungry anyway. When they get back, they can come in and have a little something. Even if they did stop and eat, they should be back pretty soon. If they stopped, it would probably be along the expressway, and someplace quick. I don't imagine he'd take her to—"

"Stop it! Just—stop it!" If you don't stop it, I thought, I'll walk out of here tonight.

144

He settled back and hid behind the newspaper he had been pretending to read.

They pulled into the driveway at eight-thirty. Frank bounded through the dining room and kitchen and out the back door. In a minute, Regina and Virgil came in alone.

"Where's your father?"

"In the garage."

"Doing what?"

"Who knows?" She looked annoyed. "Virgil's tired; he wants to go home. What did you want to talk to him about?"

"What do you mean?"

"Daddy said you wanted to talk to him."

A dull freeze came over me. What was he doing out in that garage? "I—I just wanted to know how you liked the play."

"I didn't think it was so bad," said Virgil, "but Regina didn't like it. The end was kind of a disappointment, but I guess they work on those things before they get to New York."

He went on with his review, but I had my eyes on Regina. The tilt of her head told me she was wondering the same thing I was. As Virgil continued talking, she turned and went to the dining room window. Obviously seeing nothing, she started for the kitchen, but before she reached it, Frank reappeared. His fists were clenched at his sides.

"What are you up to?" she said.

"That's what I was going to ask you."

"What are you talking about?"

"You know what I'm talking about and so does he. Sit down, both of you."

"I'm not sitting—"

"You'll do as you're told." There was a new, solid authority in his voice and Virgil was the first to bow to it. When he sat down on the couch, Regina joined him.

"Now where did you go today?"

Virgil gave a puzzled smile. "To Detroit."

Frank moved in closer on them. "I'm going to ask you just once more and I want the truth. Where did you go?"

145

Regina was fuming, but Virgil looked questioningly, helplessly at me.

"Frank," I said, "what are you doing?"

"Tracking down a lie, that's what I'm doing. They didn't go to Detroit."

"Mr. Mattison, we've got the play programs in the car. I can show—"

"Anybody can get you play programs. What about the ticket stubs? They'll have the date on them."

Virgil turned to Regina. "Have you got them?"

"No, I haven't. And he's gone crazy."

"Stop this right now," I said.

"I checked the mileage on the car before they left this morning and I checked it again just now. They've gone a hundred and fifty-five miles. Round trip to Detroit is at least two hundred and ten!"

For a minute no one said anything. Finally, Virgil spoke up. "Mr. Mattison, you must have made a mistake. We were in Detroit."

"A hundred and fifty miles is seventy-five each way. Where did you go?" He leaned over and put his face in front of Virgil's. *"What are you?"*

"Frank!"

"Get him away from us!" Regina cried.

He grabbed the boy by the front of the shirt. "I want to know right now!"

Regina tried to stand, but Frank pushed her back onto the couch. It was the first time he had ever laid a hand on her that way. Instantly, I thought of the gun.

"Seventy-five miles each way," he said to Virgil. "In what direction?"

"Frank, let him go."

"In what direction?"

I got up and went to the phone.

"Stay away from there, Irene. All I want is an answer from him."

I began dialing Bernie Golden's number, shaking so badly I

missed a numeral and had to start over. Frank rushed to me and pressed the button to cut me off. I looked him squarely in the eye and whispered, "You're sick. You're so sick I'm beginning to hate you."

"Don't say that. Don't—" His eyes finished the plea.

"Let him go home," I said. "Go upstairs and wait for me. Go now before I walk out of here tonight."

He left.

"He's nuts—he's out of his mind!" said Regina.

"That may be, but he's suffering too. You can see he's suffering. Now tell me, did you really go to Detroit? That's all he wants to know."

"Yes, we went to Detroit!"

"Just like those days you *said* you went to school?"

"So you're on his side now?"

"I'm on my own side, and I want the truth. The two of you are driving me crazy. It's not just him. Now I have to worry about whether or not you're showing up at school or if you're really going where you say you are."

"Mrs. Mattison, we really went to Detroit. He must have read the mileage wrong."

"All right, Virgil, all right. You can go home now."

"Oh, that's just fine!" said Regina. "And I'm supposed to stay here with that lunatic!"

Virgil turned to her. "He'll calm down after I'm gone."

She walked him out to his car. I waited twenty minutes. Instead of giving her the customary signal with the patio floodlight, I slipped out the back door with the intention of apologizing to Virgil. I had taken only a few steps when I heard them giggling in the car, then Regina broke into a shrill laugh. I went back into the house and signaled with the light.

When she came through the kitchen she had a faint smile on her face as though none of the last hour had happened. She breezed past me without a word.

The nightstand lamp was on when I walked into our bedroom, and Frank was lying with his arm over his eyes. I undressed in the bathroom, put on a nightgown and sat down in the rocker.

"You're pushing me to leave you. That's what you really want, isn't it?"

"That's the last thing I want."

"I can't believe that. It comes down to one of two things. Either you're not making any effort to overcome this perv—this obsession, or else it's entirely out of your control. But whichever circumstance it is, I can't live with either one."

"It's not what you think, Irene. It's not at all what you think."

"Then what is it?"

That pleading look again, but no explanation.

"I found the gun," I said.

"I know you did."

"Then you know what I found with it."

"Yes."

"Tell me why, then. Where did you get the gun?"

"It was just an impulse. I'm glad you took it. I never would have used it, anyway."

"Frank, the gun is loaded."

"It came that way."

"What did you have in mind—putting bullets in our heads while we were asleep some night?"

"Jesus, Irene, don't!"

"You haven't got much time."

"I know that better than you do. Trust me a little longer."

"I told you my time limit and I'm sticking to it. After that . . ."

After that, I didn't know.

Two days later, on Monday, I was teaching my second class when one of the office secretaries came to the door with a telephone message. It was from Vivian. I was to return the call as soon as possible. My next period was free, and I went directly to the phone booth.

She answered on the first ring. "Vivian? It's Irene."

"Can you talk?"

"Yes. What is it?"

"Frank was just here."

"What!"

"I called you just as soon as he left. Irene, I think he's dangerous."

"What did he do? What did he say?"

"He was raving. What little I could make out was about Regina. He said I had turned her against him and turned you against him. You didn't tell him about the talk we had, did you?"

"Not a word, I swear."

"I didn't think so. But he really lit into me. I was afraid he was going to hit me."

"What else did he say?"

"It was all a jumble. He kept mixing up the two Reginas and saying how nothing was his fault. That's what he kept saying: 'It's not my fault.' "

"Oh, God!"

"I just wanted to warn you. But you can't tell him I called you. For *my* sake."

"No, of course not. Vivian, what am I going to do?"

"You're going to be careful. Don't do anything to rile him up or make him suspicious. You might have to have him committed for a while . . . you know? . . . Irene? Hello?"

"Yes, I'm here."

"Just be careful, will you?"

"Yes. And thank you."

"Don't thank me. I'm sorry it's turned out this way. If you need any help, you know where to reach me."

I sat there in the booth, just trying to breathe. When I was able to think, I got the operator and told her to make my next call collect.

"Gloria, it's Irene."

"Well, we're back to the early morning calls." She chuckled.

"Gloria, I need you here. Can you come today?"

"What's wrong?"

"Everything!" I began to cry. "Everything *you* thought would be wrong nineteen years ago. God, you must have been looking into a crystal ball."

"Take it easy. Tell me what it is."

"Frank. He's sick, so sick, and there's nothing I can do! I'm

149

going to have to have him committed or else I'll kill him!"

"Stop that. What are you talking about?"

"First his sister, now his daughter. He's in love with Regina and he got himself a gun."

"What!"

"Please, can you come? I need you here."

"Do you know what you're saying?"

"I know I sound hysterical—I *am* hysterical—but it's the truth."

"All right, honey, take it easy. Do you think you can hang on until tomorrow? I could come tomorrow."

"Yes, as long as I know you're coming."

"All right, then. I'll call you as soon as I get a flight."

"Leave the message for me here at school." I gave her the number.

"I'll call the airlines right now. You're sure you'll be all right tonight?"

"Yes. Just come."

I got through the day on that single expectation. After school, I checked my mailbox in the main office and found Gloria's message. Her plane would arrive the following afternoon at five.

At dinner, Frank didn't touch a thing. He sipped on some wine and stared at the table. But he did not appear passively lost in thought; on the contrary, he had the look of someone who has just made up his mind.

"Virgil's picking me up in half an hour," Regina announced casually. "We're going to the movies."

"You're not going anywhere," said Frank.

She ignored this and started eating her pie. I waited. When the pie was gone, she picked up her plate and carried it to the kitchen, then came back through on her way upstairs.

"You heard what I said." His voice was hard enough to make her stop and turn to me.

"Are you going to let him start in on me again?"

"You step one foot out that door," he told her, "and I'll call the police. I don't want to do that to you, but I will if you force me."

"Then do it." But there was little conviction in her voice.

"I will."

Again she looked at me, but I turned away. If I just get through tonight, I thought, Gloria will be here tomorrow. Regina ran upstairs.

"I'm sorry," he said.

"Sorry for what?"

"I know what I'm doing, Irene." When his hand touched mine, it was like a jolt and I pulled back from it.

If you know what you're doing, then you're hopeless! If you know what you're doing, then you know you're driving me crazy!

"Irene, listen to me."

"I'm tired of listening to you. I'm tired of looking at you. Leave me alone tonight."

I went up to talk to Regina. Her door was closed, but I could hear her talking on the phone. She said, "Please, please," just before I knocked. She told me to wait a minute, then lowered her voice. When she hung up, I went in.

"Was that Virgil?"

"No. Betty Riley." One of her friends.

"I hope you haven't said anything to her about . . . us."

"I haven't."

"Regina, I want you to do what your father says. Just for tonight. He's more upset than usual."

She looked afraid. "What about tomorrow night and the night after? He'll find an excuse whenever he wants."

"I know, but I'm thinking of a way. . . ." What—to have him committed? Arrested? "I want you to stay away from Virgil for a few days while I decide what to do about your father."

"All right, a few days."

Frank hid in his study. Downstairs, I tried watching television, but my mind was on Gloria. Regina sat with me, next to the phone, and chewed on her fingernails.

"Expecting Virgil to call?"

"Yes. If I can't see him I can at least talk to him."

When it rang she picked it up. "It's for you," she said, and handed it to me.

"Irene, it's Vivian. Don't talk, just listen. I've been thinking

151

over what Frank said today and I'm worried about Regina. The way he kept mixing up the two of them . . . My hands have been cold all day. I don't trust him."

"I know, I know."

"Look, I have a plan. Let me bring Regina up here for a few days, maybe until the end of the week, while you figure out what you're going to do. Frank would never think of looking for her here."

"But how?"

"I can pick her up in front of her school tomorrow afternoon. You can call the school and tell them she won't be in the rest of the week."

"What about my parents? I could send her there."

"You mean they know about all this?"

"No, I couldn't tell them."

"Well, you'd have to tell them, because I'm sure that's the first place he'd go looking for her."

"You're right. But your place is such a risk. If he ever found out . . ."

"Isn't there a bigger risk having her *there?* Irene, you didn't see him as I did today. Believe me, if you had . . . Please, let me do this one thing for you, and for her."

"Yes."

"What's the name of the school and what time does she get out?"

"Old Central on Pershing Avenue. Three o'clock."

"I'll be out front. You remember my car—the black Lincoln. I'll have on a green coat."

"Okay. Maybe someday I'll be able to repay you."

"Don't worry about that. I'll be there at three o'clock sharp. When I get back here with her, I'll ring you once and hang up to let you know everything's all right."

"About what time will that be?"

"Let's see, it's seventy-five miles, so it'll be an hour and a half, approximately. About four-thirty."

I was to pick Gloria up at the airport at five. "Make it six-thirty."

152

"Fine. One ring." She hung up.

"Come into the kitchen." Regina followed me in and sat down at the table. "Listen carefully. You've heard me mention your Aunt Vivian before. That was her on the phone. You're going to stay with her for a few days up in Ridgeway. While you're gone, I'll have a chance to think what I'm going to do about your father. She's going to pick you up in front of school tomorrow, but you're to tell no one where you're going, none of your friends or that Miss McPhee, no one."

"Not even Virgil?"

"You'd better not. If your father questions him, at least he won't have to lie."

"Do I really have to go?"

"Yes. For my sake as well as yours. You can take your school books with you. But remember, not a word to anyone about this."

Later, when I went upstairs to bed, I passed by Regina's door and heard her talking on the phone again. I couldn't make out the words, but I distinctly heard her giggle and then laugh shrilly. It made me feel uneasy, and I almost opened the door. But I moved on to the bathroom, thinking maybe she really didn't fathom the seriousness of the situation. And maybe it was better she didn't. After all, she was still a child.

The next morning, I drove her to her school before I went to mine.

"Remember, don't say anything to anyone. She'll be here at three. Black Lincoln, green coat. I'll call the school tomorrow and tell them you won't be in for the rest of the week."

"Come in with me now and tell them."

"I can't. I'll be late."

"It'll just take a minute. If you do it in person, they won't be suspicious."

"Suspicious of what?"

"I've got a record now for skipping. If you call them up they might not believe it's you. They might send a truant officer around."

Despite the inconvenience, I was impressed by her concern

153

for details. If a truant officer did come to the house while Frank was there, it could be disastrous.

We went together to the main office, where I spoke to the secretary in charge of attendance. Just as I was explaining that Regina was going out of town, I was aware of a pink blouse next to me. In it was Miss McPhee. When I turned to her, she was looking at Regina sympathetically. Something in me resented that look, for it implied she knew exactly what was going on. We exchanged a quick greeting, then Regina walked with me to the front exit.

"Listen," I said, "if that Miss McPhee calls you in today to ask where you're going, don't tell her anything."

"She won't call me in."

"*If* she does."

"I won't tell her."

I bluffed my way through the day by giving the kids surprise compositions to write. I concentrated on how I was going to tell Gloria about Frank, and how I was going to tell Frank about Regina's absence.

A little after five, Gloria got off the plane, looking as beautiful as ever: tanned, sleek and self-possessed. I felt first a pang of jealousy, then a seething rage at how my life had been turned around. Years ago, anyone with eyes and minimal intelligence would have predicted that her marriage with Pat was doomed to end shortly or drag on miserably. But here she was, four children later and her marriage still intact, being summoned to witness the bitter closing rites of *mine*.

I stood at the chain-link fence outside the terminal and watched her come down the stair ramp and walk across the runway. *You cheated on your husband and are living happily ever after. Your husband wanted you to have children. You want to stay at home. Your husband has no secrets. You're living in never-never land and I'm living in hell!* To regain myself I had to turn away and walk into the terminal. In my attempt to squelch that unwarranted bitterness, I let my memory run back nineteen years to the one warning which had many voices—Gloria's, my father's, Dr. Denning's and, the night of the wedding party dinner, Vivian's. But I had ignored all the warnings, dismissed all the clues; all that courage and optimism on my part had been nothing more than romantic arrogance. Besides Frank, there was no one to blame but myself.

When she came through the door into the terminal, her face fell at the sight of mine. I knew very well what I had come to look like the past few months—the half moons under my eyes, the ashen complexion, the absence of animation in my face— but seeing her reaction to it made me feel like a crone who has had a floodlight turned on her. By the time she reached me and put her arms around me, my throat had swollen so, I couldn't speak. I clung to her, silently, while we waited for her luggage, and I held on all the way to the car. I gave her the keys and asked her to drive. We held the silence throughout the ride. When we got to the house, I made drinks, stiff ones, and sat her down in the living room. "Frank won't be home until six-thirty. We'll have time to talk first." I sat next to the phone, and part of me waited for Vivian's signal. "I can't mince words, Gloria, or give you a long preface. I want you to think back to when I first met Frank. I want you to remember anything *specific* you didn't like about him. Something he might have said or something you might have seen that I didn't." She cocked her head questioningly. "I'm sorry to put you on the spot, but I want you to be honest with me."

"You know I will be."

"I didn't listen to you then; I didn't listen to anyone. But I'm ready to listen now."

"We went over this a long time ago. You know my reaction to Frank was more a reaction to losing you. You were my mentor, my mother, a hundred things, and he was a threat."

"But if it had been a *different* man, would you have felt what you felt toward him?"

"I'm not sure. Maybe. If you had fallen as hard as you did for Frank."

"But aside from me, what was there about *him* you didn't like?"

She lit a cigarette and looked through the smoke she exhaled.

"I guess his magnanimity. The way he was always polite to me, almost unctuous, when I insulted him and treated him like shit. I thought he was either a saint or a sap or a phony, and I certainly didn't want to believe he was a saint. But then, maybe he was just smart. Maybe he figured treating me nicely was going to win him extra points with you. If that was the case, he was right."

"Yes, he was right. And I wonder now how many other things he counted on. What I wonder most is *why* he wanted me."

"Certainly you know by now."

"No, I don't. For years I thought I did. I thought I did." I knew I had to say it then or else I would never be able to say it. I had to look her in the eye and say it. "He wants Regina the way he had his sister! He wants to sleep with her. It's all he thinks about!"

At first, nothing in her face registered what I had said. Her eyes drifted to her drink and back to me. "How do you know?"

"It's so obvious, it's pathetic, the way he hovers over her, the way he hates her boyfriend. He's been spying on the boy, practically tracking down his family tree, hoping he can find something—God knows what—to use against him. He's a spectacle and he's gotten to the point where he's not even trying to cover it up anymore." I poured it all out. The beginnings of his surveillance, the immediate antagonism he displayed toward Virgil, and finally Vivian's story, which he had hidden from me all these years. "I keep telling myself this doesn't happen to people like us, you can't live with someone this long without knowing him. But I don't know him! Suppose we had had a son instead of Regina? Would this thing have stayed buried or would he have wanted me to keep having children until he got a daughter?"

"Irene, you don't think this was *planned,* do you?"

"He named her Regina, didn't he? And oh, so casually, as if the name just popped into his head. He never said a word about *that* sister. And why has he kept his family away from us? I'm telling you, I don't know what to do. One day I think this is something that has nothing to do with his love for me, that it's a sickness and he's fighting it. Then the next day he pulls the

156

same old tricks and I think no, he *wants* to follow this perversion to the end and he's planned it that way and there's nothing I can do except let him go crazy and get him into an institution. But at the same time I can't take a chance on what he might do to Regina. Or to Virgil. I'm caught. And I'm tired. I'm so goddam tired, I'm almost numb."

"How much has he admitted to?"

"He's seeing an analyst."

"Has it helped?"

"Not that I can see. You can't reverse a lifetime in just three months. But something has been touched off in him. He drove up to Vivian's yesterday and babbled about Regina and his sister. But he kept mixing them up. It's the first time he's been back home in over twenty years. I cannot believe it's a good sign."

"Has he been violent with you?"

"No, never. Just the opposite. He keeps asking me to be patient."

"And obviously you have been. Why haven't you left him before this? Why haven't you tried a separation?"

"I would have to take Regina with me and that could be the very thing that would make him snap. And . . . I can't section myself off. That's the problem. I still love him. Sometimes it absolutely repulses me to think it, to admit to it. But if this thing of his is something people can have and get over, then I can't just run out on him. I love him and want to help him, but the thought of him laying a finger on Regina . . . I think I could kill him if he did it."

"Maybe you could send Regina away. To a private school in another town."

"She'd never be willing to leave Virgil. That's another problem I haven't begun to deal with. I'm sure she's been sleeping with him from the beginning. If she ends up pregnant, I don't know what that would do to Frank. But I want you to see him, I want you to watch him when Regina doesn't show up for dinner."

She winced slightly. "Like watching a fish on a hook."

"And what have *I* been?"

"Take it easy, honey. I wasn't criticizing."

157

When Frank came home, he took one look at Gloria and stopped cold. Gloria played her part perfectly. She was cheerful and breezy and right on cue with a story of how her mother was considering a property investment and wanted her here to look at it. Frank smiled and went through the amenities by asking about Pat and the kids. But as soon as she turned her back, he gave me a wounded look mixed with fear and accusation.

Gloria took care of the dinner conversation by rattling on about the trip to Europe she and Pat were going to take and a dozen other things I barely heard. I sensed the close attention she was paying to Frank, and I wondered if he sensed it too. Finally, when Gloria paused, he looked at his watch and asked where Regina was.

"She'll be late," I said as casually as I could.

"Where is she?"

"Some club meeting."

"What club?"

"French, I think."

"Her French club meets every other Thursday. This is Tuesday."

"I think this was a special meeting about fund-raising. Anyway, she's having supper with some of her friends."

"You mean at one of their houses?"

"Yes, that's what I mean." My tone of voice told him he had gone far enough. He asked nothing more, but he stopped eating and took to his wine.

After dinner, he sat in the living room with us. He faced the window and kept staring through it. After less than an hour, he excused himself by saying he had work to do in his study.

As soon as he was out of the room, Gloria turned to me and said, "There *is* something wrong with him. I can feel it. He's absolutely panic-stricken."

For weeks, I had longed for an outside confirmation. Now that I had it, I began to shake and my whole body seemed to race downhill into my stomach. I couldn't talk, I didn't want Gloria to talk, so I turned on the television. And waited.

At nine, he came downstairs and announced he was going out for ice cream.

"And take a little ride past Virgil's?" I said. "You needn't bother. She's not there."

He paused. I knew he wanted to maintain the charade about the ice cream because of Gloria, but he also wanted to know what I knew.

"Did she call you? I didn't hear the phone ring."

"No, she didn't call and no, the phone didn't ring. I know where she is."

He managed a small chuckle. "Where, then?"

"She's on a little vacation. She'll be gone for the week."

I watched Gloria. She kept her face turned to the television, but I saw her swallow hard.

"Irene, I don't think this is anything to joke about."

"I don't, either. Especially since the joke is on me."

"Gloria, would you excuse us for a minute?"

"Sure." She started up from her chair.

"Stay where you are," I said. Then to Frank: "Does it bother you that I have someone here on my side?"

"Is she with Virgil?"

"You see?" I said to Gloria. "Everything comes back to Regina. His darling daughter. His *desirable* daughter."

"Stop it. Now where is she? What do you mean—'for the week'?"

"She's where you'll never find her. I want her away from here while I decide what to do about you. I'm going to see a lawyer. If it takes the truth to keep you away from her legally, then I'll tell the truth."

"Tell him whatever you want. Only tell me where she is right now. Is she with Virgil? Is she? Because if she is, she's in danger!"

"In danger," I mimicked. "No, she's not with Virgil. She *was* in danger, but she's not going to be anymore."

"Irene, don't toy with me. For her own good, tell me where she is. You can't play this game; you don't know what's involved. Tell me where."

I said nothing. Gloria watched. The next thing I knew, I was pulled to my feet, my shoulders gripped in Frank's hands, his face red and furious in front of mine.

"Tell me, goddammit, tell me! You don't know what might

be going on!" He began shaking me. "Tell me, tell me!"

"Take your hands off her." Gloria was standing and her voice was hard. "I said take your hands off her." He turned and looked at her. She didn't make a move and neither did he. He just stared. "Take your hands off her *now.*" His hands fell away from me. He looked as if he were going to be sick. The three of us stood there and then Gloria backed up and turned off the television. Frank collapsed into the chair I had been sitting in and put his hands over his face.

"How perfect!" he gasped. "How perfect you should be here now!" He dropped his hands and looked at her. "You were right, Gloria. You tried to save her from me at the very beginning. You were right and I should have let you do it. But now it's too late." His face drew back in a smile. His shoulders and chest began to shake, but it took a few seconds for me to realize he was not laughing. He was crying. "And so it's time to tell, and you might as well hear it too. I admired you, Gloria, and it's hard to fight someone you admire. Sit down, both of you. I don't want you standing over me this way. Please sit. Over there, together." We sat down on the couch. "You're right, Irene, everything comes back to Regina. I knew when she was born it would have to. I tried to think it wouldn't; I just willfully underestimated them. But they're strong. They're so goddam strong, it's frightening."

"Who's strong?" asked Gloria.

"Vivian. My so-called family. The kind of family neither of you would know anything about. And there's no reason why you should, except that through me Regina's part of that family. She may not recognize it, but they do. They'll try to claim her the way they tried to claim me and my sister."

His big hands hung limp over the arms of the chair, but he was breathing like a runner.

"Regina died because of them—and me. I wouldn't take her away. I promised her I would and then I didn't. I told her to wait but she couldn't wait and I just closed my eyes to it because I wanted to get out my own way, I wanted to wait until it was convenient for *me.* By then it was too late for *her.* And then she was dead." He took a deep breath and shuddered. "Irene, I must tell you something I should have told . . ." He turned his face away. "Vivian is my mother."

Gloria and I looked at each other. Her eyes said the same thing I was wondering: Was he going to become so irrational that we would have to call the police?

"Frank, Vivian is your sister."

He nodded, not looking at me. "Yes, that too." He drew breath again. "Regina and I were hers and my father's—"

"Frank, maybe you should—" But Gloria squeezed my arm and shook her head, indicating I should let him continue.

"From the beginning," he said, "I knew there was something different about Regina and me, the way my mother—or who I thought was my mother—looked at us, the way the older ones looked at us. I understood it with Regina—she had that clouded look, she was 'slow'—but I couldn't understand why they looked at me the same way. We seemed to amuse some of them and embarrass the others. Except Doris, the oldest, and my . . . mother. Doris hated us and the other one hated us and pitied us at the same time. Sometimes when we were sleeping, they would come in together and Doris would hold the pillow over our faces so no one would hear us scream and my—the other one would beat us with a piece of garden hose. Doris said if we ever told anyone she'd kill us. One night, Vivian came in and caught them. She knocked her mother to the floor and dragged Doris into the house—"

"Into the house?"

"Regina and I didn't sleep in the house. There was a shack in the backyard, an old toolshed. They put a wood stove in it and that's where we slept. Vivian used to clean it and get wood for us until I was old enough to do it. Then, this one night, Vivian caught Doris, and from what we heard from the others, she beat her to a pulp. The next morning Doris was gone for good and from then on my—Vivian's mother never stepped foot into the shack. She ignored us most of the time, but once in a while I'd catch her looking at me and I'd think she was going to cry. I remember once this hot, hot day she called me into the house and gave me a glass of lemonade and said, 'Listen, boy'—she never called me or Regina by our names—she said, 'Listen, boy, today ain't half as hot as the fires of hell. You got to watch out. God's already paid your sister by making her feeble-minded and I'm sure he's got something waiting for you too. You just remember you belong to him because even the devil belongs to him, even Vivian."

He stopped and seemed to mull this over in his head. But I could mull nothing over. To me, it was a story about someone I didn't know.

"When I was ten or eleven I began to realize why the others were crowded into three bedrooms while Vivian had her own room. Sometimes my father slept in there with her, sometimes my brothers Tom and Jack. They were the nicest to us besides Marian. Marian worked in the dime store and she used to bring us candy and little toys until Vivian made her stop. They hated each other. Later, Marian met a man, only she never brought him to the house. They moved away to get married and we never heard from her again. The night before she left, she came out to say good-bye to us and she told me to watch over Regina and keep her away from Vivian. I asked her why; she said in a few years I'd *know* why. And of course she was right. One night, Vivian and Jack came out and took Regina into the house. When they brought her back she was crying, this dull moaning. I asked her what happened. She slid her hand down her stomach and said they had hurt her. The next day she helped me nail metal prongs on the doorjamb and I got a board to stick in them. About a week later they came for her again and they broke the door down. Jack and Tom held me down and Vivian took Regina inside. Then Vivian came back and they left. That's when—when she told me Regina and I belonged to her. She stroked my hair and told me I didn't have to mind anyone but her and my father and they would take care of us. She kept saying how someday we'd all get even with Ridgeway; she'd see to that personally. We'd have money and they'd come crawling to us and then *we* could laugh at them. She said we didn't need any outsiders, not if we all stuck together. Then she started"—he shuddered—"she started kissing my neck. She said we all had to love each other, her and my father and Tom and Jack, Regina and me. The rest of the family didn't count, not if they ran out the way Doris and Marian did. I got away from her and ran for the house. In my father's room, they—Regina was in the bed making that dull moaning and my father was saying, 'It's all right, Daddy's here, Daddy's going slow,' and he was moving on top of her and when he saw me *he smiled. . . .*"

Through his words I could hear that dull moaning. It was coming from inside my head. I glanced at Gloria. Her mouth was slack, and her California tan looked tawny.

". . . Regina called to me, she called my name, but I couldn't move, and then—then he got off and Jack got on and I began to scream, and I ran to my moth—Vivian's mother's room. She was sitting there in her straight-back chair with the Bible in her lap. I begged her to stop them, but all she did was smile and say, 'They're none of mine, God has sent me a sign, they were conceived in lust but I've put lust aside, they're lust's children, they're none of mine.' She closed her eyes and started praying for me. I yelled for her to come and help me, but she didn't move, she only smiled and said, 'You can't shout down lust, boy, you have to put it aside.' "

He stopped and closed his eyes. His hands were still hanging over the arms of the chair and his veins stood out like a network of tubing. When he spoke again, his voice was distant and strangely metallic, like a noise traveling down a long, narrow pipe.

"After a while, Regina didn't cry when they took her in at night. Vivian was working at Leo's lumber company and bringing home more money than her job was worth and she was buying Regina presents and dresses. For a long time, I didn't do anything. If someone looked at me sideways at school or on the street, I was afraid they'd found out about us. I had to keep reminding Regina not to tell anyone. Then one little thing happened and it changed me and it changed Regina." He glanced at us briefly, then stared out the window. "This girl asked me to a dance. She was afraid to ask me because her father was a drunk and

163

her brothers were hoods and her sisters were whores and the whole town knew it."

"Wanda Hoople," I murmured.

"Yes. The whole town knew about her family but no one knew about us. When she asked me, she stood there, ashamed of what *she* was, and waited for me to answer. But I couldn't answer and she backed away from me like I was some kind of a prince she had no right to approach and I wanted to say, 'It's not like that, you don't know who I am,' but I didn't say anything, I didn't say a word. After that, in school, she'd slink past me with her head down and I wanted to say . . . I couldn't say it. I couldn't say it to anyone. So I turned it on Regina. One night I told her not to go with them when they came for her, I told her it was a sin, it was filthy, and she'd rot in hell for it. She started crying and moved toward me, but I pushed her away and when they came to get her, she started howling. She ended up telling Vivian what I'd said, so the next day Vivian took me for a ride in the car Leo had given her. We parked on this country road way out of town. She told me there was no place in the world for Regina and me except with her. She told me to keep my dirty mouth shut around Regina and to stop putting ideas in her head. But it was too late to undo what I had done. Regina kept after me to take her away and I kept promising her, but . . . I kept seeing her as one of *them* and sometimes when she touched me I wanted to jump out of my skin and leave her with them. But she kept begging me to take her away and I kept saying later, later. Then I got the scholarship to college. All I could think about was privacy and no noises in the night and no one to look after but myself. I told her she would have to wait, wait until I got to college, and then maybe in a year I could come get her. She said she couldn't stay there without me. She said she'd follow me, she'd go wherever I went. She knew what was really in my mind. You'll never come back, she said, you'll never come back and I'll rot in hell. And then I—" His voice broke and the words came out in spasms. "I told her she could never follow me because where I was going they wouldn't let her in. The next day she took the can of lye into the woods where no one would hear

164

her scream. And she must have died screaming. When I found her, her mouth and her eyes were wide open." He was crying again, without sobbing, and his hands were fisted. "Vivian knew why she'd done it. And she told me I was going to pay for it. I could run off to college or the North Pole, it didn't matter where, but she'd know where I was, and someday I was going to pay for it. But those few years in college, it all slipped behind me like a story I'd been written out of. They left me alone. Until our wedding. Then I knew that nothing had slipped behind me; I knew that the worst was *ahead* of me."

Slowly, he turned and faced me, and he waited. But my tongue was only a blur in my mouth, and there were no words to focus it.

"That day Vivian came to the hospital, I knew. I knew she was just beginning. Then I started hoping. Hoping she would get some fatal disease or smash up her car. But she's invincible. She's proven that much."

"Why . . . why didn't you tell me at the beginning?"

"I never planned on a beginning. When I left Ridgeway, I had accepted the fact I could never marry anyone. I thought just to be away from them, to breathe my own air, would be enough and I could live alone. But it didn't turn out that way. In a way, it was blessing not being attractive, because I never had to fight girls off. But there was a kind of girl who *was* attracted to me. Girls like Regina and Wanda Hoople, girls who hid in corners and thought the world was made for everyone else but them. And I found that somehow I made them happy. For a while that was enough. Until you came along."

He squinted and turned away as if the very memory were some harsh glare he couldn't endure.

"You came along like some cruel joke. At first, I thought . . . I even thought Vivian had hired you to lead me on and mock me. That's why I avoided you until I ran a check on you through the registrar's office and convinced myself there couldn't be any connection. But for months after that it was worse. I used to stand in front of the mirror and ask myself: 'What does she see in me? What can she love?' I decided a hundred times to tell you, but I always backed off. Then that day your parents came to my apartment, I saw who you came from and what you came from, and you held me up to them like a prize, and they took your word for it. I decided then I'd do anything to keep you and I *have* tried . . . to keep you." He turned and looked at Gloria. "But *you* knew something. Every time I was around you, I felt naked, and I asked myself: 'Why doesn't Irene see what Gloria sees?' You were a bigger threat than Vivian was. If Vivian ever tried to approach Irene, I had a story all set to counter hers. But you were a stranger and yet you sensed something; there was no way of fighting you. I had to leave that to chance."

"Frank, it wasn't that . . ." She didn't finish. I watched a tear drop from her jaw.

For a while none of us said anything. My only reaction was numbness. There was a hazy pattern forming in my head, but as it began to grow clearer, I drew back from it. Perhaps I was frightened of arriving at it by myself and needed it told to me.

"And what about Regina?" I said.

"They want her," he answered, almost whispering. "They're using Virgil. I'm almost sure he's one of them."

"But you're not completely sure."

Dear God, let the pattern get hazy again, let it disappear! Let every word he's said be a lie! Let him be insane, just let him be wrong!

"He's never lived in Fort Lauderdale. There's no record of his birth there, if that's his right name. There's no aunt living in that house, just him. Irene, it's not crazy—there's something in his face when he defies me with that smile: he looks at me the same way Vivian used to. His eyes, his teeth . . . From the beginning I suspected . . . Remember that day they were supposed to have gone to Detroit? I checked the mileage, remember? They'd only gone a hundred and fifty-five miles. Ridgeway is seventy-five miles one way, round trip is a hundred and fifty! Suppose he's been taking her up there already!"

The expressway ramp, the day she was skipping school with Virgil. They had come from the north, the same direction Vivian had come from the day we met at the restaurant. I had that

166

picture in my mind, but I couldn't speak it. I could only speak against it.

"That couldn't be," I said. "He couldn't have taken her to Ridgeway. She would have known who Vivian was."

"Why would she? She's never seen her."

What about today, I thought, when Vivian picked her up at school? What about last night—wouldn't she have recognized Vivian's voice on the phone if Virgil *had* been taking her to Ridgeway? It didn't jell. It was preposterous, as fantastic as the story he had told me about Vivian.

"Frank, I've seen your birth certificate. I saw it when we got married. Vivian's name was not on it."

"No, it wasn't. There was no doctor. They didn't register the birth until later. Naturally they didn't put her name on it."

"Then you have no proof."

"No, Irene, I have no proof. I have no proof that I love you, either, or that I've never looked at Regina the way you think I have." He moved forward in his chair. "I know I'm a selfish man, Irene, and a coward. I lost my sister because I was selfish and cowardly, and I lied to you because I was selfish. I couldn't risk losing you *that way*. But now I don't want to lose you *or* Regina! You've got to tell me where she is!"

I couldn't answer. If all this was some elaborate lie just to get Regina back home . . .

"You'd better tell him," said Gloria.

She looked at me and there was pity in her eyes. Pity where there had once been blind adoration. I wanted that adoration back, I wanted to be the rock again, I wanted to return to Irene Rutledge and start all over again.

"Tell him."

"She's at Vivian's."

"Irene, you can't joke about this. This is ser—"

"She's at Vivian's. Vivian picked her up at school today."

His face registered nothing. Until he looked at Gloria.

"My God! How!"

"I sent her. Vivian called me yesterday and told me you were up there raving."

"But why did she call *you?*"

"Because she was afraid for Regina. She offered to take her. And she was concerned about *me.*" Defensive now. "That's something I haven't had the past six months—someone being concerned about me."

He leaped from the chair. "I have to go get her!"

"You're not going without me. I'll call her and tell her we're coming together."

"No; they'll hide her someplace. They'll keep her from me!"

"Don't call," said Gloria. "We'll just drive up there."

"No," said Frank. "I'll go alone. I don't want you to see them. I don't want them to dirty you with their looks."

"You're not going alone."

"We'll all go," said Gloria.

He started for the door.

"Frank, if you leave this house without me, I'll call Vivian the minute you're gone." He stopped. "I'm going to get some answers tonight all the way around. I'll be back down in a minute."

I started for the stairs.

"Irene, we can't wait!"

"I'll be down in a minute."

Upstairs, I pulled out the bottom drawer and found the gun. I emptied my purse on the bed and stuck the gun in it. Just as I was about to switch off the light, I looked at the philodendron I had bought for Frank back in college. I wanted to shoot it to pieces and reclaim myself.

As I started downstairs, I tried dismissing everything he had told me as a fantastic, convoluted lie. He himself had implied that he had betrayed his sister Regina and, in a way, Wanda Hoople too. Perhaps the story he had told me was manufactured to betray Vivian. I almost grinned at the thought that maybe betrayals, like death, came in threes.

On the expressway, I had to tell him three times to slow down. The third time I spoke sharply, and Gloria pressed my arm admonishingly. Sitting in the middle, I sensed a bent-forward rigidity in the two of them, as if their bodies were accelerating the engine. But I didn't want speed. I wanted the car to stop and time to stop so I could think. My mind was filled with fragments, all of them terrifying yet unconnected. My body was limp and there were intervals when I had to *think* to breathe. For reassurance I slipped my fingers under the flap of my purse. The dull, cold metal of the gun calmed me until we reached the sign that said RIDGEWAY CITY LIMIT.

We crept along the main street, the only moving car. With the exception of two bars, everything was closed. The shadowy mannequins in a dress shop window, a night light burning in a hardware store, the darkened movie-house marquee—they all gave the one message small towns give when they lock up for the night: You Belong at Home. We stopped at a light, a ridiculous ritual on this empty street, and I looked at Frank. His eyes were fixed on the pavement ahead and they would remain there all the way to Vivian's. The word "hometown" struck a sardonic note in my head.

Within two blocks, the main street became residential, then gave way to overgrown empty lots, a trailer court, and finally a woods. Frank turned right onto a gravel road. There were no streetlights and there was no moon. The countryside was a blur; the road was all that was left of the world.

Then the headlights went out.

"What are you doing?" The darkness made me whisper.

"I don't want them to see us," he answered.

"Is that it?" asked Gloria.

I turned to where she was looking and saw the lighted windows of the house, which was set back a good hundred yards from the road. The light was splintered by a profusion of trees, most of them pines and evergreens. Very slowly, the car moved forward and gradually I could make out the driveway. Frank pulled into it, then angled the car so we were blocking it. He took out a handkerchief.

"Hold this over the light when I get out. Gloria, you cover up the one by your door."

"I'm not holding anything," I said. "I'm going with you."

169

"Irene—"

"I said I'm going with you."

"I am too," said Gloria. "I'm not staying out here alone."

He hesitated, then told us to get out on his side. We started up the blacktop driveway.

"We could be shot," I said, "sneaking up like this."

"Quiet."

The closer we got, the more impressive the house became. It was a large two-story affair with cathedral peaks and redwood siding. On one side of it was a swimming pool and bathhouse, on the other a four-car garage. The garage doors were closed, with two cars parked in front of them, neither one Vivian's. The back end of another car protruded from the other side of the garage. At first it was a mere outline in the darkness, but as we neared the front door of the house, there was just enough light from the drape-covered window to indicate its color. The recognition went through me in a tremor. The car was Virgil's.

"I'll stand to the side of the door. You and Gloria ring."

"Why? What are you going to do?"

"I don't want them to see me first."

We were too close now for me to protest. I thought: Thank God he hasn't got the gun.

I looked through the little diamond-shaped window in the door as I rang the bell, but all I could see was a hallway that ran into darkness. There was a large archway and a glow of light on the left, undoubtedly the living room. I rang again. I turned to Frank and Gloria and said maybe everyone was in bed. When I turned back to the window, it was filled with a man's face, and I let out a gasp. The man was Leo.

He opened the door and looked at me quizzically, then managed a small smile.

"This is a surprise," he said, eying Gloria.

He stepped back, Gloria and I stepped forward, and then I saw his face darken as Frank came into view.

"Hello, Frank. We didn't expect you . . . in our home. Vivian will be surprised."

Frank pushed past him. Leo made a slight gesture to block

him, then checked himself. Gloria and I followed Frank to the archway, which overlooked the sunken living room. Everyone's eyes were on the archway as we moved into it. The initial silence must have lasted only a few seconds, but it seemed painfully long as Vivian looked first at Frank, then at Gloria, and finally at me. Her face seemed to flicker like a jewel held up to the light: surprise gave way to amusement, amusement to satisfaction. Her head began to nod slowly, knowingly, and her mouth formed a faint, faraway smile. I looked away, at the room and the others in it. Vivian was seated in a white overstuffed chair next to the round metal fireplace. On the sofa opposite her were two women, a chubby brunette and a rather regal-looking redhead. In the two chairs flanking the sofa were an innocuous-looking man in his early fifties and Virgil. Virgil did not look at me; he was watching Frank. The only light in the room came from the logs burning in the fireplace and from a small lamp on the table near the window. The dark redwood paneling muted the light before reflecting it, softening the shadows in its glow. It was partly the lighting, partly the open spiral staircase which climbed to a second-floor hallway, and partly the three steps that separated the room from where we were standing, that gave me the feeling this was a room you *sank* into. There were no ornaments, no pictures on the walls, and all the furniture was large and modern and comfortable. It was a room designed for the body, not the eye: there was nothing to look at except the fire and each other. I looked at the fire first, then at Vivian.

"Hello, Irene," she said, still smiling. "I hadn't expected this from you. I hadn't expected this at all." She closed her eyes and opened them on Frank. "Did you threaten *her* too?" she said to him.

"How about a drink?" Leo said from behind. The rest of them had drinks. The man and the two women on the sofa looked as if they had had several. Even Vivian was glassy-eyed.

"Where is she?" said Frank.

"Just a minute," I said. "I have a few things to say and I don't want Regina to hear them."

"Then come in and sit down." Vivian motioned us to another

sofa, against the wall nearest us but outside the center circle. Gloria and I sat on it, but Frank sat on the steps. "This is my brother Tom, his wife, Alice, and my brother Jack's wife, Helen."

We all nodded. "This is a friend of mine, Gloria Malone." I turned to Virgil. "What are you doing here?"

"I was waiting for Regina outside the school," he said sheepishly. "She said I could come."

"And where is she now?"

"Upstairs, sleeping," said Vivian.

"Have you ever been here before?" I asked Virgil.

"Here? Why would I have been here?"

"What about the day you were supposed to have gone to Detroit?"

"That's where we went."

"Frank says the mileage on your car showed you couldn't have gone that far."

"I told you before, he must have gotten the numbers wrong."

Leo freshened all their drinks at the bar near the staircase. He seemed genuinely amused by me.

"What about those days Regina skipped school with you? Where did you go?"

"We rode around. Out in the country."

Frank jumped up. "What days? When was she skipping school?"

"Sit down, Frank," I said.

"When did this happen? I want to know—"

"Sit down."

"You didn't tell me?" There was hurt and disbelief in his face, but something else too. Repugnance. It chilled me, but I was not about to be distracted. Nineteen years ago, I had let my emotions snuff out my reasoning and common sense. I had married him and accepted his conditions on faith. Now, as I faced him and Vivian together, there could be no emotions, only hard and brittle logic. Gloria was with me; once again, I could be the rock. If Frank was lying, she and I would take Regina without him.

172

"Vivian, Frank says there's an error on his birth certificate."

"What kind of error?"

"An error in the parenthood."

"Well"—she chuckled— "he wasn't adopted. I hope he hasn't gone so far as to deny us."

"Then you're saying there's no mistake on the certificate?"

"I don't know. I'd have to see it."

I blurted it out. "Frank says you're his mother!"

Her eyes slid from me to Frank. "You told her that?" He didn't answer. "Well, well, well. What else have you told her?"

"That Virgil is—belongs to you," I said.

"I see. Anything more?"

"That Regina was your daughter, that your father and he"—I nodded toward Tom—"took advantage of her repeatedly until she couldn't stand it anymore."

"And what do *you* think of such a story?"

"I want to know the truth!"

"Irene," said Frank, "let's get Regina and go. She's not going to tell you anything."

"What do you say, Vivian?"

"What do *I* say? I say how is it possible you've lived with a man for almost twenty years without knowing him? You've lived with him, slept with him, paid the bills with him, had a child by him, and now, all of a sudden, you want the 'truth.' You've seen him around Regina, you've seen her reaction to him. Don't you trust what you see, Irene? Don't you trust yourself?"

The question hung in front of me like a distorted mirror. *You are the rock! Answer her! Gloria, say something!*

"You don't trust yourself," she went on. "The day you asked me to meet you, I knew that." Frank turned to me, blinking incredulously. "That's right, Frank. She's already come to me for answers. And her questions told me more than I told her."

Wait a minute, I'm running this! You're supposed to be helping me!

Frank and Vivian and the rest of them stared at me and nobody said a word. I watched Virgil get up and go to the bar for more ice and return to his chair. The movement was too casual for a first-time guest. And sitting there in the circle with the rest of them, he looked just a bit too snug.

"Did you tell me the truth, Vivian?" My voice sounded tiny. Her eyes seemed to diminish it.

"What would you like to hear? What would ease your mind the most? Which story, Frank's or mine, would be easier to adjust to?" She waited, but I couldn't answer. "Can't make up your mind?" She turned to Gloria. "What about you? I assumed you were brought along to help her. Two little peas from the same pod. You almost look alike."

Gloria spoke up, acidly. "You're a great one to be talking about peas and pods, with the *festoon* you've got here." She nodded in the direction of the group. "I happen to believe Frank."

Vivian smiled, "Well, then, Irene, there's your answer."

Frank stood up again. "That's enough. Where's Regina?"

Vivian brushed him off with a glance and looked at me. "Shall I let him go upstairs?"

"I—" I looked at Frank. His face was flushed, his eyes wild. He took a few steps across the living room in the direction of the spiral staircase. Immediately, Leo and Tom and Virgil stood up.

"You stay put," Vivian snapped at Frank. "This is my house and Regina is here with Irene's sanction. It's up to her whether or not you'll go up there."

There it was, there was the proof. She said it was up to me. They weren't holding Regina, there was no design on her, she would be delivered to me when I said so. It was up to me.

"Well?" said Vivian. "Shall I send him up?"

I couldn't look at Frank. I couldn't look at any of them. "No, I . . . no."

"Irene, for God's sake," Gloria whispered.

For God's sake, what? Nineteen years ago you saw something wrong. And you haven't seen him when he's around her! You haven't seen him when he's crazed! I can't stand any more of it and if he has lied to me—

Frank made a forward lunge. Tom rushed him with his arms

174

up while Leo moved in from the side. The three of them toppled the chair as they fell to the floor. Virgil picked up a heavy glass ashtray and held it in front of him like a tambourine.

"Put that down!" said Vivian.

They grappled on the floor behind the sofa the women were sitting on. The women didn't move. I jumped up and ran to the sofa. Leo had Frank pinned down, with his knee in Frank's back, while Tom twisted Frank's arm.

"Don't hurt him!" I screamed. "Don't hurt him!"

"They're not going to hurt him," said Vivian. *"You've* already done that quite sufficiently." She got up and walked over to Frank. She planted her feet near his head and looked down at him. When she spoke, her voice was soft and caressing. "You don't have to struggle anymore, Frank. I'm sorry it had to be this way, but you had to be shown. I told you once she would never understand. Her kind can't. You can see Regina in a few minutes, but I have something to say first. Tom and Leo will let you go if you behave yourself. Will you promise?"

"Let me go." His voice was deep and miserable.

"Promise me first. I told you you can see Regina soon. I always keep my word. You know that."

"Wait," I said. "What are you doing?"

"You keep quiet," she answered, still looking at Frank. "Do you promise?"

"Yes," he gasped.

The men came up off him. For a minute he didn't move. Then he pulled up onto his elbows, his knees, finally his feet, and dragged himself past Vivian and me to the archway steps.

"Sit down," Vivian said to me. "Over there next to your friend."

Gloria had been standing during the fracas. Now she was glowering at Vivian and not about to sit. "Irene, let's get out of here and call the police."

"You're not as smart as you look," said Vivian. "There's no need for the police. What would you tell them? You just sit down until I'm finished talking."

I sat, pulling Gloria down with me. I picked up my purse and put it back in my lap. Vivian stared at the two of us, grinning.

"You snot-nosed middle-class bitches kill me," she said. "You think the police can take care of your lives just because you pay your taxes. Virgil, get me a drink."

He took her glass to the bar. He hadn't asked what she was drinking. He knew. I saw the expressway ramp before me, his car coming down it, Regina inside. My lungs shriveled.

"I don't want to hear anything," I whispered. "I want Regina. I want her now."

"You'll get Regina, but first you'll hear me." She sipped on the drink Virgil gave her, hesitated, then nodded approvingly. "Five minutes ago, you wanted the truth, so now you're going to get it. First, I had to see how far you'd go, and you went far enough. Didn't she, Frank?"

He was sitting on the steps with his head in his arms. He did not look up or answer.

"I had your number a long time ago," she said, "that night before your wedding. I could tell you had your whole life set up like some goddam dance card. The first step was the big wedding, the big cake, the big degree from college sticking out all over your big smile. And you were big on manners too. You were so anxious to please, even when you saw how Frank felt about me. And later, when I came to see Regina when your friend here was with you—" Frank's head snapped up and he looked at me with huge eyes that made me turn away. Vivian smiled at him. "That's right, Frank, you didn't know about that. Even back then, she was riding the fence." She turned to me. "The truth is I am Frank's mother. That night before your wedding I told him to tell you. And I told him again that day at the hospital when you took Regina home. But he's always been stubborn and now he's paying for it."

"You don't need to say anything more." My stomach was filling up with disgust for both her and myself.

"Yes, I do, for your own benefit, so you'll know what *not* to do when you get Regina back. You see, you're going to have her for a very short time and I don't want you tampering with her. She's made her choice, the choice Frank should have made a long time ago. Instead, he chose to knock his head against a wall." She turned to Frank. "And it hasn't been worth it, has it, Frank? She doesn't understand you, she never could understand you. You're a different breed; it's as simple as that. No matter how hard you try, no matter how many degrees you get, you're still my son. You're still one of us."

"I'm going to be sick," I mumbled. Gloria slipped her arm around my shoulders.

"*You're* going to be sick? Well, go right ahead, because now you'll know how I felt watching you and your little family at that wedding party dinner. You'll know how you turned my stomach that night you let me in to see Regina and then again when we met at the restaurant. I know your kind, Irene. I grew up watching them. So smug in their position, so complacent with their dusted and simonized skeletons tucked away in their closets, so quick to point their fingers at someone else's misfortunes. Stupidly, I was jealous of them until my father taught me not to be. He taught me they weren't the only army in the world; we could make our own. And we have, haven't we?"

"Yes, we have," said the redhead, and the brunette nodded.

"It's sick, it's so sick," I muttered.

"Sick, is it? What would you know about it? When I was fifteen, three boys raped me behind a church. They were *your* kind and I was just a Mattison, so you can guess who would be believed and who wouldn't. I told my mother and father. My mother looked down her nose at me and prayed at the same time. But my father did something about it. He took me into his bed and showed me it didn't have to be that way. And my brothers showed me too."

"Please, no more." I slumped against Gloria.

"Too indelicate for you? Let me tell you something. This family has something you and Frank never had and never will have. There are no secrets between us. We take care of our own, we protect each other."

"The way you protected your daughter?"

"Yes," she snapped. "I protected her well until Frank polluted her mind with his filthy talk and drove her crazy. She was loved. My father loved her, Jack and Tom loved her, I loved her. How

177

do you think the rest of the world would have treated her? I'll tell you how—they would have turned her over to social services and stuck her in a home run by the state. All my mother could do was pray for her." She grinned. "Those who can't do, teach—or pray. I don't teach or pray. I run a business and we all share in it. No one in this family has to go *outside* to make a living. And we all make a very good living. I've taken care of that." She took a long swallow of her drink.

"Who does he belong to?" I asked, pointing at Virgil.

"I gave birth to him," said the brunette, "but he belongs to all of us."

"If your husband is Jack, that makes Virgil Regina's cousin," I said.

"Who her husband is has nothing to do with it," said Vivian.

"What do you mean?"

"Virgil *might* be Jack's. Or Tom's. Or even Leo's."

"Oh, Christ!" Gloria whispered.

"There's no ownership in this family," said Vivian.

"What do you call it, then?" I said. "The way you've got them all under your thumb?"

"No one's under anyone's thumb. If anyone wants to leave, they're perfectly free to do it."

"And then a few years later you go after their children."

"Only in Frank's case. He *owes* me something. He took my daughter away and he took himself away. If he'd stayed, I could have forgiven him for what he did to Regina. Or maybe if I'd had another child. But I couldn't. Cancer took care of that. So my only contribution to this family is my granddaughter, and I want her."

"You'll never get her," I said.

"You're wrong, Irene. We already have her. And you have no idea how easy it was. I was very skeptical when Virgil first brought her here last October. I thought I would have a losing battle on my hands, but as it turned out, Regina was very anxious to join us after she got to know us."

"You're lying."

"Regina is in love with Virgil. And Regina is pregnant."

Frank let out a sharp groan. I slipped my fingers under the flap of my purse.

"I think you'd better get Regina now," I said.

"I hope you're prepared for this."

"Just get her."

Vivian nodded at Virgil. He stood and went up the spiral staircase. Everyone was silent, and I thought: It'll all be over in a few minutes. We'll go away from here and never talk about it again. Regina will go to school tomorrow, I'll go to work, Gloria can fly back to L.A.

But these thoughts died with the next sound. Regina's laugh, shrill and empty, came from upstairs. I had heard it before, the night she and Virgil returned from their supposed trip to Detroit. I had heard it when she talked on the telephone to Virgil. It was filled with mockery and arrogance, perfectly matched now with Vivian's face.

"You know, don't you, that you can be prosecuted for what you've done."

Vivian chuckled. "There you go with the police again. This is a private family matter, even though you've dragged your Siamese twin here into it."

"I'll make it public if I have to."

"Irene, please," Frank moaned. "Don't talk to her."

"I'll drag you into court and show what you've done."

"And what have I done?"

"You abducted her, you and that . . . offspring."

"You're being silly. You *sent* Regina here. To get her away from her father. Even Miss McPhee knows that."

"Miss McPhee? What has she got to do with this?"

"Miss McPhee has been quite concerned about Regina's welfare. She's taken a personal interest. And I'm sure she'll take an even greater interest when she finds out Regina is pregnant."

"What are you talking about?"

"I'm talking about a little do-good twit who I'm sure resembles you. You're a teacher. How would you react if one of your students told you her father had . . . funny ideas? Miss McPhee had quite a reaction."

179

"No," Frank was whispering, shaking his head. "No, you didn't. You couldn't do that."

"*I* haven't done anything. I've never seen the woman. But Regina's been very close to her."

"What are you getting at?" I said.

"You want it straight and simple? Here it is. Regina has chosen to come to us. When the time comes, she wants to have her baby here. You're not to stand in her way. If you do, you'll get your police and your courtroom and your public testimony, only I'm afraid you and Frank will be on the receiving end. Just a few words to Miss McPhee about the *possible* paternity of the baby, a few tears from Regina. That should set a few wheels in motion."

"For God's sake," I screamed, "he's your son! Are you going to sit there and tell me you would push your own filth off onto him?"

"Call it whatever you like. Now aren't you suddenly the loving and protective wife, once you're sure of your facts!" She leaned forward in the chair, her eyes slitted. "He was my son and then he left and then you took him. I'm just taking back part of my own. We'll keep Regina. You and Frank have each other, for whatever *that's* worth now."

Another shrill laugh from above, approaching the stairs. I looked up and saw Virgil descend. Then came Regina, wearing a pink satin robe. Behind her was a tall man with salt-and-pepper hair. He held her hand all the way down the steps. I turned and looked at Frank. He was leaning forward, his mouth open and his eyes frozen.

"Jack," he whispered. His other brother.

Jack smiled and rested his arms on Regina's shoulders so that his long fingers dangled near her breasts. His face was flushed, Regina's hair snarled and sweat-soaked. For some time, no one spoke. Then Jack gathered Regina's hair in his hands, twisted it into a tail, and laid it over her shoulder. He moved to the bar for a drink. Regina sat down on the arm of Virgil's chair.

"Have you told them everything?" she said to Vivian.

"Yes."

"Regina, don't," said Frank, his voice quivering. He put out his hands. "Come to me and we'll take you home." She looked at him blandly. "We'll go home and forget all about this."

"We're not forgetting about anything," she said. "I'm going to have a baby."

"We'll take care of that. We'll get a good doctor. We'll all go away if you want to."

I listened to him beg, and I remembered my thoughts about betrayals earlier that night. The betrayals here *had* come in threes. He had been betrayed by his mother, his daughter—and his wife.

"We can go anywhere you want. We can go to California. You can rest on the beach. We'll all feel better in the sun."

Regina's eyes shifted to Gloria and she gave her a once-over smirk.

"And later you can go away to school. It'll be a new start. We'll all start over again."

"I've already made a start."

"No, honey, they've tricked you. It's not what you think it is."

"No one's tricked me," she said flatly, shaking the hair from her shoulders. "You're just jealous."

"No, Regina, that's not—" His voice broke.

My fingers moved farther under the flap of my purse. "Don't you talk to your father that way." I was crying and hating myself for it. I wanted my rage to be firm and awesome. *Where was the rock?*

"You don't have to stay," she said.

"Go and get dressed. You're coming home."

She looked questioningly at Vivian. Vivian nodded and said, "For the time being."

Regina stood up and started for the staircase. She grinned at Jack.

"You weren't raised this way!" I said, more to Jack than to her. "There's no *reason* . . ."

She stopped and turned. She gave me a long, leveling look, not like a defiant daughter, but like one woman assessing another.

181

"You should be happy," she said. "Now you can have him all to yourself. That's what you've always wanted, anyway. Now I'm out of the way."

"That is not true and you know it!"

"Yes, it is. It's just the way you are."

"The way I am? And what is that, Regina?"

"You've always gotten whatever you wanted. You're pretty and you're selfish—"

"Regina, they can't make you beautiful! That's what it comes down to, isn't it? Like the time you were sick when you were little, and you wanted to punish people for something that couldn't be helped. That's what you're doing now—punishing us."

"If that's what you want to think."

"Do you know what you're doing to your father! You did all this behind our backs, you lied to me! You made me think—"

"You thought what you wanted to think. That's not my fault. Besides, if you found out, you would have stopped me. Now you can't. You've always gotten what you wanted; now I'm going to get what I want."

"Is *this* what you want? To be shuttled around from one to the other, to be used like—like an appliance!"

"I like it here," she declared. "We're all the same here. No one's any better than anyone else. You could never stand that. You have to be superior. You and *her."* She sneered at Gloria.

Gloria snatched the bait. "What you've just shown, Regina, is that she *is* superior to you." She struck the spot. Regina made a slight movement forward before checking herself. "And I'll tell you something else. It's easy to please a crowd. But try it with one person; it takes guts and it takes work."

"Save your sermons," she said, and went up the stairs.

Through my tears, Vivian was a smiling blur slowly bending forward in her chair. "I'm glad you came tonight after all. Better than putting it off until the end of the week. Who knows"— she chuckled—"you might have had Frank locked up by then. That would have been a little messy. I'd better go help her get her things together."

"You can't have her," I whispered. My fingers pushed forward under the flap until they found the metal.

"She hasn't decided whether she wants to finish out the semester at school. If she does, she'll stay with you until June. When the warm weather comes, she can wear those Indian tops that hide everything."

"I won't let you." *I won't let you do this to Frank.* I gripped the handle and dragged it toward me.

"If she decides to quit, she can come here immediately. I've already gotten her a doctor, so that's taken care of. That do-gooder Miss McPhee might try to poke her nose into this, but I think Regina can handle her. I'm sure the two of *you* will behave yourselves. You should know by now I don't make idle threats."

She started up from the chair, smiling. Smiling. She was still smiling when she saw the gun. The smile stayed, giving a little twitch with each shot. Half sitting, half standing, she seemed to be waiting for me to finish. I dropped the gun even before she dropped into the chair.

No one moved, perhaps because she was still smiling. Even with the low gurgling in her throat and the languid closing of her eyes, she smiled, drawing my breath away. The room turned inside out and there were only shadows. One of the shadows moved immediately to Vivian, bent over her, mumbled something to the other shadows, and then came to me. It was Frank. His arm went around me, and Gloria took my hand. Two figures appeared on the staircase. There was a scream, and the room went right again.

"You crazy bitch! You killed her! You killed her!" Regina broke away from Virgil and started toward me. "You ruined everything—you always ruin everything! You killed her, you bitch!"

Frank jumped up and held her away from me. She saw the gun at my feet and began kicking at Frank in her effort to get to it. My one hand stayed with Gloria while the other went forward to retrieve the gun. Gloria called my name, made a move for my other hand, but I slid away and held my arm up in warning.

I leveled the gun on Regina.

"Don't come near me," I said. "Don't touch me or so help me

183

I'll put a bullet in that machine that's supposed to be your heart."
She drew back. When the momentary shock slid from her eyes, a grin slid into her face. "So help me."

"You'd really like to, wouldn't you?"

"Right this minute, yes, I would like to very much. Just don't *touch* me. I don't ever want you to touch me again."

"Who in hell do you think you are!"

"I know who I am, Regina." *Don't cry, stop crying.* "And *what* I am is not superior at all if you're my daughter. Now get away from me and stay away."

She yanked herself free from Frank and joined the huddle surrounding Vivian. Leo came out of that huddle. His lips were white, his face nearly purple. He started toward me.

"You stay away from me too," I said. "I want everybody to stay away from me."

Jack grabbed Leo's arm and pulled him back into the huddle. Frank sat down next to me and stroked my arm.

"Give me the gun, Irene. I won't let any of them near you."

I gave it to him and collapsed against his chest. Gloria stroked my hair.

"I love you, Frank, I do love you."

"Shhhh. I know. I'm here."

I didn't wake up until the police arrived. I don't know exactly how much time elapsed, but it had been time enough for Regina and Virgil to escape. After I had fainted, Frank had carried me up to one of the bedrooms. Leaving it, with one of the policemen gripping my arm, I was certain that it was Regina I had shot. Not until I got downstairs and saw Vivian smiling in the chair did I remember what had happened. Everyone was gathered in the living room. The two women were crying softly, sitting in their original places on the sofa. I leaned against the bar, with Frank and Gloria on either side of me.

Everyone, including the police, seemed to be waiting for something. Something turned out to be *someone.* The chief or the captain or whatever they call themselves arrived and took in the situation with one officious glance. He looked at Vivian dispassionately, then at me the same way. One policeman began to explain to him and finished with a long sigh of familiarity before he added, "Some family reunion, eh?"

Only two of the bullets had struck Vivian. The other two were found in the arm and the leg of the white chair. This, my lawyer told me, might prove beneficial to my plea of temporary insanity, but I can't remember the reason he gave. I can't even recall the trial in any sequential fashion. The wheels of justice move through verbal muck, advancing one day and sticking the next, while the people in charge argue over whether to push or pull. And my lawyer, Mr. Bates, informed me in no uncertain terms that my demeanor in the courtroom was adding extra weight to his load:

"Mrs. Mattison, I do appreciate the fact you are level-headed and cooperate with the court, but for credibility's sake your image in there has to coincide with the circumstances of our case. The jurors look more concerned than you do, and that is never a good sign. Your daughter's disappearance and her refusal to surface is extremely damaging. And I don't have to tell you what McPhee's testimony is doing for the prosecution. You've got to show some kind of reaction to things that are said, some *expression*. Otherwise, it's going to be uphill all the way to the end."

It was uphill until very nearly the end. Leo, Jack, Tom, the two wives, two of Frank's other brothers—all of them denied Vivian was Frank's mother. Frank, the prosecution contended, had manufactured the lie to delude me, he had defiled his retarded sister and driven her to suicide, and he had taken advantage of his daughter as well—hence her fear to show herself. Gloria's account of Vivian's admission and Regina's conversion pleased Mr. Bates: her frustration and rage coming out in tears (something *I* was incapable of all through the trial), she gave a vivid picture of Vivian's smug assurance and contempt. Although it made colorful copy in the papers, it ultimately would carry very little weight with the jury, for the simple reason that Gloria was outnumbered. One thing I had in my favor—and a very small thing, Mr. Bates assured me—was that Leo had waited almost

185

an hour before calling the police, time enough for Regina and Virgil to disappear. But it was Frank's car they had taken and Frank could not figure out how they had got his keys. The car was found abandoned fifty miles south of Ridgeway.

Considering the flimsiness of our case, Frank and Mr. Bates proposed a new tactic: "Your husband and I have decided it would be best if he went along with the prosecution's accusations. They've already set it up for us; all he has to do is confess he purposely misled you. You'll have a chance that way, a very good chance." Frank squeezed my hand.

"No."

Mr. Bates leaned forward. "Let me put it to you this way: it's your *only* chance."

"He's not bowing to them and neither am I. I did it once; I won't do it again."

"Irene," said Frank, "if this benefits the case, what does it matter how we bend?"

"Because it's time to break it with them. They've held on to you all these years with the truth. I won't let them hold on now with a lie."

They left, but Mr. Bates soon returned alone. He sat facing me, but he watched the pen he was twirling between his fingers. He spoke deliberately.

"History is full of martyrs who died for the truth. I have my own theory that most of them didn't happen upon a cause. They went out looking for one, one they knew could fulfill their fame-in-death wish."

"I didn't go out looking for a cause."

"No, but when you found one, you took a gun to it. All right, you made a righteous accomplishment. Now you are being offered the opportunity for a second accomplishment—getting the verdict we want. And yet you turn down that opportunity."

"I won't buy a verdict with Frank's name."

"So you'll risk a prison term and a long separation from him? Mrs. Mattison, your husband needs you more than he needs his name. You committed murder for your daughter, but you will not bend for your husband."

"I did not commit murder for my daughter. I knew she was

186

already lost to us before I fired that gun. I killed that woman for myself. I've had plenty of time to think, Mr. Bates, and I've thought about my motive. You talk about righteousness. My killing Vivian was not done out of righteousness. It was done out of humiliation and shame. Let me tell you something. I married a decent man. His decency, his integrity, his love for me, are as tangible as that pen you're playing with. For nineteen years, I had daily proof of them. But when he ran up against this— this plot, I chose to doubt him, to wipe out years of evidence with one single suspicion. I chose to believe Regina even after I caught her lying to me about school and I chose to believe Vivian, a perfect stranger, because she flattered me with some cheap sympathy. And so did I love him any better than his daughter and his mother did? Vivian knew I didn't; she told me so that night. And I shot her for it." I was proceeding calmly, rationally, and yet my throat tightened and the tears started down my face. "I'm no martyr. Far from it. I turned Regina over to his family and in a way I turned myself over to them too."

"You're distorting the situation. You seem to forget he could have told you the truth years ago."

"I haven't forgotten that. But with another woman he might have told the truth. Another woman might have made him feel safe." I took the pen he was playing with and held it tight to steady myself. "He spent all those years loving and protecting his daughter the best way he knew how. Maybe he did it wrong, but he did it single-handedly. But the failure isn't all his. It's mine too. And Regina's. *Mostly* Regina's—I can't help but believe that. I'm not going to offer him up with a lie to make Regina and myself look good. We'll just have to continue as we have been and hope."

"Then hope for a miracle."

Mr. Bates did his best to create a miracle. Our next witness was the reporter who had photographed me scrubbing the graffiti off the front of the school. It seemed most of the jurors were impressed with this, but some of them changed their expressions when the prosecution pointed out that this gesture of mine had been "extreme and reactionary."

We were nearing the end. When Frank would come to see

me, he would don a smile and reaffirm his faith in the jury. But there was always doubt in his eyes when his words ran out. Invariably, I turned the conversation to the weather and world news. We never mentioned Regina.

I rehearsed facing the verdict, although I said nothing to Mr. Bates. My resignation seemed almost sacrilegious next to his perseverance. He was still stinging from my refusal to go along with his and Frank's plan, but at the same time this fed his determination to win. There was a growing glint in his eye whenever he turned that pen round and round between his hands.

It was a Monday morning when I entered the courtroom and saw the pen not in his hands, its customary place, but stuck squarely in his pocket. He gripped my arm and whispered in my ear.

"We may have ourselves a *deus ex machina.*"

"What do you mean?"

"I have one more witness. Keep your fingers crossed."

"Who is it?"

"No one you know. Someone's volunteered to come forward. This might make all the difference."

After the opening rituals, the judge called upon Mr. Bates. "You wish to call another witness?"

"Yes, Your Honor. I call Wanda Lowell to the stand."

Peck High had its share of poor kids, mostly black and Mexican, but the relaxation of the dress code and the adoption of denim as the national uniform of youth had successfully eliminated the conspicuousness of poverty. Wanda Lowell was conspicuously poor. Her face was gaunt and sallow, her hair thin and lusterless. Her shoulders rounded to make a hollow of her chest, while her hipbones jutted forward like two tiny buttresses. The yellow and white in her dress cruelly accentuated her colorless appearance; the striped material did not match up at the seams. It was painfully apparent this woman had no time for, or perhaps no conception of, even modest vanity. I looked at her ankles, and remembering Frank's story, I half expected to see socks sliding down them into her shoes. Of course, she didn't wear socks. She wore white heels, dulled and cracked by several layers of liquid polish.

She was sworn in and gave the court her maiden name, place of residence, and former relationship to Frank. Mr. Bates began his questioning, and several of the jury leaned forward in their seats.

"Mrs. Lowell, will you please tell the court how you came to be here today?"

"I been reading about this in the paper and I seen the lies Mr. Mattison's brothers were telling about—"

"Objection!"

"Your Honor, Mrs. Lowell's testimony will clarify her accusation."

"Objection overruled. Proceed."

"Well, that's what they were," said Wanda Lowell. "It looked like no one knew Mr. Mattison's side of the story except me, so that's why I decided to speak up."

"Will you tell the court why you waited so long?"

"My husband didn't want me to get mixed up in it. I had pneumonia in January and lost three weeks at work. And I don't get paid for today, either."

Mr. Bates guided her through an explanation of how she had known Frank from the third grade on. She made it clear—and Mr. Bates underscored the fact—that the two of them had never been romantically involved.

"And you never went out with him on a date? You never had a romance with him?"

"He didn't have any money for dates. He never went out with anyone. He was too busy looking after his sister. She was retarded."

Several of the jury sat up and leaned forward.

"Now tell us about the evening you visited the Mattison house."

"It wasn't visiting; no one saw me. It was in the winter, around Christmas time. A couple of days before, I asked him to go to a school dance, the kind where the girls are supposed to ask the boys. I asked him in front of his friends and it embarrassed him. He didn't have any money to go to a dance. I wanted to tell him I was sorry, but in school there were always too many people

189

around. I knew him and his sister slept in this shack behind their house and I was going home after a baby-sitting job and their place was on the way so I figured I could talk to him alone. I took the shortcut through a field so I wouldn't have to go past the house. Well, I got nervous thinking he might get mad at me for coming around at night. I stood behind the shack awhile, trying to make up my mind. Then someone opened the back door of the house and I heard voices coming. I was scared if I ran they'd see me, so I stayed where I was. I heard them pound on the door and Regina started crying inside."

"And who was it pounding on the door?"

"I couldn't see but I could hear them. Two young men and a woman. They broke the door open and—"

"They *broke* it open? Something was blocking it?"

"I heard something crack and then something heavy fell on the floor. They got the door open and there was this kind of fight inside. Somebody got knocked against the wall."

"Were you able to look through a window?"

"There wasn't no windows."

"This shack that Mr. Mattison and his sister slept in had *no* windows at all?"

"That's right."

"I see. Go on, please."

"I looked for a window. I come around to the one side, and then around the back to the other side, and there wasn't a window. I was standing just around the corner from the front when Regina and the woman come out of the shack. Regina kept saying she didn't want to go in the house, but the woman said it's all right, he loves you."

"Who was the woman?"

"Vivian Mattison."

"When she said 'he loves you,' did she say who the man was?"

"No. She just took Regina in the house and closed the door."

"What about the two men? What were they doing while Vivian and Regina were in the house?"

"They stayed in the shack. They must have been holding Mr. Mattison down, because he kept begging them to let him go.

Then Vivian come out of the house and the two men went in. She went in the shack and there was some talking, but it was real low and I couldn't make out what they were saying. I moved around the corner close to the door and then all of a sudden it opened. I sort of squeezed myself up against the wall because if I moved the snow would crunch. Then I heard Mr. Mattison tell her he hated her and the rest of them and he was going to get the cops after them. She was standing in the door and she laughed and she said, 'You wouldn't call the cops on your mother, would you?' and he said she was a liar. She said the cops would haul him away to the nut house if he ever opened his mouth."

"And then what happened?"

"She went back in the house. She didn't even close the door to the shack. He had to do it."

"Did you go into the shack?"

"No. I ran home. I cut back through the woods and I fell on a stick. It stuck right in my leg. I still got the scar." She pointed to a spot below her right knee.

"Did you ever mention this incident to Mr. Mattison?"

"No."

"Why not?"

"It would've shamed him. That kind of thing you don't want no one to know."

"How soon after this December night did Regina Mattison kill herself?"

"Couple of months. April, I think."

"April ninth, to be exact. Did you ever return to the shack?"

"No. I never went near that house again."

"Did you have any contact with Mr. Mattison after he left Ridgeway?"

"No."

"Thank you, Mrs. Lowell." He turned to the prosecution. "Your witness."

Naturally, the prosecution did its best to discredit Wanda Lowell's testimony. How, after all these years, could she recall exact words, exact dialogue? What was her *real* interest in the defendant's husband? Was she secretly in love with him? Wanda

191

grew indignant at the last question and told her questioner she was a married woman and a mother and she hadn't come here to be insulted. I watched the jury. They were impressed.

The wrap-up came on a day of record-breaking temperatures. Collars wilted, faces drooped, magazines and newspapers were used as fans. Among the jury I sensed a definite anxiousness for the whole thing to be over with. For some of them, what had begun as a privileged adventure had now degenerated into a ritual of tedium. In his summary, my lawyer flattered them, caressed and cooled them with his mellifluous voice.

"Ladies and gentlemen, you have had the most difficult task any jury can have. You have sat through a trial which has proceeded mostly on hearsay. Yet a few facts have been produced which cannot be overlooked. One, Irene Mattison has devoted fifteen years to teaching children. She has been sensitive to their needs as well as society's needs. It was a child's welfare, her own daughter's, that drove her to murder. It was outrage over an unspeakable depravity that compelled her to pick up a gun and use it. It was Vivian Snell's clever deceit and vengeful disregard for a child's life that overruled the defendant's rational powers. And if we look closely, what other course of action was open to her?"

Not once did he turn his back on them. Instead, he leaned forward, seeking out one pair of eyes after another until he had enlisted them all. He orated but it did not sound like an oration. His tone suggested he was telling them something they already knew.

"And now we come to the question of why the defendant's daughter has failed to appear in her mother's behalf. We can't presume to know all of her motives. Regina Mattison is seventeen years old. Some of you may consider her a child, just as her mother did when it came time to protect her. But child or adult, she is a daughter who has dealt the cruelest blow to her parents— abandonment in time of need. And yet she betrayed her parents long before this. That betrayal began after the first trip she took with Virgil Evans to Vivian Snell's house. We would all like a ready answer as to why this girl joined this circle, this cult of

192

people, so completely and willingly. Of course, the obvious temptation is to lay the guilt at her parents' doorstep. But before we succumb to that temptation, let us consider the vast number of parents, many of them good parents, who have lost their children to various cults whose values are alien to those they raised their children with. And let us consider ourselves, let us consider how often all of us, as children, disappointed our parents in our pursuits. Quite simply, there was something inside Regina Mattison that made this group attractive to her, just as there was something in her mother that made them repulsive. When Irene Mattison pulled that trigger, she was doing the same thing she did the day she took a steel brush to the wall of her school. She was wiping out a plague that . . ."

And on he went until I began to cringe. I knew what he was doing was necessary, but part of me wanted to stand up and shout the real reason Vivian was dead.

I felt more comfortable during the prosecution's summary, simply because it put me on the silent defensive. Jack Rand, the principal of Peck, had cooperated with the prosecution. Although he described me as a "competent" teacher, he maintained I was "erratic" outside the classroom and stated outright that I had a contempt for authority. On the other hand, Mrs. Lorimer, our old baby-sitter, worked grudgingly with the prosecution once she found she was in over her head. They extracted from her an account of my terrible temper and my eagerness to return to work while Regina was still sick. They referred to this testimony as often as possible, and I would catch Mrs. Lorimer giving me long, apologetic stares. But of course the prosecution depended most heavily upon Miss McPhee.

"You have heard from Mr. Rand how on numerous occasions Mrs. Mattison had defied him and sought subtle ways for revenge. You have heard from Mrs. Lorimer how the defendant's temper on one occasion made a dramatic snap when a minor situation slipped out of her control. And most importantly, Miss McPhee has testified how the defendant discouraged the counselor-student relationship with her daughter." He paused and stepped backward to the corner of the jury box and pointed at me. "What you see before you is a woman who will do anything to control those around her. When she feels that control threatened, she becomes vindictive. We cannot say for sure what went on in the Mattison household, but it was something that drove Regina Mattison first to Miss McPhee and then to her father's family. There was something in that household that made Irene Mattison almost a recluse. She has had a strangely limited life. Acquaintances, but no close friends except for Mrs. Malone, who lives two thousand miles away. I submit that the defendant *chose* this excessive solitude to keep her own violent proclivities in check. She saw Miss McPhee as an intruder and encouraged her daughter to stay away from her. Vivian Snell was the second intruder, and an undeniable danger because she was a concerned relative and knew her brother only too well. That is why the defendant took a gun with her the night of the murder. Her rational abilities were very much intact. She knew that only violence could rid her of this opponent. She knew she was likely to come out the loser if there was a legal battle over her daughter. The murder of Vivian Snell was calculated. And now the defendant is calculating your sympathy. She is standing on the name of motherhood. But I ask you, where is her *daughter?*"

The jury went out. I lay in bed in my cell and smoked cigarettes during the six hours it took them to deliberate. I was prepared for defeat, for during those six hours, it wasn't Mr. Bates's summary I kept hearing. It was the prosecution's. During the few minutes I did manage to fall asleep, I dreamed of Vivian. We were holding hands, and although she had her own hair, she had my face, and the jury knew it.

Mr. Bates was holding his pen in his hand when we reconvened in the courtroom. The room was filled, the way it had been during the opening days of the trial. The jury filed into the box. Every one of them looked tired and empty; for the first time, it occurred to me to feel sorry for them.

I stood up to face them.

"We find the defendant not guilty by cause of temporary insanity."

I stood numb amid the cheering and booing until the gavel

struck and Mr. Bates gently pulled me down into my seat. A sigh whistled through his teeth. "Your miracle came through. You'd better put Wanda Lowell on your Christmas card list."

We send our Christmas cards now—the few we do send—from Long Beach. They are plain white laminated cards with "Season's Greetings" printed in red block letters. I find their simplicity soothing, and I have toned down my formerly flamboyant signature to match. Simplicity is the banner we live under; not even the holiday hysteria will set it aflutter. We have retired as far as possible from the past and past habits. Now time is there to be spent, not saved, and I've turned the burden of spending it into a luxury. It takes forty minutes to walk directly from our house to the Safeway supermarket where I work as a cashier, but I allow myself an extra twenty minutes to walk out of my way, to stop and admire a garden or to face the ocean and smoke a cigarette. I find nothing mystical about the ocean. Its surf is just another practical reminder that life is a series of simple repetitions: keep the wind down and storms at abeyance and your surf will continue with its regular rhythm. Of course, there's always the invisible, sometimes treacherous undercurrent. I feel that undercurrent now and then, unexpectedly, whenever I am taken unawares by a tall girl whose face momentarily resembles Regina's. Then the resemblance recedes, the undercurrent subsides, and the safe and soothing rhythm returns. . . .

Endings spawn beginnings, and so quite naturally the conclusion of the trial nudged us into our present routine, our change of place. The board of education dismissed me "with regret" and with the florid jargon bureaucrats use when only half committed to expediency. Public opinion, it seems, did not coincide with the jury's verdict. But the university made no move against Frank. It wasn't necessary. The number of girls who signed up for his classes plummeted to five, three of whom thought they would like to brush bodies with depravity and made advances to him. A number of the boys smirked their way through the term and asked pointed questions about the practice of incest among tribal cultures. Frank gave notice for a January departure, and we put the house up for sale. The agent warned us not to get our hopes up: our notoriety would attract a lot of curiosity-seekers not at all interested in buying a house, and once a buyer could be found, he would be certain to feel an advantage in the bargaining. For our own peace of mind, we were asked not to be in the house at all when it was being shown.

As it turned out, we sold it at a fairly small loss and went to stay with my parents for a month. My mother was valiantly cheerful and supportive and made a dress for me and a sweater for Frank. Her smiling intentions, however, were outweighed by my father, who looked as if *he* were on trial. His eyes seemed larger, liquefied, unable to focus—not on what he saw but on something within him. He was quiet most of the time, but it was a restrained silence. It broke the night he got drunk and cried in front of me at the kitchen table. He said I should never have married Frank, he had a feeling from the beginning something was wrong, it was Frank's fault the way Regina turned out, and my life was ruined, our marriage now only a charade. I didn't bother defending Frank against the insult, because I knew it was the only handle available to my father for expressing his long-term disappointment in *me*. And although I decided there and then it was time for us to leave, I resolved to wait a few days so my father wouldn't think he had driven me away. Two days later, Barry came up from Texas with his wife and kids for a week's visit. Assuming the role of brotherly protector, Barry spent his first night home making a blatant gesture of avoiding Frank. Later in the evening, Karen, Barry's five-year-old, crawled onto Frank's lap and asked him to help her with her puzzle. Under Barry's watchful eyes, Frank's hands shook in an obvious effort not to touch her in any way. She sat there smiling and babbling to him while he resisted her by quickly assembling the puzzle. When he finished, he told her to take it and show the others, then got up and played bartender to avoid sitting down again.

We left the next morning. We drove south, then west. Six days later, we arrived in Los Angeles. Gloria and Pat helped us find a furnished apartment in Santa Monica, but after two months we felt hemmed in. We decided to rent a small house and found one here in Long Beach soon after Frank got his bartending job. It was easy enough for him to get because he wanted to work the day shift.

Our life here isn't exactly meager. We play bridge on Sunday night with neighbors and on Friday night with Gloria and Pat. We work in the garden, go to the beach, to the movies, and occasionally drive up to L.A. for dinner and a concert. Sometimes, on weekends, Gloria's son Brian and his girlfriend come down for a visit. Often, Frank and Brian will lose themselves under the hood of Brian's 1956 Pontiac, his proudest possession, while Sally and I play gin rummy under the porch awning. During those afternoons, Frank is his most animated, working furiously on that Pontiac or mowing the lawn or joining us in cards. But Brian's visits are a mixed blessing. When he and Sally leave, I can see the depression settling on Frank as plainly as the Big Dipper settles on the treetop across the street from our front porch. We usually sit on the porch after Brian leaves and have two beers before bed. Rarely do we speak; we just sit and smoke and sip our beer. But it was on one of these nights I learned the truth about Wanda Lowell's testimony in court. A woman happened to pass by wearing white heels and I thought of Wanda with her dulled, cracked shoes.

"I wonder if Wanda Lowell's ever been to California."

"I doubt she's ever been more than forty miles outside of Ridgeway," said Frank.

"I wish there were something we could have done for her."

"We gave her a day's worth of revenge."

"Revenge?"

"Two days, really. The day she testified and the day you were acquitted."

"What kind of revenge?"

"She lied, Irene, and they believed her."

"Lied? How did she lie?"

"She came to see me and asked if there was any way she could help. She never came to the shack that night. I just told her the facts and the two of us worked out the story together. Then

I took her to Mr. Bates. When I saw that *he* believed her, I decided it was worth the chance. She was happy to do it."

"To perjure herself? Didn't she want anything—money or . . ."

"She wanted conspiracy. She wanted to make one big slash at the whole town and get away with it. Besides, she believed us. To offer her anything would have been insulting. It would only have shown we didn't understand her reasons."

I said nothing more about it. I'm in no position to presume or refute someone else's motives. Not even Regina's.

June first will be Regina's birthday, but since it's my birthday as well, we will get through the day without mentioning her. We get through weeks at a time without mentioning her, and then one Friday night Frank will stay on at the bar drinking boilermakers and come home to talk about her. I sit and listen and nod and wait for his soft reminiscence to become self-recrimination as he slides into his "if only"s, past and future: "If only we had moved far away years ago, while Regina was still a child"; "If only Regina would contact us just to tell us about the baby." The first few times he did this, I felt myself being pulled along to share in the recriminations. But now I can refuse because I have my protection: all I have to do is picture that thin, lightning-like scar in Brian's hair, just above his right ear, the scar he still carries from Regina. And with the rhythm of a reprise, I tell myself responsibility has to stop somewhere, that what a child is taught and what it learns are not necessarily the same thing. The thought has never accomplished a full exoneration, but it keeps Regina at the distance I need in order to go on functioning.

The mornings after the boilermaker nights, Frank hurls himself into the present. He ferrets out the weeds in the garden or washes the windows or rearranges the furniture in the living room and then takes me to dinner. Regina is not mentioned again until the next boilermaker night.

Of course, she's always here, huddling between our thoughts, defining our opposite hopes for the future. Last Saturday, Brian came down and took us to Laguna to look at pottery and antiques.

He brought us back and left at dusk, and Frank and I took up our customary positions on the front porch. A few minutes after the streetlamps came on, Frank leaned forward, gripping the arms of the chair, and squinted through his glasses. Coming slowly down the street from the direction of the highway was a green Chevrolet exactly like Virgil's. My heart backed into my lungs and stayed there until the car passed, revealing an old woman as its driver. I will never forget that momentary look on Frank's face, as if a prayer were about to be answered. When the car disappeared around the corner, it was *my* prayer that was answered.

It's natural, I know, to wish for hard and exact conclusions in life, and in that respect I am unnatural. Regardless of the consequences, Frank hopes for Regina's return. He would like to hold his grandchild and see part of himself and me in its face. I don't want that conclusion, that finality. I am resuming my position as the rock. I want nothing more than to be caressed by daily routine, working the keys of the cash register and then fixing dinner for two. The wrongs Regina and I did to each other may soften the longer we are separated, may evaporate entirely if we never meet again, and I am depending on her to recognize that. For she has my blood as well as Frank's and I pray that she too has become a rock, firmly planted and unwilling to travel the territory that keeps us apart.